Philosophy and Religion

ROYAL INSTITUTE OF PHILOSOPHY SUPPLEMENT: 68

EDITED BY

Anthony O'Hear

CAMBRIDGE
UNIVERSITY PRESS

CAMBRIDGE
UNIVERSITY PRESS

University Printing House, Cambridge CB2 8BS, United Kingdom

One Liberty Plaza, 20th Floor, New York, NY 10006, USA

477 Williamstown Road, Port Melbourne, VIC 3207, Australia

314-321, 3rd Floor, Plot 3, Splendor Forum, Jasola District Centre, New Delhi - 110025, India

79 Anson Road, #06-04/06, Singapore 079906

Cambridge University Press is part of the University of Cambridge.

It furthers the University's mission by disseminating knowledge in the pursuit of
education, learning and research at the highest international levels of excellence.

www.cambridge.org
Information on this title: www.cambridge.org/9781107615984

A catalogue record for this publication is available from the British Library

ISBN 978-1-107-61598-4 Paperback
ISSN 1358-2461

Contents

List of Contributors

Richard Swinburne, Oriel College, Oxford

T. J. Mawson, St. Peter's College, Oxford

Gerard Hughes, Heythrop College, London

Brian Leftow, Oriel College, Oxford

Richard Norman, University of Kent

Peter Cave, The Open University

Peter Millican, Hertford College, Oxford

Mary Midgley, Newcastle University

Mario von der Ruhr, Swansea University

Michael McGhee, University of Liverpool

Clare Carlisle, University of Liverpool

Douglas Hedley, Clare College, Cambridge

Robin Le Poidevin, University of Leeds

Peter Byrne, King's College, London

Introduction

In public debate the topic of religion has figured far more prominently in the past few years than anyone would have imagined likely beforehand. It cannot, however, be said that the debate has been conducted particularly constructively, or, at times, even in a civil fashion.

In order to attempt to throw light on the topic, rather than pouring yet more oil on turgid waters, for its 2008–9 annual London lecture series, the Royal Institute of Philosophy took Religion as its topic. The essays in this book are the result.

In the first four, Richard Swinburne, Tim Mawson, Gerald Hughes and Brian Leftow write very much within the great tradition of natural theology, and they are followed by Richard Norman, Peter Cave and Peter Millican who are robustly critical of religious claims. Mary Midgley then continues her long campaign against the excesses of the neo-Darwinists, arguing for what might be seen as a non-religious sense of meaning. Mario von der Ruhr, Michael McGhee and Clare Carlisle look directly at the notion of spirituality from differing perspectives. Douglas Hedley then considers the notions of sacrifice and the sacred and Robin Le Poidevin that of Incarnation and the collection closes, appropriately enough, with a careful examination of religion, pluralism and tolerance from Peter Byrne.

On behalf of the Royal Institute of Philosophy I would like to thank all those who contributed to the series and to this book, and also to Adam Ferner for his editorial and indexing efforts.

doi:10.1017/S1358246111000154   © The Royal Institute of Philosophy and the contributors 2011
Royal Institute of Philosophy Supplement **68** 2011   1

God as the Simplest Explanation of the Universe[1]

RICHARD SWINBURNE

I have argued over many years that theism provides a probably true explanation of the existence and most general features of the universe. A major reason for this, I have claimed, is that it is simpler than other explanations.[2] The present paper seeks to amplify and defend this latter claim in the light of some recent challenges.

The Two Kinds of Explanation

Explanatory hypotheses are of two kinds – inanimate (or scientific) and personal. In inanimate explanation we explain an event by means of an initial condition (or cause) C and a regularity or law of nature (N), such that these together necessitate or render probable the resulting event (E). To take a trivial example, we explain a given piece of iron expanding (E) by 'the iron was heated' (C) and 'all iron expands when heated' (N). We explain Mars being where it is today in terms of where it and the sun were yesterday and on previous days (C) and Kepler's three laws of motion (N) which together entail it being where it is today (E). In personal explanation we explain by means of a person (S) with certain powers (P), beliefs (B) and purposes (G). By a 'purpose' I mean an intention in what the person is doing; an intentional action is an action of bringing about what the person has the purpose of bringing about. We explain my hand moving (E) by means of me (S), having the power

[1] This paper is dependent on much earlier writing of mine, especially *The Christian God* (Oxford: Clarendon Press, 1994) chs. 6 and 7; *Epistemic Justification* (Oxford: Clarendon Press, 2001) ch. 4, and 'How the Divine Properties Fit together: Reply to Gwiazda', *Religious Studies*, **45** (2009), 495–8. The latter paper was a reply to Jeremy Gwiazda, 'Richard Swinburne's argument to the simplicity of God via the infinite', *Religious Studies*, **45** (2009), 487–93. I am grateful to Jeremy Gwiazda whose criticism of earlier views of mine helped me to formulate the view presented in this paper.
[2] See for example, my *The Existence of God*, second edition (Oxford: Clarendon Press, 2004) chs. 3 and 5.

doi:10.1017/S1358246111000142   © The Royal Institute of Philosophy and the contributors 2011
Royal Institute of Philosophy Supplement **68** 2011

Richard Swinburne

to move my hand (P), having the purpose of getting your attention (G) and believing that causing my hand to move will do that (B). And we explain people's purposes in terms of their desires (D) and beliefs (B). By a 'desire' I understand a kind of liability with which we find ourselves to form certain purposes which render it probable that we will form those purposes. Among our beliefs we have moral beliefs about what is good to do. Moral beliefs motivate us, incline us to do the relevant action, but they may not motivate us as strongly as non-rational desires. So sometimes we have to choose between forming a purpose involving yielding to a desire to do what is bad, or a purpose involving pursuing the good despite contrary desire.

There are however two different ways of construing inanimate explanation, depending on what laws of nature are, that is what are we claiming in claiming that 'all iron expands when heated' or (perhaps more realistically) 'all photons travel at velocity c in vacuo relative to all inertial frames' are laws of nature? We can, I think, these days quickly dismiss the Humean account that they are just assertions about what in fact happens: each bit of iron when heated in the past did expand, and each bit when heated in future will expand. For there is a physical necessity in the operation of laws of nature not captured by Hume's account. That leaves two serious possibilities. The first is that laws are real things separate from the substances (physical objects), things which determine how those substances behave. The currently discussed version of this is the view that laws are relations between universals (that is properties which may be instantiated in many different substances); 'iron', 'expanding' and 'being heated' are universals tied together (and that has to be construed as tied together in a Platonic heaven) such that when you instantiate 'iron' and 'being heated' you inevitably instantiate 'expanding'. I shall call this view, advocated by Armstrong and others,[3] the RBU (relations between universals) account. And so we explain the behaviour of a particular substance by something outside itself

---

[3] See D. M. Armstrong, *What is a Law of Nature?* (Cambridge: Cambridge University Press, 1983); Michael Tooley, 'The nature of laws', *Canadian Journal of Philosophy* **7** (1977), 667–98; and F. I. Dretske, 'Laws of Nature', *Philosophy of Science* **44** (1977), 248–68. Armstrong construes universals in an Aristotelian way (that is, as existing only when instantiated). But that will not explain why their first instantiation had the character it did, e.g. why the first piece of iron expanded when heated. That could only be explained if the universals were already tied together, and that would involve their existing before being instantiated, and so in a 'Platonic heaven'. This latter is the view of Tooley, and it is in his way that I have spelled out the RBU account.

which determines also the behaviour of other substances – e.g. other pieces of iron. The alternative view is the substances – powers – and liabilities account (SPL). This was the normal view in ancient and medieval thought, and versions of it have been recently advocated by Harré and Madden and by Brian Ellis.[4] On the SPL account the fundamental laws of nature are causal laws; and these are generalizations, not (as Hume supposed) about what in fact happens, but about the causal powers of substances of a certain kind and their liabilities (either with physical necessity or with a certain physical probability) to exercise them. Thus 'all iron expands when heated' being a law of nature is a matter of every piece of iron having the power to expand and the liability (with physical necessity) to do so when heated. Kepler's laws are generalisations about the powers of planets to move in certain ways and their liabilities to do so under certain circumstances. It is a contingent matter that things fall into a few kinds distinguished by their powers and liabilities as well as by other properties. This ultimately derives from the fact that their constituents are fundamental particles (substances, such as electrons and quarks) which fall into a very few kinds distinguished from each other by their mass, charge, spin etc; these latter being – at least in part – analysable in terms of the powers and liabilities possessed by the particles.

Although I think that the main argument of this paper can be phrased in terms of either account of inanimate explanation, in order not to make the paper too long, I am now going to make the assumption that the SPL account is the correct account. One quick reason for rejecting RBU, is the implausibility of a Platonic heaven containing universals influencing the behaviour of mundane things. Another reason is that it enables us to give a more unified account of explanation.[5] For, given SPL, all explanation, inanimate and personal, now involves substances (either persons or inanimate things) and their powers. I assume that an inanimate thing must be physical (that is, public.) The difference between the two kinds of explanation is now that inanimate things have liabilities (inevitably or with a certain physical probability) to exercise those powers under certain circumstances and so to cause effects, whereas persons intentionally exercise their powers to cause effects in the light of beliefs about

[4]   R. Harré and E. H. Madden, *Causal Powers* (Oxford: Basil Blackwell, 1975); Brian Ellis, *Scientific Essentialism* (Cambridge: Cambridge University Press, 2001).
[5]   For further argument in defence of the SPL account see 179–85 of my 'Relations Between Universals, or Divine Laws?', *Australasian Journal of Philosophy* **84** (2006), 179–89.

Richard Swinburne

what exercising some power will achieve and the purposes which they seek to achieve. Explanation of an event will now consist (in the inanimate case) in the occurrence of circumstances under which some substance (or substances) was liable to exercise certain powers. That a piece of iron expanded when heated is explained by it (S) having the power to expand (P) and the liability to exercise that power when heated (L), and by (C) it being heated. Strictly speaking no law 'all iron expands when heated' is part of the explanation. The 'law' is a mere description of the powers etc of all pieces of iron, relevant only because it entails the powers of this piece. Explanation of an event by personal explanation will invoke only S, P, B, and G; although all these factors might themselves be explained (in so far as they can be explained)by an inanimate explanation – e.g. B may be explained by the liability (L) of S to have a belief of a certain kind under certain circumstances which did in fact occur; and G may be explained by S's desire to form such purposes, that is a liability (at least with physical probability) to do so. And conversely the factors involved in an inanimate explanation might be explained by a personal explanation.

The Criteria of Correct Explanation

I suggest that an explanatory hypothesis (or theory) is rendered probably true (or likely to be true) by data (evidence) insofar as (1) the occurrence of the evidence is probable if the hypothesis is true and improbable if the hypothesis is false, (2) the hypothesis 'fits in' with any 'background evidence'(that is, it meshes with other hypotheses outside its range which are rendered probable by their evidence in virtue of the other criteria), (3) the hypothesis is simple, and (4) the hypothesis has small scope.[6] The scope (or content) of a theory is a matter of how much it purports to tell us about the world, in the range and precision of its claims. (3) and (4) are features internal to a hypothesis, independent of its relation to evidence and so determine its prior probability (probability prior to considering the evidence). While the more the hypothesis claims, the more likely it is to be false (which is what the criterion of scope says), simplicity carries more weight than scope; scientists consider some theory of enormous scope (concerned with the whole universe) probable if has a relatively

[6] For a fuller account of these criteria, but one which does not distinguish the different roles some of them play on the RBU and SPL accounts of laws of nature, see my *Epistemic Justification*, ch. 4.

simple set of laws. There may be no relevant background evidence, and then criterion (2) drops out. One case of this is when a hypothesis has very large range (purports to explain a vast amount) and so there is little if any evidence about fields beyond its range. Among large scale theories of equal scope, such as theism and rival accounts of why there is a universe of our kind, relative probability depends on criteria (1) and (3) alone; and so in the case of theories leading us to expect the evidence with the same probability (that is, satisfying criterion (1) equally well), on criterion (3) alone. Let me give you two examples – one of each kind of explanation – illustrating how, among theories satisfying the other criteria equally well, the simplest theory (simplest in an intuitive sense yet to be analysed more precisely) is the one most probably true.

Suppose we find among pages recovered from an ancient library three pages in similar handwriting of an apparently connected philosophical argument. One hypothesis is that the same person wrote all three pages. An alternative hypothesis is that each page was written by a different philosopher; all three philosophers had similar handwriting, and thought independently of the same argument which they wrote down; but only the first page of the first philosopher's text, the second page of the second philosopher's text, and the third page of the third philosopher's text have survived. The two hypotheses are of equal scope – telling us about who wrote these pages; and is such as to lead us to expect the data with equal probability. But, unless there is relevant background evidence, the first hypothesis is obviously more probable in postulating only one person writing the pages rather than three. For my second example consider a theory which renders probable the same astronomical evidence observed so far as does General Relativity. General Relativity does this (on the SPL account) by attributing to stars certain powers and liabilities to exercise them dependant on the structure of the spatio-temporal region in which they are situated; and it predicts further observations tomorrow in virtue of the same powers and liabilities. The rival theory claims that the liabilities of these things to exercise their powers will depend on the structure of their spatio-temporal region in a different way when the expansion of the Universe causes galaxies to have a certain average distance apart (which distance they will attain tomorrow) from the way they depend today. General Theory is more probable than its rival because (put in terms of laws) it consists of only one set of complicated equations and so is simpler than its rival which consists of a conjunction of two sets of complicated equations. So again simplicity is evidence of truth. In so far as General Theory gets support from other theories of physics with

Richard Swinburne

which it fits, then unless simplicity is evidence of truth, those other theories would be just as probable as rival theories adjusted in a similar way, and General Theory's rival would fit better with those rivals; and so again General Theory and its rival would be equally probable on the evidence. But they are not, and that is because of the crucial role of the criterion of simplicity.

The Nature of Simplicity

The assimilation of scientific explanation to personal explanation, consequential on adopting the SPL account of laws of nature, makes it possible to give common criteria of simplicity covering both types. So let's look at what the criterion of simplicity, when used in this way as evidence of truth amounts to. It consists of various sub-criteria. First, fewer entities (alias, substances or objects). Astronomers don't postulate an extra planet, unless thereby their data are made more probable. And the historian in my earlier example postulates as few philosophers writing texts as possible. What constitutes one entity as opposed to two? Entities require a certain causal unity to them; they stick together. But whether the parts of a physical thing stick together is matter of degree, and it's not always clear when there are two entities rather than one. (For some purposes you can treat a double-star system as one entity, for other purposes you must treat it as two entities.) But clearly an entity which has no parts is just one entity; and as such a very simple one. Secondly, fewer properties attributed to entities. Don't postulate a new property possessed by (e.g.) a fundamental particle unless it results in a gain of explanatory power. Again, the application of this subcriterion depends on how you count properties. A property defined by similarity to paradigm examples of its application, such as 'green' or 'mass' or 'bright' counts as one property; properties defined as conjunctions or disjunctions of such properties (or as having more complicated probabilistic relations to such properties) count as two or more properties. It follows from this subcriterion that hypotheses are simpler, the more accessible to observation (or experience generally) are the properties which they postulate. This can be illustrated by the well-known philosophical example of two theories to account for the colours of emeralds. 'All emeralds are green' and 'all emeralds are grue'(where 'grue' means 'green before 2050 A.D., or blue thereafter') both render the data about the colours of emeralds now (in 2010 A.D.) available equally probable. But the theory 'all emeralds are green' is more probable than

8

'all emeralds are grue', and this is because 'grue' is defined in terms of an accessible property (green) and another property (the date, whose definition in terms of what is accessible clearly has a certain complexity).[7]

Among the properties of objects are their powers and liabilities, purposes and beliefs. In explaining human behaviour we need to attribute to humans as few and as accessible such properties as will suffice to render probable their behaviour. And we need to attribute to them as few and accessible desires and moral beliefs as will explain (at least in part) their purposes; and as few and accessible liabilities to acquire beliefs as will explain their moral and other beliefs. I illustrate this for the case of powers. Someone may walk (as far as we can judge, intentionally) one mile from A to B one day at 3mph, and two miles from C to D another day at 3 mph. But we wouldn't explain his behaviour on the first day simply by his having the power to walk one mile at 3mph on the first day; and explain his behaviour on the second day simply by his having the power to walk two miles at 3mph on that day. Rather we'd explain both pieces of behaviour by his having the power over a period to walk at least two miles in a day at 3 mph. Since both previous powers follow from one equally accessible property, we attribute the latter to the person; and so we believe that in virtue of having the more general power, that person will be able to walk at least two miles at 3mph on other occasions. And so we seek to attribute to humans powers as few and as accessible as will explain their behaviour. Similarly for inanimate things – for example, we attribute to fundamental particles as few forces (that is, powers to affect other substances) as possible.

We explain the exercise of powers by inanimate things by their liabilities to exercise those powers. Liabilities are also simpler, the fewer (accessible) properties by which we distinguish them. A power of a substance is a power to exercise various amounts of causal influence; and the liability is a liability to exercise a power, and to exercise some particular degree of it under certain

---

[7] But couldn't there be a being which just recognized things as 'grue' without doing so in virtue of their colour and the date? There could certainly be a being which classified together (in virtue of their similarity to paradigm examples) the same objects as we would call 'grue' (on the grounds of their satisfying the stated definition). But he would be picking out a different property ('grue*') which – as far as his experience went – was coinstantiated with 'grue'. Yet there could be no guarantee that the two properties individuated in different ways would always coincide. We have no access to the property of being grue* and so cannot use it in our explanations of things.

Richard Swinburne

contingent circumstances. A body may exert more or less gravitational influence on another body in virtue of its liability to do so being dependent on its mass, the mass of the other body, and their distance apart. And an explanation is simpler, the simpler the mathematical relations between the degrees of the various properties and liabilities, and the simpler the mathematical entities involved in stating the relations. Such a relation or entity A is simpler than another one B, if A is defined and so can be understood without reference to B but not vice versa. For this reason multiplication is a more complicated relation than addition, numerical powers more complicated than multiplication, and vectors more complicated than scalars; and large finite integers are more complicated entities than small ones (you can't understand '5' except as '4 + 1', but you can understand '4', ' + ', and '1' without understanding the notion of '5'); and (as their name implies) complex numbers are more complicated than real numbers, real than rational numbers, rational numbers than integers. So an explanation which explains the pressure exerted by a gas on the walls of a container is simpler if it makes this depend on only three other quantities (the volume of the container, the temperature of the gas, and a constant varying with the kind of gas) rather than on four. It is simpler if the relation between the variables involves just multiplication as in the Boyle–Charles law $pv = KT$, rather than on exponentials, logarithms and square roots, for example $p = \log \hat{e} \, vk^{-1/2}T^2$. If laws of both kinds satisfied the first two criteria equally well, a law of the first kind would be more probably true than a law of the latter kind. For exponentials, logarithms and powers are defined (and so can be understood) in terms of multiplication but not vice versa. So too a law of gravity, $F = mm^1/r^2$ is to be preferred to a law $F = mm^1/ r^{2.00 \text{ (ten zeros) } 1}$ if both equally well explain the data (of measurements accurate only to a certain degree).

Likewise with purposes, desires and beliefs. A purpose to visit London and a purpose to learn to sky-dive are separate purposes, because they are not derivable from one equally accessible general purpose. But a purpose to write the first chapter of my book and the purpose to write the second chapter of my book are derivable from an equally accessible purpose to write my book; and that is why the simpler and more general description should be attributed to me, given evidence of my writing the first chapter and then the second chapter, in the absence of counter-evidence. We attribute to persons continuing accessible desires (varying with circumstances in a mathematically simple way, which give rise to purposes at appropriate times – for example, a desire to eat which increases when the person has not eaten for a long time, and decreases after eating).

God as the Simplest Explanation of the Universe

Likewise it is simpler to explain many of my beliefs by such general liabilities as the liability (at least with high physical probability) to believe what I am told and to acquire beliefs about the location of objects in my field of vision, than by separate liabilities for each belief. And powers, beliefs, purposes, desires and liabilities are readily accessible properties. In summary hypotheses of personal and scientific explanation (on the SPL account of the latter) are simpler if they postulate fewer substances, fewer (accessible) properties (including powers and liabilities), and mathematically simpler relations between them (including mathematically simpler numbers in the statement of these). These features of simplicity are features of the simplicity of the actual components (substances, properties, and the relations between them) of an explanation of some phenomenon independently of whether they are operative in other similar substances.

Natural Theology

Natural Theology of a probabilistic kind claims that the most probable explanation of the existence of the universe and its most general features is that they are caused by God. These most general features include the universal operation of simple laws of nature (that is, in terms of the SPL account, that every physical object behaves in exactly the same way codified in the simple 'laws' of nature), those laws and the initial (or boundary) conditions of the universe being such as to bring about the existence of human bodies, and humans being conscious beings, open to a finite amount of suffering and having some ability to bear it or alleviate it. (I mean by the 'boundary conditions' of the universe those general features of universe which, in addition to those captured by 'laws' of nature, the universe would need to have if it did not have a beginning, at all times if human bodies were to evolve – for example enough matter-energy.) These general features, the natural theologian's evidence or data, described in terms of the SPL account are the existence of a vast number of substances all behaving in the same simple way such as to bring about somewhere or other at some time or other in conditions of suffering the bodies of conscious humans. Natural theology needs therefore to claim that the hypothesis of theism (that there is a God) satisfies the criteria of correct explanation set out earlier better than does any rival explanation. As I wrote earlier, for very wide-ranging theories such as theism and any rivals, this will depend only on how well they satisfy criteria (1) and (3).

11

Richard Swinburne

Criterion (1) is satisfied insofar as the evidence is probable if the hypothesis is true and improbable if the hypothesis is false. I have argued elsewhere at some length[8] that if there is a God, it is quite probable that he would bring about the existence of embodied humans in conditions such as we find on earth (including limited suffering and the possibility of bearing or alleviating it) and so that he would bring about those general features of the universe just described which are necessary conditions for the existence of such humans. The basic reason for this is that God being perfectly good will seek to produce good things; humans are good things of a unique kind having – unlike God – the power to make efficacious choices between (limited) good and evil. It is therefore quite likely that God will produce them. But humans can only make efficacious choices (ones that make a difference) if they live in an embodied state in an orderly universe where they can predict the effects of their actions, and that minimally involves a universe with many substances of few kinds (protons, electrons etc) with simple powers and liabilities. But of course there are innumerable other logically possible hypotheses which satisfy criterion (1) equally well, both hypotheses in terms of many or weaker deities, and scientific hypotheses to the effect that the initial conditions of the universe and its laws of nature are ultimate and have no further explanation (e.g. in terms of God bringing them about) and eventually cause the existence of conscious beings. My concern in this paper however is only to discuss how well different such hypotheses satisfy the other relevant criterion, criterion (3), the criterion of simplicity. I now proceed to inquire, in the light of my analysis of that criterion, how well theism satisfies the criterion of simplicity, and how well any rival hypothesis either of a personal or an inanimate (scientific) kind which satisfied criterion (1) to some significant degree would also satisfy the criterion of simplicity.

The Simplicity of God

The simplest kind of explanation of the features which I have described will be in terms of some one first substance (whether some first chunk of matter-energy or a personal creator) which caused, in virtue of its powers and liabilities or its powers, beliefs and purposes, the multitude of substances of a very few kinds with their powers and

---

[8] See *The Existence of God*, chs. 6–13, and the shorter and simpler book *Is There a God?* (Oxford: Oxford University Press, 1996). chs. 4–7.

liabilities. If the universe had a beginning, the 'first substance' would be a substance which caused the emergence and evolution of the universe into this multitude a finite number of years ago. But if the universe has always existed, then this 'first substance' would be one which everlastingly keeps this multiplicity of substances in existence with their powers at all moments in time. Theism (as understood by the Christian and similar religions) postulates a person as the cause of the universe and so provides a personal explanation of its existence. This person is often called 'God'; though in the case of the Christian tradition, we must regard the first substance as 'God the Father' who according to Christianity inevitably brings about from all eternity the other two members of the Trinity.[9] Other theistic religions do not of course have this feature. So can the traditional divine properties be construed in such a way that this unique personal substance whom in future I will call simply 'God' is a simple substance and the simplest substance which can perform this explanatory role?

God is one person. So theism is inevitably a simpler theory than polytheism. To be a person at all, a substance has to live for a period of time, to have some power (to do intentional actions), some choice (whether free or not) of which actions to do, and some true beliefs. He will have to have some true beliefs about his intentional powers (what he can do); otherwise he will not be able to bring about anything intentionally. I shall assume that there cannot be a timeless person, and so that any person who exists exists and so has his properties at moments of time[10] If there could be such a person, the simplest kind of person would be an everlasting omnipotent, omniscient, and perfectly free person, a person to whose length of life, power, true beliefs,[11] and freedom of choice there are no limits;

---

[9]   A simple hypothesis is no less simple for entailing complicated consequences. Christianity claims that God the Father inevitably in virtue of his nature brings about the other two members of the Trinity, all of whom together constitute one God. (For a argument in justification of this Chrisitan claim see my *The Christian God*, especially ch. 8.) But I suggest that arguments to the existence of that one God must proceed via arguments to the existence of one person on whom everything else depends, and so to the existence of God the Father, whose postulated properties are the same as those attributed to the God of Islam or Judaism.

[10]   For argument in defence of this claim see my *The Coherence of Theism*, revised edition (Oxford: Clarendon Press, 1993), 223–9; and *The Christian God*, ch. 4 and 137–44.

[11]   It is generally agreed that knowledge is true belief not acquired by luck, although there are different views about what 'not acquired by luck' involves. I shall be arguing shortly that all the divine properties which

Richard Swinburne

or rather no limits except those of logic, since any description of what all this amounts to has got to be free from contradiction. A person is everlasting if he exists at all times, omnipotent if he can do all actions, omniscient if he has all true beliefs, perfectly free if he is subject to no non-rational desires which influence how he chooses to act. The concepts of length of time, intentional power, belief, choice, and influence on choice are concepts of properties maximally accessible; we are more familiar with paradigm examples of these properties than of virtually any other properties. The concepts of 'all', or 'unlimited' (that is having no (zero) limits) are concepts far more accessible than concepts of particular large numbers. Hence the properties of everlasting life, limitless power, having all true beliefs, being subject to no causal influences on choice are far more accessible than the properties of living for a particular large number of years, having a particular large finite degree of power, having a particular large finite number of mostly true beliefs, and being subject to fairly few non-rational desires.

A person P is omnipotent at a time t iff he has the maximum degree of logically possible power. I suggest that that amounts to this: he is able at t intentionally to bring about any state of affairs which it is logically possible for anyone at t to bring about (and the description of which does not entail that P did not at t bring it about).[12] However the notion of having an intentional power or an ability to do some intentional action is somewhat unclear. One says that someone has a power or ability when asleep, meaning by that he could exercise it if he was awake and tried to do so. One might say that someone has the ability to speak French simply because he could learn it if he tried; or even that he has the ability to speak Gaelic for the same reason even if he does not believe that there is such a language as Gaelic. But clearly he has the power in its fullest form if he can exercise it at will, is

---

I have been discussing belong to God essentially and so not by luck. So God's true beliefs will amount to knowledge. It will simplify the present discussion if I assume this already established.

[12] Philosophers have found it very difficult to analyse an intuitively simple concept of omnipotence (maximum logically possible power) in such a way as to avoid various paradoxes. For the history of attempts to analyse the concept of omnipotence, see Brian Leftow 'Omnipotence' in T. P. Flint and M. C. Rae (eds.), *The Oxford Handbook of Philosophical Theology* (Oxford: Oxford University Press, 2009). I hope that my analysis avoids all such paradoxes, but if it doesn't the concept is a simple one which makes clear the kind of qualifications which are necessary to avoid paradoxes.

14

conscious and knows that he can exercise it at will; only his will is preventing him from exercising it immediately. So omnipotence, being the maximum possible degree of power should be construed as equivalent to the following: a person P is omnipotent iff he is consciously aware of all the states which it is logically possible for anyone to bring about at t (and the description of which does not entail that P did not bring it about); and if he chooses at t to bring about any such state, it happens. Given the logical impossibility of backward causation, an omnipotent person cannot affect the past[13] or the truth of logically necessary truths, which I assume to include the fundamental moral truths.[14] Hence the choices of an omnipotent person can affect only contingent future states.

A person P is omniscient at t (in the most natural sense) iff he knows all propositions true at t. I have spelled out being 'perfectly free' as being subject to no non-rational desires influencing his choice. Clearly any agent who makes a choice is influenced by the nature of that choice, what it involves, and so by considerations of reason, the apparent goodness or badness of the action. To believe that some action is good to do necessarily gives you a desire to do it in proportion to its believed worth. The apparent good motivates, and the apparently better motivates more. What is ruled out by 'perfect freedom' are desires to do an action which is apparently bad, or ones which are stronger than its apparent worth would motivate. Hence a person who is both omniscient and perfectly free will will be moved to do an action in proportion to its actual goodness. God being perfectly free will set himself to do what he believes best; being omniscient (to the extent of knowing all necessary truths and truths about the past) he will have true beliefs about what is the best; and being omnipotent, he will succeed in doing it. So he will always do the best action where there is one. If in some situation there is no unique best action (i.e. some incompatible action would be equally good, or there is an infinite sequence of incompatible actions, each less good than the next member of the series), then God cannot do the best. But his perfect freedom will lead him to get as close to that as the nature of the good will allow; and that means that if there are several equal best actions he will do one of

---

[13]   That is, he cannot affect 'hard facts' about the past, these being ones whose truth conditions are solely in the past.
[14]   For my reasons for this assumption see for example pages 151–55 of my 'What Difference does God make to Morality' in R. K. Garcia and N. L. King (eds.), *Is Goodness Without God Good Enough?* (Lanham: Rowman and Littlefield, 2009.)

them, and in the infinite series situation he will do some good (and no bad) action. So God will be as good as it is logically possible to be, and we may call that 'perfectly good'.[15] So it turns out that God being 'perfectly free' in my sense has the consequence that while he can do evil, inevitably he will never exercise the choice to do so. In another perhaps equally natural sense of 'perfectly free' a perfectly free person would be one who could make any logically possible choice including doing evil. So why my sense of 'perfectly free' rather than the rival sense? Because it is a simpler sense. 'Perfect freedom' in my sense is simply the absence of properties, non-rational desires; 'perfect freedom' in the rival sense would be a complicating feature of God, because it would involve his being influenced by non-rational desires which alone make possible a choice of evil. So I stick with my sense.

Frequently, indeed I would have thought in most situations, there will be no unique best action for God to do. Surely, even if there were no incompatible better action for God to do, it would have been an equal best action for God to make (the universe begin in such a way as to cause) the planet Uranus to rotate in the same direction as the other planets as to rotate in a different direction. And however many planets (in our galaxy or in some distant galaxy) containing living organisms God makes, it would be better if he makes one more. And so on.

But these definitions give rise to a problem, that while there could be an everlastingly omnipotent and perfectly free person, and there could be an everlastingly omniscient person, everlasting omnipotence plus perfect freedom is incompatible with everlasting omniscience. In the absence of rational considerations relevant to his choice and in the absence of any non-rational desires influencing that choice a God perfectly free and omnipotent would have a free choice of which state of affairs to bring about before the time when the relevant state of affairs came about. But then he would have been free to choose to make any earlier belief about how he would choose false, and so only by cosmic luck could all God's beliefs have been true, and beliefs acquired by luck (see note 11) do not constitute knowledge. So omnipotence plus perfect freedom are incompatible with omniscience understood in the obvious way. On the other hand a more restricted kind of

---

[15]   William Rowe (among others) has argued that unless God always does an action better than any incompatible actions, God cannot be 'perfectly good', and so there cannot be a God of the traditional kind. See his *Can God be Free?* (Oxford: Clarendon Press, 2006). Like many others, I find this view highly implausible.

omniscience, knowing all truths about the past and all necessary truths (including the necessary moral truths[16]) is not merely compatible with omnipotence plus perfect freedom but entailed by them. This is because for any past state or any necessary truth, there are future states of affairs which can be defined by its relation to them, from which it follows that if God is to have the choice of bringing about these states, he needs to know all necessary truths and all truths about the past. For example, if God is to know that he can choose now to bring about a third world war or a prime number of planets greater than 7, he has to know that so far there have been only two world wars, and that there is a prime number greater than 7. Since omnipotence entails knowledge of moral truths, omnipotence plus perfect freedom entail perfect goodness; unrestricted omniscience is not necessary for this. Omnipotence is the simplest degree of one property necessary for a person, perfect freedom is merely the absence of certain complicating properties (causal desires), which together yield a vast degree of knowledge of a simple although not the simplest kind. ('Simple' because it is all the knowledge possible for a perfectly free and omnipotent person.) On the other hand a person omniscient in the full sense which includes knowing everything which he would choose to do, could not be perfectly free. Indeed he could not be free to any degree. He would be causally predetermined at every moment of time to do every future action which he would do on each occasion when there is no unique best action for him to do. That has the consequence that on each such occasion he would be subject to a particular non-rational desire (determining and not

---

[16]   Contingent moral truths are ones made true by a conjunction of a necessary moral truth and a contingent non-moral truth. For example, it would be contingently true that I ought to pay you £20 if I have promised to pay you £20 (contingent non-moral truth) and people ought always to keep their promises (necessary moral truth). The contingent non-moral truths which, together with necessary moral truths, create contingent moral truths are normally truths about the past – truths about past commitments or truths about what past evidence shows is likely to happen in future. Hence a being who knew all truths about the past and all necessary truths would normally know all moral truths about what would be good for him to do now. But insofar as whether an action available to such a being who is also omnipotent and perfectly free (in my sense) is good now depends on what is yet to happen (and not merely about what present evidence shows about what is likely to happen), then such a being would predetermine the future in order to enable him to do what is good now. Hence only the kind of omniscience entailed by omnipotence is necessary for God's perfect goodness.

Richard Swinburne

merely influencing him) to do this rather than that action (when there would be no reason for doing this action rather than that one.) This would make God a very complicated person. So which is the way of understanding omniscience which makes an omnipotent being the simplest kind of person? The answer is clearly the restricted kind of omniscience[17] which allows him also to be perfectly free.

The other divine properties (understood in natural ways) follow from the ones analysed above.[18] For example, since God is omnipotent, everything else that comes to exist comes to exist because he causes it or allows it to exist; hence he is in a natural sense creator of all that is. Being omnipotent, he can make things happen anywhere and learn about things anywhere without depending on intermediate causes; so in a natural sense he is omnipresent, and so is not tied down to a body, and so is not physical.

God's omnipotence is a power and so an intrinsic property. God's omniscience (in the restricted sense) is not a power or a liability[19] but a categorical state necessary for omnipotence; and it might seem that it is not an intrinsic property of God but a relation to other entities because it involves possessing (having within oneself) certain objects – all true beliefs. If that was the right understanding of omniscience, then of course God world certainly not be simple. So all depends on what it is to have a certain belief; and it is not, I suggest, possessing an object within oneself. I suggest that having a belief that p is an intrinsic property and one too primitive to be defined. But we can show what we are talking about when we talk about S's belief that p by saying that it is the sort of thing S would acquire in a certain way (e.g. by S seeing that p, or by someone telling S that p) and which makes a certain kind of difference to S's behaviour (e.g. if it follows from p, that the way to get x is to do A (and not B), and it follows from not-p that the way to get x is to do B (and not A), and S has the purpose of getting x, he will do A.)

---

[17]   For fuller discussion of this see *The Christian God*, 150–1.

[18]   In deriving this restriction I am following the convention of calling a belief about the future true now iff in the future it will be true, even when its truth is not yet inevitable. This is a convention which we do not always follow when we talk of a belief 'not yet' being true. But if we do not count a belief whose truth or falsity is not yet inevitable, as not now being either true or false, then God's omniscience can be construed simply as having all true beliefs. I do not however think that it is any less simple to understand only beliefs whose truth value is inevitable as having a truth value, than to follow our more normal convention.

[19]   Thus Aquinas: 'Knowledge in God is not ... a disposition *(habitus)*', *Summa theologiae* Ia.14.ad 1.

God as the Simplest Explanation of the Universe

We humans can have beliefs about matters about which we are not thinking. I have beliefs about what I did when young about which I am not thinking, but they are my beliefs in that – if prompted – I could bring them to consciousness. It is simpler to suppose that all God's beliefs are currently before his mind;[20] that he is currently aware of all his knowledge and so beliefs involved in his omnipotence follows from my account of his omnipotence, and these are the only ones which I am suggesting that he has. Beliefs need not be put into words; children have beliefs before they can put them into words, and when they acquire language they report that they had those beliefs. So I think that the best analogy for God's beliefs are the beliefs we acquire when we look at a scene before our eyes. Merely by looking we acquire innumerable beliefs about what objects there are, where they are, and what they look like. We are aware of these beliefs, but not as linguistic entities, and not as the brain states which causally sustain the beliefs in us. The beliefs are there in a fused pre-linguistic state out of which we can – if we choose – separate individual beliefs and put them into words (e.g. that 'there is a tree outside the window'.) We see things and acquire beliefs about them both as they are now, and (when we look at the stars) as they were thousands of years ago. Seeing involves categorizing: in seeing a tree I do not merely have a visual impression caused by a tree, but I see an object outside the window as a tree. And seeing an object thus categorized inevitably involves seeing its powers – the tree has the power to grow, to resist pressure and so on. God's beliefs are in this way just like the beliefs of which we are aware, but they concern the whole of the universe and the insides of things us well as their outsides. He sees things as they are and as they were. While our beliefs may come to us by different causal routes, it is simpler to suppose (as the traditional picture supposes) that God's beliefs come to him only by one route, directly. So too God's wider fused pre-linguistic state of belief is one integrated state of himself. It does not consist of separate items within himself, but it is a property of himself.

God's perfect freedom is, to repeat, merely the absence of the property of being influenced by non-rational desires. It is always simpler to postulate an absence than a presence. It is simpler to suppose that God has the divine properties discussed so far essentially; otherwise it would a vast accident that God continued for all time to exist and have these properties. By contrast an ordinary human person, although he

---

[20]   Thus Aquinas: '[God] sees everything at once and not successively', ibid. Ia.14.7.

Richard Swinburne

needs some power etc in order to exist, does not need to have some particular amount of power if order to be the particular human he is. And it is simpler to suppose that God does not have thisness, which would be a particularizing feature additional to his properties. (A substance has thisness iff there could be instead of it another substance with all the same properties, intrinsic and relational, as it. God would not have thisness iff there could not be instead of the actual God a different God with all the same properties, and so all the divine properties discussed so far.) But a person who does not have thisness, and for whom not merely having power (plus freedom) but having a particular amount of power (plus freedom) is essential to his being the person he is, is a person unlike any other persons with whom we are familiar. To call such a 'person' a 'person' is to use the word in a somewhat analogical sense, but one significantly similar to the ordinary notion (like an ordinary person, God has purposes and beliefs) for God to count as a person in a wide sense.

My understanding of the divine properties is traditional, except in respect of his being everlasting rather than timeless, and being omniscient only in the restricted sense.[21] My arguments however have

---

[21] That God is timeless has been the dominant theological view from at least the fourth century onwards. However, in my view the biblical authors thought of God as everlasting, and God's eternity has not been the subject of dogmatic definition. Nelson Pike's well-known book *God and Timelessness* (London: Routledge and Kegan Paul, 1970) concluded with his remark that he had not been able 'to find any basis for [the doctrine of divine timelessness] in biblical literature or in the confessional literature of either the Catholic or Protestant churches' And it is disputable whether even all western theologians of the high middle ages were committed to an explicit doctrine of divine timelessness – see R. Fox, *Time and Eternity in Mid-Thirteenth-Century Thought* (Oxford: Oxford University Press, 2006.) As regards omnisciecne, although there are a number of biblical passages which – read in their natural sense – do imply that God does not know infallibly what God or humans will do (e.g. Genesis 6:6, Jonah 3:10, and Revelation 3:5 which implies that God may change what is written in the Book of Life), most biblical passages imply that God is omniscient in the more natural sense; and the vast majority of subsequent Christian tradition is committed to that view. However this matter has not been the subject of any definition binding on Orthodox, or any definition which might be regarded by Catholics as infallible apart from the statement of the First Vatican Council that 'all things are open and laid bare to [God's] eyes, even those which will be brought about by the free activity of creatures'. (See N. P. Tanner (ed.), *Decrees of the Ecumenical Councils* (London: Sheed and Ward, 1990), 806.) However, The Council authorised no anathema against those who held a rival view; and (as far as I can see) this view is

20

God as the Simplest Explanation of the Universe

assumed that there cannot be a timeless person, and purport to show that the simplest kind of God would be omniscient only in the restricted sense. Persons other than God have more limited degrees of power and knowledge; their purposes are not influenced solely by their beliefs about what is good but by various desires for particular states of affairs whose strength is not always aligned with their beliefs about the goodness of these states. Other persons are very particular limited persons. God, defined (in the way I have spelled out) as an essentially everlasting omnipotent perfectly free person lacking thisness is a very simple substance, the simplest kind of person whose existence could explain the existence of the universe and its very general features. Hence the hypothesis of theism so construed is simpler than any hypothesis explaining the very general features of the universe in terms of a god construed in some other way. The sense in which I am claiming that God is simple is not quite the same as the sense in which later medieval theologians claimed that God is simple but it is not too far distant from it, at least on a familiar account of what that sense was.[22]

The enormous simplicity and so prior probability of hypotheses postulating omni-properties can be illustrated by a simple scientific example. Newton's theory of gravitation had three laws of motion (which are largely in effect definitions) and its law of gravity affirming of every given body, that it has the power to attract every other body in the universe with a force proportional to mm/r^2 and the liability always to exercise that power – from which it follows that each body also has the liability to be attracted by every such body with that force. These extensive powers and liabilities belong to the tiniest fundamental particle. So the power of such a particle extends over physical objects to the ends of the universe and that

---

not mentioned in the 1992 *Catechism of the Catholic Church* (London: Geoffrey Chapman, 1994) which 'aims at presenting an organic synthesis of the essential fundamental contents of Catholic doctrine' (9).

[22] For that familiar account, which may only be applicable to the later medievals, see my *The Christian God*, Clarendon Press, 1994, ch. 7. For these thinkers God's simplicity was a matter of his not having parts, and all his essential properties being the same as each other and the same as God. I claim that God has no parts, and that (not having thisness) he is whatever instantiates his essential properties. I claim that God has just one essential property – everlasting omnipotence – together with the absence of a property. For a rather different account of Augustine's views on God's simplicity, see Brian Leftow, 'Divine Simplicity', *Faith and Philosophy* **23** (2006), 365–380.

21

covers quite a range of the extent of God's power, though of course in no way comparable to it in strength; and its sensitivity to other physical objects, which we may compare to God's knowledge of them, also extends over quite a range of what God knows about. If there was no quantum indeterminism and we could make measurements with infinite accuracy, merely measuring the movements of one particle could tell us an enormous amount about the distribution of massive bodies throughout the universe; and measurements on several particles would tell everything about this (given the contingent truth of Newton's theory). The considerable probability of Newton's theory on the evidence available in 1689, far greater than that of the infinite number of rival theories which could have been postulated and would have predicted the evidence equally well, derives from the enormous simplicity of its omni-properties, ones which have considerable similarity to the omni-properties which theism attributes to God.

The simplest inanimate explanation of the universe is less simple than God

Could there be a physical object as simple as God (understood in the way developed above) which could provide an inanimate explanation of the existence of a universe with the very general features described above? The normal kind of 'first substance' postulated by physicists is an extended substance – a 'vacuum state' or a very compressed chunk of matter-energy. But such a state has parts and so is less simple than God. But physical cosmology could postulate one unextended substance, a particle, as that from which all else evolved (or on which all else depended, if the universe did not have a beginning). It would need to be a physical object of a certain kind in having certain properties, powers, and liabilities. The normal kind of physical substance would have powers of particular mathematical quantities (such as the attractive and repulsive powers of mass and charge) and liabilities to exercise them under certain physical conditions. These would need to be fairly specific powers and liabilities (some mathematically precise mass and charge for example) if they were to make it probable that it would bring about a universe with substances of few kinds with the same simple powers and liabilities as each other, of a human-body producing kind; and this specificity would make the hypothesis of the existence of such a substance more complicated than the hypothesis of theism. The singularity of the Big Bang would have to have all or at least (given a certain amount of indeterminism) most of the details of the future development of the universe built into it.

But could we not instead merely suppose that this physical object had the power to produce a good universe, and the liability always to exercise that power, and that would explain why we exist (because of the goodness of humans existing) and the other general features of our universe (the details of which were not predetermined but constitute one of the ways in which the universe would be good)? The power could be exercised by producing an appropriate sort of Big Bang. Given my earlier claim that laws of nature are to be analysed in terms of the powers and liabilities of substances, this is the nearest we can get to John Leslie's hypothesis that goodness has a propensity to exist.[23]

However even if such a physical object could do the explanatory work, it would not be nearly as simple as God. Like God, it could be essentially unextended, everlasting and lack thisness. The physical object's power to create the good would however be a limited power and so less simple than omnipotence (which can only be had by a being which can choose to act). And it would also need another power, the power to prevent any other substance bringing about the bad, and the liability always to exercise that power. Theism does not need a corresponding second power and liability, because it follows from divine omnipotence (plus perfect freedom) that every other substance only exists and produces effects insofar as God allows it to do so. The liabilities always to exercise these powers would be properties of the physical object additional to its powers. Yet being physical (and so public), it couldn't simply have *those* liabilities. A physical object (unless it is the only physical object) must have a location – there must be somewhere where it is (relative to other physical objects), and that means that there must be some detectable effects of it in one place which are not detectable elsewhere. (If a physical thing is here rather than there, here and not there is where it impedes the motions of other objects, or can be detected by a Geiger counter, or from where it emits light, or whatever.) So if the first physical substance were everlasting and so existed alongside other physical objects, its liability to produce effects must be manifested more or differently in one place than others, and that makes that property not a very simple property. (If however it ceased to exist after the creation of the physical universe, and so did not exist alongside other physical objects, it would not be everlasting and so would be less simple than God for a different reason.) So the

---

[23] See his *Value and Existence* (Basil Blackwell, 1979).

properties of a first physical object (additional to being everlasting, unextended, and lacking thisness, which God also has) would make it far from being very simple. In addition to the properties common to both God and a first physical substance, God would be merely omnipotent and perfectly free, but the latter, as we have seen, is simply the absence of something -and absence is always simpler than presence. I conclude that the powers and liabilities which we would need to ascribe to the single particle hypothesis (the simplest kind of inanimate explanation of the orderliness of the universe there could be) would be less simple than the properties of God – essential everlasting omnipotence (plus perfect freedom), from which all the other properties follow. So the hypothesis of theism provides a simpler explanation of the very general features of the universe than does any inanimate explanation. And it will be evident that the primary reason for that is that moral beliefs motivate; and so a conscious being needs less in the way of properties than does an inanimate one to cause the same effects.

And even if the hypothesis of one physical first substance were just as simple as the hypothesis of God, its propensity to create the good could not explain certain more particular features of our universe which would only be good if they were brought about by God. Vast numbers of religious experiences apparently of God would not be good unless there is a God. Interactive prayer would be deceptive. And our universe contains so much suffering that it would probably be overall a good universe only if its creator were to suffer with his creatures;[24] and that is something that only a person can do. I conclude, for two separate reasons that God (understood in the way which I have developed) is the simplest kind of cause of our universe there could be.

Oriel College, Oxford

---

[24] See my *The Resurrection of God Incarnate* (Oxford University Press, 2003), 44–5 for the obligation on a creator to share the suffering of those whom he causes to suffer for the sake of some great good. The argument which I use this point to develop here is that a good-producing physical object would have to produce a world with less suffering than would a good God who is prepared to share that suffering with creatures whom he makes to suffer for the sake of a great good.

This paper has been published, with the kind agreement of the Royal Institute of Philosophy, in *European Journal for the Philosophy of Religion* **2** (2010), 1–24.

Explaining the Fine Tuning of the Universe to Us and the Fine Tuning of Us to the Universe

T. J. MAWSON

I shall start, if you will permit me, by indicating how I shall be under-standing a couple of crucial terms, what I shall be meaning when I talk this evening of 'the universe' and of 'God'.

By 'the universe', I shall mean the physical reality that we encounter in everyday life – we presume – and all things causally connected to it which admit, at least in principle, of scientific explanation. So, I shall mean to include by the word 'universe' not merely the observed universe, but also the unobserved – sections of space-time beyond our light cone. If, as the Everett interpretation of Quantum Mechanics suggests, each time a quantum state 'collapses' as we might put it,[1] the universe branches, then all the branches taken to-gether make up one universe in my sense of universe. Similarly, if the space-time that started with the Big Bang and which we'd ordina-rily suppose was the entire universe is in fact a bubble created by a mother space-time system, then that mother space-time system is the universe and what we'd ordinarily suppose was the entire universe is in fact merely a part of the whole. If the Big Bang was caused by a collision of higher-dimensional membranes, then the membranes *et al.* are, collectively, the universe. And so on. I won't labour the point with more examples, the point being that, as I shall be using the term, the universe includes all and only entities the explanation of which would be part of a completed science.

By 'God' I shall mean the God of classical theism: a supernatural person who is omnipotent, omniscient, perfectly good, and creator of everything other than Himself. I take it that the existence of such a God is logically possible. And I also take it that, were God to exist, He would – of necessity – not be a part of any universe as, were He to exist, He would lie outside scientific explanation in prin-ciple. The God of classical theism is – by definition – the creator of everything other than Himself, so, if He exists, He is the creator of

---

[1]   'Collapses' then needs scare quotation marks as, on the Everett interpretation, instead of really collapsing, every component of the wave-function lives on in some branch or other.

doi:10.1017/S1358246111000075   © The Royal Institute of Philosophy and the contributors 2011

Royal Institute of Philosophy Supplement **68** 2011

our universe, whatever its nature may be (branching, bubble, *et cetera*), and of any other universes that there might be too.[2]

This evening I shall be considering the probability of every possible universe being actual, what I shall call the 'maximal multiverse hypothesis'. I shall be considering its probability relative to that of God's being actual, the 'God hypothesis' if you will. And I shall be considering their relative probabilities on the evidence provided by certain general features of the laws of nature which we take to be operative in our universe, what might be called the 'fine tuning of the universe to us' and the 'fine tuning of us to the universe'. (I shall explain what I mean by fine tuning in a moment.) As well as considering the relative probability of these two hypotheses on the evidence provided by fine tuning, I shall also be considering the probability of the evidence on these hypotheses as that is, I take it, relevant to their relative satisfactoriness as explanations of that evidence. I've focused on the maximal multiverse hypothesis and the God hypothesis as these two hypotheses are, I am assuming, the simplest naturalist and supernaturalist hypotheses that one might suggest as explaining the fine tuning. The simplicity of the maximal multiverse hypothesis is an issue to which I shall return in due course; the relative simplicity of the God hypothesis amongst supernaturalist hypotheses is one that time considerations force me to assume.[3]

---

[2]   The use of 'universe' and 'God' then necessitates that if there is a God, he exists outside any and every universe. If God exists, it is not then strictly-speaking correct to say we live in a universe in which God exists. Rather, we should say we live in a world in which God (and at least one universe) exists. See note 31 on page 185 of Richard Swinburne, *The Existence of God* (Oxford: Oxford University Press, 2004).

[3]   I do argue for it elsewhere, e.g. my *Belief in God* (Oxford: Oxford University Press, 2005), part I. In doing so, I follow in broad outline Swinburne, who argues that polytheism, for example, has a prior probability lower than classical theism (in e.g. Richard Swinburne, 'The Argument to God from Fine-Tuning Reassessed', in Neil Manson (ed.), *God and Design: The Teleological Argument And Modern Science* (London: Routledge, 2003), 107) due to its complexity. As well as its simplicity, the God hypothesis has its plausibility as a metaphysical necessity on its side relative to alternative supernaturalist hypotheses. Suppose that we allowed that a hypothesis positing the pantheon of Greek gods was as simple as classical theism and raised to the same extent the probability of the fine tuning that we observe. Unless the fact that the pantheon of Greek gods existed would be as plausibly necessary were it to obtain as the fact that the God of classical theism existed would be necessary were it to obtain, the God hypothesis would nevertheless be a better explanation of the fine tuning and the existence of the Greek pantheon is less plausible

In considering these hypotheses I shall be allowing myself then to think that in principle the probability of various explanatory hypotheses which make reference to things beyond the universe – specifically other universes or God – might be raised or indeed lowered by our discovery of features of this universe.

Some people are of course very chary of talking of probabilities in this area for they hold exclusively to a frequentist understanding of probability, thinking that whenever one talks of probability one is gesturing to a series of trials and talking about the relative frequency of a certain outcome across that series. Where that sort of background is lacking, such people say, attributing probability to a hypothesis doesn't make sense or perhaps – more minimally – makes sense but

---

as a necessity (if it obtains) than the existence of the classical theistic God is plausible as a necessity (if it obtains). So, even suspending judgement on its relative simplicity, we are justified in starting with a presumption that classical theism is to be preferred as a potential explanation of the fine tuning over Greek polytheism and, as the same considerations apply *mutatis mutandis* to other supernaturalist hypotheses, over these too. Were the proponent of Greek polytheism or an alternative supernaturalist hypothesis to assert his or her religious beliefs as beliefs in metaphysically contingent things and assert that the metaphysical contingency of his/her explanation didn't undermine its truth, we might agree. Were he/she to maintain that its contingency didn't undermine its explanatory value, we should disagree. Greek polytheism and other supernaturalist hypotheses, if they present themselves as metaphysical contingencies, just push the fine tuning up a level. (And if, as just mentioned, they present themselves as metaphysical necessities, they are less plausible as such than classical theism.) We shall come upon this issue again in the main text when discussing the first naturalistic model for explaining the fine tuning of the constants; the higher-level fine tuning remerges on it, prompting the move to the maximal multiverse model. The notion of plausibility in play here is certainly a difficult one, but the same notion is in play in other areas of Philosophy too, whenever one judges of things that they are metaphysical necessities. (The fact that nobody has yet built a time machine such as that depicted in H. G. Wells' story *The Time Machine* is more plausible as a metaphysical necessity than the fact that nobody has yet built a space ship capable of interstellar travel.) This notion is not, I suggest, reducible to the notion of simplicity or even universally conjoined with it: it may be in some cases that that which is relatively complex appears more plausible as a metaphysical necessity than that which is simpler. There being nothing at all would be simpler than there being something, but – given that there is something – we know that there being something is more plausible as a metaphysical necessity than there being nothing.

is something for which one cannot have any reasons. Obviously in the case of the hypothesis that there's a God or indeed the hypothesis that there's not a God, we don't have this sort of background, so, such people maintain, we can't talk of the probability of such hypotheses being true. We can't stand back and look at say a 1000 universes and see – for example – that 900 of them are created by God and only 100 are brute facts, thus concluding that it's 90% probable that theism is true and only 10% probable that atheism is true on the evidence given to us by the existence of a universe. We can't do that, so we can't talk of probability here. Well, that's what some people say and I admit that it is *prima facie* plausible. But I don't think it's *ultima facie* plausible. On reflection it can be seen to be an overly restrictive understanding of probability. To see why, engage in the following thought experiment with me if you please.

Suppose that scientists had discovered that the universe was composed of a certain type of fundamental particle each one of which had inscribed on it in Times Roman zero, point zero, zero, zero, some-tiny-size font, 'This Particle Created by the God of Classical Theism'. What would we say to someone who, on being made aware of this startling discovery, said this? 'My notion of probability is such as to mean that I cannot allow that this evidence raises the probability of Theism for it does nothing to allow me to stand back and look at multiple universes, observing the frequency with which this property is conjoined with God and the frequency with which it is conjoined with no God.' Well, we'd surely say that they'd just shown themselves to have an overly restrictive notion of probability. That sort of evidence – had it been forthcoming – really would have raised the probability of there being a God beyond reasonable doubt and anyone whose notion of probability is such as to mean that they'd say that it wouldn't is someone whose notion of probability is one we have *ipso facto* good reason to reject as exhaustive of legitimate notions of probability.

Now we'll all have noticed that we're not actually in a universe where scientists have discovered that written on every fundamental particle is a small but unambiguous message purporting to be from the creator. But we are in a universe where scientists – and indeed philosophers – have discovered lots of interesting things and some of these, I suggest, have a bearing. Let's turn to the scientists first.

Scientists tell us that had the Big Bang had slightly more force, then the universe would have expanded at such a fast rate that no stars, planets, or life could ever have formed. Had it expanded slightly more slowly, everything would have collapsed back in on itself under gravitational attraction before life could have formed too. As well as that which controls the force of the Big Bang, there are a number of other quantities in the laws of nature, and scientists are approaching consensus on what are the maximum deviations in these quantities that would nevertheless have allowed life to have formed. Thus, they tell us, the Cosmological Constant could only have deviated by a factor of one over ten to the power of 120; the ratio of Electrons to Protons by one over ten to the power of 37. And so on. There are, I believe, currently thought to be about twenty of these things. Of course some of these things may be shown in future to be derivable from others or two or more from something more basic than any of them, but we'll be left with at least one, even in a completed science.[4] We may thence be led to picture our universe as one amongst many possible universes, in each of which the same natural laws operate, yet in only a very few of which life is possible as in only a very few of which do these constants manage to hit just the right values, thus concluding that our universe is 'fine tuned' to life; universes which permit life are uncommon in what we might therefore call the immediate 'wider landscape'[5] of other possible universes, universes with the same laws as ours but different constants. And this fact, it might be suggested, needs explanation, an explanation best provided – it has often been suggested – by the God

---

[4]   There are many good discussions of these things, e.g. John Leslie, *Universes* (New York: Routledge, 1989); Martin Rees, *Just Six Numbers: The Deep Forces that Shape the Universe* (New York: Basic Books, 2000); John Barrow, *The Constants of Nature: From Alpha to Omega* (London: Jonathan Cape Collins, 2002); Robin Collins, 'God, Design, and Fine-Tuning', in Raymond Martin and Christopher Bernard (eds.), *God Matters: Readings in the Philosophy of Religion* (New York: Longman Press, 2002); and Rodney Holder, *God, The Multiverse, and Everything: Modern Cosmology and the Argument from Design* (Aldershot: Ashgate, 2004).

[5]   I talk in terms of 'landscape' as does Susskind (Leonard Susskind, *The Cosmic Landscape* (Little Brown and Company, 2005), *passim*) although with something slightly different in mind; Leslie talks in terms of a 'local area of possible universes' (op. cit., 138). There is room for confusion here between considering the landscape/area being talked of as a landscape/area of possibilities, or one of actualities. In fact Susskind's term 'landscape' refers to different solutions to string theory which are instantiated via Linde's eternal inflation model and so form part of the one actual universe in my sense of universe; he calls this the 'megaverse'. These things are glossed over rather in the main text, but not in a way that affects the validity of the argument.

hypothesis.[6] Thus, the 'fine tuning' version of the Design Argument.[7]

By far the most common objection to the fine tuning version of the Design Argument may be put as follows: 'Fine tuning can't be in need of explanation because we couldn't observe a universe which wasn't fine tuned. We wouldn't be here to think about it if it hadn't happened, so the fact that it has happened isn't worth thinking about.' This, despite its almost universal appeal, is, I take it, shown to be misguided by thought experiments such as the following, which I adapt from Swinburne.

> A terrorist ties you up in a room with a machine. The machine is linked up to a bomb which will, if it explodes, kill you. You see the terrorist put ten ordinary packs of cards into the top of the machine. He tells you that the machine will thoroughly shuffle these cards and then select ten at random and drop them into a little tray at its front. Only if the ten it dishes out are all aces of hearts will the bomb not go off. He leaves you. The machine whirs away. The first card comes out – it's an ace of hearts; the second, another ace of hearts; the third, ace of hearts; and so on. In fact, all ten are aces of hearts. The machine goes silent; the worrying red light on the bomb turns to green. You have survived.[8]

This would require some explanation. The chances of ten aces of hearts being dished out in a row if the machine worked as the terrorist said it did are very small and the fact that something very improbable has happened needs explanation in terms of something that would make it less improbable, for example the machine selecting cards on a basis which actually gives it a preference for aces of hearts. If

---

[6] Of course gods other than the classical theistic God could explain the fine tuning, but the classical theistic God hypothesis is the simplest god hypothesis and the most plausible as a necessary truth, so it is the one that should be preferred. See previous note.

[7] Of course, much depends on how 'life' is taken. Carbon-based life of the sort we are familiar with obviously occurs in less possible universes than life on more relaxed understanding. But the proponent of the argument characteristically urges that life *per se* requires some degree of structuring and in the vast majority of possible universes there is not sufficient structuring to allow it to arise however relaxed (yet plausible) a definition of life one operates with. Certainly the sort of life on which we'll be focusing needs this structuring.

[8] T. J. Mawson, *Belief in God* (Oxford: Oxford University Press, 2005), 145.

the terrorist came in and brushed off your survival as not needing explanation, as not being a fact which gave you a reason to suspect that the machine was not as he had described, you would give him short shrift, even shorter shrift than you would be inclined to be giving him *qua* terrorist anyway. It may be true that you could not have observed any other outcome, but another outcome was – if what the terrorist told you was correct – immensely more likely. So, from the fact you have survived, you have reason to believe that what the terrorist told you was not correct.[9]

Similarly then, if there were nothing outside the universe, there would be no process selecting values for these constants, constants which have to be finely tuned for life to be possible. The fact that they have the values they do would then be a matter of random chance. That is a possibility. But then the probability of their coming out in the way that they have would have been fantastically small in the one and only universe. It's far more likely then, so the argument goes, that there's something outside the universe, in some sense selecting these values. From the fact that the universe is fine tuned to life, one has reason to believe that there's almost certainly a fine tuner. At this stage, another objection is usually raised:-

If the machine had dished out what we'd all think of as a random selection of cards and the bomb gone off as a result, then that state of affairs – the bomb's being set off by just that particular selection of cards – would have been just as improbable as is the state of affairs of its ending up not being set off as a result of the ten cards all being aces of hearts. Yet one would not say that the bomb's going off in this manner needed an explanation. Or, if one thought that even this would need an explanation, one would be thinking that it would do so due to some more general feature of it, for example that it would be a contingent happening, and due to one's holding approvingly in one's mind the principle that contingent happenings need explanation. To go down that road however would be to take oneself outside the territory of the Design Argument and into that of the Cosmological Argument. To stay an argument from fine tuning then, the improbable feature which one takes to be evidence of a fine tuner has to be *special*, special by reference to a standard

[9] Although see Elliott Sober, 'The Design Argument', in W. Mann (ed.), *The Blackwell Companion to Philosophy of Religion* (Oxford: Basil Blackwell, 2004).

For a very full and balanced discussion of observer selection effects, see Nick Bostrom, *Anthropic Bias: Observation Selection Effects in Science and Philosophy* (New York: Routledge, 2002).

objective enough to mean that it would have applied regardless of what had happened.[10]

The proponent of the fine tuning argument may reply to this by saying that surely life *is* special, if not the life of slugs or beetles, then the morally sentient life of rational, conscious, significantly free agents such as ourselves. We in this room – he or she may insist – simply *are* more important than a similarly massive collection of non-sentient, unconscious, non-agents, for example a pile of rocks lying on the surface of a desert. That's why, if a meteorite were to hit this building and destroy all of us, it would have destroyed something more important than if it had hit the desert and destroyed the rocks. Anybody who really didn't believe that rocks were less important than life of our sort would be someone who didn't know what – or rather who – to prioritize saving when fire engulfed both an orphanage and a Geology Museum.

Such a response, whilst I would maintain in every respect true, would not go far enough.

The universality of at least some values – by which I mean their holding throughout the universe – need not be questioned by the opponent of the fine tuning argument pressing this objection. The point at issue here is the putative *trans*-universality of at least the value of life of the sort we are concerned with – its holding *across* universes. (Remember: in the case of the ten aces of hearts needing an explanation, they did so because the outcome was special *by standards which would have obtained regardless of what outcome had obtained*.) In other words, the opponent of the fine tuning argument may concede that, say, significant freedom for morally sentient creatures such as ourselves is a good everywhere within this universe, whilst maintaining that its absence from, for example, a universe consisting of just one hydrogen atom isn't a relative deficiency in that universe; after all, it's certainly not bad for anyone in that universe that they don't enjoy significant freedom; it's not bad for anyone as there's no-one there for whom it can be bad.

The trans-universality of at least some values is less obviously correct than the universality of at least some values, but, I believe, it is correct nevertheless. We can, I suggest, see that a universe

---

[10] M. C. Bradley, 'The Fine-Tuning Argument: The Bayesian Version', *Religious Studies* **38** (2002), 382–385, discusses this point, although in discussing it in terms of objectivism, he does not draw out the requirement of what I call the trans-universality of value. A naturalist realism is, I take it, a version of objectivism, but would not be sufficient for the fine tuning argument to go through.

consisting of only one hydrogen atom, for example, would have certain good features: it can be imagined to have a certain simple beauty about it (although of course there'd be no-one in it to appreciate that beauty); there would be no suffering in it; there would also be no shameful viciousness or wilful ignorance. But there would equally-certainly be bad features of a universe consisting of only one hydrogen atom: as I say, there'd be no-one in it to appreciate whatever beauty it had; there'd be no pleasure; no justifiable pride, virtue, or knowledge in it. If there's not going to be any significant freedom in a universe, then adding to it morally sentient creatures in all respects other than their lack of freedom like ourselves would certainly make it worse, because then this deficiency would not only be bad, but there would be people for whom it was bad. But the fact that adding morally sentient people to a universe where there is never going to be any significant freedom would make it even worse shouldn't blind us from the fact that it was in one respect at least bad beforehand, in not containing such goods as the presence of morally sentient beings entails. That, in any case, would be my view. I am spared from having to defend it further as it is not needed to support my final conclusion. For the moment then I shall proceed on this assumption, noting in due course when it drops out.

For the moment then, allow me to assume that if the universe is fine tuned for the life of morally sentient significantly free creatures such as ourselves, it is fine tuned for something that is trans-universally valuable. The sort of life enjoyed by beetles might be trans-universally valuable, but the claim that it is trans-universally valuable is not so plausible as the claim that the sort of life enjoyed by us – morally sentient, rational, conscious, significantly free creatures – is trans-universally valuable. If a meteorite destroyed a planet populated entirely by beetles, the loss to the universe would be on any plausible account less great and thus less obviously a loss than if a meteorite destroyed the Earth. So, the fine tuning of the universe to life such as ours is the most obviously special (as well as improbable) feature and thus the best place to start a fine tuning argument from. Even on the assumption that this sort of life is trans-universally valuable, I would contend that so far the proponent of the fine tuning version of the Design Argument has given us no reason to posit any *extra-universal* fine tuner.

Were our universe in fact one where each of the values of what are then somewhat misleadingly called 'constants' is 'tried out' somewhere or 'somewhen', as it were, then what I previously called the 'wider landscape' of other possible universes would actually be encompassed within this universe and thus the fine tuning of which

T. J. Mawson

I have so far made mention would disappear. Perhaps ours is an oscillating universe, where each Big Bang is the other end of a Big Crunch, the curvature of space-time gradually altering with each crunch and bang towards being life-permitting. Perhaps the higher-dimensional membranes are multiply colliding, or bubble sub-universes frequently emerging from the mother universe, each 'trying out' one of the possible values that what we call 'constants' might take. In any of these cases, the fine tuning spoken of so far would not need an extra-universal (i.e. outside the universe in my sense of 'universe') fine tuner.[11] It is this very fact that explains the attractiveness of views of this sort to some scientists. (Confusingly – given my use of the terms 'universe' and 'multiverse' – these views are sometimes called multiverse views.) According to some such scientists, the fine-tuning of the force of the Big Bang, for example, does need an explanation, but it gets an explanation that doesn't posit anything God-like from the fact that the wider universe (in my sense of 'universe'; those propounding these views often call this wider whole the 'multiverse'), has parts which instantiate each of the different values that the relevant constant might in principle take. The same thing goes for the other constants. If Swinburne's terrorist tried his machine out enough times to make sure that every possible series of ten cards was eventually dished out, then of course one of his victims would eventually end up surviving.[12]

Such a view might seem then to make the fine tuning disappear, but in fact it merely relocates it to a higher level, in the natural laws that, for example, determine the evolution towards life-permitting

[11] Examples of such theories would be Susskind's (*The Cosmic Landscape*) and Smolin's (Lee Smolin, *The Life of the Cosmos* (Oxford: Oxford University Press, 1997)). To make the outcome we are concerned with a statistical certainty, we'd need to formulate these hypotheses so that they involved an actual infinity of oscillations or what have you. Otherwise the outcome would just tend towards a statistical certainty as the number of oscillations or what have you tended towards infinity.

[12] Here and elsewhere I assume certain things about how one may speak of probabilities even when considering sets of possible outcomes with an infinite number of members. In doing so I set myself against some of what is said in Timothy McGrew, L. McGrew and E. Vestrup, 'Probabilities and the Fine-Tuning Argument: A Sceptical View', *Mind* **110**:440, 1027–1038. This is discussed in Graham Oppy, *Arguing about Gods* (Cambridge: Cambridge University Press, 2006), 205–207. See also Swinburne, 'The Argument from the Fine-Tuning of the Universe', 185–188 referring back to 168–172 and Jeffrey Koperski, 'Should we Care about Fine-Tuning?', *British Journal for the Philosophy of Science* **52** (2005).

conditions of the oscillating universe. If the universe as a whole (in my sense) creates space-time subsystems randomly or in an evolving way such that a life-permitting subsystem, whilst improbable in any particular instantiation or oscillation, becomes a statistical certainty over the infinite range, there is still fine tuning in that it is still a general feature of the universe that it permits in principle life-conducive space-time subsystems to come into being, rather than confines what may come into being to parameters that necessitate lifelessness. Thinking in terms of our imaginary persistent terrorist, the fact that he feeds *ten* packs of cards into the machine on each occasion he tries it out, rather than say nine (which would of course then render it impossible for anyone to survive it however many times he tried it out[13]), permits – indeed over an infinite number of runs makes a statistical certainty of – a victim surviving. So there is higher-level fine tuning even here.

There is another hypothesis that suggests itself as the natural extension of the one we have just been considering. It pushes one step out. On the hypothesis we've just been considering, the universe had one set of natural laws, but varied in the values various 'constants' took in sub-systems within that universe. A natural extension of this hypothesis, what I shall call the 'maximal multiverse' hypothesis, would assert that every possible universe is actual. The higher-level fine tuning which remained on the previous hypothesis disappears on this one: the maximal multiverse hypothesis explains more; as well as explaining why the 'constants' are as they are (they're every value that they can be somewhere) it explains why the natural laws are as they are (they're every form they can be somewhere). Thus, it is preferable. The moral of the story so far then might be summed up as follows: on the assumption of the trans-universality of the value of life of our sort, you should think that the fine tuning of the universe to this sort of life needs explanation and, if you're going to believe in a naturalistic explanation of this fine tuning, you should believe in the maximal multiverse.[14]

[13] This is assuming that the machine works as the terrorist describes it, of course.

[14] Compare David Lewis, *On the Plurality of Worlds* (New York: Basil Blackwell, 1986) and Max Tegmark, 'Many Lives in Many Worlds', *Nature* **448** (2007). It will be noted that I am ignoring one common objection to multiverse theories; that they are 'unscientific'. Of course I would dispute the claim that is sometimes made, that multiverse theories are unscientific as there is no evidence in favour of them; the fine tuning of a universe to the sort of life on which we're focusing is evidence in favour of them. 'But such models don't provide causal explanation', someone might say.

What I am suggesting then is that an infinite number of infinitely variable universes would explain the existence of the fine tuning we have hitherto discussed at all levels. If you're a terrorist who can link enough devices to enough other devices according to enough principles, you'll find yourself trying out a bomb/card set-up such as Swinburne's, infrequently to be sure, but an infinite number of times to be sure too, and thus a victim will, now and again, survive. If you stick enough animals in front of enough pieces of equipment, then, sure you'll get a frustrating proportion of slugs in front of typewriters and monkeys in front of vacuum cleaners, but you'll occasionally get a monkey in front of a typewriter; and – if you do it enough times – this occasional happening will eventually lead to monkey Shakespeare. So it is a certainty that in a maximal multiverse composed of an infinite number of infinitely variable universes 'somewhere' in the maximal multiverse, there'll be a universe like ours.[15]

At this stage, we appear then to have two reasons to suppose that the maximal multiverse hypothesis is a better explanation for the fine tuning of our universe to us than Theism:-

---

Indeed, the maximal multiverse has explanatory power, yet the explanation it provides is not causal; so much the better then, I would reply, as anything which explained the universe causally would itself be part of the universe (if the causal explanation was a scientific one) or God or something similar (if not).

[15] I take it that this is the solution to what Hacking calls the problem of the 'inverse gambler's fallacy'. *Pace* Hacking (Ian Hacking, 'The Inverse Gambler's Fallacy: The Argument from Design. The Anthropic Principle Applied to Wheeler Universes', *Mind* **96** (1987), 331–340). If you were a surviving victim of the terrorist we are imagining, and you knew the machine to work as the terrorist had described it, you *could* then conclude from your survival that it was more likely that the terrorist had tried his machine out many times than that he had tried it out only once. And the simplest hypothesis that has him trying it out many times is the hypothesis that he has tried it out an infinite number of times. The fact that we know that there aren't these sorts of actual infinities within our universe is why we are not intuitively drawn to such a hypothesis. We don't know that there are not the relevant sort in the case of the situations that concern us in the main text. There is then another objection to the theory, that actual infinities are not physically realizable. Copan and Craig explore this in Copan and Craig (Paul Copan and William Lane Craig, *Creation out of Nothing* (Grand Rapids: Baker Academic, 2004)). I ignore this in the main text as my overall conclusion does not depend on this objection failing.

Firstly, and most obviously, on it, the probability of our universe existing is one. Given that on the hypothesis every possible universe exists, so, on the hypothesis, our universe – being possible – *has to* exist. Theism, by contrast, in picturing the existence of the universe as the result of a free choice on God's part, a choice which – being free – He did not have to make in the way that He did, may be able to raise the probability of this universe existing on the hypothesis, but it cannot raise the probability of its existing on the hypothesis to one.[16] Of course, we're primarily interested in the probability of the hypothesis on the evidence, not that of the evidence on the hypothesis, but, as an explanation of some evidence, a hypothesis that gives that evidence a probability of one is in that respect at least the best sort of explanation one could ever get.

Secondly, the maximal multiverse hypothesis is simpler than the Theistic hypothesis.[17] The maximal multiverse hypothesis might

[16]   There are a number of possible universes which are not fine tuned to life of the sort we're interested in, yet which plausibly have certain good-making features and which God may have chosen to create in virtue of these features. We have considered one such universe, a universe with just one hydrogen atom in it, and suggested that it would have the good-making feature of a certain sort of beauty. It's not then that fine-tuned-for-life-of-the-sort-we're-interested-in universes are the *only* ones that God might have good reason to create. But this doesn't matter for the argument; as long as a fine-tuned-for-life-of-the-sort-we're-interested-in universe would be 'quite likely to occur' (Richard Swinburne, 'The Argument from the Fine-Tuning of the Universe', in J. Leslie (ed.), *Physical Cosmology and Philosophy* (New York: Collier Macmillan, 1990), 155) on Theism, then whatever other universes are more or less likely to occur on the God hypothesis in addition is beside the point (although see discussion in main text concerning the explanatory power of the maximal multiverse hypothesis relative to the God hypothesis in raising the probability of the evidence to one). Of course, merely assessing the probability of the evidence on the hypothesis will not get one very far in assessing the probability of the hypothesis on the evidence, since an inherently improbable hypothesis may give a high probability to the evidence; hence the unavoidability of prior probabilities and – I would concede – the unavoidability of using simplicity, as it strikes one, to judge of these. But it is the unavoidability of just this sort of thought process which, as we shall see, forms the basis for the most powerful version of the Design Argument. So this can hardly be an objection to my argument.

[17]   Some suggest that simplicity considerations favour the God hypothesis over the maximal multiverse hypothesis (J. P. Moreland and W. L. Craig, *Philosophical Foundations for a Christian Worldview* (Intervarsity Press, 2003), 487, and Holder, op. cit., 16). It is an implication

seem *prima facie* much more complicated than the hypothesis that there's one universe and one God, but it is not really more complicated in the way we care about when comparing hypotheses.

Simplicity considerations operate on types of entity as well as tokens of a type. The maximal multiverse hypothesis is simplest on types of entity; there's only one type of thing, universes. The God hypothesis is simplest on tokens of type; on it (at its simplest) there are only two tokens, one each of two types of thing, the first God and the second the universe. I suggest that simplicity with regard to type is to be preferred over simplicity with regard to token and thus that the infinite number of infinitely variable universes hypothesis is actually a simpler hypothesis than the God hypothesis.[18] If you

---

of the final argument that I shall advance that, ultimately, we cannot advance above brute intuitions here. It has been suggested that since Kepler's and Ptolemy's laws of planetary motion involve equations with common variables, at least the number of free parameters in those equations can be compared and relative simplicity judged thereby (David Dowe *et al.*, 'Bayes not Bust! Why Simplicity is No Problem for Bayesians', *The British Journal for the Philosophy of Science* **58** (2007), 709–754), although some (Malcolm Forster, 'Bayes and Bust: Simplicity as a Problem for a Probabilist's Approach to Confirmation', *The British Journal for the Philosophy of Science* **46** (2003), 399–424) would deny even this. However this issue is to be resolved, it seems plausible that nothing similar is possible when comparing the God hypothesis to a multiverse hypothesis. Swinburne suggests, in essence, that a hypothesis is simple insofar as it involves few substances and few properties, but this is not unproblematic as the properties in turn need to be simple ones (not grue/bleen-type ones), which just pushes the problem on a stage. All that being so, the approach taken in the main text, to pump an intuition with a thought experiment and then move on, is, I suggest, the only approach to take. See though Richard Swinburne, *Epistemic Justification* (Oxford: Oxford University Press, 2001), 83–102. It may also be worth pointing out at this juncture that my final conclusion doesn't depend on the maximal multiverse hypothesis being simpler (in that it says that even if it's simpler, we should still prefer the God hypothesis).

[18]   This is also the view of David Lewis, the most prominent exponent – although for quite different reasons – of the maximal multiverse hypothesis. See also Bradley, 'The Fine-Tuning Argument: The Bayesian Version', *Religious Studies* **38**:4 (2002), 389. Arguably the situation is not so clear cut as I make out in the main text: some of these universes – lots of them indeed – contain types of thing that don't exist in our universe, e.g. new sorts of particles (sorts that are physically impossible in our universe), so one might argue that my saying in the main text that on the maximal

think you might disagree with me, consider the following. For this thought experiment to work, one needs to sweep from one's mind the fact that one knows certain things about poppies and fields, e.g. that there cannot be an infinite number of poppies in a field as each poppy takes up a certain amount of space and no field can be that big. With this background information swept from one's mind, consider then the following:

You have just come upon a field in which, as far as the eye can see, poppies wave gaily at you; they stretch over the horizon in every direction. One person with you suggests the hypothesis, 'These poppies never end; there's an infinite number of poppies in this field'. Another suggests the following, 'There's a huge but finite number of poppies and at least one other type of flower in this field'. Surely you would favour the former hypothesis, even though it posits infinitely more tokens than the latter, which posits one more type. Why, when each would equally well explain the data – poppies stretching out as far as the eye can see? It must be simplicity, mustn't it?

So what, if anything, can be said *against* the maximal multiverse hypothesis? There is something, and it is something decisive. Let us approach saying it somewhat obliquely, by looking at a danger to which the maximal multiverse hypothesis *need not* succumb.

---

multiverse hypothesis, there is only one type of thing, universes, is too quick. My intuitions go as they do as I suppose that physical stuff (whatever universes are made up of) is fundamentally one type of thing and spiritual stuff (whatever God is made up of) is fundamentally another. This raises then the general problem of how we are to determine whether two objects, A and B, are two tokens of the same fundamental type or one token each of two types. Insofar as A and B may be discriminated between (and thus plausibly are numerically distinct), there will be some qualitative difference between them in virtue of which we make the discrimination and, in *lieu* of anything else, this could always be used as the hook off which to hang a claim that they are tokens of two types of thing. 'We should not be talking of A and B as two peas in a pod', someone might say, 'but rather as one A-pea-in-a-pod and one B-pea-in-a-pod'. But, I take it, some concepts strike us as gerrymandered: in the situation I am imagining, it strikes the majority of us that two peas in a pod, A and B, are not tokens of two types of thing, but rather two tokens of the one type of thing, a pea in a pod; indeed peas are just one type of thing whether they're in a pod or not. In deciding which concepts are gerrymandered however, we will be drawn back to judgements of simplicity. See previous note and later discussion in the main text.

T. J. Mawson

It may look as if the maximal multiverse hypothesis, in making every possible universe actual, 'explains too much'. It might appear to suggest that *whatever* feature of the laws of nature was discovered and posited as giving reason to believe in God, the maximal multiverse hypothesizer could, on his or her hypothesis legitimately, explain it by saying, 'Well, every possible thing happens somewhere and this is somewhere after all'. If that *were* what the maximal multiverse hypothesizer could always – by his or her own lights, legitimately – say regardless of the feature, then that would surely be implausible.

We may imagine a modified terrorist example to bring this implausibility out.

The situation is as in the original example except that the terrorist tells you that the machine will dish out *twenty* cards selected at random from the *twenty* packs it shuffles. As before, only if the first ten are aces of hearts will you live, but only if the next ten are aces of hearts *as well* will you be given a Singapore sling to toast your good fortune. The first ten are aces of hearts; you survive; the next ten are aces of hearts too; the terrorist enters, mixing your Singapore sling.

The terrorist can brush off your surviving by pointing out that he's used the machine an infinite number of times, but he cannot brush off your getting the Singapore sling by pointing out that he's used the machine an infinite number of times. Why? The Singapore sling needs an explanation – I take it – precisely because of those people who do manage to survive only a tiny proportion go on to enjoy a Singapore sling in addition. Assuming the terrorist tries his machine out an infinite number of times, people – an infinite number of people indeed – will survive and people – an infinite number of people indeed – will enjoy Singapore slings, but amongst the set of people who survive (amongst whom you may safely number yourself after the tenth card has been drawn) the frequency of Singapore sling drinkers is very low; the chances of you getting a Singapore sling after you've survived are the same as the chances of you surviving in the first place and those are very small, very small indeed.[19] That being so (and a Singapore sling being – I am taking it – something rather special, even if only to humans), the Singapore sling needs an explanation of a new sort.

This must be right for a reason we have already come across: the maximal multiverse hypothesis should not be able to leave as not requiring any explanation beyond itself a discovery that every fundamental particle had written onto it 'This Particle Created by

---

[19]   I am then assuming that the machine shuffles each pack separately and then draws a card in turn from each shuffled pack, rather than mixes the packs in together with one another during the shuffling process.

40

the God of Classical Theism'. And it need not: the maximal multiverse hypothesizer can explain why such a discovery would indeed be in need of an explanation that took one beyond the maximal multiverse hypothesis by pointing out that, amongst those universes which are conducive to life of the sort we are concerned with, the frequency of those with such messages written on their particles is extremely low. So, the maximal multiverse hypothesizer must – but can – leave the door open to the possibility that there may turn out to be features of our universe that need an explanation which takes one beyond the hypothesis, i.e. features which show the maximal multiverse hypothesis to be explanatorily inadequate, 'Singapore sling' features if you will. Now we have noted that the door is open, let us go through it.

So far we have been considering the fine tuning of the universe to us, or – more specifically – to us *qua* morally sensitive and significantly free creatures (morally sensitive and significantly free creatures being better contenders for being trans-universally valuable than beetles.) Let us now turn to consider the fine tuning of us – or, more specifically, us *qua* morally sensitive and significantly free creatures – to the universe. We shall concentrate on a feature of our relationship to the universe that one need not posit is trans-universally valuable; one need only recognize that it is a feature which is valuable to us and this nobody will deny. (So at this stage in the argument, the assumption of the trans-universality of values is dropping out.) It is a feature that has been discovered and the significance of which has been pointed out, not by scientists, but, pleasingly, by philosophers – arguably Kant and certainly, more recently, Walker.[20] The feature is the continuing tractability of the universe to the process of induction as we find ourselves engaging in it.

---

[20]   Walker attributes it to Kant in Ralph Walker, *Kant* (London: Routledge, 1999), ch. 11; there are also versions in e.g. Ralph Walker, *The Coherence Theory of Truth* (London: Routledge, 1989). There is a parallel here with worries as discussed by e.g. Davies (Paul Davies, *The Goldilock's Enigma: Why is the Universe just Right for Life?* (London: Allen Lane, 2006), ch. 8) that multiverse theories make versions of Bostrom's simulation argument more pressing or they make more pressing the hypothesis that we are probably so-called 'Boltzmann brains' (see esp. discussion in R. Collins, 'The Fine-Tuning Argument', *forthcoming* in W. L. Craig and J. P. Moreland (eds.), *The Blackwell Reader in Natural Theology* (Oxford: Blackwell)), worries which do not arise on the hypothesis of 'a God who is no deceiver', as Descartes might have put it. As well as the line of thought explored in the main text (which applies induction primarily to time going forward [although secondarily, in a later note, to time going backwards too]), we might consider Penrose's (Roger Penrose, *The Road to Reality* (London:

T. J. Mawson

The process of induction is the process of believing that the future will resemble the past in the broad sense that the simplest laws that can be made to harmonize with past experience will continue to hold in the future. This principle lies at the root of all action. As Walker puts it, 'Alternative, counter-inductive procedures are conceivable, whereby the future is expected to be different from the past; but no experience of the failure of induction would make us adopt counter-induction instead. For the counter-inductivist's reaction to the observation that past futures have not resembled past pasts is to expect that this will now cease, and that in future things will turn out as his inductivist rival would anticipate.'[21] Induction's inescapability then is secure, but its

---

Vintage Books, 2004)) argument, which applies it to space going outwards. As Holder put Penrose's argument in an email to me: 'The creator had 1 in 10 to the power 10 to the power 123 universes to choose from, only one of which would be as ordered as ours. However, to make life you only need a solar system's amount of order. To make only a solar system, surrounded by chaos, by the random collisions of particles, which is all that is required to make life, the order required is much less than this, though still vast. It is 1 in 10 to the power 10 to the power 60. Since 10 to the power 10 to the power 123 swamps 10 to the power 10 to the power 60 completely, what that means is that although a universe with order 1 in 10 to the power 10 to the power 123 exists with probability 1 if all possible universes exist, the probability of ... [creatures such as ourselves] observing such a universe is only 1 in 10 to the power 10 to the power 123'. He suggests a helpful analogy, drawing on the typewriter one. 'Suppose you have a monkey typing and life corresponds to its coming up with "To be or not to be, that is the question". It is much more likely to come up with that than the whole of Hamlet, so it is vastly more probable that "To be or not to be, that is the question" is surrounded by junk than the rest of Hamlet, let alone the whole of Shakespeare. Thus ... [creatures such as ourselves] are far more likely to find ourselves in a solar system surrounded by total chaos than in a totally ordered universe'. It is of course less obvious that it is valuable to creatures such as ourselves not to live in such a spatial 'oasis' than it is that is valuable to us not to live in such a temporal 'oasis', which is why I think this variant of the argument is weaker than the one discussed in the main text. Matters are similar, I suggest, with regards to certain features of our universe which one might think are 'over designed'. For example, the proton lifetime is at least 2×10 to the power of 32 years, i.e. at least ten to the power of 22 times the age of the universe, which is vastly longer than needed for life to form. It is less immediately plausible that a universe 'special' by being over designed in this way is evidence of God. We shall return to some of these issues at the end.

[21] Ralph Walker, *Kant* (London: Routledge, 1999), 171.

42

applicability – *its continuing to work* – is not, a point that Hume was first to press upon us and that Goodman has since made all the more pressing.

Goodman famously introduced to the philosophical lexicon two portmanteau words, 'grue' and 'bleen'.[22] We may define them – following him in spirit if not letter – thus: an object is grue in colour just if it is green before time *t* (where time *t* is a particular but arbitrary time in the future, let us stipulate then whatever time it is that will be two seconds after I finish speaking this evening) and blue after time *t*. An object is bleen in colour by contrast if it is blue up until time *t* – blue up until two seconds after whatever time I finish speaking – and green thereafter. Goodman pointed out that we all believe (or at least think we believe) that emeralds are green and thus believe that we are thinking that the future will resemble the past when we think that emeralds will stay green tomorrow. However, as he also pointed out, the evidence we have collected to date – all of it of course being collected before time *t*, before two seconds after I have finished speaking this evening – equally well supports the claim that all emeralds are grue. Someone to whom the concepts of grue and bleen came naturally, in expecting nature to continue on as it has done in the past, would thus expect emeralds to stay grue, which in our terms would amount to their expecting them to change from green to blue. But *we* are not such people and it is *we* who get things right, get them right time after time. Walker again: 'Nature keeps on working in such a way as to meet our expectations: yet our expectations are based on nothing more secure than the accident that we normally classify in one way rather than another – that we use the concept "green" rather than the concept "grue".'[23] This is a remarkable co-incidence, the equivalent of a continuing run of aces of hearts, a continuing succession of Singapore slings being mixed up for us by the universe.

The most frequent first reaction to this point is to say that grue is a more complex concept than green, but (a) this is not obviously so from any transcendent standpoint and (b) it is irrelevant.

With regards to (a): a person who had been brought up using grue and bleen would have to have what would strike them as our hopelessly time-indexed terms 'green' and 'blue' translated for them. An object is green in colour, we would have to explain – trying our best to meet their incredulous gaze steadily – just if it is grue up until

---

[22]   Nelson Goodman, *Fact, Fiction, and Forecast* (Harvard: Harvard University Press, 1955), ch. 5.
[23]   Ralph Walker, *Kant*, 172.

two seconds after Mawson's lecture and bleen thereafter. An object is blue, we would continue, if it is bleen up until two seconds after Mawson's lecture and grue thereafter. They would be astonished that we projected such 'bent' predicates as green and blue. 'Why are you expecting emeralds to change colour at that time?' they would ask us. 'Why not believe as we believe', they would say, 'that emeralds will continue to be the colour they always have been, grue?' On hearing this, we would naturally think that our positions were precisely the reverse: 'It's not *us* who are believing that things will change', we'd protest. And we'd think our fates were reversed too: 'it won't be *us*', we'd think, 'who will have to say, "My goodness, you grue/bleen projectors were right; emeralds have changed from green to blue or — as you so rightly predicted — they've stayed grue!".' Rather, we would think, it would be them who'd have to say to us, 'My goodness, you green/blue projectors were right all along; emeralds have changed from grue to bleen or — as you so rightly put it — stayed green!' That's what we'd confidently expect alright, but what are our grounds for such a confident expectation? Not, it appears, the relative simplicity of green and blue over grue and bleen.[24] In any case, moving onto (b), the relative simplicity — even if it could be established — seems irrelevant to our concerns. What if grue and bleen were more complex by some concept-transcendent standard? What is to say that our universe will turn out to be as simple by this standard as we suppose it to be?

Evolution cannot help us here, because — so far — evolution has of course, like everything else science might draw upon to explain anything, only operated in the past and thus it cannot yet have selected against grue/bleen projectors whose time t is in the future, e.g. those who happen to have it set at the time, whatever that is, two seconds after I finish speaking this evening. It just *couldn't* have harmed us *yet* if we happened to live in one of those logically possible universes where everything goes along just as in the universe we suppose ourselves to be in up until two seconds after I finish speaking and then takes what from our green/blue projecting framework would strike us as a radical turn and what would strike someone from a grue/bleen projecting framework as no change whatsoever. It's no good saying, 'But we just don't live in a universe where things change colour arbitrarily', for that is precisely what is at issue: what reason do we have to suppose this

---

[24]   But see Swinburne, *The Existence of God*, 88, n. 10.

from the fact, which we may grant,[25] that we don't live in a universe where things have changed colour arbitrarily in the past (haven't changed by reference to our, apparently arbitrary [see point (a)], standards of arbitrariness that is)? 'Well, it would be simpler (at least by our standards) if things did continue the same (by our standards)' is of course true, but then what reason we have to suppose that that which is simplest (by our standards) will continue to obtain is again just the point at issue. In short, there can be no solution to this problem from any feature of this universe, for whatever feature this universe is posited as having and used in the putative explanation will be indistinguishable by us on the evidence we have collected to date from a feature which is about to break down by reference to our standards of simplicity and sameness, a feature the time t of which is about to arrive. So, if we cannot solve this problem, even in principle, with resources drawn from within the universe, if we are to solve this problem, we must go outside the universe. The maximal multiverse model posits entities outside the universe; does *it* have the resources with which to provide an explanation of the continuing fine tuning of us to the universe? No, it certainly does not.

On the maximal multiverse hypothesis, as every possible universe is actual, so for every moment that passes for a creature in a universe without recalcitrant experience demolishing its inductively-based expectations, there are an infinite number of creatures in other universes who, whilst hitherto having shared that creature's happy fate, now find their continuing experience recalcitrant in the most extreme ways. For every emerald that stays green over a moment in the actual universe, there is another universe that was precisely as ours up until that moment in which it goes blue; in another, it goes red; in another, yellow; in one universe that is exactly like ours up until this moment, it turns into a glass of water; in another, it turns into a glass of claret; in another, a banana. And so on. On the maximal multiverse hypothesis, as every possible universe is actual, so from the fact that, roughly speaking, there's an infinite number of ways one might go wrong when one believes something about the future and only one way in which one might go right, there are an infinite number of people just like us up until this moment who are about to go wrong. On the maximal multiverse hypothesis then, the evidence we have collected to date through our experience does nothing to

---

[25]   But see next note for further reflection on this grant and its dubious status on the maximal multiverse hypothesis.

reduce the probability of us being about to discover that we're one of the ones who was about to go wrong when we suppose that emeralds will stay green. The chances on the maximal multiverse hypothesis of the next Singapore sling being served up to us by a compliant universe are infinitely low. Yet they keep being served up to us, with every moment; there's another, there's another, there's another.[26]

[26] A possible counterargument (suggested to me by Swinburne) is as follows: Given that creatures exist for a period that is long enough for them to sustain thought concerning their universe and given that most time periods are longer than the fifteen or so billion years that this universe has taken to generate us having these thoughts (because almost all periods are longer than that), it is not very unlikely on the maximal multiverse hypothesis that creatures having these sorts of thoughts will find themselves in a universe in which induction has worked and continues to work for periods a lot longer than fifteen or so billion years. Someone might argue that on the maximal multiverse hypothesis we may consider the issue as analogous to one where a barman with an infinite amount of time ahead of him intends, over that time, to stop serving repeated Singapore slings to all but one of the infinite number of customers to whom he starts off serving them. This being so, he will of course disappoint an infinite number of his customers each time he does his rounds around the Long Bar (it is a very long bar). But – in order to leave himself enough people to disappoint later by failing to serve them the Singapore slings they've come to expect – the frequency with which these disappointed customers are distributed around the Long Bar is infinitely low. So, were you a customer, in seeing the bar man coming towards you on one particular round, you could be almost sure that he wouldn't disappoint you on that round. (This is not, it will be noted – an inadequacy of the analogy raises itself here – as a result of your performing an induction along the following lines: 'Well, he's never disappointed me in the past, so ...'. Rather, it is the result of your performing a calculation of this sort: 'the people he disappoints on any round of the bar have to be infinitely thinly distributed and thus the chances of my being one are infinitely small.') So, the continuing tractability of our universe to induction as we find ourselves utilizing it is indeed a feature which needs explanation, someone pushing this line might concede, but it gets an adequate explanation in terms of the maximal multiverse hypothesis, an explanation no better indeed than the one in terms of God, but no worse either. However, this counterargument does not work. Just as the ways in which the universe could diverge from the present in the future and surprise us are more frequent in logical space than are those in which it could continue more or less according to our expectations, so the ways in which the universe might converge on the present and not be anything like we suppose our history to have been are more frequent than those in which it does so more or less via the processes we suppose it to have followed. The issue

Unsurprisingly (in that it could hardly do worse), the God hypothesis does better at explaining the fine tuning of us to the universe; in fact, it does much better.

The reason God would have to create, from within that set of possible universes that are conducive to morally sentient significantly free creatures, a universe which is consistently inductively tractable is easy to see: these creatures' moral sensitivity and significant freedom would be in vain, devoid of the necessary conditions for responsibility, to the extent that the world around them proved unpredictable. Of course at the extreme, without any inductive tractability at all, creatures could not *be* morally sensitive – often knowing what they ought to do – or significantly free – able, in principle, to choose whether or not to do as they ought. So, pending a conclusive argument in favour of the trans-universality of the disvalue of lack of moral sensitivity and significant freedom, we cannot draw out with confidence a reason God would not have created such a world. But in a world that was not entirely inductively intractable but just significantly less inductively tractable than ours (for example, irregularly, but on average every five minutes or so, the laws of nature as its inhabitants had been led to think of them might 'suspend' themselves for a moment or two in localised patches before re-establishing themselves), creatures could plausibly retain at least some moral sensitivity and significant freedom, but – in proportion to the unpredictability of their world – they would find that they would nevertheless not end up doing that at which they had aimed; their freedom would be – in proportion to their universe's inductive intractability – evacuated of its moral significance and to this extent, this world would be bad for them. So, given that God had – if needs be one can say, whimsically – decided to create a world with morally sensitive and

---

here then may be put as one of whether we have any reason to think that induction has worked in the past. In a maximal multiverse most people like us (except for some of their relational properties) believing induction has worked in the past are in a temporal 'oasis'; in other words, they are mistaken in thinking it has worked in the past. Even amongst that relatively rare group who find themselves with what they take to be good evidence that it has worked in the past (it doesn't seem to them as if they're in a temporal oasis), the majority are mistaken. In essence then, the force of the argument in the main text may perhaps better be put like this: either abandon the view that one knows induction has worked in the past (absent supernatural intervention) and that it will continue to work in the future (absent supernatural intervention) or abandon the maximal multiverse hypothesis and believe instead in the God hypothesis.

significantly free people in it, He would then have good reason, indeed overwhelming reason, to create it with natural laws that were to a large extent inductively tractable to them, the more inductively tractable, the better His reason for creating it.[27] Of course, a universe where things proved as inductively tractable to its morally sensitive and significantly free creatures as ours has done to us up until a certain time and then took a radical turn would be a universe where the morally sensitive and significantly free creatures had enjoyed effective freedom up until that time, and God might plausibly be argued to be acting permissibly were He at that time to disestablish the harmony (although of course He could not disestablish it whilst preserving His creature's effective freedom and thus responsibility), especially were He to do so as a metaphysically necessary means to some higher end. But this sort of end to the pre-established harmony is not only compatible with Theism, it is exactly what most variants of Theism predict: we will continue to be permitted to act freely and with responsibility just up until the end of the world, the Last Judgement.[28]

[27] There is a variant of the Problem of Evil to be addressed at this stage then: given that the universe does sometimes do unpredictable things, how is this to be reconciled with its being created by the classical theistic God? But this is a topic for another paper.

The sort of inductively tractable universe that God would have good reason to create creatures of our sort in would only require of course inductive tractability at the level of the sorts of objects and actions which had moral salience for such creatures; our easy understanding of sub-microscopic properties, e.g. the more recondite recesses of Quantum Mechanics, would not have its probability appreciably raised by the hypothesis that the universe was created by God; nor would the discovery that Quantum Mechanics is easily understandable by the majority of people exposed to it increase the probability of the God hypothesis. This would be or is (depending on how easily one believes Quantum Mechanics is in fact understood) another bit of 'over design'.

[28] I am grateful for having discussed another solution – although not one open to someone holding the maximal multiverse view – with Walker, who is now more sympathetic to it than he was when he first wrote on this topic.

We may posit that there is a metaphysical distinction between what we might call 'real' properties (green and blue, for example), on the one hand, and what we might call 'non-real' ones (grue and bleen, for example) on the other; and we may posit that there is a metaphysical principle dictating what we might call 'an ontological preference' for universes which instantiate real, rather than non-real, properties. These posits, taken together, would then explain (to a greater or lesser extent, depending

With that, it is time to conclude. Allow me to sum up our findings.

Our argument has progressed as follows. Initially, it appeared that the best explanation of the fine tuning of *the universe to us* – a fact which *did* need explanation on the assumption of the trans-universality of the value of life of our sort – was the maximal multiverse hypothesis. That hypothesis raises the probability of this universe existing to one and, it was argued, is simpler than the God hypothesis. By contrast, the God hypothesis raises the probability of this universe existing to less than one and, it was argued, is more complex. *However*, as we went on to see, regardless of the trans-universality of any value, the best explanation of the continuing fine tuning of *us to the universe* is the God hypothesis. On the maximal multiverse hypothesis, the probability of any universe in which there are morally sensitive and significantly free persons being a universe which those persons can more or less consistently understand through induction is infinitely small. On the God hypothesis, that probability is one. As it is infinitely small on the maximal multiverse

---

on the strength of the preference posited) why we find ourselves in a universe where things are green and blue, rather than grue and bleen. One might suggest that we could get away with positing an ontological preference for real simplicity and letting the rest take care of itself: given that green and blue are, one may contend, really simpler than grue and bleen, and given that it would be really simpler for creatures to be directly aware of the really simple properties, rather as Russell thought we are directly aware of universals, from this preference for real simplicity alone we could explain why it is that we find ourselves in a universe where things are green and blue and where we have managed to discover this feature and innumerable other similar features. We cannot of course posit an ontological preference for what would be really simpl*est*: ours is not the really simplest world (for there is stuff – a whole universe at least – in it). So we would need to posit a preference for 'relative real simplicity' and work from there. In that this preference is being designed to do the job God's choice in creation does on the God hypothesis and may, in principle, be reworked and reworked without limit until it does so, it would be futile to maintain that strategies of this type will *inevitably* leave unexplained something the God hypothesis explains. But there is something rather unsatisfactory about them nonetheless, indeed precisely because they seem so *ad hoc*. Going down this road, it seems, we may in the end be left with a Parfitian 'selector' that is less plausible as a necessity than the God hypothesis. Some of these issues come up in my 'Why is there anything at all?', in Y. Nagasawa and E. Wielenberg (eds.), *New Waves in Philosophy of Religion* (London: Palgrave Macmillan, 2008), but I do not feel I have plumbed the depths and hope to be able to return to it at a later date.

hypothesis and one on the God hypothesis, so these hypotheses exclude one another: if there were a God, He would not have created any universes where there were morally sensitive and significantly free beings who found their universes significantly inductively intractable and there are an infinite number of these on the maximal multiverse hypothesis. The hypotheses excluding one another in this way means that we must abandon one of them. Taking all of these things into the balance then, it is obvious which one we should abandon. We should conclude that, despite its rational attractiveness in explaining the fine tuning of the universe to us in a more conclusive and arguably simpler manner than the God hypothesis, due to its abject failure to explain the continuing fine tuning of us to the universe, we should discard the maximal multiverse hypothesis and instead believe in the God hypothesis. The God hypothesis is the best explanation of the fine tuning of the universe to us and the fine tuning of us to the universe.[29]

St Peter's College, Oxford University

[29] I am grateful to Sophie Allen, Rodney Holder, Dennis Lehmkuhl, Richard Swinburne, and Ralph Walker for their comments on a draft of this paper. I am also grateful for the chairmanship of Anthony O'Hear at the meeting of the Royal Institute of Philosophy on 10th October 2008 where this paper was delivered as a lecture and for the questions and comments which he and those attending the lecture provided on that occasion.

What can God Explain?

GERARD J. HUGHES

1. Introduction

In this paper, I shall be arguing for what I hope is a modern version of a very traditional view, which is that God can explain two very basic phenomena: the first is the existence of the universe as we know it: the second is the particular way in which the universe is organised. I shall also, though briefly, try to counter the view that the totally unwelcome features of our universe make it impossible to reconcile the universe as it is with anything like traditional theistic belief. This project, however, is quite a daunting one. So I would wish to make it clear right at the start that, while I would claim that my views are reasonable, and indeed more reasonable than belief in the denial of these views would be, I still do not hold that it is unreasonable for someone to reject each of the conclusions for which I shall argue. For plainly anyone, whether myself or any opponent, can be both reasonable and mistaken.

The project is, as I have said, daunting. In particular, it has to overcome the arguments for three contrary positions. These positions are

a)   That no explanation for the existence of the universe is necessary.
b)   That in any case the notion of 'God' is too hopelessly vague to be genuinely explanatory.
c)   There is no explanation of the moral character of this world which is compatible with anything like traditional theism.

I shall try to undermine each of these counter-claims. In order to do so, I shall begin by offering some very general considerations concerning the notion of explanation itself. Partly I do this for the sake of clarity: but also because I think it important, at any rate in passing, to try to determine which difficulties are inherent to the very notion of explanation itself, and which are specific to explanation used in a theist context.

2. What is Explanation?

If we leave aside for the moment the explanation of personal behaviour, the most obvious kind of explanation consists in exhibiting

doi:10.1017/S1358246111000051   © The Royal Institute of Philosophy and the contributors 2011
Royal Institute of Philosophy Supplement **68** 2011

Gerard J. Hughes

some particular event as falling under a general rule or law. We are satisfied with an explanation when we can say 'That's just what one would expect to happen in the circumstances'. Of course, in order to do this successfully we need to have carefully identified which are the relevant features of what happened. We are all capable of jumping to conclusions which are either just plain wrong, or else not perfectly accurate. To this extent, the notion of 'explanation' need not involve anything with which Hume would not have agreed. For nothing so far is inconsistent with saying that an explanatory 'law' is simply a summary of what previously has happened in our experience – what Hume calls, a pattern of 'customary', by which he means constant, succession. Of course Kant considered this account of causal explanation as fatal to the whole project of Enlightenment science; and argued that Hume's supposedly basic notion of 'experience' itself presupposed the kind of causal necessity which Hume would ascribe to a projection on our part.

It is often rapidly affirmed that Kant is right on this point and Hume wrong. But it is worth considering how far Hume's more sceptical picture could take him. Hume could certainly accommodate the fact that our laws of nature regularly undergo refinement (and, occasionally, outright rejection); for in his terms, we might find that constant conjunction was not quite constant; and that our notion of what was constantly conjoined with what can and should often change. Nothing in this to disturb a scientist – such refinements of the laws of nature are commonplace. Nevertheless, does it not appear that on Hume's view, absolutely anything might happen at any time; for all we know, we live in a world of cosmic coincidence? Strictly speaking, I believe Hume would accept that. Nonetheless, he might point out that, by coincidence or not, our world is like that – regular and therefore predictable. Hume could argue that the assumption that the coincidental patterns of constant conjunction will remain constant happens to serve us very well. If Humean scientists continue to make this assumption, they will be at no practical disadvantage relative to their colleagues who believe that there is necessity in things. The two assumptions are operationally equivalent. Kant is being needlessly alarmist to suggest that Humeans inevitably undermine the whole scientific project. Of course, it is conceivable that there be a one-off event, a happening which forms no part of any constant conjunction of experiences; and that such an event would be totally inexplicable in Humean terms. But he might retort that such an event would be equally inexplicable on anyone's terms, and he would be right.

Nonetheless, the necessitarian scientist, if I may so describe someone who believes that there is a causal necessity in the way in which things in the world interact, will not rest content with this Humean account of explanation. It has several shortcomings. Firstly, it gives little or no guidance for distinguishing between what could be random conjunctions and genuinely causal connections. Thus, a Humean might be disposed to infer that day causes night, and night day; the conjunction is perfect, and there is no Humean reason to look further for anything more explanatory. Again, every bicycle produced in Britain is smaller than the dome of St Paul's cathedral; but the necessitarian scientist would not be willing to suppose that the Dome somehow limited the size of British bicycles; or indeed of all bicycles worldwide. But for the Humean, no conjunction, provided it is constant, is any more or any less significant than any other. None is more worth taking as the basis for further research than any other. Nor, as it seems to me, is it simply a matter of causal beliefs 'supporting counterfactuals', as the phrase goes: as if to say, 'If St Paul's were to be demolished, bicycles might well turn up which are truly enormous by contemporary standards' Neo-Humeans might try to offer that absurdity as the reason why they too would take my example as ridiculous. But, in default of any experience of post-Dome bicycles they would have no psychological Humean inclination to suggest any such thing. The absurdity assumption is groundless in their own terms.

One way in which the necessitarian scientist might claim to differ from the neo-Humean is that he is constantly in search of mechanisms to account for the relationships between the properties of things. Often enough, the models have a primitive simplicity about them, and might almost be seen as sophisticated variants on Humean billiard balls. Sub-atomic particles typically have mass, and hence can possess kinetic energy and can be launched at one another to produce splitting, and so on. To be sure, scientists often produce complex equations in their attempts to formulate accurate scientific laws, and they would perhaps speak of such equations as 'models' for reality. But it seems to me that they are not in general content with such abstract models, and would much prefer if they could interpret these equations in terms of things which are within our everyday experience. We are well acquainted with billiard balls, and with things being split apart into smaller bits; we can understand strings vibrating at different frequencies; at a pinch we can understand such vibrations as occurring in ten dimensions. We can visualise water going down a dark hole and never coming out again. We use such models not only as visual or imaginative aids; but, at least sometimes, as pointers to entities which lie totally beyond our direct experience. Perhaps the line between helpful metaphors and ontological commitment is not

Gerard J. Hughes

always clear, either to non-specialists like myself, or to scientists themselves. I suppose that talk of colliding sub-atomic particles is to be taken literally, but that curved space, black holes, and ten-dimensional strings are metaphors – but I am far from sure. But in either case, scientists can be stimulated to look for further particles – the Higgs boson, which, though itself of zero mass, might explain why other things have mass, would be one instance. What sense of 'explain' is being invoked here, one might wonder?

At any event, my point is that all this kind of research is quite difficult to reconcile with Hume's general position, and that of his contemporary empiricist followers. It is not so much that they cannot re-interpret each step once it is taken (if indeed they can do that much) but rather that the entire inspiration for this kind of research and for that kind of imaginative construction of hypotheses is difficult to justify on purely Humean grounds. Surely the best explanation for the success of contemporary science is that it correctly assumes a realist account of the meaning of physical laws, and of at least some realities which we can only metaphorically describe. It is for this reason that Kant was in the end right, and Hume wrong. But notice that to say '…but surely', as I have just done, is not really an argument: it is an appeal to some kind of unargued for intuition of what is and is not reasonable.

But by far the most difficult aspect of contemporary science, as it seems to me, is to determine what requires explanation, and when explanations have reached the point at which they can justifiably be said to be complete. Consider the following examples:

a) We can correlate the half life of radioactive substances with their chemical composition, and so give a statistical probability for the proportion of atoms which will decay in that time: but we can at present give no explanation of why any given individual atom decays rather than any other. Einstein and Bohr disagreed about whether some further explanation was necessary.

b) We can correlate the power of gravitational attraction of an object with its mass; but to many scientists this still leaves gravity itself as quite mysterious. Yet the attempt to explain it by postulating graviton-particles seems rather a desperate expedient. Is the mass/gravity connection, then, simply a brute fact, not further to be explained?

c) Neuroscientists and philosophers are both divided about whether consciousness and the content of our concepts and beliefs can be explained simply in terms of the activity of the neurons in our brains. On the one hand, if we were to postulate a perfectly developed neurology, so that we could produce a 'constant conjunction' between neural states and conscious states, it still seems to many neuroscientists and many philosophers that the conjunction would not constitute an adequate explanation at all: and to others it would seem clear that once the neurology was perfectly established, there would be nothing further to be looked for, so the explanation must be satisfactory.

So far as I can see, these three examples show no signs of being resolved to everyone's satisfaction. There is perhaps an assumption on the one side that everything that can be known must be accessible to the methods of physics, even if at present we have not developed our physics sufficiently; and on the other, there is an equally deep-seated conviction that none of the proposed correlations is what is needed to provide a satisfactory explanation. We might have to be content, at least for the moment, either to resign ourselves to the fact that even the best explanations might seem seriously inadequate: or to suppose that there may be properties of the things in our material world which are not accessible to the methods of physics; or that there may exist entities which are not material objects at all. But how to decide between these possible conclusions?

It is time to try to sum up this long – yet no more than preliminary! – section. What we mean by 'explanation' should at least reflect the methods of scientific research, whose assumptions can perhaps be justified by the success which adopting these assumptions has produced. I think these assumptions can be listed as follows:

1. That the 'laws of nature' represent our best efforts to give precise accounts of the causally necessary ways in which the properties of things interact with one another.
2. That we would hope that the entities referred to in these laws actually exist independently of our theories, even though we cannot always directly experience such entities.
3. Ideally we could perhaps give literal descriptions of the entities referred to in our mature theories, but at least in the interim we often can do no more than offer mutually correcting metaphorical descriptions; and not always can we even do so much.
4. That we do not have a clear notion of the point at which the desire for further explanation is irrational.

The difficulties involved in each of these claims are serious: I suggest that they are well known, and I claim that they arise quite separately from any problems about theism.

Gerard J. Hughes

3. What can God explain?

A. The existence of the universe

Before trying to decide whether or not God can explain the universe, there are therefore two prior issues which must be tackled. The first is whether there is any need to explain the universe at all; and the second is whether any kind of explanation is even possible.

Various attempts have been made to show that the universe simply needs no explanation at all. Here is a modernised version of something which Kant said. Kant insisted against Hume that there was every justification for speaking of causal necessity in the world of our experience. But he maintained that, although it was not indeed senseless to speak of causal explanations outside the realm of possible experience, there was no way in which such a use could be validated. He also maintained that there was no legitimate way of showing that the necessary being – whose existence he accepted – had any of the properties one might look for in God. Well, then: the law of the conservation of energy is one of the most fundamental laws of physics. It states that, though the distribution of matter/energy in the universe is varying all the time, the total energy in the universe cannot change. But if it cannot change, then the energy in the universe is just 'there', and is therefore a plausible candidate for the status of necessary being. No further explanation is required.

This argument, I suggest does not work. There are perhaps two reasons for supposing that the world did in fact have a beginning. The first derives from a philosophical puzzle about infinity which troubled both Aristotle and Aquinas along with other medieval Aristotelians. It might be argued, they said, i) if the universe had no beginning, then it must already have existed for an infinite number of days; but ii) there cannot actually exist an infinite number of anything. Hence iii), the world cannot have existed for an infinite time, and so must have had a beginning. It is a matter of scholarly discussion in what sense Aristotle did say that in a sense an infinity can exist; but it seems that he meant no more than that one can be in the middle of a process which need have no end.[1] William Lane Craig has argued, I believe convincingly, that the theoretical mathematics of infinity cannot without intolerable paradox simply be applied to the actual world; and that the two premisses of the above argument are sound if taken to be true of the

---

[1] See Jaakko Hintikka, 'Aristotle's Infinity', *Philosophical Review* **75** (1966/2), 107–118.

actual world. If time had no beginning we would already have had an infinite number of days, and that is impossible.[2]

But if the universe did have a beginning, then it does require an explanation. Appeal to the laws of physics will not satisfy this requirement. For the laws of physics describe the way in which things in the universe actually behave. They do not cause things to behave in that way. If no universe exists, there is nothing for the laws of physics to describe, and nothing of which they can be true. So the law of the conservation of energy, while it states that where energy exists, it exists in an unchangeable amount, is vacuous in the case where no energy exists at all. Accounts of the Big Bang extrapolate backwards to a point at which the universe would be infinitely small, infinitely hot, and infinitely dense. It seems to me reasonable to suggest that the implications of this are that at that 'point' there can be no physical object which has those properties. At the limit, the universe does not exist. Fred Hoyle accepted this argument, and was not happy with what he took to be its theistic implications. It was this that motivated him to consider an alternative model of the universe, the steady state theory. But this has been convincingly refuted by the experiments of Hubble, Penzias and Wilson which show that the universe is expanding, and that its expansion began some 15 billion years ago.

It is more difficult to argue that the universe needs no further explanation if it did in fact begin at a point in time in the past. For quite generally, science would simply not accept something coming into being without trying to find some explanation of why it did. Nevertheless, there is here a very deep conflict of philosophical intuitions and it is always hard to get behind an appeal to intuitions, or to adjudicate between conflicting ones. So, consider these examples:

If astronomers observe the sudden appearance of a bright light in some portion of the sky, they will, let us suppose, explain it in terms of a previously unsuspected supernova; they will not be content until they have fitted it into the pattern of regular behaviour which characterises such exploding stars, and to trace that behaviour in turn to most basic patterns of physical interactions. But why does such an occurrence need an explanation at all? If the neo-Humeans are right, there seems to me to be no particular justification for saying that it has to be an instance of some pattern or other; there is no clear reason why it might not be a one-off event. Why, then, can it not simply happen without cause, without explanation? If the

---

[2] William Lane Craig, 'The *Kalam* cosmological argument', in William Lane Craig (ed.) *Philosophy of Religion: A Reader and Guide* (Edinburgh, Edinburgh University Press, 2002), 92–113.

reply to this question is that most things happen as part of a repeatable pattern, does that assertion itself not require support in two respects: even if most things are part of a pattern, why should this be one of the ones that is?; and in any case do we need to ask why most things exhibit regular succession? The necessitarian will, of course, argue that the best explanation of the success of scientific research is that the basic assumptions which researchers make are in fact correct, and that a key assumption is that things necessarily react with one another in ways which are determined by their natures. But as I have mentioned above, this is not quite a clinching argument, since the neo-Humean could still try to maintain that all he needs for scientific success is to assume that events in the world just happen to be patterned without any necessitation being involved at all. Provided it works, he does not need to explain why it should. The key claim the neo-Humean needs to make is that such an assumption of cosmic coincidence needs no form of realist justification; what he cannot consistently do, as it seems to me, is to claim that it is justified because it has worked well so far, unless 'justified' simply means 'convenient'. To the necessitarian realist, the Humean picture seems impoverished and profoundly unscientific: to the neo-Humean, the realist view seems to make basic assumptions which are at once unnecessary and unverifiable. In my own view, there is at this level no knock-down proof; but it seems to me on balance more reasonable to adopt a view which underlies most scientific research, and which can give a rationale for distinguishing between pseudo-correlations and causal connections.

Suppose, then, that at this point the eager theist leaps in to claim that it is more reasonable to hold that the universe needs an explanation, and that the explanation is God. Surely the obvious rejoinder is to question whether that is an explanation at all; for does it not lack two of the features which we would normally consider absolutely fundamental to any genuine explanation?: it does not offer any lawlike correlation; and it provides absolutely nothing in the way of a model whereby we can gain any understanding. If the theist appeals to the notion of causation, the problem is that at least on most theistic views divine causation is, to say the least, not very similar to intra-worldly causation. The net result is that to appeal to God as an explanation is to do no more than give a name to the problem, but not really to offer any kind of explanation at all.

The force of this criticism can, I believe, be blunted, but not conclusively overcome. Firstly, the theist can say that we would indeed not expect that a transcendent explanation should have the same explanatory characteristics as a scientific explanation of worldly phenomena in terms of other worldly powers. In the nature of the case, the explanans is not going to be an item in our world; and indeed, given how hospitable contemporary science is to worldly explanations in terms of things which are in principle unobservable, and to which we attribute some very strange properties indeed, we can perhaps not afford to be too inhospitable to an explanatory Something which would be timeless and not a material object at all. Indeed, it is precisely down this avenue that Aquinas urges us to go. He advocates that in using the word 'God' we adopt a definition of convenience, a nominal definition, 'whatever it takes to explain the world' because we have no knowledge of anything better to use. We do well to remember that the brisk conclusion of each of his Five Ways, 'And this we call God', uses the term 'God' precisely in this non-committal stipulative sense; he claims to have established no more than that the universe does need an explanation. To say more will require a great deal of further philosophical effort.

B. Order or Design?

To fill out the nature of this minimalist explanation the theist, in my view, is going to have to use at least some of the considerations more traditionally considered in connection with the so called 'argument from design'. Once again, though, they will have to be used with considerable caution. There are several reasons for this.

It is difficult to suppose that there could exist anything at all which did not in some way and at some level exhibit some kind of order or structure. I think it safer to assume that a totally non-orderly universe is simply not possible. On that assumption, there is nothing remarkable in the fact that our universe is orderly. Rather, the question needs to be whether the orderliness is of such a kind as to need some kind of further explanation. The well-known argument based on what is called the 'anthropic principle' at least recognises this requirement. It seeks to meet it by arguing that the very accuracy of the orderliness required for the evolution of intelligent beings such as ourselves is so demanding that it has to be purposeful. In short, the degree of orderliness is such that it can be explained only as deliberately aimed at producing beings such as ourselves. I think this argument is at best problematic. Here are my reasons:

i) While it is indeed true that, so far as we can tell, very small variations in any of the basic constants in physics will have extraordinary large effects, the conclusion to be drawn from this need not, and I think should not, be limited to observations about what would have been the fate of human kind if the set-up were even marginally different. If the argument is going to work at all, it is going to have to deal with the universe as a whole, not just with 'us in our small corner'. And in any case it might be argued that the anthropic principle is especially vulnerable to arguments connected with the Problem of Evil. On this point, more below.

ii) It is of course true that the universe is very delicately balanced in such a way as to produce the kinds of being that it contains. To say that, however, is little more than a tautology: any universe will of necessity be fine-tuned in such a way as to produce exactly what it produces. That in itself says nothing about purposefulness or design.

The point is whether the particular arrangement of this universe requires explanation at all, and, if it does, whether that explanation has to contain any element of intelligent design. Once again, it seems to me not to be unreasonable to deny that any such explanation is necessary. Indeed, such a position is all the more plausible because the relationship between a transcendent cause and its effects is even less transparent than ordinary intra-cosmic causal relationships. Moreover, we are extremely ignorant about vast areas of the universe, and not really in a position to assess its functionality as a whole with respect to any purported purpose or design that it may exemplify.

On the other hand, it is perhaps striking that a universe should produce even one planet in which beings appear who do entertain such notions as purpose and point and intention; and who without undue anthropocentrism can appreciate beauty and elegance and value in many of the things that this planet contains. It is common to give short shrift to poor old Paley and his watch; but I wonder is this fair? The fact that such astonishing complexity as is to be found in our earth itself, let alone in the universe as a whole, can be truly describable in terms of comparatively few fundamental laws is in itself remarkable; and is something which we would in ordinary human activities take to be a sign of intelligent planning and elegant economy of design. Given that there are good reasons to suppose that there does exist a first cause of the universe, it is not unreasonable to conjecture that that cause must itself entertain some such notions as point and purpose, given that the universe which it brings about contains beings such as ourselves who naturally operate on the basis of such attributions to one another.

Two caveats are in order. Firstly, I am not for one moment denying that our universe, our planet, and everything within it has in different ways evolved from things which were much simpler – from the baryons and quarks and other primitive particles which first emerged from the big bang. The most complex life-forms, such as ourselves, have evolved over billions of years. Secondly, neither am I at all trying to say that each stage of the process is somehow purposive in itself. Thus, I believe it is the case that the mutations which led to the evolution of the feather long antedated the development of organisms that could fly. The process which produced a feather was not itself somehow 'aiming at' helping birds, even though eventually the environment would be such that for some organisms the possession of feathers turned out to be an advantage. If there is purposiveness in the universe, it is that the design of it taken as a whole exhibits purpose, rather than simply that at various times those entities which were better adapted to their environments tended on the whole to be better survivors. Just so with Paley's watch: the watchmaker intends the gears to turn the hands on the dial; but the clockwork itself is not purposeful; it is a blind mechanical process. The exception to this would be those higher animals, including ourselves, to which it is appropriate to ascribe intention and purpose. The significant fact about it all is that there are beings such as ourselves who can see, or at least claim to see, purposiveness in the cosmos as a whole, and that such a process from start to finish can reasonably be seen to be more than an immense chain of adaptation to the environment, whether on the part of inanimate entities or of living organisms.

Once more, I am not arguing that such a conclusion is the only one which can be drawn beyond any reasonable doubt; I am arguing only that such an overall interpretation is not at all an unreasonable one; indeed I believe that on the balance of probabilities it is likely to be correct. In which case, that the transcendent cause of the universe is not in space/time, is not a material object, and is intelligent and purposeful goes at least some way towards establishing that it is in fact God. The dispute is not dissimilar to the well-known dispute in neuroscience, about what will count as a satisfactory explanation of consciousness and of human choice. The reductionist and physicalist reply to this question is not absurd, for it is indeed hard to pin down whether more explanation of our human consciousness and choices is required than one couched in terms of the complexities of our cerebral electronics. Yet that electronic explanation still hardly seems to add up. What 'more' consciousness, or agent causation adds to pure neurology, or, as I would urge here, to cosmology, is a matter of rational assessment, which is much more than geometry or logic or physics.

Gerard J. Hughes

C. 'The Problem of Evil'

Many of the approaches to what is in general called 'the problem of evil' assume that the task of anyone who wishes to deal with the problem is to show how appeal to the existence of a God with the traditional attributes of omniscience, omnipotence and omnibenevolence can explain all the undesirable features of this world. I think that this approach is doomed to failure, and that the most that the theist might hope to do is to explain why it is reasonable to believe in such a God despite the state of the world. The general line of argument is to show that there is no justification for blaming God unless it can be shown that this world could not be the best possible world. If we cannot establish that God can reasonably be blamed, then there is no reasonable ground for saying that the world as it is cannot in the end be explained by the existence of a good God.

The first step in this argument is to suggest that we have no clear criteria for evaluating the worth of worlds overall. It is no secret that even were we to agree, as in general terms we might well, on which actions or features of our world are valuable, admirable or in some other way to be evaluated positively, we are much less likely to find clear grounds for evaluating complex states of affairs overall. Two brief illustrations might serve to illustrate the point.

The first concerns predatory animals. If a leopard kills a deer, is this a good or a bad state of affairs? Plainly at least the initial answer is going to be different, depending on whether one considers the action from the point of view of the leopard and her cubs, or the dead deer, or the herd of deer, or the ecological balance of the wildlife on the Serengeti Plain as a whole. Similar considerations might apply to the relationships between mosquitoes and humans, or the AIDS virus and humans, and the overall balance between humans and the rest of the organisms in the world. We are naturally inclined to consider at least the second set of questions from the human point of view; and certainly a God's eye view, even if there is a God, is not readily available to us.

Or consider some comparative values, such as the achievements of the human mind, the beauties of music and the arts, the deep value of love at its best. One might reasonably think that on balance these things together outweigh even the terrible sufferings which disfigure the history of our world. That thought might explain why we think that Earth is a better place than the moon, despite the fact that there is no suffering on the moon. In the same way, we might think that the earth now, when humans and other animals have evolved, is a richer and better place overall than it was millions of years ago when there were no life-forms on earth capable of suffering. Of course, there are no scales on which such a balance can be tested; nor is there any mathematical procedure for measuring which of these values outweighs the other. Still, it is at least reasonable to think that Earth as it is now is a good place overall, and to say that if this is true for Earth, there is no reason for denying that the same is true about the Universe as a whole.

I claim that this is a 'reasonable' point of view. By that I mean that it is a view which a thoughtful and well-informed person could believe there to be good grounds for accepting. I do not claim that it is the only reasonable point of view. Indeed it seems fairly obvious to me that there are very many questions about this world and this universe about which many different and indeed incompatible views can reasonably be defended, and no one of them conclusively established. It is just like the way in which it is built into our system of justice that there are often several mutually incompatible views which can reasonably thought to be true on the balance of probabilities. Indeed I think that statement itself is true beyond any reasonable doubt.

I would argue, then, that it is not unreasonable to suppose that this world is good overall.

On the other hand, to establish that much, if indeed I have established that much, is not sufficient. It seems to me that if one is going to claim that the existence of this world can be explained in terms of a good God, one has to show that one can reasonably believe that this is the best possible world. We humans can perhaps operate with a distinction between strict duty, on the one hand, and on the other, heroic deeds over and above the call of duty. We can perhaps blame people for failing in their duty, but not blame them for failing to be heroic. I think, however that higher standards have to be applied to a God if such a being is to be thought worthy of worship. Leibniz was right: God surely would be obliged to do the best that is possible.

But might this be the best possible world? Once more, it seems to me that there is no way of establishing beyond reasonable doubt that the world could overall be better than it is. Not that this has been a widely shared view, it has to be said. Hume, in a famous passage in the *Dialogues Concerning Natural Religion* suggests that if anyone were told in advance that they might experience a world made by an all powerful and omnibenevolent God, they would be mightily disappointed to be told that this was it. Instead, they might conclude that it was the work of an infant deity, as yet unpractised in the arts of creation. With more experience, he might have grasped how the 'great springs of nature' could be tweaked to produce a more moderate climate, creatures that did not need pain to stimulate them, world without illnesses and misfortunes. It takes little imagination to suggest many obvious improvements.

I certainly do not trust/believe in the various efforts to demonstrate that every unfortunate event still contributes to the goodness of the whole. Efforts along these lines have been made: that suffering strengthens character, that disasters can punish humans for their wrongdoing, and that even if the good do suffer and the evil prosper, the balance will surely be restored. But surely suffering can embitter or crush people as well as strengthen character; and however much we might need to believe that righteousness is ultimately vindicated, this is, as Kant said, a postulate rather than a demonstrable truth. Efforts to explain that even the most horrendous or tragic events are all really providential seem to be at best incredible, and at worst morally outrageous.

Equally, however, the naïve Humean assumption that an omnipotent God must be able to fine-tune the great springs of nature in such a way as to satisfy our more idyllic imaginations seems to me equally untenable. If even an omnipotent God creates a limited world, it follows that in such a world some things are possible and others not. From what contemporary physics tells us about our own universe, it is clear that the patterns of causal interactions are extremely restricted; even the most minute changes in any fundamental law would have incalculably wide-ranging effects. Selective tuning – to provide an atmosphere which is breathable, recirculates water, and shields us from the worst aspects of solar radiation, yet without any risk of flash floods, droughts, or skin-cancer – is just not causally possible, so far as we can see. Descartes is right to admonish us not to allow our powers of imagination to limit our beliefs about the omnipotence of God. Universes quite unlike ours may indeed be possible: but if they are quite unlike ours, then comparisons to determine whether they are better or worse than ours will not be possible. And if they are like ours, we know as a matter of scientific fact that they will inevitably have causal limitations against which the Humean imagination is quite literally powerless.

4. Conclusion

If I am right, the conclusions of this paper are modest, reasonable, and important.

They are modest, in that I do not claim, nor do I believe, that I have shown that postulating the existence of God makes the origins of the universe clear, nor that the sense in which God explains a material world is one which we can clearly grasp. They are modest, also, in that I do not claim that atheism, or agnosticism on any of these matters is an unreasonable position to adopt. To be sure, just as there are indefensible versions of theism, which owe more to prejudice and passion than they do to reason, so there are such versions of atheism or religious agnosticism. All I wish to claim is that believing that there is a God does answer questions which cannot be dismissed without that dismissal being itself arbitrary.

That these are reasonable conclusions is certainly not to say that this is the only reasonable view which can be taken on such matters. But it is to say something about its place among the rest of our reasonable beliefs. For I claim that to conclude that there is a God is certainly not to deny or to try to sideline the achievements of science; nor is it to try to slip such a belief into the places where we do not yet have scientific explanations for things in our world. I am not, in that sense, offering anything like a 'god of the gaps.' Rather I am saying that the very features of our intelligence which best account for the successes of our scientific endeavours are just those which can reasonably prompt us to claim that, where science must come to an end, there are reasonable questions which can still be asked, and reasonable answers which can be given in theistic terms.

And finally, that this conclusion is important is simply a corollary of the fact that it might indeed be true. For if it is true, it does provide a context in which our scientific endeavours can be seen as giving us some understanding of God: and while that conclusion does not give a meaning to life, as if without it our lives were meaningless as they stand, it does provide an additional level of meaning which can be welcomed with all reasonable delight.

Campion Hall, Oxford

One Step Toward God

Much of traditional natural theology offers causal explanations- e.g. for the universe's existence and ability to host our sort of life. But a less-remarked strand offers ontological explanations, claiming that theories involving God are the best answers to ontological questions. Leibniz, for instance, wrote in the *Monadology* that

> If there is a reality in essences or possibilities, or... eternal truths, this reality must be founded on something existent... and conse- quently on the existence of the necessary being in whom essence involves existence... without (God) there would be nothing real in the possibilities – not only nothing existent, but also nothing possible.[1]

Though Leibniz barely gestures at the argument, what he wants to claim is that the ontology of modality requires God, and this is reason to believe that God exists. Nor does he treat God as a cause of possi- bility; he thinks instead that God's nature makes possibility claims true, offering an ontological explanation (an account of what sort of entity makes a sort of claim true[2]) rather than a causal one.[3] Again, Alan Rhoda and Dean Zimmerman offer God as a response to a truthmaker problem arising on presentist views of time.[4] Augustine made a similar move on the problem of universals. In an early work, he puts forward the premise that if there is anything superior to human reason, there is a God.[5] He then argues that 'immutable'

---

[1] ##43–4, in *Leibniz: Philosophical Writings*, tr. Mary Morris, (London: J.M. Dent and Sons, Ltd., 1938), 10.

[2] This is one way to give an ontological explanation. There are others- e.g. one can explain what set-talk is really about, or in what it consists for a set to exist.

[3] G. W. Leibniz, 'On Nature's Secrets', in C. I. Gerhardt (ed.), *Die phi- losophischen Schriften von G. W. Leibniz* (Berlin: Weidmann, 1875–90), vol. vii, 310.

[4] Alan Rhoda, 'Truthmakers and God', *Pacific Philosophical Quarterly* **90** (2009) 41–62; Dean Zimmerman, 'The A-Theory of Time, Presentism and Open Theism', in Melville Stewart (ed.), *Science and Religion in Dialogue* (Oxford: Wiley-Blackwell, 2009), v. 2.

[5] Augustine, *De Libero Arbitrio* II, vi, 54–6.

doi:10.1017/S1358246111000063   © The Royal Institute of Philosophy and the contributors 2011
Royal Institute of Philosophy Supplement **68** 2011   67

(i.e. necessary) mathematical truth is superior to human reason.[6] It emerges that such truth has its foundation in a realm of Platonic mathematical objects, which turn out to be somehow identical with the Platonic Forms.[7] So at one level, Augustine's premises are that

1. if something is superior to human reason, God exists, and
2. something is superior to human reason.

But given that his case for (2) is really a case for a Platonist account of attributes, at another level, we can see Augustine's premises as

1*. if a Platonist account of attributes is true, God exists, and
2*. a Platonist account of attributes is true.

I hold no brief for Platonism, but Augustine's idea of arguing God's existence *via* the claim that the true theory of attributes involves God seems to me worth pursuing. The theist theory of attributes I defend could be called nominalist or Platonist: nominalist in that it invokes only concrete particulars, Platonist in that it invokes something (God) outside spacetime and is structurally similar to Plato's theory. My full case for this theory has three broad parts. One shows that it can in fact do the full range of work one wants from an attribute-theory.[8] One argues that non-theist forms of nominalism either do not do some of this work or do some of it at greater ontological cost. The last rejects non-theist forms of realism because they generate unacceptable metaphysics of concrete substances. If I'm right, the theist view gives one overall the best account of substance and attribute and ought therefore to be believed. My full case, then, is matter for a book, not a paper. Here I can only offer one piece of it, which is why all I do here is take one step toward God. I begin by explaining some problems to which Platonism was an answer, what Plato's answer was, and how Augustine's answer improved on it. This shows *inter alia* that inclusion of a theist element can in fact improve a theory of attributes. I then state a theist account of attributes which modifies Augustine's, begin my argument for it by addressing one non-theist form of nominalism, then answer three objections to the theist account.

---

[6] Ibid., xii.
[7] Ibid., xvi.
[8] See my 'God and the Problem of Universals', *Oxford Studies in Metaphysics* **2** (2006), 325–56.

Attributes, predication and Platonism

Predication raises some of the oldest ontological questions. If I say that an apple is red, I attribute being red to the apple. Being red, then, is something I attribute, an attribute. Questions that arise here include just what if anything an attribute is and what it is to have an attribute. Since a predication is true just if its subject(s) has (have) the attribute we predicate, these amount to the question of what makes predications true.

Plato gave the first theory of attributes and predication: that corresponding to most predicates is an abstract entity, a Form, and if there is a Form for the predicate 'F', things to which 'F' applies are Fs by standing in a relation, participation, to the Form of F.[9] Plato did not make clear what 'participation' is.[10] But it is at least likeness grounded on some sort of real dependence: anything's being F consists in its depending on the paradigm F, The F, for a likeness to The F.

There are three sorts of reason we are not all Platonists. Plato's theory has internal difficulties: the Third Man argument, the difficulty of understanding participation, the strangeness of the Forms. Plato's theory is uneconomical: it adds hosts of abstract entities to our ontology. Forms are also suspect on broadly epistemological grounds. As Platonism developed, middle- and Neo-Platonists used God or gods to replace the Forms. Plutarch replaced them simply with God.[11] Alcinous replaced some Forms with ideas in the mind of God.[12] So did Plotinus.[13] Augustine combined the moves, replacing with God the Forms for attributes God can share with creatures and with God's concepts the Forms for attributes creatures alone can have.[14]

Religious motives may have played a part in this. But I think the Platonists got all godly about it for largely philosophical reasons: using God and His concepts to take the Forms' place makes progress on Platonism's philosophical problems. We don't have a good grip on

[9]   See e.g. Plato, *Phaedo, Republic*.
[10]   For discussion, see e.g. Charles Bigger, *Participation; a Platonic inquiry* (Baton Rouge: Louisiana State University Press, 1968).
[11]   Plutarch, 'On the Delay of the Divine Vengeance', in Phillip De Lacy and Benedict Einarson, trs., *Plutarch's Moralia VII* (Cambridge, MA: Harvard University Press, 1959), 550d, 195.
[12]   Alcinous, *The Handbook of Platonism*, tr. John Dillon (N.Y.: Oxford University Press, 1993), ch. 9, ll. 33–5, 16.
[13]   *Ennead* V, 5.
[14]   *Retractions*, i, 3, 2; *83 Different Questions*, 23, 46; *De Gen. ad Litt.* I, 4, #9.

participation. But if God replaces some Forms, participation in these cases becomes depending really on God for a likeness to God. If God can act in the world, it is clear at one level what this comes to: it is being helped by God to be in some way or degree Godlike. At a deeper level, how clear this is depends, of course, on how well we understand what it is for God to act in the world. But it is at least clear that this is efficient causation, if of an unusual sort. We hadn't even this much grip on what Plato meant by participation. So the God-move gains us something philosophically. If God's concepts replace other Forms, participation in these cases becomes depending really on God for being such as to satisfy His concepts. If God can act in the world, it is also clear at one level what this comes to, and so again, the God-move replaces Plato's cloudy picture with one a bit clearer. Again, while Forms are *sui generic*, gods are persons of a sort, albeit an unfamiliar sort. We're already in the business of offering a non-naturalist theory, if we're Platonists; the concept of God is not less intelligible than that of a Form; and the allied mysteries lessen a bit if God takes the Forms' place.

Again, while Forms are abstract; God is concrete, being a cause. One might reply that God's concepts are abstract, and so no gain is made in moving Forms into His mind. Plotinus, oddly, would've disagreed: as he saw it, each divine idea was a minor god.[15] *We* can instead pare divine concepts away, in favor of divine mental events. Again, Forms are myriad; Augustine pared deities down to one. He had of course religious reasons to do so, but the move gets strong support from Ockham's Razor. One God can do all the philosophical work other versions of Platonism did with many gods, so there is just no philosophical basis to multiply them. Again, Forms don't seem to permit a good epistemology. A God able to cause events in the world can cause us to have certain sorts of knowledge. Finally, consider the Third Man.[16] Participation involves likeness: anyone's being a man involves likeness to The Man. Now likeness is symmetrical. So if men are like The Man by being men, The Man is like men in respect of being a man – The Man is a man. So one must ask what it is for The Man to be a man. Plato reasoned that if The Man is a man, it has something in common with other men. So there is a Form, Man, in which they all participate. But Plato also held that no Form can participate in itself. If so, there is another Man, common to the initial Man and all other men – and so *ad infinitum*. For theistic Platonism, though, there is in place of The Man a

---

15   So e.g. V 8.
16   For which see Plato, *Parmenides*, 132a1–b2.

divine concept (in my variant, a divine mental event). A concept (or event) is not a man. So the Third Man dissolves, at least for Forms replaced by divine concepts. I suggest a line on Forms replaced by God below.

There thus was good philosophical reason for classical Platonists to take a theist – and even monotheist – turn.[17] So we might see behind Augustine's (1*) the premises that

3.   if Platonism is true, its best version is true, and
4.   The best version of Platonism includes theism.

(3) is plausible. If Platonism is true, we must decide between its versions to see what the whole truth is. We do so by seeing which version has the greatest theoretical virtues – scope, simplicity, parsimony, etc. This (we hope) selects out a theory it is most rational to believe: Platonism's best version. And though the move is hardly beyond controversy, we take it that what is most rational to believe is most likely true. I have suggested why a classical Platonist might incline to (4).

I now begin my case for a theist solution to the problem of attributes, and hence for God's existence. I first outline my theist story about predication. I then begin my case against other theories of attributes by comparing this view with one version of nominalism. I do not argue first that theism is possibly true. One way to show that Ks are possible is to display an actual K; an argument that God actually exists is *ipso facto* one that He possibly exists.

Theism: the basic story

To give my theist story, I return to Plato. Plato need not have gotten in Third Man trouble. A Platonist can say that The Man and other men are men in related ways. For them all, being men includes being like The Man (contentfully, rather than in virtue of sharing such transcendental properties as self-identity). Men other than The Man depend really on The Man for this likeness. The Man is contentfully like The Man. So it is a man. But it does not have that likeness by depending really on itself. It has that likeness by being itself. It is like itself because it is identical with itself: what makes the Man a man is that it is the Man. Thus there is no Form in which The Man and other men all participate. This is a 'no ontology' view of The Man's

---

[17]   Which is of course not to say that their best course was to retain Platonism in some form or another.

being a man. We get this for free given that it is The Man. Thus the Third Man evaporates. This strategy applies too to Forms God eventually replaced. On this approach, at an abstract level, the Platonist story about predication involving Forms becomes that

P. (x)(Fx iff (∃y)(y is the paradigm F and (x = y or x is appropriately related to y)).

That is, the paradigm F is F *per se*, just by being itself. For other Fs, being F is bearing a relation to the paradigm F.[18] What makes F-predications true is always of one or the other sort. This account is not outré. We don't jib at

X is one meter long = df. (∃y)(y is the standard meter and x = y or x is length-congruent with y).[19]

Augustine adopts (P), adding that

5. if it can be the case that God is F and some concrete non-divine being is F, God is the standard/paradigm F[20], and
6. if God can be F and no concrete non-divine being can be F, then if God is F, God is F *per se*[21], and
7. if some concrete non-divine being can be F and God cannot be, God's F-concept provides the standard.

(7) raises the specter that God's concept of evil will provide the standard evil. Augustine's doctrine that evils are lacks of goods provides an answer to this; Aquinas used this to say in effect that God has no concept of evil as such, merely concepts of goods whose

---

[18] Obviously a regress threatens here. This does not distinguish Platonism from other forms of realism – each has to deal somehow with the relation between an abstract item and the concrete thing of which we predicate a property – or from trope theories, which face parallel questions about 'compresence'. Nor does it distinguish Platonism from nominalism. In some forms of nominalism a relation takes the place of participation (satisfaction, resemblance) and parallel questions arise about this relation. In other forms no relation does – on a set theory of attributes, there can be no relation of membership. As we see below, this brings its own difficulties.

[19] One could of course simplify to 'is the standard meter and x is length-congruent with y', but equally one could simplify (P) to 'is appropriately related to y.'

[20] And the appropriate relation is resemblance: this is a resemblance-nominalist component of his theory.

[21] This is part of the content of Augustine's claim that God 'is what He has' – on which see my 'Divine Simplicity', *Faith and Philosophy* **23** (2006), 365–80.

absence He notes – and since evils are just absences, that is all He need do.[22]

I alter Augustine: I parse divine concepts away. I say that talk of them is fiction. If I can make this claim good, I can provide the explanatory power of Augustine's theist Platonism without positing abstract entities of any sort. What makes something a cat on my account is its dependence not on a divine concept but on certain bits of God's mental life. These are just primitively events with a particular causal role in God's mental economy, such that when appropriately involved in the execution of a divine intention, cats result. This is no worse than a realist's saying that a universal or Form, cathood, is just primitively cathood – that it does not have to instance another property, being cathood, to have this character. Explanation runs out somewhere; these seem reasonable stopping-points.

I also make it part of the theory that

8.   every substance is either God or a concrete non-divine particular, and for all x and t, if x is a concrete non-divine particular, if x exists at t, God conserves x in existence at t.

(8) is standard theism: for all x and t, if x is concrete and not God and exists at t, God wills that x exist at t, and this contributes causally to x' existence at t. If x has existed for some period open toward t, this is contributing to causing x to continue to exist. This does not imply that only God causes concrete creatures to continue; it could be that God provides a necessary but insufficient condition for continuation. If x has not previously existed, God's willing x to exist at t constitutes creating x at t.[23] This might be a simple case of creation *ex nihilo*. But God can also cause x to begin to exist *via* creaturely intermediaries; God can conserve or create by willing there to be created causal chains that begin or sustain creatures' existence. So my preferred theist theory consists of (P), (5), (6), (8) and

9.   if some concrete non-divine being can be F and God cannot be, being F consists in being conserved in dependence on those divine mental events which lie behind fictional talk of God's having an F-concept.[24]

---

[22]   E.g. *Summa Theologica* Ia 15, 3 *ad* 1.

[23]   Thus I use 'conservation' in a slightly extended sense which includes creation as a special case.

[24]   Every theory of attributes owes an account of the referents of abstract terms apparently naming attributes, e.g. 'wisdom', Wisdom is what 'makes' the wise wise. In Plato, 'wisdom' named a Form, and to be wise was to participate in that Form. In Augustine it named a divine concept, and to be wise

Brian Leftow

God conserves Fs as Fs just if those events figure in the right way in the intention which directs His conserving power. This employment gives rise to the right sort of causal dependence on them. This kind of constant conservation threatens occasionalism, the doctrine that only God causes any event: if first God conserves me as a boy and then He conserves me as a man, it might seem to follow that by switching how He conserves me, God causes me to become a man. But the most that would follow here is overdetermination or part-causation- perhaps both God and my biology account for this. I do not think it is over-determination, either, because (I submit) it can be the case that causation among creatures accounts for what it is that God conserves. It might e.g. be that causal processes in some water account for the fact that by conserving the water-molecules individually, first God

---

was to either be divine or satisfy that concept. On my view, it names a complex of divine mental events with the ontological role Forms and divine concepts filled, and to be wise is either to have the divine nature or for those events to cause one to be like God in a particular way.

Every theory of attributes also owes an account of second-order predication, e.g. of what makes it true that wisdom is a virtue. The theory as so far stated concerns attributes of God and of concrete non-divine beings. Attributes are neither. Thus I am free to offer a different sort of account of second-order predication. For Plato, wisdom was a virtue because it participated in the Form of virtue. For Augustine, I presume, what made it true that wisdom is a virtue was the divine nature, which 'contained' wisdom and so settled its nature. There are three cases to consider: attributes only God can have, attributes only creatures can have, and attributes the two can share. On the first I say what Augustine did: the truthmaker is the divine nature. On the second I say it is the events themselves: what makes it true that doghood is an animal-kind may be that the doghood-event has the causal role of making dogs dogs and thereby making them animals, or perhaps that the doghood event necessarily recruits the animality-event when it operates to make dogs dogs. On the last, we must distinguish whether the attribute is God's essentially or accidentally. If essentially, the truthmaker is again the divine nature. One divine accidental attribute creatures can share is preferring Gandhi to Hitler. This has the attribute of being a preference. It has it essentially, by its own intrinsic content, and has it as it is in God, whether or not any creature comes to share it. It also has accidental attributes, e.g. being the preference Leftow mentioned in a long footnote. It has that due to what I did.

One can also ask what attributes *are*, on a given view. For me, there are no such things. On my account of what it is to have an attribute, strictly speaking there is no such thing as an attribute had, as in resemblance nominalism.

74

conserves some liquid and then He conserves some ice. For reasons of space, though, I cannot pursue this further.

Theism vs. class nominalism

One recommends a theory of attributes by rebutting arguments against it, showing its rivals' problems and showing that it can do the work one wants of a theory of attributes. Here I can offer only one comparison, with one current view, which holds that attributes are sets. I raise six problems for the set theory, and show that the theist view does not face them. There are also questions one can raise for the theist view which do not arise for the set theory. I answer some below, and answer more elsewhere.[25] If some such answers work and no worse problems arise for my view, then if my work does at least as much metaphysical work as class nominalism, class nominalism's problems suggest that my view has an edge on it. And that it does at least the work is clear, since theists can easily eliminate sets in favor of certain divine mental activities.[26] I argue below that my view in fact does more of the ontological work one wants out of a theory of attributes than the set view. If I'm right about this, my view faces fewer problems than the set view and does more ontological work. I also suggest that it does this view at less ontological cost. If correct, all this constitutes a fairly strong case that my view is preferable to the set view.

Flouted intuitions

Class nominalists like Quine, Quinton and David Lewis hold that attributes are sets of their instances.[27] This creates metaphysical

[25]   'God and the Problem of Universals', *Oxford Studies in Metaphysics* **2** (2006), 325–56.
[26]   See Christopher Menzel, 'Theism, Platonism and the Metaphysics of Mathematics', in Michael Beaty (ed.), *Christian Theism and the Problems of Philosophy* (Notre Dame, In.: University of Notre Dame Press, 1990), 208–29.
[27]   W. V. Quine, *Word and Object* (Cambridge, Mass.: MIT Press, 1960), 209–10, 267; W. V. Quine, *Theories and Things* (Cambridge, Mass.: Harvard University Press, 1981), 100, 107 (strictly speaking, Quine would say that we should replace attributes with sets, not that attributes *are* sets, but his point is that sets are what ought to be playing the roles we tend to give attributes); David Lewis, *On the Plurality of Worlds* (Oxford: Basil Blackwell, 1986), 50–69; Anthony Quinton, 'Properties and Classes', *Proceedings of the Aristotelian Society* **58** (1957–8), 33–58.

worries. We tend to think that attributes give their bearers their characters: what makes the apple red is that it has a color, redness. Class nominalism reverses this. A set is redness – the set of red things – because all and only the things in it are red.[28] So the red things' being red helps make a particular set redness. (Had these items been in this set, but not been red, the set would not have been redness.) On class nominalism, then, bearers give attributes their characters, not *vice-versa*. But *ceteris paribus* it's best to preserve in our metaphysics as much as we can of our intuitive ideas about attributes. The theist view doesn't share this problem. The divine mental events of which we speak fictionally as concept-possession were what they were before God created anything. They do not derive from red things the character in virtue of which things appropriately related to them are red, and appropriate relation to them is a red-maker.

Again, on class nominalism, being redness turns out not to be an intrinsic property, for whether a set has it depends on whether anything other than its members is red. But this is odd: surely whether something is redness should depend on its own content alone. On the theist view, again, God's red-producing mental events had their full character when He alone existed. So having this character is intrinsic to them. This implies that their content is entirely narrow, but this is a claim without cost, for in the case of God's pre-creative mental events there is no pressure toward externalism.

A metaphysical commitment

Again, on class nominalism, if time really flows or passes,[29] there are many rednesses over time, since many different sets are successively the red-set as new things come to be red and old ones cease to be red. We thus have to answer the question of what the red-sets all have in common that makes them all redness. This question looks

---

[28] I suppose a class nominalist might try to deny this, claiming that the set just is primitively the set of red things. (My thanks here to Gonzalo Rodriguez-Pereyra.) But if a set of a trout and a tuna is such because it contains a trout and a tuna, I can't see why things would be different with the set of all and only red things.

[29] That is, if an 'A theory' is true, or if time is 'dynamic'.

hard. It will not do, for instance, to say that they are all members of a set, the set of things that are ever rednesses, because if time really passes, whenever there is a new red-set there is also a new set of red-nesses. Even if time passes, this question does not arise on any other theories of attributes. Thus class-nominalism may be the sole view to require a theory on which time does not really pass. A large commit-ment about the nature of time is a cost: it is better to have a view neutral on this.

Being red vs. being in the red-set

Again, on class nominalism, 'A is red' predicates membership in the set of all and only red things. So what makes it true that A is red is that A belongs to the red-set. Which things are red determines which set this is. Red things' being red thus has to be something other than their belonging to the red-set, or it can't determine which set is the red-set. Putting this more carefully, on class nominalism,

A is red = df. A ϵ R and R is the red-set.

But as we've seen, that A is red helps explain it that R is the red-set. So that A is red is logically or explanatorily prior to R's being the red-set. But what is prior to one conjunct's obtaining is prior to the con-junction's obtaining. So that A is red is logically or explanatorily prior to *A ϵ R and R is the red-set*. But what is prior to the conjunction's obtaining can't consist in its obtaining.

Approaching this another way, on class nominalism, what makes it true that A is red is that A belongs to the red-set. So for reasons seen, on class nominalism, A's being red is something other than that which on class nominalism makes it true that A is red. Yet it should be the case that A's being red makes it true that A is red. The theist view escapes this problem. Things' being red consists in their being appropriately related to certain divine mental events. This is also what makes it true that they are red. Now that last bit might strike some as odd: surely, they will say, what it consists in to be red is (say) being such as to reflect and absorb certain wave-lengths of light. The theist needn't demur. There are two ways to take such 'consists in' statements. In one, they give the metaphysical constitution of having the property: this is the story involving God. All theories have such a story, involving universals, tropes, resem-blances, classes, concepts, etc. The other sort of 'consists in' state-ment gives the content of the property. This is where light enters the picture.

Brian Leftow

Can we see that apples are red?

Again, what makes it true that the apple is red is that the apple is red. This is observable. So what makes it true that the apple is red is observable. But on class nominalism, what makes it true that the apple is red is that the apple belongs to the red-set. This is not observable, because neither sets nor the membership relation are.[30] If being red is being a member of a set, it is not an observable property. This is not just because we do not see all the red things. When we see six glasses, the six exhaust a set's membership, but we do not see that the glasses are a member of their set. We observe the six, and infer the membership. Though we see all six members, we do not see the set: abstract entities can't reflect light. If we see a group, that is because a group is not abstract. Seeing the group is seeing *them*, i.e. the glasses.

It won't do to say that when we see the apple, we see what it looks like to belong to the red-set. There is nothing it looks like to belong to a set, because membership has no effects, and so no observable effects. It won't do to appeal to the content/constitution distinction either. For a way of putting my point is that the class nominalist's constitution story isn't compatible with the property's content: nothing which consists in set membership is observable. The theist's constitution story is compatible with the theist content story: the apple's reflecting and absorbing light is the tip of a causal iceberg whose submerged depth is divine. If things' being red is their being disposed to interact with light a certain way, at a deeper level it is their being constantly caused to have this disposition – and of course it can be both. Belonging to a set can't confer a reflectancy property, nor is having the reflectancy necessary for belonging to the set,[31] nor does belonging to the set depend on having the reflectancy,[32] nor does an item's being thus-reflective suffice for the set's being the red-set.[33] Thus there is no clear way for the content of belonging to a set to be a reflectancy,[34] and in fact, as noted earlier, a

---

[30]   *Pace* Penelope Maddy, *Realism in Mathematics* (Oxford: Oxford University Press, 1990).

[31]   Unless perhaps the reflectancy is an essential property of what has it. But redness is plausibly accidental in all cases.

[32]   Again, unless being red is essential to the red thing.

[33]   Unless it is the only red item.

[34]   This remains true regardless of the possible exceptions noted in the previous footnotes, for they are precisely special cases. For the content to be a reflectancy, the conditions mentioned would have to hold in all cases.

disposition to appear red *isn't* part of the content of belonging to the set, because belonging to the set presupposes having it. We might next ask whether when we see an apple's redness, we see a sign of its being a member of the red-set. We certainly see it looking as it will look just if it belongs. But we believe we can observe the apple's being red, not just signs of it.

Theism has an edge here. Red-making divine mental causal relations to apples have observable effects. When we see a red thing, the mental causal relations are among the (distal) causal conditions of our perception. We see effects of being rightly related to them. So in one sense of the phrase, we see what it looks like to be rightly related to them. So we see what it looks like to be red. What else would we expect to see? One might reply that a thing's being red should be directly, not indirectly observable. But perhaps it is, on the theist account. If we let causal mediation suffice for rendering states of affairs only indirectly observable, no state of affairs whose effects are not causally immediate to the eye (or the brain?) will count as directly observable. It's not clear that a parsing which lets something as causally removed from us as a reflection-event count as directly observable will not let the thing's being red count as directly observable, even on the theist account. One might reply that seeing the thing should suffice for seeing it to be red (given normal perceptual capacities and conditions), and this isn't so on the theist story. But it is: it's just that on the theist account there is a further, distal causal story behind our so seeing the thing.

The coextension problem

Again, class nominalism has a well-known problem with contingently co-extensive attributes:

10. the set of unicorns = the set of centaurs = ø. So   (premise)
11. unicornhood = centaurhood.   (10, class nominalism)
12. All identities are necessary. So   (premise)
13. Necessarily unicornhood = centaurhood.   (11, 12)
14. Possibly some unicorns are not centaurs. So   (premise)
15. possibly the set of unicorns ≠ the set of centaurs. So   (14, set identity-conditions)
16. possibly   unicornhood ≠ centaurhood.   (15,   class nominalism)
17. ¬(13).   (16, modal rule)

Brian Leftow

Since a contradiction has emerged, something has to go. But (10), (14) and the set identity-conditions are unassailable, and rejecting (12) is unappealing. One move is to say that there is a role, collecting all and only unicorns, playing which is sufficient to make something a world's unicorn-set and so its unicornhood, and this role is played by different sets in different worlds. This lets the class nominalist deny that class nominalism gets us (11). It suggests that instead, unicornhood is e.g. a pair of the unicorn-set and the unicornhood-role, centaurhood a pair of the centaur-set and the centaurhood-role, and so the attributes are distinct even if there are neither unicorns nor centaurs.

But a role is an attribute, and so on class nominalism a set. Perhaps the unicorn-role in a world W is the unit set of W's unicornhood. Or perhaps it is a set whose members are W's unicornhood and all W's unicorns. I see no other plausible proposals if every world has its own unicorn-role. Either way, if there are neither unicorns nor centaurs, the centaurhood and unicornhood roles wind up identical, and so we still get (11). What's required, then, is that the unicorn role be a trans-world set, one containing every world's unicorns coupled with that world's unicornhood. This generates a different set to conjoin with W's unicorns than is conjoined with W's centaurs, even if W lacks both, and so keeps unicornhood and centaurhood distinct. But this generates a commitment to possibilia, merely possible unicorns.

Once this commitment rears its head, rather than talking about roles, the class nominalist can deny (10), by bringing non-actual animals into the sets to distinguish them. But if we do this in one case, we have no principled reason not to do it everywhere else: and so class nominalism winds up committed to possibilia to instance all possible attributes. This is a far larger ontological cost than positing one God, in terms of both individuals and kinds posited. It is also a far more radical revision of our general ontology: theism posits one unusual actually existing individual, while possibilism requires us to believe in things that either do not exist or are not actual but are unicorns- and gods. If possibly God exists, then even if He does not actually exist, the possibilist must accept that there 'is' a God- just one that doesn't happen to exist, or be actual. Even if there are irredeemable defects in the standard concept of God, there are surely other concepts nearby without these. If the problem is (say) that omnipotence and moral perfection are incompatible, there are the consistent concepts of someone just like God save for being not quite omnipotent and someone just like God save for being not quite morally perfect. Even if both are concepts of necessary beings and there are

80

reasons to deny that there could be more than one near-divine necess-ary being *per* possible world, there are also consistent concepts of con-tingent near-Gods, and so surely there are possible worlds in which such things exist. So the possibilist must at a minimum accept that many possible worlds contain near-Gods – just (again) ones that doesn't happen to exist, or be actual. Some might think this fortu-nate, but the ontologist must judge that a non-existent or non-actual near-God is a stranger beast than theism believes in. So class nominalism avoids the contingent coextension problem only by taking on ontological commitments due to which a theist theory wins against it on economy grounds if it can do at least the ontological work class nominalism does and has no insuperable internal difficulties.

The membership relation

A last problem for class nominalism is that it creates difficulties for the metaphysics of sets. ZF is the generally accepted theory of sets. At least within the confine of ZF set theory, on class nominalism, there is no such thing as the membership relation, $\in$. For $\in$ is a relation, an attribute. It links every member to every set of which it is a member. So within class nominalism, $\in$ is a set of pairs, each con-taining a member and a set. $\in$ has members: the pairs. So there are also pairs consisting of a pair and $\in$, and these pair-sets are in $\in$. So $\in$ is a member of a member of itself. This conflicts with ZF's axiom of well-founding. So ZF rules such a set out. Mathematicians do consort occasionally with non-well-founded sets, but philosophers prefer more respectable company. The class nominalist, then, must deny the existence of a membership relation. But without a member-ship relation to relate members to sets containing them, how can we understand the difference between sets containing an item a and sets not containing a? I see seven options.

The identity option

Quine suggests identifying singletons with their members. There is then no difficulty understanding what makes {a} different from {b}: it is just whatever makes a differ from b. We might consider extend-ing this to other sets: saying that '{a, b}' is just a plural referring device that picks out a and b, that '{{a}}' differs in sense from '{a}' but has the same referent, and so on. This would turn set

Brian Leftow

theory into an elaborate notational device whose sole ontology is ur-elements. Whatever the charms of this, the class nominalist can't accept it. The class nominalist believes in sets to be attributes. This device eliminates sets. One could instead combine it with some ideas of David Lewis to eliminate non-sets, but that is surely a non-starter.[35]

An Intrinsic property?

If identity won't take the place of a membership relation, we might try to take containing a as an intrinsic property of {a}, not a relation between {a} and a, and so the difference between {a} and {b} vis-à-vis a as a matter of having this property. But this is mysterious. And it makes it equally mysterious why {a} cannot exist if a does not. If containing a is an intrinsic property of {a}, it should be possible for {a} to exist and have the property though a does not exist: if a's being F entails that b exists or has some attribute, Fness is *ipso facto* an extrinsic property. Yet of course, {a} can't exist without a. Further, if {a} contains a, {a} contains something: if there is such a property as containing a, there is presumably a property of containing something, which appears just where we thought we had a membership relation. On class nominalism, this property is a set, whose members are all the sets which contain something- all the non-empty sets. But then it contains itself, and so is non-well-founded. So ZF won't permit it.

Constituency work

We might next consider taking a as a constituent of sets containing it. But if a is a constituent of {a}, is there any more to {a} than a? There isn't some further entity to which the brackets correspond, which when added to a gives us a singleton. A singleton doesn't consist of a collecting lasso and the thing collected. So if a is a constituent of {a}, there is nothing more *to* {a} than a. Yet that can't be right either, because it seems to imply that a = {a}. Again, Quine has suggested this identity, but if we limit it to singletons it does not

---

[35]   That is, one could start from Quine's move, eliminate non-sets, then treat non-singleton sets as Lewis does in *Parts of Classes* (London: Blackwell, 1991).

fully explain the difference between sets containing and sets not containing a (non-singletons also contain a), and if we generalize it we eliminate sets or non-sets. It can't be that {a} consists of constituents, {a}'s only constituent is a, there is nothing 'out there' to account for the non-identity of a and {a}, and yet a ≠ {a}. There is nothing to account for their non-identity if a is a constituent of {a}; in fact, a ≠ {a}; and if a is a constituent of {a}, {a} consists of constituents and {a}'s only constituent is a. So a is not a constituent of {a}.

Constitution

We might next appeal to constitution, a relation which (say some) obtains between statues and the blocks of which they consist. This relation can be 1:1. We might say that a *constitutes* {a}: that a's existence generates {a}'s, and a is not a constituent of {a}, but is instead related to it somewhat as a block of marble is to a statue. The problem here is what to make of the constitution-relation. Some treat it as contingent identity.[36] Such proposals just fall under my treatment of identity above. Some treat it in terms of shared temporal parts.[37] This is a non-starter if sets are not in time, as many think. If they are in time, still this amounts to the claim that for some period of time, an item is both a and {a}. But this would have to be the whole period of their existence – a cannot outlive {a}, nor *vice-versa* – and necessarily so if set theory is necessarily true. So in this particular case, we would have it that one item is both a and {a} and the two are not even possibly distinct: which boils down to the identity proposal already discussed. Some proposals treat constitution as relative identity or its close kin.[38] In the case at hand this would require finding a sortal under which a non-set and a set can coincide – probably a non-starter. Finally, some treat constitution as a relation between distinct but coinciding entities. The

[36] So e.g. Allan Gibbard, 'Contingent Identity', in Michael Rea (ed.), *Material Constitution* (NY: Rowman and Littlefield Publishers Inc., 1997), 93–125 and George Myro, 'Identity and Time', in Rea, *op. cit.*, 148–72.
[37] So e.g. David Lewis, 'Counterparts or Double Lives?', in Rea, *op. cit.*, 126–47.
[38] Michael Rea, 'Sameness Without Identity: An Aristotelian Solution to the Problem of Material Constitution', *Ratio* **11** (1998): 316–328.

best-developed account of this is Lynne Rudder Baker's. Her official definition is this:

> X constitutes y at t = df. there are distinct primary-kind proper-
> ties F and G and circumstances favorable to the existence of Gs
> such that X has F as a primary-kind property,
>   X is in G-favorable circumstances at t, it is necessary that an
> F so situated at t have a G spatially coincident with it, y has G
> as a primary-kind property, X and y spatially coincide at t, y is
> the only G spatially coincident with x at t, it is possible that x
> exist but not have a G spatially coincident with it, and if x is of
> one basic kind of stuff, y is of that same basic kind of stuff.[39]

If a thing is necessarily accompanied by its singleton, any circumstance is singleton-favorable; more generally any circumstance containing a and b is {a, b}-favorable. Sets don't consist of stuff, and
as usually conceived don't spatially coincide with anything. There
is also a difficulty about primary-kind properties: in the context of
class nominalism, these can only be sets, but it's not clearly licit to
appeal to sets in trying to give an account of a relation basic to
making sense of what a set *is*. So the account seems simply not
to apply to this case. If we say that sets are where their members
are, the account applies if we ignore the worry about sets and eliminate the clause about possible non-coincidence and stuff-clauses.
We must also eliminate the sole-coincidence requirement. If a is a
member of many sets, and sets are where their members are, presumably they all spatially overlap a; if we retain sole coincidence as a requirement by requiring not just overlap but complete coincidence,
the account will only apply to singletons. With these moves made,
we'd be saying that constitution for sets reduces to spatial coincidence with their elements. But this seems inadequate. Coincidence
is a symmetrical relation. Its presence can't explain the asymmetry
of membership: {a} and {{a}} coincide, so why does only one constitute the other? Whatever moves we make, further, we're left with a
more basic difficulty, which applies too if we leave the constitution-relation primitive, as in Wiggins. On set-Platonism, the constitution relation is a set. If constitution replaces the member-set
relation, constitution simply becomes our new relation that isn't
there.

---

[39]   Lynne Rudder Baker, *The Metaphysics of Everyday Life* (Cambridge:
Cambridge University Press, 2007), 161.

Armstrong

Our fifth alternative grins and bears it. Armstrong embraces the non-existence of ∈, rather than seeing it as a problem. He sees ∈ as un-needed: he holds that the existence of a and {a} is all we need to make it true that a is a member of {a}. The truth of the relational proposition 'supervenes' on these though the relation does not exist.[40] But this won't do. It might just be a way to say that it is primitive, non-relational fact about {a} that a is its member – i.e. that this is a non-relational property of {a}. If it is, I've already dealt with it. If not, it is just 'solving' the problem by magic if we can point to nothing about the singleton that makes a its member. And if a is not in an intrinsic membership-relation to {a}, not a constituent of {a}, nor 'in' it as a block of marble is 'in' a statue it constitutes, there is no such intrinsic thing to be had. We need the relation as something given in reality to explain what it is about the set that lets it help make the relational proposition true.

Whatever {a} is, it is the unique entity to which only a bears the membership relation. If the member-set relation is not intrinsic- and it is hard to see how a relation to something spatial could be intrinsic to something non-spatial – we need an extrinsic membership relation. If so, being a set is an extrinsic property- what makes something a set is that something has to it a relation of membership. And something extrinsic, a relation between a and {a}, makes it the case that a is a member of {a}. Jubien contends that if sethood is extrinsic, it turns contingent that a given entity is a set, and its members are its members:

> We ordinarily think it is essential to (the unit set of the moon) that it (has) the moon as a member. (But) there is... no plausible external source for... the necessity of the moon's membership... So it looks like the idea that sets... aren't intrinsically sets could be upheld only by abandoning (this) essentialist tenet...[41]

But there is nothing incoherent about the idea of an extrinsic essential property. Perhaps I am essentially the result of the meeting of sperm S and egg E to form a zygote, and that zygote's splitting in

---

[40]   Armstrong, *Universals*, 56. If this broad approach is right, then strictly all it would take to make the relational proposition true is the existence of {a}, though the set's existence entails a's.
[41]   Michael Jubien, 'Straight Talk about Sets', *Philosophical Topics* **17** (1989), 93.

Brian Leftow

two. If so, I essentially share a possible world with the other bit of that zygote. A set's extrinsic essential attributes may include its relations to its members.

Identity and existence

Rodriguez-Pereyra suggests that being a member of {a} is the property of being identical to a and such that {a} exists.[42] On class nominalism, this conjunctive property is a set, and so are its conjunct properties. As class nominalism identifies properties with the sets which are their extensions and having properties with belonging to those sets, identity with a is the set, {a}, having this property is being a member of {a}, and being such that {a} exists is the set of things such that {a} exists. Both conjunct properties are problematic on class nominalism. To see the problem with the first, recall that on Rodriguez-Pereyra's account, a ∈ {a} =df. a has the property of identity with a and is such that {a} exists. But on class nominalism, the first really asserts that a ∈ {a}: Rodriguez-Pereyra's definition turns circular. The problem with the second property is that everything is such that {a} exists. So there is a set of things such that {a} exists only if there is a universal set – and there is not. If one appeals instead to a universal proper class, then the same proper class will be being such that {b} exists, being such that {c} exists, etc. So these all wind up as the same attribute. But they are not. They are not even necessarily co-extensive; in worlds in which a exists but b does not, everything is such that {a} exists but nothing is such that {b} exists. Leaving this aside, their identity means that if we conjoin class nominalism, a universal proper class and Rodriguez-Pereyra's suggestion, it follows that being a member of a is the property of being identical with a and such that {b} exists. Finally, consider the conjunction as a whole. If properties are just sets of their extensions, this property is just {a}. So if we conjoin class nominalism with Rodriguez-Pereyra's suggestion, the relation of membership in {a} is just {a} itself. I can make no sense of this – certainly if sets presuppose membership relations, but also even if they do not. So whatever the merits of Rodriguez-Pereyra's suggestion, it does not sit well with class nominalism.

---

[42] Gonzalo Rodriguez-Pereyra, 'How not to trivialise the identity of indiscernibles', in P. F. Strawson and A. Chakrabarti (eds), *Concepts, Properties and Qualities,* (Ashgate, 2006), 217–8.

Type theory

We might last consider moving to a typed class nominalism, saying that there are many membership relations, not one: that if the highest type-level of any member of set S is level n, S is of level $n + 1$, and so the relation linking S to its members is of level $n + 2$. On such an account, we never get a non-well-founded membership relation: if a membership relation R is a set of level n, then R's membership-relation to any set must be of at least level $n + 2$. There is no ontological bloat here; if there are sets at all, these sets all exist anyway. But this puts class nominalism at a disadvantage in simplicity to any theory that can get by with a single relation between properties and their instances. Moreover, it sits ill with the iterative conception of set. The guiding thought of the iterative conception is that a set's existence presupposes only lower-level items: thus every set has as members only ur-elements or sets formed at lower points in the set hierarchy.[43] A non-empty set presupposes the existence of its members- and exists just if they *are* its members. If that's right, it presupposes a membership relation as well as the existence of its members. If sets cannot presuppose items from higher levels of the hierarchy, and their existence presupposes a membership relation's existence, relations between sets and members cannot be sets of higher levels of the hierarchy.

On class nominalism, each membership relation is itself a set. And on the iterative conception, sets presuppose the existence only of sets from earlier or lower in the hierarchy. The iterative conception, then, seems inconsistent with ZF and class nominalism. So it seems that class nominalism is false if ZF and the iterative conception are true. Theism, however, is compatible with both – and a structuralist account of both would allow for items involving God to take sets' place as the items bearing the structure.

Putting them to work

Attributes are invoked to do a variety of philosophical work. I have already suggested that God can do at least as much of this work as sets. That is enough for the purposes of my argument. But in fact, God can do more than sets, and showing this will strengthen my

[43] So George Boolos, 'The Iterative Conception of Set', in Paul Benacerraf and Hilary Putnam (eds.), *Philosophy of Mathematics*, 2nd ed. (Cambridge: Cambridge University Press, 1983), 493.

Brian Leftow

case. Immanent universals are the gold standard here. So I frame my discussion in terms of jobs they are invoked to do. I've shown elsewhere that God can do all the work immanent universals can do.[44] I do not claim that a theist theory of *attributes* does all this work. Rather, my theist theory commits ontologically only to God plus created concreta, and I remain within the bounds of that theory as long as I do all the needed work with only the ontology it permits. I now argue that sets (with or without concreta) can't do some of this work.

Universals provide referents for abstract singular terms and so help make statements involving abstract terms true: that courage is a virtue is true if the universal *courage* has a particular relation to the universal *virtue*. 'Courage' could refer equally well to the realities behind talk of a divine concept. But there are well-known difficulties in pressing sets into this role.[45] And they are not helped even by expanding the sets to include possibilia.

Universals help ground modal truths: there can be more cats than there ever have been because universals are always further-exemplifiable. So too, there can be more cats than there ever have been because God's cat-concept is always further-satisfiable – God can always make more. Some necessities can be traced to universals' contents and relations (e.g. of incompatibility, grounded on their contents) – and so too, these necessities can be traced to the contents and relations of the realities behind divine-concept-talk. Sets have their members essentially. So it is not the case that there can be more cats because the actual cat-set can have more members. If there can be more cats, another set can be the cat-set (though not another *actual* set, if there are no possibilia), but the actual cat-set contributes nothing to this being so. Actual concrete non-divine particulars don't always provide the possibility of further cats, either. For more cats will be possible even if the world comes to contain only non-divine concreta that essentially could neither cause cats to be nor turn into cats. Granted, it would still be true in that case that past things could have turned into or caused more cats – but this gives us only that there could have been more cats, not that there can be more cats. So it seems that sets and actual non-divine elements can't do all of immanent universals' modal work. If the cats include possibilia, there can be more cats because there are merely possible cats, not because there are merely possible sets of cats. So even if we move to

[44] Leftow 'God and the Problem of Universals'
[45] See e.g. D.M. Armstrong, *Universals* (Boulder, Colo.: Westview Press, 1989), 33–6.

88

a possibilist version of class nominalism, the sets won't do the work here. Only the possibilia do. Further, sets don't have incompatibility relations, as universals or divine concepts may. What are incompatible are (say) belonging to the cat-set and at the same time belonging to the dog-set- but nothing about the sets explains this. The class nominalist needs (I think) again to appeal to possibilia- the incompatibility can *be* the fact that nothing is a possible cat-and-dog. Once the class nominalist has brought in possibilia, sets are in many cases idle wheels. And I have already suggested that possibilia are a greater ontological cost than God is.

Again, causes (we think) effect what they do in virtue of their properties: if water's coming into contact with salt dissolves the salt, this is because of their molecular structures. The theist can say the same, only adding that having that molecular structure consists in depending on the realities behind talk of a divine concept of such a molecule for being such as to satisfy it. This amounts to saying that the molecules are always being caused in a particular way to have the structures they do – which does not deny the structures their causal role, any more than being caused to speak denies the speaking its causal role. On class nominalism, our target claim becomes that causes effect what they do in virtue of belonging to (some) sets they belong to. But membership doesn't seem a causally relevant relation. Perhaps the class nominalist is best advised to reject the claim that causation is due to properties, saying instead that particulars just do cause what they do. But the loss of an intuitive thesis about causality is legitimately counted as a cost of the position, a cost theism needn't pay. Again events seem to lose their role as causal relata on class nominalism- at least on any theory that takes events to involve exemplifying properties at times. For on class nominalism, this becomes things' belonging to sets at times. And again, set-membership isn't causally relevant. So how could an event be a causal *relatum*, on this sort of account plus class nominalism?

Universals would ground resemblance. Intuitively, cats are alike *qua* cats. Being cats makes them alike. It explains their resemblance. Realists about universals can accept this: their all being cats is their having the same universal property, cathood. I accept this too, and say that what explains their resemblance is their all depending on the same divine mental events. Cats are termini of causal paths with one origin. One could object here: that cats are cats is a fact about *them*. On my account, it is a fact about their relation to something *outside* them, something extrinsic – and that's odd. But it's not clear that relations to God are extrinsic. God is omnipresent. He is in some sense everywhere. So He is within the boundaries of every cat. A cat's relation to items within it are intrinsic. Again, relations to a necessary being come out intrinsic on many accounts of being intrinsic, e.g. Yablo's.[46]

In the order of explanation, first cats are cats, which suffices to make them all alike, then they are for this reason members of the cat-set. What explains cats' resemblance must precede it in the order of explanation. So membership in the cat-set can't ground resemblance. So the class nominalist must argue that while cats do resemble, it is not because they are cats. Rather, they just resemble as a whole; respects of resemblance don't enter the account, save as defined in terms of overall resemblance as wholes. This gives up on doing the work of explaining resemblance, and so constitutes another respect in which the realities behind divine concept talk can do more work. Further, showing the overall-resemblance account to be tenable would take one a long way toward showing the tenability of resemblance nominalism, of which it is a central thesis. If resemblance nominalism works at all, it arguably works without identifying attributes with sets.[47] So I suggest that class nominalists face a dilemma here. They can say that resemblance needs to be grounded in property-identity, and then admit that they can't do needed ontological work. Or they can defend the claim that resemblance needn't be grounded in identity of property – and then try to show that this doesn't undermine their position.

Overall, I submit, a theist theory of attributes does more work than a class nominalist theory, and does it at less overall ontological cost. So we have reason to prefer a theist theory to class nominalism-unless of course the theist view has still worse problems of its own.[48] I close by considering three objections it is bound to raise.

[46] Stephen Yablo, 'Intrinsicness', *Philosophical Topics* **26** (1999), 479–505.
[47] As in Gonzalo Rodriguez-Pereyra's version (*Resemblance Nominalism* (Oxford: Oxford University Press, 2002).

[48] This sort of comparative argument raises a question: even if I could show that the theist theory is more reasonably believed than any other, it might not follow that it is more reasonable to believe it than to withhold judgment on the whole matter, perhaps with the sense that if that's the best answer, there must be something wrong with the question. In reply: withholding judgment would be reasonable if there were no positive arguments for the victorious view (i.e. if the case for it were *purely* comparative), if it seemed likely that there were further theories to be had, if there were independent reason to consider the question flawed and if the question were minor, tangential and (so to speak) optional rather than required. None of these conditions is met here. Predication is fundamental to our conceptual

Three questions for the theist view

The theist view set out above raises at least three objections. One is that it seems automatically to lose out in comparison with any non-theist view. Universals, for instance, do not raise the problem of evil – one need not explain the presence of evil in the world to

---

apparatus, and attributes are fundamental to any ontology. So if the ontology of these things is a legitimate question at all, it cannot be a minor or tangential one to any metaphysician. Whether some ontological questions are substantive, non-verbal and answerable is becoming an issue after a long abeyance (see e.g. David Chalmers, David Manley and Ryan Wasserman (eds.), *Metametaphysics* (Oxford: Oxford University Press, 2009)). But the debate does not focus on the problem of attributes in particular, and those who argue that not all ontological questions are equal in these respects do not seem to see the question of attributes as one of the 'bad' ones. Only one fundamentally new theory has emerged since the Middle Ages, and it (mereological nominalism) has not actually been held, but merely mentioned as an option: so the likelihood of something both fundamentally new and very attractive seems small. Finally, there *are* positive arguments for the theist view: that it does the work we want of such a theory, that it is parsimonious, and that it permits a good epistemology of predication. To say just a bit about the last: one can ask about what justifies common-attribute claims, and about whether the scheme of common attributes we ascribe to things really 'cuts nature at the joints'. We call many things dogs, but do they really have a kind in common? At one level, all attribute-theories are on a par: we ascribe common kinds due to likenesses we notice, no matter what the truth about attributes is. On another, they are not. On concept-nominalism, kinds just *are* concepts we predicate. On Van Inwagen's theory of properties something relevantly similar is true (see Peter van Inwagen, 'A Theory of Properties', *Oxford Studies in Metaphysics* **1** (2005)), 107–39. On either, if a kind-concept applies in common, that is all there is to it: *ipso facto* the things to which it applies share a kind. These theories bring a strong epistemic guarantee for our kind-scheme with them. However, a guarantee that strong is implausible: surely we are *able* to get kinds wrong. I hope to show elsewhere that concept nominalism is simply untenable and that van Inwagen's view does so much less needed ontological work than my own that whatever epistemic differences there are between the two are not sufficient to tip the scales van Inwagen's way. My own view can appeal to the goodness of God as reason to believe that we are so made as to attain some truth about kinds over time. This is (I think) the strongest sort of epistemic guarantee that stands a chance of being correct. More needs to be said, of course, but I suggest that in light of these things, withholding judgment may not be the most reasonable move.

assert realism. So there is a large problem for theist views which seems likely to outweigh difficulties in their non-theist rivals. But actually one deals with evil partly just by arguing that God exists. If God exists, there are sufficient answers to all arguments from evil. A reason to believe that God exists, then, is reason to believe that there are such answers. So any good argument for God's existence is just as such a minimal response to the problem of evil. Now as long as one hasn't seen more than this sort of minimal response, one may reasonably give theism less credence than one might have: if (say) an argument might on its own lead one to assign theism a credence of .7, lingering doubt that a viable account of evil is really to be had could reasonably lower that credence, perhaps to below .5 despite the argument. But despite this, it could be that if we consider only the problem of attributes, a theist theory provides the best answer. Even if that answer could not convince fully save as part of an overall package of arguments including arguments about evil, it would be worth giving, for a viable treatment of evil may well be available. Further, whether the project of explaining evil is worth looking into depends in part on how much better theist answers are than their rivals; in advance even of considering a theist theory, there is no way to show that its advantages do not justify the extra work, nor that they are not big enough to incline one more toward theism than toward its rivals even in advance of that work. So while evil is a problem for theism and not (say) realism, there is no reason to think it must outweigh theism's advantages over (say) realism in the theory of attributes.

Conservation

My theist theory requires that divine conservation be a possible sort of causality. The causal role of conservation is to explain non-probabilistically why the universe begins or continues to exist. No natural cause can do either. This is obvious in the case of beginning: the universe's beginning to exist is the appearance of the first natural items able to cause.[49] Again, no matter what natural causes we appeal to, it is compatible with their operation that history cease. It is possible, even physically possible, that time stop at any

---

[49]   If the first event was a fluctuation in 'quantum vacuum' by which an initial zone of expanding space and matter appeared, then the universe did not in the text's sense begin to exist unless the vacuum itself appeared, for the vacuum is a natural item able to be a cause.

point: General Relativity could be satisfied in a spacetime of any size, and so one which stopped just then. For it to be a non-probabilistic natural law that E-type events follow C-type events is for it to be a law that if history continues long enough after a C-type event, there will be an E-type event. Even the conservation laws, crudely put as 'mass-energy is neither created nor destroyed', do not entail that history will continue, for they are more precisely put as claims that the amount of mass-energy in the universe remains constant in every state of the universe, and this fact is compatible with there being a last state.

The laws do not guarantee that history will continue. They at most make it probable that it will. So a non-probabilistic explanation of the universe's persistence would require a different, non-natural sort of causation, involving a cause whose action eliminated the possibility that history cease – one whose action is incompatible with its effect's not occurring. Now it is not possible that an omnipotent will be thwarted. So while no natural cause's operation can entail that time will last long enough for it to have a given effect, if an omnipotent will decides that time shall last long enough, it cannot fail to do so. Divine conservation, then, is just a causation fit to do this particular explanatory job. Divine conservation involves a primitive causal connection: it just is a fact that if God wills that x continue to exist, x continues to exist, because God so wills. But we find good reason in the explanatory work they would do to posit other primitive causal connections. It is not clear why we should treat this case differently.

Again, competitor theories of attributes that introduce new ontology also introduce new primitive relations between their posits and the particulars which bear properties. Realism posits universals and also exemplification to tie them to particulars; trope theories posit tropes and also compresence to bind them to one another in particulars or exemplification to bind them to particulars which are not just trope-bundles; set theories introduce membership. In each case, the theories need the relations, and posit in them just the properties needed to perform their theoretical work. The theist theory's use of conservation is no different – though it has perhaps a slight epistemic edge in that the theist can rightly claim that the relation was not invented to solve this problem, but instead has its home outside the theory of attributes. Competitor theories that introduce no new ontology (concept – and resemblance-nominalism) also do without special relations: concepts bear satisfaction-relations to concreta and the important relation in resemblance nominalism is just ordinary likeness. But I hope to show elsewhere that concept nominalism is simply inadequate and resemblance nominalism solves its problems only at an ontological cost much greater than theism's. If I'm right, the theist need worry only about competitor theories of attributes that also introduce special relations, and it is not clear that conservation is the worst posit to make.

Conservation is apt to sound like magic: God wills it, and just for this reason it is so. At one level, this resemblance is a good thing for theists. We have all read stories of wizards who say words and by so doing cause effects. We understood those stories. We had no idea how such a world could work, but we could vividly imagine the world working that way. In so doing, it is unlikely that we were imagining etc. anything metaphysically impossible. The very vividness and completeness of the imagination involved is evidence against that. We were imagining a world with radically different natural laws than ours, where laws link the occurrence of words with the occurrence of effects. It is part of the idea of conservation that there is a set of natural laws which link certain sorts of thought words with events outside the mind.[50] The more strongly something we imagine is like something whose possibility we're trying to assess, the more evidence the ability to imagine is in favor of the possibility. So the imaginability of a magic world is considerable evidence in favor of the possibility of conservation.

This isn't to say that believing in conservation is like believing in magic. Believing in magic is believing in something we know doesn't work, that purports to explain things for which better explanations are available and even known. So believing in magic is either irrational or a function of defective information, or both. Belief in conservation is neither. We don't know that conservation doesn't work or doesn't occur. And conservation, if it occurred, would explain something for which no other explanation seems possible. The concept of a world in which magic works is like the concept of a world in which conservation occurs. It doesn't follow that belief in conservation and belief in magic have the same epistemic status. The epistemic status of belief in conservation is more like that of belief in a fundamental, brute-fact physical causal connection. Conservation, if it occurred, would be a brute-fact though lawful causal connection between God's volitions and the existence of creatures. It could not be otherwise: there is nothing in virtue of which conservation works except the nature of God's power, i.e. the nature of God, and it is a brute, not further explained fact that this is as it is.

[50]   Ultimately, laws about the nature of God – as (I'd argue) other natural laws are ultimately about the natures of other sorts of being.

Do we really need God?

One might also ask whether God is a more complex piece of equipment than we really need to handle attributes. God has (we may think) many attributes not needed to make my theory go. If so, the most my argument really warrants is a stripped-down semi-deity: even if it succeeds, it is best taken not as an argument for God's existence, but as one for the instancing of a description which falls short of full deity. This problem of course afflicts many sorts of natural theology: a first cause or an intelligent designer need not (one can argue) have all the other divine attributes.

I reply that the best version of a theory broadly like mine includes more standard divine attributes than one might think. To begin: on the theory, whatever is F is the paradigm F, or conserved by it, or conserved by a being with appropriate mental events. It's conceivable that there be many paradigms or conservers, that many beings split the appropriate mental events between them, that nothing both is a paradigm and has any of the right mental events, etc. But it's obviously more parsimonious to combine all the roles in one being, and there is no countervailing reason not to. So if ontological parsimony is a guide to truth or at least reasonability, the most likely true or at least most reasonable version of my sort of theory will be that at any time, at most one being plays all these roles for all attributes. The one-being version ties the others in its ability to explain the facts; the tie-breaker must come from elsewhere, and rules against the others.

Again, on the theory, there must be at least one conserver at all times at which anything other than a paradigm has an attribute. It's conceivable that there be different ones at different times, and none at all when nothing which is not a paradigm has an attribute. But it is more parsimonious to have one being play all the roles at all times at which anything plays them. This being will either persist at all times, even when there is nothing to conserve, or disappear when there is nothing to conserve and reappear when there is. If we hold that this being persists even when there is nothing to conserve, we must say why and how it persists. But we need not say why it ceases, why it does so when it does, why it pops back into existence when it does, what brings this about, or what secures its identity over the gap of non-existence, and intuitively all this is more (and harder) to explain. If we do not make the parsimonious move, we have different beings playing the role at various times. Then we have to explain for each that ceases why it does, and why it does so just then. For any that re-appear after an interval we must answer all questions above. For any that do not but have successors which have not previously appeared, we must explain why the successors appear, why just when they do, and what brings this about. All this is a complicated story. The parsimonious move, then, gets added support from the fact that it has (probably) the simplest, easiest further explanation to supply. In the abstract, it seems likely that the conjunction of answers to the questions about less parsimonious versions will be less plausible overall than the conjunction for the parsimonious version – if only because there seem likely to be more independent conjuncts to the answer, and where the conjuncts of a theory are independent and each has an epistemic probability of less than 1, the more the conjuncts, the lower the epistemic probability of the conjunction. So the most plausible version of the theory will have a single eternal being always available to play the metaphysical role described for all attributes.

The theory is a metaphysically necessary truth if true at all (just as it is necessary if true at all that actual attributes are universals, or tropes). It's conceivable that different beings play the metaphysical role in different possible worlds, but if we have just one being do it in all worlds, we need not explain why there are many across worlds, and why there are the ones there are in different worlds. There is no good argument against the necessary-being version of the theory. This being is concrete, since it is a conserving cause, and there have been arguments that there cannot be concrete necessary beings: but I dispose of these elsewhere.[51] If we say that one being is in all worlds, questions arise about why it is necessary and why there are not also others. But it's plausible that necessary beings are so just because of the kind of thing they are, and to the second we may just say that Ockham's Razor bids us not believe in others unless one being of this sort can't do all we want of it: and if it is necessary, it can do all we want. If there is just the one necessary being, then its being there is just one brute fact across all possible worlds; if there are many beings across all possible worlds, either there are many brute facts (which as brute are minimally plausible additions to the theory) or there are many explanations of why there is this being, not that, in a given world, and their sheer number is reason to think that the theory will be much less plausible

---

[51] 'Swinburne on Divine Necessity', *Religious Studies* **46** (2010), 141–6 and 'Divine Necessity', in Charles Taliaferro and Chad Meister (eds.), *The Cambridge Companion to Christian Philosophical Theology* (Cambridge: Cambridge University Press), 15–30.

for including them. So overall, the necessary-being version of the theory seems likely to be the most plausible.

This being would conserve all other concreta at all times in all possible worlds. Now we believe that the universe had a beginning. A being that conserves all things at all times conserves them even at their origins: and on the part of the cause, conservation at the universe's origin is just creation *ex nihilo*. That is, what the conserving cause does is fundamentally the same in each case, namely make the difference between there being and there not being a segment of universe-history. So this being will also be a creator *ex nihilo* in worlds where a universe begins to exist. I would argue that nothing could be both necessarily existent and composed of matter: hence I would argue that this being would be immaterial in any world in which it was necessary. On the theory, this thing has *per se* any properties it both has and conserves in others. As these include existence, it is not itself conserved in existence by anything else.

So far, I've suggested that the most plausible version of the theory involves a single eternal, necessary, immaterial, uncreated creator *ex nihilo* and conserver. This being is divine, though, only if it knows and wills. So the next question is whether it does: why not a conserving cause whose inner states aren't mental?[52] Well, one either does or does not believe in immaterial items with mental events. Those who do have been happy to hold that any concrete immaterial thing has mental events.[53] Some who don't may be happy to grant that if there *were* such things, they would have mental events. They would have non-transcendental properties. *Ex hypothesi* they would have neither physical nor distinctive abstract-entity properties. Other than some natural kinds, we have little idea what other sort of non-transcendental property they could have. So the need to fill in the blanks on them somehow will strike some as weak reason to think they would have mental properties. Again, if some immaterial concreta would have mental properties and some not, there would presumably have to be something else different about the two sorts to explain this: there certainly is where the things lacking and possessing mental events are physical. Difference in kind – 'the one with mental events is a human soul, and the one without isn't'– doesn't provide any explanation we can grasp. So with no idea what other sorts of non-transcendental intrinsic states they might have, we must choose between an unexplained difference with regard to mental

---

[52] Jurgen De Wispelaere pushed this point with me in another context.

[53] Thus Descartes, in holding that the principal and essential attribute of a soul is to be thinking, and so too Aquinas, *Summa Contra Gentiles* I, 44.

Brian Leftow

events or the claim that all immaterial concreta, as such, would have mental events. The latter seems more plausible. So the question 'why not one without mental events?' is likely to be put only by some who think that whatever has mental events is physical. Among these, functionalism is the leading theory of the mind.[54] So I point my further reply at a functionalist, by considering how a conserving machine (henceforth Con) might work, given the actual character of the world. I argue that Con most likely turns itself on and off in non-random ways, and the ways it does so are grounds for ascribing mental events to it.

If Con exists, it is not always switched off, for if it were, nothing other than itself would ever exist. So Con must either switch on and off, or be always on. But it is unlikely that it always switches off and on randomly. If it did, then whether Con provides a sufficient or merely a necessary condition of conservation, it very likely would sometimes so switch off as to cause things to lapse from existence randomly. This does not (we believe) happen on the macro-level. So either Con does not always act randomly or there has been a remarkable run of luck, with random off-switchings for various items always just happening to occur when they had already ceased to exist (or were just doing so) for other reasons, and perhaps Con's 'going random' so timed as to produce this result. It is also likely (though less so) that Con does not ever for any extended time act randomly. It thus seems likely that if Con exists, it switches on and off non-randomly to conserve things in the patterns in which we see them appear and disappear, or else is always switched on to provide a standing necessary causal condition for conservation of whatever it conserves.

If Con is always 'on', though, then in non-probabilistic conserving causation – and so (I suspect) all conservation at the macro-level – conditions among conserved entities as time moves toward t constitute the rest of a causally sufficient condition for conservation at t, and this 'triggers' the conservation. If this is how things work, the presence of appropriate conditions just before t entails the occurrence of conservation, and so history's continuance up to t. I have already argued that this is not the case: that it is possible, no matter what has occurred to things other than Con just before t, that such things' history end without ever reaching t. If this *is* possible, then nothing just before t infallibly triggers or entails Con's action. Instead, there are conditions before t which provide an opportunity

[54] For some important expressions and criticisms of the view, see Ned Block (ed.), *Readings in the Philosophy of Psychology* (Cambridge, Mass.: Harvard University Press, 1980).

98

for Con to turn itself on for t, and it does or does not do so, with the possibility of doing otherwise.

If Con exists, then, it is most likely that Con switches on and off non-randomly to conserve things in the non-random patterns in which we see them appear and disappear. Given that Con does turn on and off, that it does so non-randomly might seem a trivial claim, for one might doubt that Con's action could count as random. Con's contribution to the world is part of what determines the patterns we see. So whatever the world's regularities are, Con's output is one factor determining them, and so if there are any, one might think, Con's activity will appear lawful, not random. I suggest, though, that if Con's activity is *truly* random, then it is likely that eventually its pattern changes. It is likely, in other words, that some lawlike regularities involving things' beginning and ceasing to exist eventually alter, and perhaps be replaced by no discernible regularity at all. Con's activity, if it *is* random, can also *appear* random, by contrast with its previous pattern and with patterns in events other than beginnings and ceasings to exist. Because this could happen, it has content to say that Con does not act randomly. Con acts regularly, and some of these regularities do not change over time. If a ball moves toward a wall, the ball does not disappear, and reaches the wall if it has enough momentum: this is *inter alia* because Con continues to contribute to the ball's existence. Thus Con's non-random activity is a major part of the reason we live in a world of regularities.

Things are Fs *inter alia* because Con conserves them as Fs, on my view. Further, on my view, whether or not Con is personal, different internal states operate in conserving Fs as Fs than operate in conserving Gs as Gs. If Con has no mental events, (9)'s talk of the states behind F-conservation fictionally involving concept-possession is very fictional indeed, but the theory demands that *something* in what Con uses to conserve Fs as Fs differ from what Con uses to conserve Gs as Gs, else there will be nothing in reality to distinguish being F from being G. If something does differ, then Con logs in the current state of the world it conserves, in the form of the current pattern of activation of these states. If Con conserves a frog, Con's frog-conserving states are activated. So there is information about the state of the world encoded in Con's inner states. They represent the state of the world – that it contains a frog – if only as rings in a tree represent the tree's age, and their changes represent changes in the world.

We can use the regularity of Con's activity to argue that while earlier states of the physical world do not determine Con's current activity, Con in fact logs in the content of the world's earlier states somehow – minimally, by retaining some record of the sequence of activations of its inner states – and therefore produces output apt to maintain earlier regularities. For if this is not the case, Con's maintenance of these is an improbable cosmic coincidence. The coincidence could be that though Con's output is random and not based on the past, it just happens to be what's needed to continue them. If Con's output is not random but not past-based, the coincidence runs this way. As non-random, Con operates entirely out of an inner program, switching on and off its conservation of various things. As it is not past-based, the program is not responsive to conditions before these things begin or cease to exist (perhaps Con keeps no records). Further, earlier parts of the program in no way causally condition the content of later parts; if anyone wrote it, the author of each instant's worth had no knowledge of the content of other instants. (Otherwise the program's later output would be in a way at least partly past-based.) If conservation involves co-operation between Con and conserved things, the program is not responsive to the availability of things to co-operate or keyed to providing them earlier to have them for use later. But it just so happens that this program so regulates conservation that a lawful physical world results, and if co-operation is needed, it is available enough of the time for there to be regularities about beginning and ceasing to exist.

Lawful regularities are much more likely on the assumption that Con currently has information about the world's earlier state and bases its current output on this, whether it has that information from without or by keeping records within. So the fact that there are natural laws strongly supports this thesis. But if Con logs in the earlier world's state and then produces appropriate current output, it has internal states somehow encoding this information, internal states which somehow process this information, and internal states which produce outputs at least partly determined by this information. Trees do not do internal processing on or produce responses to the content of their rings. It thus seems plausible to view Con as *inter alia* an information-processing machine, and Con's inputs as providing it information.

It seems, then, that if there actually is a conserver, it turns itself on and off, initiates its own activity whenever it acts, does so with full possibility of not doing so, has internal states which somehow represent external information, and produces activity based on processing of these states' content, activity appropriate to maintaining a law-governed universe. Con's representation of external information is mental (as vs. the tree-ring sort) if the states encoding the information are mental.

The relations between Con's input, inner representational states, internal processing and output look in outline like those functionalists claim to constitute mental systems. For functionalism, to be a mental state is to be a state with a particular functional role in a causal system of such states, mediating between environmental input and (at least possible) behavioral output. If any of Con's states is somehow caused from without to represent states of the universe, it plays the role of a perceptual belief. If Con works entirely from internal records, the states providing these play the role of memory beliefs. Con is not controlled from without and is self-activating; those of its states which trigger output in response to information from the environment or remembered information seem to play the role of intentions or volitions. But whether any of these really is a mental state depends on the overall character of the system in which it is embedded, for functionalists.[55] This in turn depends on whether what takes us from input to output is of the right sort to count as mental.

Suppose for instance that Con is simply equipped *ab initio* with a huge program which pairs one response with every possible set of inputs.[56] In this case it is not plausible that Con's inner setup constitutes a functionalist mind. If this is not how Con works internally, then Con has its inner representations, its possible responses, and taking it from one to the other something which falls short of pairing one response with every possible set of inputs. It has instead some sort of programming which selects an output based on the inputs and some inbuilt algorithm(s). If the algorithms uniquely determine the selection, though, we have again a setup which simply pairs one response with every possible set of inputs-only the pairing isn't (so to speak) written out in advance. Given what we've seen so far about Con, though, it is unlikely that this is how Con works within. For if Con works this way within, external conditions determine (and together with Con's condition just before t entail) that conservation shall occur and history shall continue. So Con must have a different internal setup. To have one different in the required respect, Con needs algorithms which work probabilistically: which might given the same inputs at least sometimes lead to different responses. If Con has these, Con is a probabilistic automaton: which is what the early 'machine state' version of

[55] So e.g. David Braddon-Mitchell and Frank Jackson, *Philosophy of Mind and Cognition* (Oxford: Basil Blackwell, 1996), 52.
[56] As in Ned Block's 'Blockhead' example (Ned Block, 'Psychologism and Behaviorism', *Philosophical Review* **90** (1981), 5–43).

functionalism took us to be.[57] Functionalism has evolved beyond the 'machine state' version, but its core idea remains near the center of later functionalist views. So I submit that functionalists are ill-placed to push the question 'why not a conserver without mental events?' For when we look at how Con must act, it appears that Con has mental states as functionalists understand such states, or at least states enough like functionalist mental states that a functionalist's denial that they are mental looks strained. Thus to both dualists and functionalist materialists it should seem likely, based on how Con acts if Con exists, that Con has both beliefs and intentions.

It is a further question whether Con's beliefs are true. As we do not know how Con logs information in, we have no reason to suppose that a medium or its perceptual faculties will somehow distort incoming data and lead to inaccurate representation of the world's state, or that Con has immaterial memory traces which somehow decay over time. Now Con operates by way of algorithm. Algorithms may encode goals, if only those of their programmers: a thermostat algorithm which is biased toward selecting a lower temperature encodes a goal of cooling rooms. Whether we can infer accuracy from Con's output activity depends on what we suppose about the goals encoded in Con's algorithms. If Con's goals include maintaining certain natural regularities, Con's output suggests an accurate encoding of the world's state. If Con's goals include radically altering the regularities, Con's output suggests a wildly inaccurate encoding so interacting with the goal that acting (so to speak) with the intention of altering regularities but based on wildly false beliefs leads to just the output needed to maintain the regularities. However, if Con has a mind, principles of charity apply in interpreting its activity as they do in reading the activities of other humans: which suggests that we should favor accuracy and fulfilled goals over inaccuracy and thwarted goals. Further, Pr (Con maintains the regularities/Con has mostly true beliefs and the power to maintain regularities and has maintaining the regularities as a goal) is high, while Pr (Con maintains the regularities/Con has mostly false beliefs and the power to maintain regularities, and has altering the regularities as a goal) is not high: for there are many ways Con's beliefs could be false which would not lead to Con's maintaining the regularities, given its powers and goal. So we should hold that Con has mostly true beliefs and an intention to maintain regularities.

[57]   Hilary Putnam, 'The Nature of Mental events', reprinted in Hilary Putnam, *Mind, Language, and Reality* (Cambridge: Cambridge University Press, 1975), 429–440.

To do its job, further, Con must log in the entire state of the universe: and so if it has a mind, it is at every time at least well on the way to omniscience about the universe's state just before then and just then. If Con is to have enough concepts (speaking fictionally) to provide all possible non-divine attributes, it will have to possess (speaking fictionally) all possible concepts of non-divine attributes. What take the place of an F-concept on my account, again, are events with a causal role such that when appropriately tokened, Fs result. So for every possible non-divine-attribute-concept F, Con can bring it about that there is an F. This gives it at least a large chunk of the traditional range of omnipotence.

Nothing can be more perfectly one meter long than the standard meter, at least on the reading of 'standard meter' which treats the meter as whatever length that particular metal bar in Paris happens to have. So suppose that Con is actually the paradigm – standard-F. If nothing at a time can be more F than the standard F, then however great an F could appear at t, Con will have also to be at least that F by t. So at all times, Con's level of Fness, where it is the paradigm F, must be at least as great as any other F that could appear just then.

In sum, then: while it would be possible to formulate complex versions of my sort of theory in which no single being has anything approaching the divine nature, the best version of the theory involves a being which is eternal, necessary, uncreated, immaterial, creator/conserver, very knowledgeable and powerful and as perfect in relevant respects as any other thing that might co-exist with it.[58] Were Richard Dawkins to learn that something had just these properties and no more, I doubt he'd say 'well that's that, then – atheism is true'. Western monotheists would happily call it God even if it falls short of the standard perfect-being package. And of course, nothing rules it out that this being *does* have the rest of the perfect-being package: a being could well have the requisites for performing a role in the best version of my theory and much more besides.

Oriel College, Oxford

---

[58]   To have something that looks *very* like God, we would have to add that it is morally perfect. If we enrich Con's concept with moral perfection, we gain an additional, epistemically-based argument for the truth of my view – but I can't develop this here.

What do Religious Believers Believe?

RICHARD NORMAN

A common response to Richard Dawkins' assault on religious belief has been that he is attacking a straw man. The beliefs of religious believers, so the protest goes, are not as crude and simplistic as the ones which he attributes to them. Here is Terry Eagleton's comment to that effect:

> Imagine someone holding forth on biology whose only knowledge of the subject is the *Book of British Birds*, and you have a rough idea of what it feels like to read Richard Dawkins on theology. Card-carrying rationalists like Dawkins...invariably come up with vulgar caricatures of religious faith that would make a first-year theology student wince.[1]

Undeniably, Dawkins does set up an over-simplified picture of religious belief and commitment as the target of his attack. In this paper I shall try to do justice to the various forms which the religious stance takes, both for ordinary believers and for theologians and philosophers of religion. Taking into account the complexities and subtleties, I shall aim to assess the extent to which they remain vulnerable to criticisms in the manner of Dawkins.

Rationalism and Fideism

I use the term 'religion' as a shorthand for 'theistic religion', and I shall concentrate entirely on the case of Christianity, since it is the only religion with which I am adequately familiar. I take the core content of traditional Christian theistic belief to be the assertion of the existence of a *personal* god – a being to whom it makes sense to attribute cognition and will. As Richard Swinburne puts it, 'By a person I mean an individual with basic powers (to act intentionally), purposes and beliefs.'[2] It is also essential to religious belief that the existence of such a being must play some kind of *explanatory* role

[1]   Terry Eagleton, 'Lunging, Flailing, Mispunching', *London Review of Books* 19 October 2006.
[2]   Richard Swinburne, *Is There a God?* (Oxford and New York: Oxford University Press, 1996), 4.

doi:10.1017/S1358246111000117   © The Royal Institute of Philosophy and the contributors 2011
Royal Institute of Philosophy Supplement **68** 2011

Richard Norman

in our understanding of reality. The ancient Epicureans acknowledged the existence of gods in the sense of beings who enjoyed an ideal life of unperturbed bliss somewhere in the *intermundia*, but these beings played no role in the workings of the universe and a knowledge of them was held to be irrelevant to an understanding of the world around us; that is what makes Epicureanism a characteristically non-religious philosophy. In contrast, then, a distinctively religious belief in the existence of a god or gods must give such beliefs an explanatory status. Typically, the kind of explanation which is supposed to be provided is *purposive* explanation – hence the requirement of a personal god. Religious explanations claim to explain not just *how* the universe came into existence and continues to operate, but also *why* – understood to mean: with what intentions and for what purposes. That is what makes an explanatory deity more than simply a synonym for the causal workings of nature.

As we shall see, not all religious adherents place explanatory beliefs at the heart of religion, and there is a strong strand in contemporary Christianity which plays down the element of belief altogether. For the time being, however, I want to focus on the version of religious belief which is intended to play this explanatory role. It is this which gives Dawkins his target. Theistic explanations have been rendered redundant, he thinks, by the success of scientific explanations. Hence there is no longer any rational case for the existence of the god posited by theistic explanations. And if religious belief cannot be rationally defended, then it is just blind faith.

This is obviously too quick. As Dawkins knows perfectly well, there are plenty of intelligent religious believers who fully embrace scientific method and scientific explanations; they are not biblical literalists and they have no time for the naivety of creationism. They see theistic explanations not as competing with scientific explanations on the same terrain, but as having a separate role to play at the point where science leaves off. They accept the need to provide rational arguments for why scientific explanations are insufficient, and why theistic explanation is also necessary. Those rational arguments have to be taken seriously.

I have said that, according to this account, theistic explanation has a different role from scientific explanation. But the view of what that role is will necessarily be shaped by a view of the nature of scientific explanation and its limits. So although the theistic explanation is not seen as a scientific explanation, it is what we might call *parascientific* explanation. Its scope is set by claims about where scientific explanations properly leave off and how they are supposed to dovetail with explanations of a non-scientific kind. A classic example of such a parascientific explanation now much in favour is the so-called

106

'fine tuning' argument. According to this argument, if the fundamental scientific laws and the basic physical constants had been even slightly different from what they are, the 'big bang' would not have led to a universe like ours, with its galaxies and stars and planets, on at least one of which there are living beings, including conscious beings such as ourselves. Some further explanation is therefore needed, and it cannot be a scientific explanation, since scientific explanations must appeal to precisely those basic laws and constants which stand in need of further explanation. The best explanation, it is then suggested, is a purposive explanation – that those basic laws and constants were fixed by an intelligent deity who *knew* that they would generate our universe and who *intended* that they should do so.[3]

What makes the 'fine tuning' argument a good argument, it is said, is that it provides the *simplest* explanation of why the initial conditions were such as to lead to our universe and the existence of beings such as ourselves. Dawkins has responded that this is to misunderstand the requirement of simplicity in explanations. The theistic hypothesis may be simply stated, but the existence and agency of such a being stands much more in need of explanation than what it is supposed to explain.[4]

On this point Dawkins seems to me to be right. Indeed, I think that the problems go even deeper than he supposes. He sees the problem for the fine-tuning argument as essentially an infinite regress problem: 'A designer God cannot be used to explain organised complexity because any God capable of designing anything would have to be complex enough to demand the same kind of explanation in its own right' (109). And he assumes, I think, that any possible candidate for an explanation of the existence of an intelligent designer would itself have to be a scientific explanation akin to the evolutionary explanation of the existence of intelligent life on our planet. I would myself want to add that the supposed theistic explanation of the initial conditions of the universe also faces insuperable metaphysical difficulties. It would itself require further explanations of, for instance:

• how such a being could know what scientific laws and physical constants would produce a universe such as ours;

---

[3]   Some examples of this line of argument are: Richard Swinburne, *The Existence of God* (Oxford and New York: Oxford University Press, 1979), and *Is There a God?*; John Polkinghorne, *Belief in God in an Age of Science* (New Haven and London: Yale University Press, 1998), *Science and Theology* (London: SPCK, 1998), and many other works; Keith Ward, *Why There Almost Certainly Is a God* (Oxford: Lion Hudson, 2008).
[4]   Richard Dawkins, *The God Delusion* (London: Bantam Press, 2006), 134ff, esp. 109 and 148–150.

Richard Norman

- how such a being could create, *ex nihilo*, matter having those properties;
- how this intelligent being could exist without any physical embodiment;
- how a non-physical being could act on matter.

An explanation which genuinely met the requirement of simplicity would be economical in the sense of explaining as much as possible without invoking processes or mechanisms which are themselves more inexplicable than the original phenomena to be explained. The 'fine tuning' argument fails to meet that requirement. I accept that it is, in one sense, not in competition with scientific explanations, and as such can claim to provide a basis for religious belief which is not 'refuted' by scientific theory. But it is in competition with scientific explanations in this sense: that it must satisfy the same standards for what can count as a good explanation, including standards of simplicity and economy. It fails to do so.

Here is a second popular proposal for the kind of non-scientific explanation which theistic belief is supposed to provide. God, it is said, is the explanation of 'why there is something rather than nothing'. The problem is that it is very difficult to see how anything could constitute such an explanation. Theism does not do so. It purports to explain one thing (the natural universe) by reference to the existence of another 'thing' (God). Any explanation, scientific or otherwise, is bound to take that form: the explanandum is explained by reference to the explanans, so something has to be taken as given in order to provide the basis for the explanation.

At this point it is sometimes objected that theistic explanation does not take that form, because 'God is not an entity alongside other entities'. Here is Eagleton's review of Dawkins again:

> Nor is he [i.e. God] a principle, an entity, or 'existent': in one sense of that word it would be perfectly coherent for religious types to claim that God does not in fact exist. He is, rather, the condition of possibility of any entity whatsoever, including ourselves. He is the answer to why there is something rather than nothing. God and the universe do not add up to two, any more than my envy and my left foot constitute a pair of objects.[5]

I am not sure what is meant by saying that God is not an 'entity'. Clearly he is not an individual of the same kind as any other individuals – not located in space and time, and therefore not individuated in

---

[5] Eagleton, 'Lunging, Flailing, Mispunching'.

the manner of other things or persons. But if he is not in *some* sense an existent entity, then it is difficult to see how he can constitute an explanation for, or a 'condition of the possibility of', anything.

It may indeed be that the question 'Why is there something rather than nothing?' is not really a request for an explanation at all. Wittgenstein, in the *Tractatus*, famously says 'Not *how* the world is, is the mystical, but *that* it is.'[6] That is precisely *not* a call for an explanation. It is, perhaps, a way of expressing the feeling of wonder at the thought that there might have been nothing at all. That thought can induce a sense of metaphysical vertigo, and perhaps this is why we might reach for the word 'mystical'. But it is not a thought which appropriately invites the response 'The reason why there is something rather than nothing is that God willed it to be so.' That response would still leave things mysterious, but it would banish the sense of the mystical – the sense that nothing could possibly count as an answer to the question. Posing the question does not, therefore, provide a space for theistic belief.

I have looked very briefly at two possible ways of claiming that the success of scientific explanations leaves room for a different, non-scientific explanation, of a kind which belief in a personal deity can provide, and that the need for such an explanation therefore furnishes a rational basis for religious belief. A great deal more could be said in defence of such claims, and of others like them, but they are all likely to fail for the same reasons. Either they will purport to explain when explanations are not what is needed, or they will fail to meet the requirements of a good explanation. Explanations do not have to be scientific explanations, but they do have to match up to the same standards for what is to count as a good explanation – at the very least, they should not leave things even more inexplicable.[7]

The fact remains, nevertheless, that many theists do try to meet the challenge of the success of science by producing rational arguments of this kind. And the efforts of theistic rationalists such as Swinburne, Polkinghorne, Ward and others are more sophisticated versions of

[6]   Ludwig Wittgenstein, *Tractatus Logico-Philosophicus* (London: Routledge & Kegan Paul, 1922), 6.44.
[7]   I do not have space to discuss here other possible ways of providing a rational basis for belief in the existence of a personal deity, such as appeals to religious experience of the kind defended by Ward, (*Why There Almost Certainly is a God*, ch. 7). I say something about appeals to religious experience, and why I think they fail, in my *On Humanism* (London: Routledge, 2004), 41–2, and in 'The Varieties of Non-Religious Experience', in John Cottingham (ed.), *The Meaning of Theism* (Oxford: Blackwell, 2007).

Richard Norman

the vague intuition entertained by many religious believers, that God is needed to explain things which science cannot explain. That is why Dawkins' sweeping accusations of irrationalism are far too dismissive. He says:

> Christianity, just as much as Islam, teaches children that unquestioned faith is a virtue. You don't have to make the case for what you believe.[8]

Attempts at rational justification may fail, but unsuccessful arguments are still appeals to rational argument, not simply to 'unquestioned faith'. Dawkins implicitly acknowledges this when he engages with the arguments and attempts to show that they are insufficiently cogent. Rather than accusing all religious believers of irrationalism and a recourse to 'unquestioned faith', his criticism would be better put in the form of a dilemma. *Either*

> (a) religious believers attempt to provide rational arguments for their belief, in which case their arguments, though not refuted by science, fail to meet the standards for a good explanation,

or

> (b) they eschew the appeal to rational argument and assert that religious commitment rests ultimately on non-rational faith.

Though Dawkins is too sweeping, it has to be acknowledged that there is indeed a strong fideist and irrationalist strand both in modern theology and in popular religion. Karl Barth for instance, often held up as the most important theologian of the twentieth century, maintained that since God is 'wholly other', we cannot aspire to knowledge of him by means of our merely human powers of reason. Natural theology he saw as a blind alley. For Barth, we can know God only insofar as he chooses to reveal himself to us, and this he has done above all through Jesus of Nazareth.

Any such appeal to revelation as the basis of religious belief is bound to be fideistic. Since there can be no self-authenticating revelation, the claim that any supposed revelation is an authentic revelation of the true god has inescapably to be an act of faith. For all their sophistication, such theologians cannot avoid the circularity which is happily embraced by so many ordinary religious believers: 'I believe in God because his existence and nature is revealed in our holy book, and I know that what is in that book is true, because it is the word of God.'

[8]   Dawkins, *The God Delusion*, 306.

When I refer to a strand of theology and religious discourse as 'fideist' and 'irrationalist', I do not mean that it is devoid of intellectual content. It can go along with an abundance of scholarship devoted to Biblical exegesis, textual criticism, historical enquiry, and the articulation and defence of the finer points of doctrine. What makes it irrationalist is the refusal of the need for rational justification of the core beliefs which underpin the whole edifice. This tendency is still alive and well, and can take highly intellectualised forms. Here, for instance, is a representative of the current theology which calls itself 'radical orthodoxy', drawing on postmodernist clichés about the plurality of 'narratives', the failure of any overarching meta-narrative, and hence the supposed dispensability of any notion of objective truth.

1. The end of modernity, which is not accomplished, yet continues to arrive, means the end of a single system of truth based on universal reason, which tells us what reality is like.
2. With this ending, there ends also the modern predicament of theology. It no longer has to measure up to accepted secular standards of scientific truth or normative rationality...
3. In postmodernity there are infinitely many possible versions of truth, inseparable from particular narratives. Objects and subjects are, as they are narrated in a story. Outside a plot, which has its own unique, unfounded reasons, one cannot conceive how objects and subjects would be, nor even that they would be at all.[9]

How convenient. At a stroke it becomes possible to ignore rational criticism and to brush aside any demand for the rational defence of religious belief. When Dawkins describes Christianity as teaching that 'unquestioned faith is a virtue' and that 'you don't have to make the case for what you believe', he is over-generalising, but he does have legitimate targets.

Sideways Moves

So far I have been talking about religious *belief*. I have treated religious commitment as a matter of accepting certain beliefs, and

[9] John Milbank, 'Postmodern Critical Augustinianism: A Short *Summa* in Forty-two Responses to Unasked Questions', in Graham Ward (ed.), *The Postmodern God: a Theological Reader* (Oxford: Blackwell, 1997), 265.

Richard Norman

I have argued that the rationalist and the fideist accounts of such beliefs, though they should not be lumped together, each remain in their different ways vulnerable to Dawkins-style objections. I need now to consider an increasingly common suggestion from contemporary religious adherents – that religion is not primarily constituted by 'beliefs' in the sense of factual or propositional beliefs. John Cornwell, in his riposte to Dawkins, says:

> You think religion is "a persistent false belief held in the face of strong contradictory evidence". I am sure you realise that this hardly exhausts the meaning for most people, still less those who study it academically – theologians, philosophers, historians, and anthropologists. Religion, of course, is only partly involved in actual beliefs or doctrines, and these beliefs, if truly religious, are rarely held (except by fundamentalists) to be literal explanations of the world... Religion's activities, its rituals, its mythologies, hymns, meditations, prayers, chants, poetry, images, parables, legends, taboos, and sacramentals (by which I mean holy objects, such as candles, incense, oils, vestments, holy water) are principally symbolic, often appealing to deep levels of folk memory.[10]

Clearly, if religion does not involve a commitment to the holding of factual beliefs, it stands a much greater chance of being immune to the kinds of objection which Dawkins levels at it, that we should obtain our factual beliefs from the sciences and that this leaves no space to be filled by religious beliefs. But as we shall see, it makes an important difference whether Cornwell and others want to say that religion is 'only partly' a matter of beliefs, or whether it is *not at all* a matter of beliefs. I shall look at three possible sideways moves which can be made by religious adherents, all of them hinted at in the quotation from Cornwell – three deflationary accounts of religious commitment which play down the element of belief. They are understandings of religion in terms of (a) practices, (b) metaphors, and (c) stories or myths.

1. Religion as practices

It is obvious that practices of the kind listed by Cornwell – prayers, hymns, rituals and so forth – have been central to the character of

[10]   John Cornwell, *Darwin's Angel* (London: Profile Books, 2007), 43–44.

all major religions, including Christianity. What is less obvious is whether it can plausibly be claimed that these, rather than beliefs, are the centrally defining features of religion. One such attempt is the work of the theologian George Lindbeck. In his book *The Nature of Doctrine* he proposes what he calls a 'cultural-linguistic model' of Christian doctrine, which he contrasts with a cognitivist propositional model (as well as with an 'experiential-expressive' model).[11] Like many other recent theorists of religion, he draws on Wittgenstein's concept of 'language-games' to argue that, though avowals of belief are inescapably present as elements of doctrine, they get their sense from the religious practices and rituals in which they are embedded.

Any such account as Lindbeck's will find it hard to deny that assertions of belief are either explicit, as in the reciting of creeds, or implicit, as in the addressing of prayers and praises, in religious practices. That being so, it seems to me that some form of cognitivism is bound to re-emerge. Accordingly, Lindbeck's account falls back into seeing the practices as a *guide* to propositional beliefs rather than an *alternative* to them. He says, for instance, that religious sentences

> acquire enough referential specificity to have first-order or ontological truth or falsity only in determinate settings... The theological and doctrinal uses of, e.g. "Christ is Lord" are important... but they are not propositional. For Christian theological purposes, that sentence becomes a first-order proposition capable... of making ontological truth claims only as it is used in the activities of adoration, proclamation, obedience, promise-hearing, and promise-keeping which shape individuals and communities into conformity to the mind of Christ.[12]

This passage revealingly oscillates between suggesting that 'Christ is Lord' is not a propositional claim at all, and suggesting that it *becomes* a propositional truth claim when it is used in religious activities. That tension is surely inevitable. It is difficult to see how religious practitioners can meaningful engage in prayer without believing that there exists a being to whom such prayers can appropriately be addressed, or can engage in the activities of praise and worship without believing that there is a being who is the proper object of such praise and worship. And this is typical of the way propositional claims are bound to re-emerge in 'practice' conceptions of religion.

[11]   George A. Lindbeck, *The Nature of Doctrine* (Louisville: Westminster John Knox Press, 1984).
[12]   Ibid., 68.

It is not surprising, therefore, that Lindbeck often shifts to employing the notion of language-games in ways which make the contrast with propositional truth-claims less stark. Sometimes he speaks of religious language games as categorial frameworks. And since he then has to acknowledge that different religions appear to offer different and incommensurable categorial frameworks, thus raising the spectre of relativism, we find him re-introducing the idea that one particular set of categories may be more 'adequate to reality'.

> Thus the questions raised in comparing religions have to do first of all with the adequacy of their categories. Adequate categories are those which can be made to apply to what is taken to be real... A religion thought of as comparable to a cultural system, as a set of language games correlated with a form of life, may as a whole correspond or not correspond to what a theist calls God's being and will.[13]

Talk of 'categorial adequacy' slips imperceptibly into talk of 'categorial truth' (e.g. on page 51), and though he continues to contrast this with 'propositional truth', the commitment to truth-claims has inescapably re-emerged.

Sometimes, again, he rephrases his contrast as one between doctrines understood as propositional truths and doctrines understood as 'rules' or 'regulative principles'. Once more, however, the contrast is set up only to collapse.

> It is beyond the scope of this essay to examine the historical evidence for a regulative rather than propositional interpretation of the ancient creeds, but... three regulative principles at least were obviously at work. First, there is the monotheistic principle: there is only one God, the God of Abraham, Isaac, Jacob, and Jesus. Second, there is the principle of historical specificity: the stories of Jesus refer to a genuine human being who was born, lived, and died in a particular time and place. Third, there is the principle of what may be infelicitously called Christological maximalism: every possible importance is to be ascribed to Jesus that is not inconsistent with the first rules.[14]

The first two of these 'regulative principles', and perhaps even the third, look remarkably like propositional beliefs. And that, I have suggested, is bound to happen. The practices make no sense

---

[13]   Lindbeck, *The Nature of Doctrine*, 48, 51.
[14]   Ibid., 94.

without beliefs. We are then back with the question of whether the beliefs can be rationally supported, and whether their possible explanatory role has been usurped by the success of scientific explanations. We have still to consider, however, the other deflationary accounts of religion, and it may be that the apparent propositional claims and beliefs can be re-interpreted as 'mythological' or 'metaphorical'. We shall see.

2. Religion as metaphors

Here is Cornwell, addressing Dawkins, again:

> When theologians attempt to describe God's reality ... they are all too well aware of the trap known as anthropomorphism: of treating God as a human creature, Yet it seems pointless to remind you that thousands of studies have been published on this theme down the centuries emphasising ... the impossibility of speaking about him in anything but inadequate terms. Those inadequate terms are broadly speaking metaphorical and analogical.[15]

It is indeed important to do justice to believers' insistence that the nature of God surpasses human understanding, and that humans have to grope for the right language, which will always elude them. The question is then *how much* of religious language and beliefs can be construed as metaphorical, and whether it can plausibly *all* be said to be metaphorical (or analogical or symbolic), as Cornwell might seem to imply.

There are obvious candidates for a metaphorical interpretation. Talk of 'God the Father' is clearly to be construed as a metaphor. God cannot sensibly be thought to stand in a biological relationship either to Jesus, his 'son', or to those human beings who address him as 'our Father'. The metaphor is intended to capture, perhaps, a certain combination of moral authority, creative power, and loving care. And once 'father' is construed as a metaphor, there is room for feminist theologians to suggest that the metaphor of motherhood also has a role to play, perhaps as capturing better than 'father' the qualities of nurturing and compassionate devotion.

There is a tendency to run together the metaphorical, the analogical, and the symbolic as features of religious language, and it is indeed not always easy to tell which term is the most appropriate, but we can

[15] Cornwell, *Darwin's Angel*, 48.

see how any of these labels has the potential to secure intellectual respectability for religious beliefs. The six-day creation story at the beginning of *Genesis* can be read as a metaphorical or symbolic representation of the process of creation by divine power and intelligence over billions of years. The miracle stories can be read as metaphors for the healing power of compassion. The resurrection of Jesus can be seen as a metaphor for the triumph of goodness over apparent defeat and death. In all such cases, the invoking of metaphor serves to rebut the charge that these beliefs lack credibility in the light of a scientific world-view.

I want to insist, however, that religious language cannot be *entirely* metaphorical (or analogical or symbolic). If it were, then there would be no grounds for identifying it as distinctively religious in the first place. It must be possible to say at least something in non-metaphorical terms about what the metaphors apply to and why they are appropriate. Take again the example of 'God the Father', and the suggestion that this points to the combination of God's power and authority and love. It is possible to defend the metaphor as appropriate only if it can plausibly be maintained that there *is* a being whose relationship to the natural world and to human beings invites such a description. Discussion about whether 'father' or 'mother' or some combination of the two is the more appropriate metaphorical description presupposes that we can appeal to experiences of a non-human power and love at work in the world, and can test the metaphors against that experience. And it is difficult to see how such a discussion could even get off the ground without the acceptance of what I identified earlier as the core element of traditional Christian belief: the existence of a personal god possessing powers of cognition and will. Talk of metaphor therefore cannot obviate the need to make a case for the non-metaphorical truth of that belief.

Consider this passage from Lucretius:

> Mother of Aeneas and his race, delight of men and gods, life-giving Venus, it is your doing that under the wheeling constellations of the sky all nature teems with life, both the sea that buoys up our ships and the earth that yields our food. Through you all living creatures are conceived and come forth to look upon the sunlight.[16]

---

[16] Lucretius, *De Rerum Natura*, Book I, lines 1–5, in the translation by R. E. Latham, *The Nature of the Universe* (Harmondsworth: Penguin Books, 1951).

The invocation of Venus is for Lucretius a metaphorical description of nature and the procreative power of sexual desire. We know, from everything else in the poem, that he rejects the idea of divine beings playing any directive role in the workings of nature. That is what makes his world-view an uncompromisingly non-religious one. What is it, then, that distinguishes the Christian metaphor of 'God the Father' from Lucretius' metaphor of Venus as the mother of all living things? It can only be the non-metaphorical belief that there does exist a personal being separate from the natural world, with creative and benevolent intentions and purposes.

Janet Soskice, in her thorough and rigorous discussion of metaphor and its place in religious language, argues that in an important sense metaphors are irreducible.

> No metaphor is completely reducible to a literal equivalent without consequent loss of content, not even those metaphors for which one can specify an ostensive reference. When we speak of the camel as "the ship of the desert", the relational irreducibility of the metaphor lies in the potentially limitless suggestions that are evoked by considering the camel on the model of a ship: the implied corollaries of a swaying motion, a heavy and precious cargo, a broad wilderness, a route mapped by stars, distant ports of call, and so on.[17]

Soskice's example demonstrates one sense in which metaphors can be said to be 'irreducible' – in respect of their scope and suggestiveness. But this does not make them irreducible in the sense of having *no* literal equivalents. It does not invalidate my claim that we still have to employ at least some literal equivalent of any metaphor in order to identify what makes it appropriate. This is precisely what Soskice herself does with her example of the camel as 'the ship of the desert'. She provides literal equivalents – the swaying motion, the precious cargo, and so on – which show very effectively why the metaphor is appropriate. Agreed, they do not exhaust the suggestiveness of the metaphor, but if we were unable to say at least some things like this in literal terms, we would be incapable of seeing what makes the metaphor a good one. The same goes for the use of metaphor in religious language. Religious beliefs cannot be *entirely* metaphorical. They must include some non-metaphorical truth claims. And those truth claims need to be rationally justifiable.

---

[17]   Janet Soskice, *Metaphor and Religious Language* (Oxford: Clarendon Press, 1985), 95.

Richard Norman

3. Religion as stories ('myths')

Cornwell to Dawkins again:

> ...your separation of fact and fiction, true and false, reality and imagination, science and everything else, could not be more plain.... The Gospels are not factual (because they have all those factual inconsistencies, as you note), therefore the Gospels are fiction. So are you inviting your readers to infer that poets, dramatists, novelists are not concerned with truth-telling either? It's one thing, I suppose, to suggest that Christ's Sermon on the Mount contains no truths, but do you really wish your readers to accept that writers such as Chaucer, Shakespeare, Dickens, Dostoevsky ... the entire canon of world literature ... is just so much *untruth*? Fiction?[18]

The view of religious doctrines as stories is perhaps the most popular of the sideways moves which I am considering. It is sometimes formulated in terms of 'myths' rather than 'stories'. I won't dwell on possible differences of emphasis between the two terms. I take myths to be stories which are hallowed by tradition. That may be too simple, but the important question raised by both terms is whether religious doctrines should be seen as having the kind of significance and the kind of truth ascribed to imaginative creations such as plays, poems, novels and fables, and whether that is a better model than the model of scientific truth and can avoid the implication that scientific theories and religious doctrines are competing on the same ground.

As with metaphors, we need to ask: how extensive is the assimilation of religious beliefs to stories supposed to be? That stories feature prominently in religions in general and Christianity in particular is undeniable. The parables told by Jesus in the Gospels are clear examples. The beginning of *Genesis* can easily be read as a 'creation myth' comparable to the creation myths of other cultures and not in competition with scientific hypotheses. The narratives in the Old Testament need not be assessed for historical accuracy. The Garden of Eden and the Fall, Cain and Abel, Noah and the flood, Abraham and Isaac, Joseph and his brothers, Moses and the exodus from Egypt: these are stories – wonderful stories – which encapsulate valuable insights into human experience. Are the Gospel narratives to be read in the same way, as Cornwell seems to suggest? All of them?

---

[18]   Cornwell, *Darwin's Angel*, 34–5.

And is even the overarching narrative of a divine creator and his purposes for mankind to be treated as an imaginative fiction?

An early and influential comprehensive version of the 'religion as stories' thesis was Richard Braithwaite's paper 'An Empiricist's View of the Nature of Religious Belief', published in 1955. The first part of the paper defends the common view that the important feature of religions is their moral content: 'My contention... is that the primary use of religious assertions is to announce allegiance to a set of moral principles...'[19] A problem for this position, he then recognises, is that different religions may well be expressions of the same moral values.

> How then can religious assertions be distinguished into those which are Christian, those which are Jewish, those which are Buddhist, by the policies of life which they respectively recommend if, on examination, these policies turn out to be the same?[20]

It is in order to deal with this objection that he introduces the emphasis on stories.

> The really important difference, I think, is to be found in the fact that the intentions to pursue the behaviour policies, which may be the same for different religions, are associated with the thinking of different *stories* (or sets of stories)... It will be the fact that the intention to follow this way of life is associated in the mind of a Christian with one set of stories (the Christian stories) while it is associated in the mind of a Buddhist with thinking of another set of stories (the Buddhist stories) which enables a Christian assertion to be distinguished from a Buddhist one.[21]

Braithwaite's formulation of the connection between stories and ways of life is somewhat crude: they are 'associated in the mind'. Since the publication of Braithwaite's paper, much philosophical work has been done on how imaginative narratives can embody truths, including moral truths, which illuminate the human condition and help us to understand our lives. The view of religions as stories can draw on this work, and religious stories can then take their place among the stories which play this role.

---

[19] Richard Braithwaite, 'An Empiricist's View of the Nature of Religious Belief', in Basil Mitchell (ed.), *The Philosophy of Religion* (Oxford: Oxford University Press, 1971), 82.
[20] Ibid., 84.
[21] Ibid.

But the question then arises: why should religious stories have a special status in this respect? Stories can be valuable, but not just any stories will do. Some stories (religious and non-religious) are powerful and illuminating and inspiring, some (such as much popular fiction, not to mention the stories conveyed through other media such as films and television) are trite, sentimental, sexist, and sadistic. We have to assess and select, and it seems highly implausible to suppose that the upshot of our assessment will be to buy into a package deal consisting of all and only those stories linked to a particular religion. As Cornwell himself says, we have Chaucer, Shakespeare, Dickens and Dostoevsky. He and other Christians may set the Christian stories on a par with the classics of the literary tradition, but why should they be given a unique status? They could be given such a status if it could be backed up by claims about an authoritative divine revelation which guarantees that these particular stories are divinely inspired – but that would take us back to the contestable factual truth-claims which the emphasis on stories was intended to avoid.

A possible response might be that the Christian stories have been transmitted over generations and have stood the test of time as sources of inspiration. That might be why some defenders of religion as a set of stories might prefer to use the term 'myths' and might suggest that it is these that have a special power to meet our needs. Again, however, that is not a sufficient reason for focusing exclusively on the stories of one particular religious tradition such as Christianity. What about the power of the ancient Greek myths – Pandora's box, Prometheus and the gift of fire, Daedalus and Icarus, the Rape of Persephone, and so many others. These seem to me to embody deep truths about despair and hope, about human resilience and the defiance of adversity, about the dangers of overweening confidence in technical contrivances, about the natural rhythms of death and rebirth. That does not commit me to an allegiance to ancient Greek religion – it doesn't make me an Olympianist.

But the Christian stories are *our* stories, it might be said. They have a special status because they are the legacy of our own cultural tradition – they are central to our cultural identity and that is why they are the ones which we live by. Perhaps – but only on a limited view of 'our culture'. The myths of Greece and Roman occupy almost as important a place in the culture as do the Christian stories, and both of them are parts of a wider cultural tradition which is replete with stories of all kinds.

The Religion of Identity

The emphasis on *identity* does, however, take us to the heart of the problem posed by my title. For most religious 'believers', I suggest, religion is primarily a matter of identity rather than belief. Historically that has always been the case. People have adhered to a religion because it has been the shared framework of understanding and devotion inherited unquestioningly from the society in which they have been born and raised, not because of any independent assessment that its beliefs are true. The idea that one might choose one's religion is a very late arrival. In contemporary multicultural societies adherence to a particular religion is often the badge of identity of a sub-culture; many people see themselves as Muslims or Hindus because their roots are in the relevant immigrant community. Christians, whether committed or nominal, see themselves as such because Christianity is the tradition with which they identify. And many thinking Christians, confronted with the difficulty of providing a cogent intellectual justification for traditional Christian beliefs, will, if they are honest, acknowledge that their religion is a matter of who they are rather than what they believe.

An essay by Nicholas Lash, in response to Dawkins, makes this point very explicitly. Dawkins, he says, 'takes it for granted that to "believe in God" is to be of the opinion that God exists.'[22] This preoccupation with beliefs in the sense of opinions represents a complete misunderstanding of religion:

> To be a Jew, or a Christian, or a Muslim, is to be a member of a particular *people*: a people whose identity is specified by particular habits of memory and ritual, of understanding and relationship and hope.[23]

We can see from this quotation how an emphasis on identity and community membership goes naturally with an emphasis on practices rather than beliefs. And since the beliefs nevertheless remain an ineradicable part of the picture, Lash also employs the characteristic recourse to the emphasis on metaphors and stories. He puts to Dawkins the following question:

> ...given the *centrality* of this insistence, in Christian thought, for two millennia, on the near-impossibility of speaking

---

[22]   Nicholas Lash, 'Where Does *The God Delusion* Come From?', in *Theology for Pilgrims* (London: Darton, Longman and Todd, 2008), 7.
[23]   Ibid.

appropriately of God, is it ignorance or sheer perversity that leads him wholly to ignore it, and to treat all statements about God as if they were characteristically taken, by their users, as straightforward and literal description? ...most Christians are not fundamentalists. They know that they do not comprehend the mystery of God, and that what we say is said in metaphor and parable.[24]

I take Lash's essay to be a particularly clear and articulate statement of the position adopted at least implicitly by many, often the most sensitive and thoughtful, of his fellow-Christians. Their Christianity consists not in a set of intellectual beliefs about the origin and nature of the universe, but in membership of a community with which they share a way of life and particular practices, rituals and observances. And if challenged on the traditional beliefs of Christianity, they are likely to fall back on the construal of these as metaphors and stories rather than as literal factual truth-claims. A position such as this then incorporates all three of the sideways moves which I have been discussing – the emphases on practices, metaphors, and stories – because it sees these as defining features of a particular community, membership of which makes one a Christian.

What are we to make of this? I offer, first, two brief practical comments. On the one hand, a religious commitment of this kind stands a good chance of being, in one way, benign in its practical consequences. It stands in contrast to a religion of dogmatism and textual fundamentalism. Christians of this ilk are least likely, in particular, to suppose that their moral views can be derived from a literal reading of particular Biblical texts. They can be flexible and liberal in their interpretation of the traditional teachings. They need not find themselves trapped by Biblical pronouncements on, for instance, sexual behaviour, homosexuality, or gender relations. (Whether they are nevertheless trapped in the authoritative pronouncements of ecclesiastical leaders and institutions will depend on which church they belong to.)

My second practical comment is more negative. I recognise the appeal of religion as communal identity, but I am not convinced that it is what we need now. We know all too well the possible consequences – the lethal consequences – of a religion of identity. I am not suggesting that Christians who feel an attachment to the rituals of choral evensong, or Jews or Muslims or Hindus who value their cultural roots, are indistinguishable from latter-day crusaders and

---

[24]   Ibid., 8–9.

jihadists. Nevertheless, in a diverse society facing dangers of fragmentation and internal conflict, we should be looking for the cultural ties which bring people together rather than the religions which divide them.

But what about the intellectual status of the religion of identity? By putting the weight on community membership, and by downplaying the role of beliefs, understood as factual truth-claims, in favour of practices and metaphor and stories, can it avoid a conflict with scientific understanding in which it would face defeat, and can it thereby secure immunity from rational criticism?

Let me first recall my critical comments so far. An emphasis on practices, I suggested, faces the problem that the practices appear to presuppose beliefs. Prayer makes no sense without a personal deity to whom the prayers are addressed. Praise and worship make no sense without a being who is the object of adoration. Intercession for forgiveness makes no sense in the absence of a god who knows and forgives. The traditional beliefs which underpin the practices may then be construed in terms of metaphors and stories. But if they consist *entirely* of metaphors and stories, there is nothing to make them distinctively religious. They are metaphors and stories which any atheist can embrace as part of a common cultural stock. You don't have to be a Christian to see praise of the Creator as an expression of awe and wonder at the beauty of the natural world, or to respond to the stories of the nativity and the crucifixion which pervade literature and music and the visual arts, alongside many other stories.

This was where the appeal to community identity came in. Giving a special status to these particular practices and metaphors and stories can be seen as a token of membership. What makes them distinctively religious is that they are the distinguishing marks of a particular religious community.

Is that a coherent and watertight position? I do not think that it is, straightforwardly, intellectually refutable. I do think that it is inherently *unstable.*

I have posed the question: do those Christians who put so much weight on metaphors and stories understand what appear to be the 'beliefs' of their religion as consisting *exclusively* of metaphors and stories? My impression is that, typically, they simply do not press that question. To put it rather brutally: they do not explicitly accept that they have *no* non-metaphorical religious beliefs of a traditional kind, but if they are challenged on the plausibility of any *particular* belief they are always able to fall back on the reinterpretation of it as a metaphor or a parable or a myth.

Richard Norman

If they were to press the question, they would face a dilemma. Jettisoning *all* the traditional non-metaphorical beliefs would loosen the bonds which unite the religious community. Because the metaphors and stories are so much a part of the wider culture, the boundaries which separate the religious community from that wider culture would become increasingly porous, to the point of eventually disappearing.

Conversely, if the metaphors and stories are to have a special status as the possessions of a distinctive community to which the secular humanist does not belong, they must be tied to at least *some* non-metaphorical factual beliefs. If talk of 'God the Father Almighty' as 'maker of heaven and earth' is to be more than a metaphorical way of talking about the creative power of natural processes, then it must point to some inescapably metaphysical belief, however vague, about the existence of a creator distinct from the natural world and in some sense personal. If the Gospel narratives are to be seen as more than stories which must take their place alongside other tales of inspiring teachers and moral visionaries and martyrs for a cause, then there must be a commitment to at least some factual claims about the life of Jesus, his survival of physical death, and his special relationship to the creative intelligence which is called 'God'. Those metaphysical beliefs and those factual beliefs then have to be capable of rational justification, and of being defended against criticism from a scientific standpoint.

I do not think that they can be. And on this point at least, I think that Dawkins is right.

University of Kent

With and Without Absurdity: Moore, Magic and McTaggart's Cat

PETER CAVE

> Fish (fly-replete, in depth of June,
> Dawdling away their wat'ry noon)
> Ponder deep wisdom, dark or clear,
> Each secret fishy hope or fear.
> Fish say, they have their Stream and Pond;
> But is there anything Beyond?

Here is a tribute to humanity. When under dictatorial rule, with free speech much constrained, a young intellectual mimed; he mimed in a public square. He mimed a protest speech, a speech without words. People drew round to watch and listen; to watch the expressive gestures, the flicker of tongue, the mouthing lips; to listen to – silence. The authorities also watched and listened, but did nothing.

The incident – 1986, Zagreb, Yugoslavia – says much. It is a tribute to humanity: the young man's ingenuity, courage and force for freedom. It may also be condemnation of humanity: the authorities' desire for power, conformity, repression. The incident displays human absurdity – a protest speech without words. A protest was being made, as all could tell. Yet the law – the law against protest – remained unbroken. The protestor obeyed the law's demand not to speak, yet spoke. The police were dutiful in stopping protest, yet allowed protest. Our humanity enables us to see our lives as filled with incongruities and tensions such as the above – yet also with aspirations and achievements, also as above. Our humanity encourages a smile.[1]

Absurdities

Rupert Brooke's 'Heaven'[2] and the young man's protest introduce the paper's topic: absurdities within and without religion, life with and

[1] This and some of the later paragraphs related to humanism are taken from my *Humanism: a Beginner's Guide* (Oxford: Oneworld, 2009).

[2] The paper's opening is but the first few lines from Rupert Brooke's splendid poem. It is printed whole in numerous collections

doi:10.1017/S1358246111000038   © The Royal Institute of Philosophy and the contributors 2011

Peter Cave

without absurdity. One absurdity is simply that of believing in a 'beyond', a transcendent, a god or gods, without evidence, without good reason.

'Absurdity' as used here focuses on incongruity, a clash, an extreme example being an explicit contradiction of the form p & not-p. 'She came from Dungerness, but not from Dungerness.' In the incongruity of a protest speech without speech, there is a sense of clash, but we readily understand what is going on: a mimed speech is not 'really' a speech, yet may have the same effect as a speech – or even more. We can assert out loud that the protester is miming a protest speech, yet that is something that he must mime, if wishing to express agreement within his silent constraint. He is constrained; we are not. We are more detached, as we also are when judging Brooke's pondering fish. The clash between an attached view and a detached view – between perspectives – recurs in this paper.

Incongruities, as seen with 'Heaven', drive humour: jokes, puns and cartoons, usually involve a clash; we expect one outcome, but find ourselves suddenly confronted with something rather different. A husband says, 'Darling, I missed you.' How loving we feel – but he next says, 'I must fire again!' The scene is cast in a different light. We abruptly see things differently; we are given a new vantage point.

G. E. Moore may appear far removed from all this, but he drew attention to the absurdity of someone asserting a proposition of the form: p, but I do not believe that p. This is Moore's Paradox, as it became labelled courtesy of an impressed Wittgenstein.[3] It is absurd for me to assert or think, 'Today is Friday, but I don't believe that today is Friday,' yet the proposition that I express seems the same as that expressed by others without absurdity, and one that may be true, namely, 'Today is Friday, but Peter Cave doesn't believe today is Friday.' I cannot possess the vantage point on my current beliefs that is possessed by others. In trying to secure that vantage point, detached from my current beliefs, I lapse into absurdity. We shall return to Moore's Paradox.

I am a humanist, an atheistic humanist. 'Humanist' hereafter applies to atheists who recognize the force of moral values, the

---

and also in my *Humanism*, op. cit. note 1. Its last few lines conclude this paper.

[3] See G. E. Moore, *G. E. Moore: Selected Writings*, (ed.) Thomas Baldwin (London: Routledge, 1993), 207–12 and Ludwig Wittgenstein, *Philosophical Investigations*, tr. G. E. M. Anscombe (Oxford: Blackwell, 1953), II.x.

sense of fellow feeling and the possibility of lives flourishing.[4] Religion, for humanists, forms one arena for absurdities. Indeed, some religious believers themselves view religion as such an arena. Humanists may feel superior. 'At least we do not live by absurdities as religious believers do.' This paper challenges that assertion, by displaying some similar absurdities in reason, through some paradoxes, and some absurdities at the heart of human life. Arguably, the paradoxes of reason are contrived and the resultant absurdities can be dissolved. Unarguably, people can live well without the absurdities of religious belief.[5] The absurdities of human life though – well, they seem to be ones that we – believers or no – cannot live without while remaining recognizably human.

Absurdities in religion cannot be laughed off in the way of laughter at the absurdities in humour. Religious beliefs, however absurd many such beliefs may strike us, can be dangerous. With a supposed god or gods, or the one God, on their side – and, hereafter for ease, let us merely mention God, without the caveats – religious believers may be deaf to reason, blind to evidence, and untouched by appeals to humanity. How can anything compete, so to speak, with the declarations of an omnipotent, omniscient deity! If scriptures, religious leaders or revelations tell believers, for example, that homosexuality is wicked, then appeals to humanity, to reason, to toleration, hit a brick wall, a scriptural reading rendered as stone. If a revealed 'God's word' announces that apostates should be killed, then invoking common humanity is unlikely to carry much weight. If divinely inspired scripture insists that Adam and Eve were directly created by God six thousand years ago, then all the evidence for evolution will be re-interpreted. None of this is to deny that many, many religious beliefs and believers are kindly and humanist driven; and humanists must, of course, recognize that much of humanity seems drawn to a divine beyond – as are Brooke's fish.

Religious absurdities lead many to reject religious belief; and religions' potential dangers provide motivation to encourage some

---

[4]   This is not intended as a formal definition of 'humanism' and, of course, many humanists are agnostic at some level or other. Restriction to atheists here is merely for simplicity of exposition. Indeed, many agnostics are really atheists who yet highlight the fact that they could be mistaken. Similar highlighting would leave some to speak of being a-'fairies at the bottom of the garden'-ist.

[5]   This is not to say that religions lack value. They have influenced many lives for the better and, of course, have been instrumental in generating some wonderful literature, art and music. It is silly to try to perform a calculation of overall harm or benefit.

others. Of course, humanists' stress on reason and evidence ought not to suggest that humanists are devoid of passion, opposed to absurdities of humour, and never hold contradictory beliefs or perform terrible deeds; but humanists often think – aspire, hope, trust – that, once religions' absurdities have been exposed, life's puzzles may be ironed out, at least to some extent. Human cooperation, rationality, and empathy may come to the rescue, not over the solar system's collapse and humanity's eventual destruction, but over how our lives may be improved and how best to view meaning in life and of death.

Many lives, indeed, could go much better, without religion – just think of countries dominated by Islamic governments – but I doubt whether any of us can iron out life's creases and wrinkles, the conflicting perspectives, tensions, and incongruities that we live by and die by. I doubt the good sense of even wanting so to do. Here, humanistic ironing is not the project. The project, as implied, is merely to remind us that, arguably, all is not well in the land of reason – and in life – if we seek to avoid absurdities. Maybe we can patch up reason, but not life.

Magic

One absurdity which draws the eye is magic. The beautiful young lady is being sawn in half, or so it seems. We experience a clash: what we seem to be seeing clashes with what we yet know to be so. Once we learn more, learn how the act is performed, we may lose the excitement; yet we may still be unable to see what is really happening. More mundanely, we know that the drawing can appear as a duck and also as a rabbit, but when we see the rabbit, we cannot also be seeing the duck.

With conjuring tricks, we are typically aware that there is an explanation in terms of everyday procedures, maybe speeded up, and we can be immersed in the magic of the trick, while knowing that it is just a trick. No weird laws of nature are being manifested or well-known laws broken, concerning hats, rabbits or ladies in many parts. We can be both enmeshed within the magical exercise and yet detached, knowing it is just magic. There is kinship here with how we can believe in, be moved – even to tears – by the characters in a novel, a play or opera, while knowing they are but fictional. In some way, we occupy two vantage points, closing eyes to the resultant incongruity.

For some people, magic can be more than mere conjuring tricks. Ritual activities, incantations, uses of occult knowledge – some use these with the intention of manipulating people and objects in ways unknown to the physical sciences. Some people stick pins in dolls, burn effigies, or chant curses, to bring about bad happenings to victims. These are no mere symbolic acts; they are believed to have causal powers. At an everyday level, a lover loses a ring and may believe that, as a result, the relationship is at an end.

Many of us engage in little rituals. We ask to be buried together, but not because we anticipate holding hands in death. We place flowers on graves, but not because we believe that corpses or onward souls will experience the scent and beauty – and final decay.[6] These are things that we do. Of course, many religious activities are also symbolic, but for some believers they possess causal powers, as if magical. Many Christians believe the bread and wine of the Eucharist, in some way, really are converted into Christ's body and blood. Religious believers may pray that their children survived a disaster unscathed, believing that their prayers *after* the accident may yet affect the accident. Such beliefs, for many of us, are akin to believing that the young lady really has been sawn into two. Such beliefs are, as John Maynard Keynes once said, instances of hocus-pocus.

Religious absurdities

Belief in God as omnipotent, loving and requiring worship, seems akin to belief in magic or collapse into fiction. We shall take up the fiction later; but let us briefly sketch three particular clashes in religion to compare them with those in reason and life. The three concern reflective motivation, religion-ism and immunization.[7] They are additional to the central puzzle, namely, the existence of religious belief when there seems no good evidence or good reason for such belief.

Reflective motivation

Many, many religious believers think that a necessary condition for reaching heaven is to obey God's commands. Perhaps this is to misunderstand the religious texts, but the puzzle, the absurdity, arises from what many, many religious people believe, whether or not the belief is true – and their belief may well be based on many sermons

---

[6] I believe this quip derives from G. K. Chesterton.
[7] These three puzzles, including 'Sympathy for the Devil', are discussed in more detail in my *Can a Robot Be Human? 33 Perplexing Philosophy Puzzles* (Oxford: Oneworld, 2007).

preached from many pulpits about the many wages of sin. One godly command is a moral one, namely, that we ought to help others, and, most importantly, that we ought to do so for the sake of those others, not to benefit ourselves. The puzzle is that this leaves believers who seek to follow God on this matter in a seemingly impossible position.

Christian believes that, by acting morally, he will reap the benefits of passing the moral test at heaven's gate. His motivation is to secure the heavenly end and avoid the hellish. Perhaps Christian was a pretty immoral character before he came to believe in God and grasped what God commanded. After a little reflection, he reasons, 'There is no point in my helping others; this is because what motivates me is my desire for heaven (or fear of hell) and that makes the whole point ... er ... pointless.' To pass heaven's moral test, he needs to act morally, without any self-interested motivation, yet he clearly possesses a self-interested motivation. Christian's simple aim of achieving heaven seems, paradoxically, to prevent his doing what is required for heaven.[8]

Being motivated by a heavenly afterlife need not contaminate being motivated by the plight of others. People can be genuinely motivated to help others for their own sake and be genuinely motivated to do what is required to reach heaven, yet because they fail to realize that helping others is a means of increasing heavenly chances, there is no problem. Christian may be able to take this path by developing ignorance. He could set about helping people, albeit with the wrong motive yet, over time, come genuinely to be helping them for their sake, forgetting the link with heavenly entry. Indeed, you may be motivated to do X, knowing that X brings about Y, yet not be motivated by Y. That is easily seen when Y is undesirable, but not so easily when Y is desirable and desired.

For Christian to have the right motivation, we need him to help others, even without the consequence of the increased likelihood of heaven. As Christian is a seriously committed religious believer, can he make sense of such a possibility: of there being no God; of not wanting to go to heaven? If he is unable to make sense of it, he cannot assess what he would still do in, for him, such a senseless world. The answer perhaps is that no requirement exists for him to be able to carry out the 'Would I still?' test, just that it be possible for someone to carry it out. Step forth the atheist – now, arguably,

---

[8] There are many puzzles with some similarity to this. Think of a Groucho Marx wanting to belong to a club if and only if it does not want him – or of Catch-22 where requesting to be grounded ensures that one fails to satisfy the conditions for being grounded.

in a better position, with a better vantage point, than Christian for evaluating his true motivation.

Religion-ism

Let us turn to the second religious puzzle: religion-ism. Consider two individuals, one brought up Christian and firmly remaining committed to Christianity, the other brought up Muslim and firmly remaining Muslim. They are reflective individuals; they recognize that had they been brought up differently – in the faith of the other – they would have been committed to different religious beliefs. Importantly, these two believers, unlike many believers, recognize in a detached way that evidence for Christianity is of the same strength and character as that for Islam. So, the counterfactuals concerning what they would have believed are not akin to our believing, 'Had we been brought up in the Middle Ages, then we would have believed the Earth the centre of the universe.' In this astronomical example, we understand that we now have more and better evidence.

Knowing that their particular religious commitments depend so heavily on their upbringing and culture – and knowing that there is no worldly evidence or tests to show one religion is right, the other wrong – each believer would seem irrational in holding fast to her belief. It seems a prejudice in favour of one religion over another: religion-ism. Non-believers find it utterly absurd that, say, a Christian Sophie can be so confident in her Christianity while agreeing that, had she been brought up a few miles away, across a border, she would be Muslim, confident in Islam. We may make our example vivid, by supposing our two individuals identical twins who, at birth, became separated, growing up as described. Had they been switched at birth, then Sophie would now be committed to Islam. Reason suggests that they should suspend belief. Of course, they may respond, 'Ah, but this is faith' – but this sounds akin to responding, 'Ah, but this is superstition', or to insisting that the young lady really has been sawn in half and stuck back together.

Immunization

Believers typically maintain that God is all good and loving – and also all powerful, including all knowing – yet evils, in the form of numerous sufferings, exist. Lest we forget, right now, millions of people are suffering malnutrition, natural disasters, disease or war. Think also of particular, more homely cases – of toothaches, pains in dying and

Peter Cave

seeing loved ones dying. Add to these the sufferings of non-human animals. Many, many of these sufferings seem gratuitous. Indeed, John Stuart Mill stressed that, looking around the world, we find considerable evidence to blacken any deity's name, not much evidence for praise. Believers are accepting a clash, an incongruity, between the divine characteristics and how the world is. Non-believers usually find this absurd.

Humanists use reflections concerning this well-known problem of evil to point to the non-existence of an all-powerful, all-good God. Perhaps, indeed, we should have sympathy for the Devil: the Devil is overlooked when there is such evidence for a malign superpower, assuming the world is any evidence at all for the supernatural. If the world is evidence for anything supernatural, we perhaps should move to the position of believing there to be supernatural powers, in conflict, one for good, and one for evil – something like the Zoroastrian position. This would be the most rational religious belief – which perhaps explains why there are so few Zoroastrians.

Reasoning absurdities

Many believers are trapped within one or other of the three absurdities or puzzles above. Yet reflective reasoning and logic give rise to similar puzzles. There is the well-known liar type of paradox. 'The proposition expressed by this sentence is not true.' On the surface, if true then absurdly it is not true; and if not true, then absurdly true. Here are three puzzles, again only briefly sketched, which seem to leave us baffled over what to believe and hence do.[9] They are Surprise, Newcomb, and Chalice.

Surprise

This well-known paradox tells of students being informed by a truthful teacher of a noon examination one school-day next week. It is a surprise examination in that, whichever day it occurs, the students will have no good reason to believe on that morning that it will take place that day.

'Well, it can't be on the last day, Friday', think clever students, realizing that by Friday it would not then surprise, Friday being the only

---

[9]   For discussion of these three paradoxes, their sources, relations to other paradoxes and further references, see my *This Sentence Is False: an Introduction to Philosophical Paradoxes* (London: Continuum, 2009).

day left. 'With Friday ruled out, it cannot be on the Thursday; so Thursday must be ruled out.' Thus the reasoning continues, the days being knocked out one after the other. Clever students conclude that there can be no such surprise examination. They face the week with a complacent smugness, not bothering to revise. Of course, one day that week then smugness is intruded upon: an examination is given – and it surprises. The clever students, having not revised, may now fail the examination, while students unable to conduct such 'clever' reasoning have revised and pass. Clever students have been too clever by half, or at least by one eighth.[10]

On encountering the paradox, people are often impressed by the tale's days ahead, but it is difficult to see why the quantity of days should be the puzzling source. After all, the puzzle arises because clever students project themselves to the Friday morning unexamined, understanding the teacher's announcement to imply that even a Friday examination would surprise. Ridding ourselves of the window-dressing of the days, we move to an austere version. To register this revision, let us hereafter speak of the Surprise Party.

If told of a surprise party this very evening, you may well be surprised at being told; but you can hardly now be surprised by the party. Surprise parties, to be surprises, require secrecy, mouths to be kept shut. Of course, the surprise may be for someone else, or the announcer may be mis-speaking. After clearing away such quibbles, you realize that the informer, firmly believed truthful, is telling you that there will be a surprise party for you this very evening. What are you to make of what you have been told?

You will probably not know what to think. However, being perceptive, you then reflect, 'Hold on, in my not knowing what to think about the party, I am certainly not believing that there will be one – and so, when it happens, it will be a surprise.' You now see how the announcer can be speaking the truth after all; but that flips you back into believing that the party will be given, and hence into not being surprised. And so, you reel, round and round.

Newcomb

You are a contestant in a long-running television show. You face two boxes. One is open, and the contents, £10,000, can be clearly seen. The other is a surprise box, its contents hidden. You need to

---

[10]   This quip derives from Ted Honderich.

choose whether to take both boxes or the surprise box only. The surprise box is either empty or contains £1,000,000, its contents determined by a mind-reader's prior assessment of your character and the choice you will make. If the mind-reader judged that you will two-box, then nothing has been placed in the surprise box. If she judged that you will one-box, taking only the surprise box, then £1,000,000 will have been placed in the box.

The show has run for many years, and, whenever players have selected both boxes, the surprise box has been empty – or has been empty in 99.99% cases. That latter qualification highlights that the jackpot win, of the million pounds together with the £10,000, is possible: maybe very, very occasionally the mind-reader makes a mistake; mind-reading can be tiring.

You want to secure the most money possible. What is it rational to do? There are two conflicting lines of reasoning, both powerful. Given the evidence of the mind-reader's mind-reading success, it is surely rational to select the surprise box only, for she will have correctly predicted your choice. This 'evidential' argument clashes with the 'causal' or 'already there' argument. 'Look, the money is already there – or not – so you may as well take both boxes.' We are not proposing backward causation or that your choice could now cause the £1,000,000 (if present) magically to vanish. Suppose, indeed, that you could actually see what is in the surprise box: what sight could lead you not to two-box?

Most philosophers support the 'already there' reasoning. Were they to do so in practice, the evidence overwhelmingly suggests that they would leave the show pretty grumpy, having secured only the £10,000: the mind-reader would have anticipated their philosophical preference in the reasoning. Participants who allow the mind-reader's past success to dominate their reasoning, thus taking the surprise box only, nearly always end up with the £1,000,000. Ideally, to maximize winnings, you need to get into the position of sincerely wanting to one-box (so the mind-reader puts in the million pounds), yet incongruously ending up two-boxing.

Is the successful mind-reader possible in theory? Well, such a reader could be successful with different player-types: some players, for example, may come over as very greedy grabbers, who would grab at both boxes without reflection; other players may be timid, always inclined to take one rather than two. (And, of course, there are further factors concerning the relative sizes of the money involved and the contestants' wealth.) Is a successful mind-reader possible, though, when operating with those participants whom the puzzle addresses, namely those whose decisions result solely from rationality? Rationality – good reasoning – points, as seen, to no single convincing answer as to what to do. So, the mind-reader, it seems, cannot consistently and successfully predict the choices of players, if their choices are based solely on rationality. This prompts the deep question: how do choices and reasons relate to the neurological causes and effects that lead to the words we utter, the movements to take two boxes, for example, rather than just one?

Chalice

Here is a prefatory tale, unlikely, but generator of no paradox. You are a philosopher at a banquet, medieval in style, sitting beside an extremely wealthy and eccentric lady, Lady Bountiful. The time is an hour or so before midnight. She points to the chalice of wine. She tells you, truthfully, 'If you drink this potion at dawn, I will give you the castle of your dreams, with servants at your beck and call, unlimited wealth for the rest of your life.' You have no scruples: you would love such wealth, such life-style – such luck. There is no catch, no trick, no snag, except that, as the lady explains, the chalice is poisoned, a heady brew, an unpleasant concoction. The potion will leave you struggling with intense pains for a couple of days; but then all will be well. There are no side-effects, no damage. Masochist you are not, but the pains are worth the pleasure of the reward. This is no paradox.

Paradox arises when Lady Bountiful's offer is as described, except for one key difference. You are in better luck, or so it seems. Lady Bountiful is offering you the immensely valuable estate; the only condition now is that at midnight you must intend to drink the nasty potion at dawn. There is no need actually to drink it; *merely intending* is sufficient. Surely, this revised offer is so much better than the original one. Intending to do something is so much easier than doing it – and, in this case, intending to drink from the chalice causes no pain, in contrast to the drinking.

With the Lady's offer before you, you reason as follows. 'I want the wealth, so obviously I will intend to drink. Ah, but that is enough. With the intention achieved, there is nothing more I need to do, so, of course, I shall not need to let a sip from that vile phial touch my lips. Oops! That means that I'll lack a genuine midnight intention to drink. If I intend to do something, I cannot also be set on not doing it.'

But you really do want the wealth, so the reasoning may continue. 'Reluctantly and sadly, I now see that I had better truly intend to drink the potion. To hell with rationality! I'll just drink it. But

Peter Cave

hold on… I cannot help but realize that there will be no good reason to drink it when the time comes. A poisoned chalice, yes; but also a poisoned offer! It's an offer I cannot take up.'

This is no puzzle for wealth-seekers who do not reflect. They intend to drink and, indeed, they may go ahead – or may, if receiving the keys to the castle before dawn, realize drinking is not then needed. Poor philosophers, paradigms of rationality, have a bad time: they remain poor. Yet it is, of course, possible sincerely to intend to do things and yet fail to do them; athletes intend to win, yet lose; students to study, yet sleep instead; and lovers intend to make the earth move, yet it remains unmoved.

Comparisons: corrosions and detachments

'The chief danger [...] is scholasticism – the essence of which is treating what is vague as if it were precise and trying to fit it into an exact logical category,' writes F. P. Ramsey, with the early Wittgenstein in mind.[11] What follows is no strong attempt at regimentation, at forcing the religious absurdities into the same categories as the reasoning ones. The claim is not that there are perfect parallels. Rather there are some wavy lines entangled.[12] Let us look at a few pairings; various ones are possible.

Let us try Chalice with Immunization. With Chalice, the midnight intention to drink the poison at dawn is corroded by the reflective awareness that there would be no good reason to carry out the intention. If faced with the offer from Lady Bountiful, we should need to blind ourselves, at least at midnight, to what it would be rational to do in the future – rather as Odysseus had himself bound to the mast, to avoid succumbing to the sirens' song. Compare with Immunization: believers in the loving, omnipotent, all-good God need to blind

---

[11]   F. P. Ramsey, 'Philosophy', *The Foundations of Mathematics*, ed. R. B. Braithwaite (London: Kegan Paul, 1931), 269.

[12]   For display of a common structure to the three reasoning paradoxes, see Laurence Goldstein and Peter Cave, 'A Unified Pyrrhonian Resolution of the Toxin Problem, the Surprise Examination, and Newcomb's Puzzle', *American Philosophical Quarterly* **45.4** (2008), 365–76. For more work on these paradoxes, with further detail, see R. M. Sainsbury, *Paradoxes*, 3rd ed. (Cambridge: Cambridge University Press, 2009). Chalice is usually known as 'Toxin'. All three paradoxes continue to be discussed in the journals.

themselves to the gratuitousness of the suffering in the world, or embrace the suffering as, paradoxically, a sign of love and benevolence. In Chalice, we should need to be planning to drink, even though it would be absurd to drink. With Immunization, believers are committed to God even though the commitment sits incongruously, absurdly, with the world's suffering. We should expect the world's suffering to corrode the belief.

We turn to Newcomb and Religion-ism. If, as players, we could sincerely want to one-box, yet end up two-boxing, all would be well; but the awareness of the reason to two-box corrodes the one-boxing desire. Players need, when being assessed by the mind-reader, to be blind to any convincing two-box reasoning. With Religion-ism, believers committed to their religion in the way described, manage, it seems, to resist the force of the corrosive counterfactuals 'Had I been brought up differently...' despite awareness of them. It is that which generates the absurdity. It is similar to the way mentioned earlier in which we may immerse ourselves in a play, moved by its characters, while knowing 'it is just a play'.

Finally, let us place Surprise with Christian's Reflective Motivation. You do not know what to make of the surprise party announcement: how can the announcer have been speaking the truth? Yet once you doubt his truth-telling – 'I don't know what to believe' – you can see how he could have spoken the truth: 'the party can be given', but that immediately corrodes the lack of belief in the party; and the puzzle returns. With Christian's reflection, once he gives up trying to get to heaven, then if he does still help others for their sake, he can get to heaven. Of course, once he sees this, then the purity of his intention is threatened again by corruption and the puzzle may return.

Considering all six puzzles, we call in Moore's Paradox for they all possess kinship with the form: p, but I do not believe that p.[13] Moore's paradox involves the impossibility of my separating how the world is from my current beliefs of how the world is. Others can do that for me, but I cannot directly do so for myself. I can readily recognize that I had mistaken beliefs, will have mistaken beliefs, and may have them now; but, in expressing how the world is, I am expressing my belief of how the world is. I cannot detach myself from my beliefs in the way that others can be detached from my beliefs. Let us see how this feature plays with the six puzzles. Let us mix them differently.

[13] Ramsey, *The Foundations of Mathematics*, 369–70.

Chalice has a player (as we may term the recipient of the offer) intending to drink, binding himself to drink, and blinding himself to the sensible later plan not to drink. He cannot sincerely assent to a Moorean conjunction such as, 'I intend to drink, but I shall not do so.' We, as detached observers, though, may note his sincere intention, yet anticipate that later he will see the pointlessness of actually drinking: 'He intends to drink, but won't do so.' With Reflective Motivation, Christian wants to help others solely for their sake: if he manages to do so, then it is difficult for him to step back and recognize that this aids his heavenly entry – without undermining that entry. We, as detached observers, can see his behaviour as aiding others for their sake and as being means to heavenly entry: 'By helping others for their sake, Christian will get what he wants.'

Turning to Surprise and Newcomb, in the minimal Surprise we indeed have the form of Moore's conjunction, for the hearer is trying to embrace in the first person, what she has been told and what may well be true. She is trying to embrace, 'There will be a party, but I don't believe there will be.' That is absurd. In Newcomb, we have a player trying sincerely to want to one-box when being assessed by the mind-reader, blinding himself to the two-box wisdom: he cannot hold to, 'I choose to one-box, yet shall take two'. We, as detached observers, though, may judge that possibly could happen – without absurdity. Maybe he sincerely chooses to one-box, yet somehow or other ends up two-boxing.

The remaining two puzzles are Immunization and Religion-ism. They both have believers seeming to manage to embrace the absurdities that thwart the relevant participants of the other puzzles. With Immunization, believers hold fast to an omnipotent and all-good God, when faced with good opposing evidence. Non-believers, detached, see the believers' states as absurd, as ones in which they wittingly believe that the God of Love exists despite the overwhelming contrary evidence.[14] Sophie, the believer as set out in Religion-ism, believes in Christianity, blinding herself to the corrosive effect of the 'Had I been nurtured in Islam...' counterfactual. 'Sophie believes in the Christian God rather than the Islamic despite no superior evidence for the former' is not absurd for us to assert from our vantage point; yet Sophie's assertion, 'I believe in the Christian God rather than the Islamic despite no superior evidence for the former' strikes many non-believers as absurd.

[14] There is a similarity with Harman's Paradox where if one knows that p, surely any evidence against p is misleading evidence and should be ignored. For outline, see Cave, *This Sentence is False*, 101–2.

Tertullian embraced religious absurdity: he declared that the Son of God was born and then died and that, because it is absurd, it is to be believed.[15] Quite what he meant is open to question, but some believers do readily recognize absurdities in their religious belief. They stress that their relationship to God is not that of a standard belief that an item exists. They may, indeed, speak of faith, of trust, of belief *in*. We may see this – and shall see this – as casting religious belief in a new light. Before that light, what is to be said about the reasoning puzzles? Well, arguments still rage; but one simple and persuasive thought is that impossibilities are built into the tales' premisses. Lady Bountiful simply sets the impossible task of intending to do something, knowing that, when the time came, it would be crazy to do that something. Arguably, Newcomb sets circumstances such that it is not possible for the mind-reader to be relevantly reliable in her predictions; and Surprise has the announcer magically knowing the belief states of recipients on receiving baffling information.

Belief: 'Clarissa loves me'

How may we cope with the religious absurdities, other than dismissing God – and viewing religious believers as simply embracing absurdity? Let us take up the thought that the 'belief' element of much religious belief is indeed rather different from regular belief.[16] After all, sense can sometimes be found in what sounds nonsensical, if the seeming nonsensical is cast in a new light. A tribe new to the telephone apparently described telephone messages as 'messages on poles'. Later, when they encountered the wireless, wireless messages were referred to as 'messages on poles without the poles'.[17] We can grasp what was meant.

Suppose I yearn for Clarissa – and believe that Clarissa secretly loves me. In seeking loving demonstration, I invite her to the opera, ask her round for drinks and send her earrings. My offers are spurned. My conclusion is that opera is not her cup of tea, that she is a non-drinker and

---

[15]   For discussion, see Bernard Williams, *Philosophy as a Humanistic Discipline* (Princeton: Princeton University Press, 2006), 3–21.

[16]   That God is usually taken to be a necessary existent may also suggest that belief in his existence is rather different from typical belief in items existing. For more on arguments concerning God, see Cave, *Humanism: a Beginner's Guide.*

[17]   Reported by John Wisdom. See the title paper in his collection *Paradox and Discovery* (Oxford: Blackwell, 1965), 133–4.

that she lacks desire for earrings. When, the following week, I see her at the Royal Opera House, sipping champagne, some splendid earrings jangling – well ... ? Maybe, I conclude she plays hard to get. Suppose she resists all my subsequent amatory advances. Suppose she sends round her husband, threatens a court order – and eventually calls the police. If I still protest that she loves me really, it is time to recognize that I no longer have a belief, but suffer a forlorn hope, desperate obsession, or mental state requiring medication.

Perhaps our reflections on religions' absurdities suggest that religious belief is all too much, or too little, to be typical belief, whatever traditional believers say. Rather, religious belief is a way of seeing the world: it casts the world and our lives in certain lights. Of course, alcohol can cast the world and lives in a light different from that of the sober; indeed, we may be tempted by Housman's 'And malt does more than Milton can/To justify God's ways to man.' Religions with their rituals and stories can, though, have value as ways of seeing the world – and not just a value similar to the temporary intoxications from grape or grain.

The suggestion, sometimes played, is that to believe that God exists is not to think that there exists a supernatural item that could be discovered, an item for which there is evidence. To believe that God exists is to treat the world in certain ways with certain attitudes, concerns, regular beliefs and intentions. People who read the world in the light of Christian scriptures may see it differently from those who read it in the light of, say, Darwinism and nothing more. So-called belief in God as an existent being, with the related religious beliefs, involves a web of stories, moral motivations, rituals and more. The web is best understood as expressing commitment to a way of life, be it to help the poor or – for that matter – kill the infidels. On this understanding – and a few religious believers agree – many religious claims, practices and scriptures amount to expressions of moral intentions, combined with a mixture of exemplary stories, some poetry and some empirical claims promoting certain ways of living. For some Christians, stories of Jesus' death, the events of the Last Supper and the good Samaritan parable, all lead to living agapeistically – that is, in brotherly love. Richard Braithwaite, an empiricist philosopher, gave explicit voice to this approach and, on this basis, I believe, entered the Church of England.[18]

[18] This approach is found in Richard Braithwaite, *An Empiricist's View of the Nature of Religion*, (Cambridge: Cambridge University Press, 1955). A seminal paper on this is John Wisdom's 1944 paper 'Gods', reprinted in his *Philosophy and Psychoanalysis* (Oxford: Blackwell, 1953), 149–68.

Most believers, of course, take their godly belief to be that there literally exists some supernatural being, that Christ really rose from the dead, and that God directly speaks to them. The proposal that religious beliefs amount only to highly important lifestyle commitments carries with it the thought that traditional theists are mistaken in treating their religious beliefs as involving genuine beliefs about an existent necessary being – a little in the way that I am mistaken about my psychological state directed towards Clarissa. A few who attend church or synagogue make no such mistake; they think of themselves as non-believing Christians or Jews, that is, atheists who yet value the religious tradition, rituals and morality.[19]

However gently humanists may suggest this approach to the religious – perhaps emphasizing the value that great fiction, myth and art, be it religious or no, may have for encouraging good living – traditional believers insist that God literally exists. I may then reply, 'It's just a way, a valuable way, of seeing the world, leading, say, to encouraging brotherly love, and being in awe of the beauty of flowers, mountains and sunsets.' They respond, 'But God really does exist.' Paradoxically, I may agree – for I may take those words to mean that the speakers really do possess the commitments mentioned. This is where the 'really's multiply. 'But, really really, really God exists.' 'Yes', I answer, 'Really, really, really you are committed to loving your fellow man and being in awe of sunsets and so forth.'

The resort to understanding certain basic beliefs as more akin to lifestyle commitments or approaches to the world is not unknown in other arenas of life. Some suggest that 'the future resembles the past' and 'every event has a cause' are best understood as expectations or rules for investigation – though, in contrast to religion, without these we cannot live. Casting things in different lights, expressing different attitudes, need not thereby be arbitrary, without foundation. It may dovetail with believers' talk of insights and added depths. Life is not 'really' a gift from God, but observations about life as divinely given may encourage respect and pious feeling not solely for humans, but also for other creatures and the natural world around us. Odd pictures of the world may help us to handle the world. Think of how physicists speak of 'charms' and how chemists picture molecules. Of course, some pictures hinder our understanding: consider how geneticists' lapses into 'selfish' genes have wrongly led some to conclude that humans must be selfish. One big difference between scientific pictures and religious pictures is that at least scientific theories lead to

---

[19] I have in mind, for example, Martin Rees (now Lord Rees of Ludlow) regarding Christianity and the late Peter Lipton regarding Judaism.

experimentations and testable predictions; but, we should note, the pictures and tales drawn by religions lead to ways of living – some that humanists welcome; some they rightly flee.[20]

Life: muddling through

One approach to religious absurdities and ways of seeing is to highlight the fact that we do not need to believe in God to have flourishing lives – after all, many flourishing people do not believe in God – though I, even as an atheist, would regret the loss of the kaleidoscopic delights ranging from absurd tales of revelations to uplifting religious words and music. Religious or not, there are, though, some deep absurdities that we all live by, yet which we often shrug off. We shall move from love to free will to the self – and then to the beyond.

Larry loves Ludmilla – yet Larry's love of Ludmilla must be because of her various characteristics. Larry's love rests on his experiences, knowledge and beliefs concerning Ludmilla; and they rest on Ludmilla's qualities – physical, emotional, intellectual and so forth. He may adore her smile, her coquettish walk and talk; he may value her kindness, the flick of her hair and her entrancings. We could list away: he loves her because she has qualities F, G, H and so on. Once we have the list, the paradox presents. Larry loves a Ludmilla-type rather than this particular Ludmilla. If someone else comes along with Ludmilla's qualities, Larry should love her just as much.

'No, only this Ludmilla', Larry insists. We then ask, 'Well, what is it about this Ludmilla?' If an answer is given, then we may be able to add it to the F, G, H list – and off we go again. Larry ought, it seems, to settle for any Ludmilla look-alikes when Ludmilla is out of town. Of course, the answer may be that love develops through a joint causal history of intertwined lives. That causal history cannot now be repeated: it ties Larry, a particular, to this particular Ludmilla here. Although Ludmilla's qualities are repeatable, in the sense that other items could have those same qualities, Ludmilla and this particular intertwining cannot be repeated. She is irreplaceable as far as Larry is concerned – well, for the moment.

Many items in our lives are readily replaceable. We do not mind which particular item we have of a certain type, so long as of the

---

[20] John Wisdom tells of a woman trying on a hat, looking in the mirror, undecided, unsure whether the hat would quite do. After a pause, her friend announces, 'My dear, it's the Taj Mahal.' The look of indecision leaves the face in the mirror; the woman now sees what is wrong about the hat. See 'The Logic of God', in Wisdom, *Paradox and Discovery*, 2–5.

right type. That glass of wine or this? No matter – as long as they are same size, quality and cost. Yet most people think differently about friends and lovers, about spouses and family – even about cats. Such items are not treated solely as ones of a certain type. The irreplaceability stance also applies to certain inanimate objects. Heirlooms form obvious examples: a curl of hair, a worn gown, a torn postcard can be 'irreplaceable', even if the proposed replacements are indistinguishable from the originals, be they as shabby as the originals are now.

No doubt, we could live without love, though it is difficult to see how we could live with treating others merely as of a type and being treated as such ourselves. The particular/qualities problem to one side, we frequently hold others and ourselves morally responsible, open to praise and blame – unless the doings are without, or outside, the agents' control. True, when things are abnormal, we often withdraw accolades of responsibility. The mentally ill avoid prison, but gain psychiatric units. The sane, though, we treat as if they have control over what they do; but have they any more ultimate control than the insane? A sudden high wind blows a mother against her son, knocking him to the ground. That is not the mother's fault; yet when the mother hits the child out of anger – that is her fault. Could she have controlled that anger? She might have tried, yet failed. And if she failed to try, was her character such that she could have tried? Perhaps she could not. Successful hard workers differ from failed hard workers, yet the successful are lucky to possess their abilities, their nature and nurture. Yes, there is a difference between the industrious and lazy; but presumably such character differences result from a mixture of nature and nurture – and unexpected events – all outside the control of the relevant individuals. Machiavelli spoke of the significance of Fortuna in how our lives turn out. Harold Macmillan, when asked about the determination of policy, replied, 'Events, dear boy – events!' People, we feel, should not be praised or blamed for their luck or unluck – yet a matter of luck or unluck it is, that we are who we are.[21]

Treating people, in the main, as responsible agents, or at least *as if* responsible, is essential to our human relationships. If we did not, we should regard others as biological cogs and springs, as blobs. That is, of course, dangerous, for we cannot properly admire – befriend,

[21] This is the well-known puzzle of moral luck which seems to be the traditional free will problem in modern dress. Bernard Williams introduced the expression as an oxymoron: see 'Moral Luck' in his *Moral Luck: Philosophical Papers 1973–1980* (Cambridge: Cambridge University Press, 1981), 20–39.

resent, praise, blame – cogs, springs or biological blobs: we use such items as but means to ends. Our treatment of people 'as people' manifests an emphasis on man's dignity, on his autonomy – an emphasis oft found in religions, yet which sits incongruously with God or Allah demanding worship; and an emphasis found in humanism, yet which sits incongruously with scientism, with explaining everything in terms of scientific laws, towards which some humanists are drawn. If murderers are but cogs in a causal machine completely determined, then, as offenders, they vanish. Our moral indignation is no more appropriate than rebuking an earthquake. Yet even if we are causally determined to do what we do, paradoxically we still have to make choices. If told of the prediction of our choices – even our own prediction of what we shall do – we may still, it seems, choose to do otherwise.[22] From the vantage point possessed by others, Mary is bound to do X; yet Mary may be unable to accept that she is so bound.

Over such matters, such matters hinted at through Newcomb, we muddle through. Richard Dawkins, fine defender of humanism, writes that our brains 'are separate and independent enough from our genes to rebel against them'.[23] Putting to one side how brains can rebel: if, on the one hand, the rebellions stand outside causal explanations, then they are mysteries closed to scientific investigation – presumably not Dawkins' position. So, let us clasp the other hand: if our resisting certain tendencies has causal explanations, then why do those resistances count as free choices, as Dawkins seems to think, whereas those explained genetically do not?

We muddle through – and the muddle arises, in part, because we are baffled by the 'I'. What is this subject – an enduring subject? – that sometimes freely chooses, yet sometimes is battered by storms both physical and emotional? What is this 'I' that asks to be loved? 'Love me for *me*, not for my coquettish walk and whimsical ways.'

One way of seeing the absurdity residing in 'I' is via the thought experiments found in Locke and Thomas Reid and enhanced in recent decades by Williams, Parfit and Zuboff.[24] One saga from

---

[22] This gives rise to a paradox of contrary choice, or self-knowlege. See 'Mary, Mary, quite contrary' in Cave, *This Sentence is False*, 153–5.
[23] Richard Dawkins, *The Selfish Gene*, 30th anniversary edition (Oxford: Oxford University Press, 2006), 332.
[24] Bernard Williams, *Problems of the Self* (Cambridge: Cambridge University Press, 1973), Derek Parfit, *Reasons and Persons* (Oxford: Oxford University Press, 1984), and Arnold Zuboff, 'One Self: The Logic of Experience', *Inquiry* **33** (1990) 39–68. For a presentation of how

Williams involves your knowing that someone will be tortured tomorrow, but needing to establish whether that someone will be you. That someone will be a person with all your psychological states, yet not your body – or with your body but none of your psychological states. The puzzle comes down to the following dilemma, assuming you lack yen for torture. 'Should I hope that *this* body is not tortured, whatever the psychological states, or should I hope that whichever body carries these psychological states is not tortured?' Neither 'continuity of body' nor 'continuity of psychological states' seems an essential condition for me to be me. Even if we see identity as depending on the disjunction of those two conditions, we still encounter familiar replication and fission thought experiments that can leave us baffled.

Moving away from such metaphysical speculations, we muddle through more practically with regard to how we view our 'true identity'. Athletes seek fairness in sport: we want to see what runners can truly achieve 'by themselves'. Performance-enhancing drugs are banned; yet not performance-enhancing training. We muddle through, often pretending there is clarity, when in fact there is chaos, cloaked chaos.

Stepping outside

The three life puzzles mentioned – love, free will, and self – all involve the absurdity or clash that arises when the attached vantage points meet the detached. Attached, Larry loves this Ludmilla; yet if he could step back, anyone similar should do. Attached, I praise and blame others and myself, yet stepping back, I may see all the actions as caused and outside the agents' free control. Attached, well, we cannot help speaking of ourselves, yet, detached, we become at a loss over what to identify as the 'self'.

For a final piece of absurdity arising through stepping back, seeking further detachment, we meet Pushkin, a cat once owned by John McTaggart Ellis McTaggart, the distinguished Cambridge philosopher.[25] In cold winters, surrounded by the snows or winds of the Fens, people who visited McTaggart's college rooms would be

---

to some extent we may be the same person, and to some extent not, see Ardon Lyon, 'Problems of Personal Identity' in G. H. R. Parkinson (ed.) *An Encyclopaedia of Philosophy* (London: Routledge, 1988), 441–62.

[25] These considerations are taken from my *What's Wrong with Eating People: 33 More Perplexing Philosophy Puzzles* (Oxford: Oneworld, 2008). Such muddles are also discussed in my *Humanism* op. cit. note 1.

Peter Cave

astonished to see his cat enjoying pride of position fireside front, while McTaggart shivered in a corner. 'Why ever do you give the cat the best position?' they would ask. 'Because,' replied McTaggart, 'that's the best it gets for a cat.'

We reflect on life. We reflect not just in philosophy seminars, but at work, at dinner – and in the stillness of nights without sleep. Of course, sometimes we may feel the feline life is preferable. I remember the reflection well from my mother, when the going was tough. None the less, most of us value being a person far more than being a cat. Only we humans can investigate and evaluate, aware that we so do. Only we humans can explore skies so high and oceans so deep. Only we humans can marvel and wonder at fact and fancy. We discover mathematical truths and apply them to the world; we send our imaginations soaring through art, literature and music. We demonstrate kindness, loyalty and beauty – and laugh at jokes. There is far more to human life than to the feline. We value them more.

We stepped outside lives to evaluate the human over the feline, just as Hume so stepped when concluding that man's life is of no greater importance to the universe than an oyster's. Indeed, Sophocles' detachment led him to speculate that the happiest are those not to have been born. Some of us cannot resist seeking a vantage point detached, undistorted by preferences and position, yet which is still, incongruously, a vantage point from which to evaluate. That probably is without sense, yet we readily recognize degrees of distortion in our views of the world. Think of the head spinning after too much partying, of thoughts clouded by current woes. We step outside in order to see more clearly, or to see the bigger picture or a picture un-spun; but once we push on further, we fall into obscurities, of maybe wanting to choose what sort of people to be, yet with no basis on which to choose.

A mouse's life, as Thomas Nagel writes, is not absurd; a human life is.[26] A mouse's life contains no incongruity; a human's does. The mouse scurries about, satisfying desires, never stepping outside her life for the bigger picture, never reflecting on the significance of her scurry. We humans can – or think we can – step outside, taking up a more detached vantage point, be it from the universe's edge, or from nowhere at all. There indeed we reach the absurdity, the clash, between the importance we give to our life and its seeming unimportance from outside. Yet, no sense can be made of mattering, or not mattering, from a viewpoint that is really neither point nor view.

[26] Thomas Nagel, *Mortal Questions* (Cambridge: Cambridge University Press, 1976).

'What if in reality my whole life has been wrong?' That question, asked by Tolstoy's Ivan Illyich, may make us uneasy. As we grow older, we may become ashamed of our past: we may reflect on wasted years, spot mistaken turnings, recognizing occasions when we failed to stand up for what we believed. Our lives, as wholes, may be judged to be seriously wrong compared with standards once embraced or embraced now. We may even try to step outside our lives, wondering whether all our standards – our desires, aspirations, lives – are themselves all wrong. Some then shudder, repent, and turn to God as eternal judge. Humanists, of course, reject the eternal judge. Yet, with or without the judge, there exists a mish-mash of recognized values: freedom, happiness, promise-keeping, respect, rights, welfare, mercy – and virtues, such as courage, generosity, justice. There are finer values: courtesy, decency, beauty and grace. What should we do when such concerns conflict, as, unnoticed, they often do, and, noticed, they sometimes do? What indeed should we do when concern for just a single value generates conflict – when, for example, if Orson soothes Andrea, Zoe is distressed; and if he soothes Zoe, Andrea is distressed.

'It is a matter of judgement', some say. True, we want to *judge*, not decide on throws of some dice or whims of the day; but how do we judge? When judges with expertise and experience, in the House of Lords or the American Supreme Court, speak of weighing the evidence, balancing factors, yet reach opposite conclusions – with three judges, for example, concluding that free speech was infringed and two judges concluding the opposite – is accepting the majority view as the right answer any better than spinning a coin? We may also note that, had certain other expert judges been appointed or been sitting, then the overall decision could well have been different. More mundanely, people seek fairness in, for example, parking fines; yet what constitutes fairness here? Should fines be at a fixed level, or should they vary according to vehicle size or value, driver's income or wealth? With moral dilemmas, people often think that, detached, there must be *the* answer, determining which one of various alternatives ought to be taken, given the circumstances. Often, though, there is, in that sense, no right answer. It is not as if there is some path that is the one right path, known by God, but undiscoverable by humans who are too attached, too involved, in the happenings. It is difficult to believe that even an all-knowing God would know the 'right' way and level to set parking fines.[27]

---

[27] Perhaps I should not be so doubtful. With regard to the Sorites puzzles, some hold the curious epistemic position that there really are sharp dividing lines between heaps and non-heaps and between reds and oranges, though we cannot spot them: see Cave, *This Sentence is False*, 80–1.

Peter Cave

*

Humanists accuse godly believers of absurdities, yet, as maybe seen above, we all live lives with some absurdities – with some conflicting perspectives. We face ethical dilemmas: we juggle incommensurable factors from different vantage points. We may be bewitched by the desire for the black or white, yet right answers often involve 'to some degree' and 'in some respects'. There are many examples, from voting procedures to taxation, where fairness and reasonableness have to be invoked, yet where what counts as fair and reasonable can be moveable posts or areas of greyness. What weight do we, or ought we to give to mantras such as 'everyone has a right to life,' when we choose expenditure on the arts, or vote for reduced taxation, instead of more aid for those suffering badly, the dispossessed of the world?

Although we cannot live without judging on such matters as the above, without speaking of 'I', without assessing others and ourselves, losing the self often helps to give meaning to our lives. Whatever we enjoy – be it immersion in philosophical thought, laughing at banana skin slips, reading novels, moving with music, playing the piano, even watching football – when we look back, we often discover that we were lost in the reflections, the story, the emotions, the music, the game. Religious believers, indeed, can be lost in their faith. When the last page is turned, or the credits roll or the applause thunders, we are brought up sharp, brought back to the world. This is most odd; it may even tempt us to think that, after all, there is a lot to be said for the life of the non-reflective Pushkin, even for the Sophoclean 'the happiest are those never to have been born' – for then one's 'self' is truly lost. Yet we know well that here lies mystery, that things are not as simple as that. In some way, we were aware of enjoying the novel, the play, the music – and yet, in another way, we did not exist, save in as far as we were distracted by some whispering or sensations of overheating. Such mysteries provide a pull towards the mystical.

We can lose ourselves in our everyday lives, unaware of the absurdity. Step back and reflect on those lives: now the absurdities, tensions and muddles mentioned above fill our view; but they too have value for many of us. We may smile wryly. Pity Pushkin: he knows of no absurdities, of no smiles. Yet pity us too – for we cannot know for certain how our lives finally work out.

'Pity us', did I say?

Knowledge of how our lives are ultimately viewed, if viewed at all – from a detached vantage point – may be knowledge best not to possess; but what is worth having is the mishmash, the muddles, the mêlée of life itself. With philosophy an analytical and reflective art, we have here engaged reflection. It is, though, fitting to emphasize that *not* reflecting also brings value, brings meaning. There can be paradoxical delight in simply surrendering, as perhaps Pushkin does, to mosaics of colours and sounds, from scuffling leaves and storms of snow to a skylark ascending over a heath. There is charm in saying nothing, in saying nothing at all. There is charm in – experiencing.

And yet religious believers seek more – they seek the divine, the eternal, to bring forth meaning. Well, humanists have little scope for the eternal. All the things we value, however rare, however small, that give point or meaning to our lives – the friendships, loves and absurdities; those soundscaped memories entwined with shared entrancings and glances that magically ensnare and enfold; the intoxications of wines and words, and wayward musings and music, even city sounds, with which we wrestle into misty slumbering nights, our senses revived by sparkling waters, much needed at dawn; the seascapes of wild waves, mysterious moonlights and images and widening skies that stretch the eyes – do indeed all cease to exist; and curiously the most enchanting are, as implied, oft those within which we lose ourselves and also cease to be – yet that they, and we, existed at some time remains timelessly true, outside of all time.

For lovers of eternity – of the 'beyond' – that is as good as it gets. And that good manifests another absurdity – incongruity, puzzle – for here on Earth we have sense of the abstract, of the timelessly true; here on Earth we image the fish and their unlanded heavenly land, their pond beyond; and here on Earth we smile at such tales, smile at such absurdity, feeling better for the smile – and for the absurdity.

Fat caterpillars drift around,
And Paradisal grubs are found;
Unfading moths, immortal flies,
And the worm that never dies.
And in that Heaven of all their wish,
There shall be no more land, say fish.

The Open University

149

Twenty Questions about Hume's "Of Miracles"*

PETER MILLICAN

Hume's essay on the credibility of miracle reports has always been controversial,[1] with much debate over how it should be interpreted, let alone assessed. My aim here is to summarise what I take to be the most plausible views on these issues, both interpretative and philosophical, with references to facilitate deeper investigation if desired. The paper is divided into small sections, each headed by a question that provides a focus. Broadly speaking, §§1–3 and §20 are on Hume's general philosophical framework within which the essay is situated, §§4–11 and §19 are on Part 1, §12–18 are on Part 2, and the final three sections §§18–20 sum up my assessment of his arguments.

1. Is "Of Miracles" Consistent with Hume's Inductive Scepticism?

Hume's discussion of miracles is commonly alleged to be in serious tension with the somewhat sceptical views developed earlier in both the *Treatise* and the *Enquiry*.[2] Traditionally, he has been interpreted as an extreme sceptic about induction, one who argues that "as far

* This paper was completed whilst enjoying the delightful hospitality and stimulating environment of the Institute for Advanced Studies in the Humanities (IASH) at Edinburgh, in the role of Illumni David Hume Fellow. I am profoundly grateful to the Edinburgh Illumni and to IASH for giving me this opportunity. I should also like to express my appreciation of innumerable helpful discussions with members of the excellent Hume Society, with particular thanks to Lorne Falkenstein, Don Garrett, and David Owen.

[1]   Hume's *Enquiry* was originally published as *Philosophical Essays concerning Human Understanding*. Hence Section 10, which provoked controversy right from the start, quickly became known as his "essay" on miracles.
[2]   For example by Broad (1917, p. 92), Flew (1961, p. 171), and Larmer (1996, pp. 29–32).

doi:10.1017/S1358246111000105

as the competition for degrees of reasonableness is concerned, all possible beliefs about the unobserved are tied for last place" (Stroud 1977, p. 54). And if this is his view, then the case he makes in "Of Miracles" – that miracle stories cannot be inductively established – seems a pointless exercise. To such an undiscriminating sceptic, belief in Jesus's resurrection, or a weeping statue, or any other alleged miracle, must be no less (and no more) justified than commonplace inductive beliefs such as that the Sun will rise tomorrow, or that my pen will fall if released in mid-air. Is he not then simply inconsistent in comparing miracle stories unfavourably with everyday and scientific inductions?

If there is indeed an inconsistency here, however, this is more a difficulty for Hume's philosophy of induction than for his position on miracles. Most of his work – from the *Treatise*, through the *Essays* and *Enquiries*, to the *History* and the later works on religion – is thoroughly infused with the empirical scientific spirit of an investigator attempting "to introduce the experimental method of reasoning into moral subjects" (as declared by the subtitle of the *Treatise*). In this respect, the inductive commitment of his essay on miracles is entirely typical. And in fact there is no inconsistency between Hume's philosophy of induction and his empirical method; quite the reverse. His inductive "scepticism" – as presented in Sections 4 and 5 of the *Enquiry*, is encapsulated in the claim "that, in all reasonings from experience, there is a step taken by the mind, which is not supported by any argument or process of the understanding" (E 5.2). This unsupported step – the assumption of uniformity whereby we extrapolate from observed to unobserved and "expect similar effects from causes, which are, to appearance, similar" (E 4.23) – has instead a non-rational basis, in an animal instinct which Hume calls *custom* (E 5.6). Later, in Section 9, he goes on to highlight the corollary, that human inference to facts about the unobserved is fundamentally similar to that of the animals, based not on rational insight into how things behave, but instead on a crude natural instinct to expect more of the same. All this has a sceptical potential which Hume fully recognises (E 12.22), but he does not follow it through by claiming that all induction is equally worthless, and instead proceeds to build *positively* on his crucial result, by emphasising our *need* for the assumption of uniformity rather than its non-rational basis. Any sceptic who urges us to discard it "must acknowledge, if he will acknowledge any thing, that all human life must perish, were his principles universally and steadily to prevail" (E 12.23). So we are stuck with the assumption of uniformity, because we cannot live without it and are anyway psychologically unable to abandon it; moreover the sceptic can provide no persuasive reason why we should not rest content with it. Though not itself rationally founded, therefore, it is worthy of our assent, and is even able to provide an appropriate criterion of rational empirical judgement. Thus the upshot of Hume's "mitigated scepticism" (*E* 12.24) is not to undermine human reason, but rather to bring us face to face with its nature and humble animal origins. Induction remains "that reasoning, which can alone assure us of any matter of fact or existence" (*E* 7.27), and hence it is on induction that we must rely if we are to have any well-founded belief concerning such matters of fact as the trustworthiness of reporters and the occurrence (or non-occurrence) of miracles. There is thus no inconsistency whatever between Hume's "scepticism" concerning induction and his inductive assessment of the evidence for miracles.

2. What Does Hume Mean by "Probability" and "Proof"?

Even once the general principle of inductive extrapolation from observed to unobserved has been accepted, such inference is not always straightforward, because our experience does not always follow consistent patterns. Section 6 of the *Enquiry*, "Of Probability", considers how psychological associative processes, analogous to custom, operate to generate proportionate degrees of belief in such cases. But it is at the beginning of his discussion of miracles that Hume casts this issue most clearly into a *normative* light, showing how a commitment to induction can point the way towards appropriately *rational* judgements. Observation teaches us that some patterns in our experience have been uniform, whereas others have varied; hence induction itself should lead us to expect a similar mix of uniformity and variety in the future. Hume accordingly draws a distinction between induction from phenomena which have been "found, in all countries and all ages, to have been constantly conjoined together", and induction from those which "have been more variable" (*E* 10.3). In the next paragraph, he uses some technical terminology to capture this distinction, a refinement of a standard dichotomy inherited from John Locke.

Locke's *Essay concerning Human Understanding* of 1690 had influentially drawn the distinction between *demonstrative* and *probable* reasoning (*Essay* IV xv 1), roughly equivalent to the modern distinction between *deductive* and *inductive* arguments. In *Treatise* Book 1 Hume follows this Lockean usage, but at *T* 1.3.11.2 he remarks that it is infelicitous, in a passage largely repeated in the *Enquiry*:

Peter Millican

> Mr. Locke divides all arguments into demonstrative and probable. In this view, we must say, that it is only probable all men must die, or that the sun will rise to-morrow. But to conform our language more to common use, we ought to divide arguments into *demonstrations*, *proofs*, and *probabilities*. By proofs meaning such arguments from experience as leave no room for doubt or opposition. (*E* 6.0 n. 10 – footnote to the heading of Section 6 "Of Probability")

In the *Enquiry*, Hume accordingly reserves the term "probable" for inferences specifically from *inconstant* experience.[3] And so he speaks instead of "moral reasoning" or "reasoning concerning matter of fact" when he wishes to refer to the broader Lockean category of non-demonstrative reasoning, which encompasses both *probabilities* and *proofs*. A proof, thus understood, is an inference from *constantly repeated and exceptionless* experience, such as my inference that the sun will rise tomorrow, based on my uniform experience of its having risen every day in the past. It is this technical sense of "proof" which Hume intends throughout his discussion of miracles, for example in the famous passage that immediately follows the *E* 10.3 paragraph quoted above:[4]

> A wise man, therefore, proportions his belief to the evidence. In such conclusions as are founded on an infallible experience, he ... regards his past experience as a full *proof* of the future existence of that event. In other cases, he proceeds with more caution: ... He considers which side is supported by the greater number of experiments: To that side he inclines, with doubt and hesitation; and when at last he fixes his judgment, the evidence exceeds not what we properly call *probability*. All probability, then, supposes an opposition of experiments and observations, where the one side is found to overbalance the other, and to produce a degree of evidence, proportioned to the superiority. (*E* 10.4)

The remainder of Section 10 is devoted to spelling out the implications of this prescription of wisdom, as applied to the specific case of testimony for supposed miracles.

---

[3] With the exception of *E* 4.19, which refers to "probable arguments" in the broader Lockean sense.
[4] The *Enquiry* does sometimes use the term in a more everyday sense, for example at *E* 7.14, 8.14, 8.22 n. 18, 11.30.

3. Is "Of Miracles" Philosophically Serious, or a Scurrilous Addition?

Sir Amherst Selby-Bigge, in the Introduction to his edition (1894, §5 and §12), influentially alleged that Hume included the discussion of miracles in the first *Enquiry* merely to spice up the work and provoke public notoriety, rather than for any serious philosophical purpose. But this dismissive judgement is quite wrong. First, the essay is of significant philosophical interest in its own right, and provides the most developed application of Hume's theory of induction to a case of conflicting evidence, showing how in practice he combines his general epistemology of mitigated scepticism with normative critical standards.[5] Secondly, his choice of topic for this role is by no means gratuitous, because testimony was central to the early-modern discussion of non-demonstrative evidence, as one of the two *grounds of probability* identified by Locke:

> ... The *grounds of [Probability]*, are, in short, these *two* following: *First*, The conformity of any thing with our own Knowledge, Observation, and Experience. *Secondly*, The Testimony of others, vouching their Observation and Experience. (*Essay* IV xv 4)

So it is quite natural that Hume – having devoted Sections 4–6 of the *Enquiry* to the first of these grounds (i.e. conformity with our own observation and experience) – should go on to discuss testimony. And it is also entirely typical of the time that such a discussion should culminate with a consideration of miracles, just as it had with Locke:

> Though the common Experience, and the ordinary Course of Things have justly a mighty Influence on the Minds of Men, ... yet there is one Case, wherein the strangeness of the Fact lessens not the Assent to a fair Testimony given of it. For where such supernatural Events are suitable to ends aim'd at by him, who has the Power to change the course of Nature, there, under such Circumstances, they may be the fitter to

---

[5]   This illustrates the point made in §1 above, that Humean "inductive scepticism" is entirely compatible with drawing distinctions between strong and weak inductive evidence (according to how well each inference conforms to the basic assumption of underlying uniformity). His "scepticism" is not indiscriminate, because he insists that the Pyrrhonian's "undistinguished doubts" should be "corrected by common sense and reflection" (*E* 12.24)

procure Belief, by how much the more they are beyond, or contrary to ordinary Observation. This is the proper Case of *Miracles* ... (*Essay* IV xvi 13)

Hume wholeheartedly agrees with Locke that, in general, claims contrary to "the ordinary Course of Things" are to that extent less credible. Where he most conspicuously differs from Locke is in denying that miracles should constitute any exception to this general rule.

4. Is Hume Right to Treat Testimonial Evidence as Inductive?

Hume's treatment of testimony starts by applying his previously-stated principles of probability:

> To apply these principles to a particular instance; we may observe, that there is no species of reasoning more common, more useful, and even necessary to human life, than that which is derived from the testimony of men ... our assurance in any argument of this kind is derived from no other principle than our observation of the veracity of human testimony, and of the usual conformity of facts to the reports of witnesses. (*E* 10.5)

He then follows through his argument of *Enquiry* Section 4 by insisting that the "general maxim" (*E* 10.5) established there – that all inference to unobserved matters of fact depends on extrapolation from experience – applies just as much to testimonial evidence as to any other. So while Locke treated testimony as a second, and apparently independent, "ground of probability", Hume effectively reduces it to a form of inductive evidence.[6] He goes on to refine this approach, by taking into account the specific nature of the testimony:

> And as the evidence, derived from witnesses and human testimony, is founded on past experience, so it varies with the experience, and is regarded either as a *proof* or a *probability*, according as the conjunction between any particular kind of report and any kind of object has been found to be constant or variable. ... Where ... experience is not entirely uniform on any side, it is attended with an unavoidable contrariety in our judgments, and with the same opposition and mutual destruction of argument as in every other kind of evidence. ...

---

[6]   The same treatment is sketched in the *Treatise* at *T* 1.3.9.12, which briefly anticipates its application to miracles.

> This contrariety of evidence ... may be derived from several different causes; from the opposition of contrary testimony; from the character or number of the witnesses; from the manner of their delivering their testimony; or from the union of all these circumstances. ... There are many other particulars of the same kind, which may diminish or destroy the force of any argument, derived from human testimony. (*E* 10.6–7)

Again we see echoes of Locke, who had mentioned the "Number", "Integrity", and "Skill" of the witnesses, and the "Consistency" and "Circumstances" of the testimony (*Essay* IV xv 4), but gave no indication of how these are to be weighed against each other. Hume fills this gap by explaining – consistently with his inductive methodology – that any such judgement should depend on how reliable the testimony of each kind has actually turned out to be in practical experience.

It is sometimes objected that testimony cannot be "reduced" to induction in this way, because it serves as a fundamental source of information which must be accepted as reliable from the start if we are ever to learn anything significant.[7] Hume's own discussion, moreover, seems to take for granted that we know from personal experience various things – such as that all men must die (*E* 6.0 n.10) – which in practice are known almost entirely on the basis of others' testimony and hence *their* experience. So unless we start by accepting that their testimony can be relied on, it seems that we cannot acquire this broader experience on which our inductions are supposed to be based. Fortunately we know Hume's response to this objection, which was pressed by George Campbell (1762, I §2, pp. 37–8). In a 1761 letter to Hugh Blair (who had sent him Campbell's manuscript), Hume implicitly acknowledges that his use of "experience" is ambiguous:

> Sect. II. No man can have any other experience but his own. The experience of others becomes his only by the credit which he gives to their testimony; which proceeds from his own experience of human nature. (*HL* i 349; Hume 1748, p. 165)

Here he appears to be saying that although *strictly*, all experience is personal, nevertheless facts attested by those one trusts (such trust being based on personal experience) can *appropriately* be accorded the same honorific status. He also makes similar remarks in the

---

[7]   See in particular Coady (1973; 1992, ch. 4). Traiger (1993) mounts a defence, arguing that Hume does not presuppose an epistemically individualist and reductionist conception of testimony.

Enquiry itself and in his essay "Of the Study of History" (para. 6), saying how reading and conversation can "enlarge ... the sphere" of our experience (*E* 9.5 n. 20) and even "extends our experience to all past ages" (*Essays*, p. 566). In "Of Miracles", at least, the ambiguity indeed seems harmless. After all, Hume is not here taking issue with ordinary facts founded on widespread and concurrent reports: these are not in dispute, and so can be accepted as though they were personally experienced. The debate concerns only claims that are generally recognised to be extraordinary, outside the common course of nature, and moreover widely disputed. Someone might reasonably decide to investigate these kinds of claims more critically than others, but there is no reason why suspension of belief in them should imply any general rejection of testimony. Indeed one reasonable way of proceeding might be to develop the inductive measures that Hume recommends, by assessing – both on the basis of our own personal experience *and* the accepted testimony of others (including, possibly, academic literature on cognitive biases) – what kinds of testimony are most to be trusted. In short, Hume has no need to dispute the claim that we must start by taking testimony for granted to build our knowledge of the world.[8] But this in no way impugns his proposed targeted investigation of testimony for alleged miracles, nor his pursuing that investigation on inductive principles.

5. How Does Hume Apply these Principles to the Case of Miracles?

It is only after having set out his general approach to the assessment of testimony, and having drawn attention to a range of relevant factors (as quoted from *E* 10.6–7 above), that Hume turns his attention – in the very next sentence – towards the topic of the miraculous:

> Suppose, for instance, that the fact, which the testimony endeavours to establish, partakes of the extraordinary and the marvellous; in that case, the evidence, resulting from the testimony, admits of a diminution, greater or less, in proportion as the fact is more less unusual. (*E* 10.8)

Here the unusualness of the reported event is identified as one additional factor that bears on the credibility of testimonial reports.

---

[8]   Moreover the first sentence of *E* 10.5, quoted at the beginning of §4 above, suggests that he agrees. Note also his comment at *E* 10.28 that "some human testimony has the utmost force and authority in some cases".

But Hume then immediately isolates this particular factor, and views it as balanced *on the other side of the scale* against the characteristics of the testimony that incline us to believe it. He soon goes on to present the most extreme possible case of such "counterpoize" (*E* 10.8), where the reported fact

> instead of being only marvellous, is really miraculous; and ... *the testimony, considered apart and in itself,* amounts to an entire proof; in that case, there is proof against proof, of which the strongest must prevail, but still with a diminution of its force, in proportion to that of its antagonist. (*E* 10.11; my emphasis).

Two very important points should be noted here. First, Hume's argument so far has treated a miracle as just an extreme case of an extraordinary event, and the general principles involved in this treatment are no different from those that he applies to any other extraordinary event. Secondly, in sketching out how the counterpoise takes place, Hume has understood the strength of the testimony – "considered apart and in itself" – as yielding a single overall measure of *proof* which can then appropriately be weighed against the strength of the counter-proof that arises from the unusualness of the alleged event. The stronger of these two proofs "must prevail, but still with a diminution of its force, in proportion to that of its antagonist". So the confidence we place in the testimony (or – depending on which way the scales point – in the inductive evidence against the supposed event) will depend on the extent to which the testimonial proof (or alternatively the proof from experience) over-balances its antagonist. The picture that results is something like this:

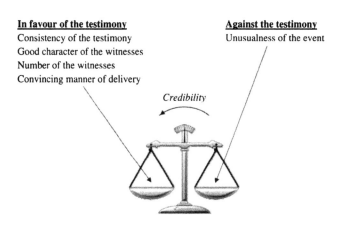

In favour of the testimony	Against the testimony
Consistency of the testimony	Unusualness of the event
Good character of the witnesses	
Number of the witnesses	
Convincing manner of delivery	

Credibility

Peter Millican

Thus the *overall* credibility depends on this contest between *the proof constituted by the inductive evidence in favour of the testimony "considered apart and in itself"* (weighing down on the left-hand tray) and *the proof constituted by the uniform evidence of nature against the reported event* (weighing down on the right-hand tray). We have "proof against proof", with the overall credibility given not by either "proof" individually, but by the result of weighing them against each other.[9] In the setup illustrated above, this will be indicated by the direction of the pointer at the top of the scales once they have settled.

6. Does it Make Sense to Weigh "Entire Proofs" Against Each Other?

All this should seem fairly commonsensical, as long as we are careful to remember that Hume is using the term "proof" in the technical sense explained in §2 above. In this sense, even an "entire proof" can – without contradiction – be outweighed by another proof that is stronger, a point that he explains further in the 1761 letter to Blair:

> The proof against a miracle, as it is founded on invariable experience, is of that *species* or *kind* of proof, which is full and certain when taken alone, because it implies no doubt, as is the case with all probabilities; but there are degrees of this species, and when a weaker proof is opposed to a stronger, it is overcome. (*HL* i 350; Hume 1748, p. 165)

Hume does not spell out in detail how the strength of a "proof" is to be assessed, but much of what he says – both in the *Enquiry* (e.g. *E* 6.4, 10.4) and in the *Treatise* (e.g. *T* 1.3.11.5, 1.3.12.15) – suggests a model based rather crudely on numbers of instances. Suppose I experience an *A* which is *B*, then another, then yet another, and so on. "The first instance has little or no force: The second makes some addition to it: The third becomes still more sensible

---

[9]   This point is very clear from Hume's text, and refutes outright the interpretation of John Earman (2000, p. 41; 2002, p. 97), which would instead involve a calculation, *prior* to the weighing operation, of two overall judgements – namely the conditional probability (given the testimony) of the event, and of its absence – which are then put in the balance against each other. For more on Earman, see Millican (2003) and cf. also Millican (2007a, pp. 170–1 n. 9).

[i.e. noticeable]; and 'tis by these slow steps, that our judgment arrives at a full assurance" (*T* 1.3.12.2). If this pattern continues, and every *A* that I encounter is a *B*, then eventually my consistent experience will constitute an "entire proof", enabling me to go on inferring with complete confidence that each subsequent *A* will be a *B* also. But the "gradation from probabilities to proofs is in many cases insensible", and there seems to be no clear line where the one changes into the other.[10]

Perhaps this absence of a clear line between "probability" and "proof" is unimportant, given that Hume's notion of proof itself involves – as we have seen – a flexible rather than absolute standard. In line with his letter to Blair, it seems appropriate to interpret a "proof" as involving experiential evidence so strong that, were it standing alone without any countervailing evidence on the other side, it would suffice to give a reasonable person "full assurance" without any element of doubt. There are plenty of everyday cases where we feel such assurance (e.g. my confidence that the Hertford College "Bridge of Sighs" did not rotate in the air last night), but this need not involve a denial of *any possibility* of error.[11] I can recognise that Descartes' evil demon, a mischievous wizard, or divine action are all *epistemological possibilities*, but that alone will not lead me to harbour any doubts about the Bridge of Sighs' nocturnal movements. However I could perhaps *imagine* testimonial evidence so strong as to dent this complete confidence, and if such were to come my way, I would be faced with the sort of contest of "proofs" that Hume envisages. So far, therefore, his position seems to make reasonable sense.

---

[10] Hume's wording suggests that the line will be crossed at the point when "our judgment arrives at a full assurance", a psychological rather than normative criterion. But it seems quite plausible that "full assurance" should eventually become normatively appropriate given sufficient accumulation of evidence, especially given our practical incapacity for reliably assessing, or reasoning in terms of, tiny probabilities (e.g. it does not seem feasible to maintain a psychological doubt corresponding accurately to a probability of one in a thousand, let alone one in a million).

[11] Nor does Hume treat it as effectively conferring an error probability of "flatly zero", as claimed by Earman (2000, p. 23; cf. 2002, p. 95), which would beg the question against any miracle report by ruling out from the start any possibility of testimony outweighing such a proof. Fogelin (2003, pp. 43–53) rightly attacks Earman's claim.

Peter Millican

7. How Should Hume's Maxim be Interpreted in Probabilistic Terms?

Just two paragraphs after explaining his balancing of proofs, Hume reaches the famous Maxim which is the culmination of Section 10 Part 1:

Hume's Maxim

The plain consequence is (and it is a general maxim worthy of our attention), "That no testimony is sufficient to establish a miracle, unless the testimony be of such a kind, that its falsehood would be more miraculous, than the fact, which it endeavours to establish; ..." (E 10.13)[12]

One might think that evidence "sufficient to *establish*" some event would need to prove it beyond reasonable doubt, but it seems clear from the context that Hume is requiring only that it should render the event *more probable than not*:

When any one tells me, that he saw a dead man restored to life, I immediately consider with myself, *whether it be more probable*, that this person should either deceive or be deceived, or that the fact, which he relates, should really have happened. *I weigh the one miracle against the other*, and according to the superiority, which I discover, I pronounce my decision, *and always reject the*

---

[12]   Here, for simplicity, I am considering "Hume's Maxim" as being only the first part of the relevant sentence, which continues: "... And even in that case, there is a mutual destruction of arguments, and the superior only gives us an assurance suitable to that degree of force, which remains, after deducting the inferior." For a discussion of this second part, see Millican (2003, §7). In brief, Hume's talk of the "mutual destruction of arguments" (in a situation where the testimony's falsehood is even less likely than the miraculous event) can be given a clear and coherent mathematical interpretation, in terms of an inductive "credibility" measure which varies between 1 and -1, and whose value is typically assessed (in line with the inductive "straight rule") by the balance of positive over negative instances divided by the total number of instances, i.e. $(p-n)/(p+n)$. Such an interpretation is suggested by T 1.3.11.9–13, and this same measure can be applied in the case of convincing testimony for miracles by treating p as the initial probability of the miraculous event (e.g. 3 in a billion) and n as the initial probability of the testimony's falsehood (e.g. 1 in a billion). This then gives a very good approximation to the probability suggested by the mathematics of §8 (and note 16) below, translating from credibility (0.5 in this case) to conventional probability (0.75) using the formula $P = (C + 1)/2$.

greater miracle. If the falsehood of his testimony would be more miraculous, than the event which he relates; *then, and not till then, can he pretend to command my belief or opinion*. (*E* 10.13, my emphasis)

The first two sentences here assume an unsurprising inverse relationship between degrees of probability and of miraculousness. And only in the case of an exact tie, it seems, will Hume fail to "pronounce his decision" in favour of the more probable event (thus rejecting the greater miracle). Hence if the testimony's falsehood is more improbable than the supposedly miraculous event – even by a tiny fraction – "*then ... can [the testifier] pretend to command my belief or opinion*".[13]

Bearing these points in mind, Hume's Maxim can be translated into probabilistic terms as follows:

It is a general maxim ... "That no testimony is sufficient to render a miracle more probable than not, unless the testimony be of such a kind, that its falsehood would be even less probable, than the fact, which it endeavours to establish ..." (adapted from *E* 10.13)

Its intended basis is clear, because Hume's discussion sets up a trial of strength between the human testimony and the inductive "testimony of experience" (concerning what happens in nature, independently of the testimony). The testimony we are considering in the crucial case is exceptionally strong, of a type whose typical probability of falsehood f is tiny. But here this exceptional kind of testimony has been presented in favour of an event of a type M whose expected probability of occurrence m is also tiny. Nevertheless the testimony for M has been presented, so we have "proof against proof", and one of these tiny probabilities must be actualised. Either M genuinely occurred, in which case the human testimony is true and the inductive testimony of experience is "false", or alternatively M did not occur, in which case the human testimony is false and the inductive testimony of experience is "true". Understood in this way, the overall credibility of the miracle report indeed seems to reduce to a straightforward comparison of strength between the human testimony and the testimony of experience. Hume's derivation of his Maxim accordingly seems very straightforward, concluding that we should believe a miracle-report only if f (the probability of such testimony's being

---

[13]   This suggests that Hume intends his Maxim as both a necessary *and* sufficient condition for credibility of miracle stories, though his initial wording implies only a necessary condition. In what follows, I ignore this complication.

Peter Millican

false) is even less than m (the probability of such an event's occurring).

8. Can Hume's Maxim be Derived Mathematically?

All this might seem to justify Hume's Maxim, but there is a key assumption underlying his argument, to which I have already drawn attention in §5 above (and which is clearly presupposed by his talk of the testimony "considered apart and in itself", and "testimony ... of such a kind ..."):

Hume's Independence Assumption
Different "kinds" of testimony (specified in terms of the character and number of the witnesses, their consistency and manner of delivery etc.) carry a different typical probability of truth and falsehood *independently of the event reported*.

To see the importance of this assumption, suppose instead that it were not possible to identify "kinds" of testimony with their own typical probability of truth and falsehood. In that case, when speaking of "the probability of the testimony" we could only be referring properly to the probability of a *particular item* of testimony (i.e. a "token" rather than a "type"),[14] which asserts the occurrence of one *particular event*, and since that item of testimony would be true if, and only if, the event truly occurred, this would make it impossible to separate coherently *the probability of the testimony* from *the probability of the event*. Hume's Maxim would then at best be trivial.[15]

If, on the other hand, we adopt the Independence Assumption, then the Maxim can be derived very plausibly. To see this, let us as before focus on a particular kind of testimony – whose typical probability of falsehood is f – which on some occasion either asserts, or denies, the occurrence of a particular type of event M – whose

[14] Those who have tried to understand Hume's Maxim in probabilistic terms have generally overlooked this crucial distinction between a "type" and a "token" interpretation as introduced in Millican (1993, pp. 490, 495 n. 8). In Millican (2003) I argue in detail against the interpretations of Earman (2000, 2002), Gillies (1991), Holder (1998), Howson (2000), and Sobel (1991), though it now seems to me that *any* such "token" interpretation is ultimately bound to be inadequate for the simple reason given here, so detailed discussion of the mathematics is superfluous.
[15] As critics from George Campbell (1762, I §6, pp. 99–103) to John Earman (2000, p. 41; 2002, p. 97) have alleged. But this is certainly a misinterpretation, as pointed out in §5 above (cf. especially note 9).

probability of occurrence is m. If the reliability of that kind of testimony is probabilistically independent of what is being reported, then we can apparently calculate the probability of a "true positive" and a "false positive" report as follows:

True positive (miracle occurs, and is truly reported)

$$Pr(M \ \& \ t(M)) = Pr(M) \times Pr(true\ report) = m.(1 - f)$$

False positive (miracle does not occur, but is falsely reported as having occurred)

$$Pr(\neg M \ \& \ t(M)) = Pr(\neg M) \times Pr(false\ report) = (1 - m).f$$

If positive testimony has been given, therefore, this testimony will be probably true only if a "false positive" is less likely than a "true positive", and hence in accordance with the formula:

$$Pr(M/t(M)) > 0.5 \rightarrow (1 - m).f < m.(1 - f)$$

which simplifies to:

$$Pr(M/t(M)) > 0.5 \rightarrow f < m.$$

This result neatly corresponds to Hume's Maxim, since its right-hand side is exactly equivalent to saying that *the falsehood of the testimony, considered apart and in itself* is more miraculous (i.e. less probable) than *the event reported, considered independently of the testimony*.[16]

9. Is Hume's Maxim of Practical Value?

If his Independence Assumption legitimately applies to testimony for miracles in this way (for doubts, see §19 below), then Hume's Maxim does indeed provide an appropriate "check" (E 10.2) on human credulity. To illustrate how such a restraining mechanism can work

[16]   Moreover the mathematical argument here can be seen as a more precise version of the informal reasoning in the final paragraph of §7 above, which spells out what seems likely to have been Hume's own route to his Maxim. The value for $Pr(M/t(M))$ implied by this reasoning is given by the formula $m(1 - f)/(m(1 - f) + f(1 - m))$ as explained in Millican (2003, §4).

in practice, let us consider a non-miraculous example. Suppose, then, that I want to know whether I suffer from some genetic condition G which afflicts one person in a million. I have no evidence either way, but a test is available which seems very reliable, in that whoever is tested, and *whether they actually have the condition or not*, the chance that the test will give a correct diagnosis is 99·9%, and an incorrect diagnosis only 0·1% (so Hume's Independence Assumption applies). When I later leave the clinic in distress at having tested positive for G, how convinced should I be that I do indeed have that condition?

Repeated experience with audiences of undergraduates and others indicates that most people would judge my likelihood of having G in this situation to be very high, but in fact the reverse is the case, as Hume would recognise. As I stumble out despondently through the clinic door, he might greet me with a consoling comment something like this:

> *Consider whether it be more probable, that this kind of test should be mistaken, or that you should really have condition G.*[17] (cf. *E* 10.13)

Given that the test is wrong one time in a thousand, while G afflicts only one person in a million, there is clearly a far greater likelihood of a mistaken test than of my actually suffering from G. And so a positive test does relatively little to indicate that I actually have the disease: in fact, it changes the probability from a negligible one in a million to the only slightly more worrying one in 1,002.[18] Hume's Maxim, therefore, is entirely correct in this case, and it also gives the correct answer for other relevantly similar cases: if, for example, we change the "initial probability" of the disease to more than one in a thousand, then the test indeed becomes credible. The practical value of the Maxim is thus evident in these individual scenarios, and perhaps even more so when assessing proposals for mass medical screening.

[17] Note that this is quite different from asking: "Which is more probable, in the light of this result: that this specific test is mistaken in saying that you have condition G, or that you really have condition G?", which would be trivially equivalent to asking whether the test result makes it more probable than not that I have the condition. Earman's interpretation (cf. note 9 above) would imply that Hume's Maxim expresses just this useless equivalence.

[18] Consider a population of a billion, of whom one thousand have the disease while 999,999,000 do not. If all were tested, we would expect 999 true positives against 999,999 false positives.

10. Does Hume Consider a Miracle to be a Contradiction in Terms?

The discussion above has made little mention of *miracles* as such, but has focused quite generally on the assessment of testimony for events that seem improbable based on past experience. In §7 we saw how Hume's famous Maxim could be derived entirely on this basis, by closely follow-ing his own text and taking advantage of an equivalence between "more miraculous" and "less probable" which he himself implicitly endorses. So far, then, it seems that miracles play a role in his main argument only as extreme instances of initially improbable events.[19]

If we confine our attention to the main argument of *Enquiry* 10 Part 1, this impression is indeed entirely correct. Miracles feature signifi-cantly only in the famous paragraph 12, which I deliberately ignored at the beginning of §7 above, precisely in order to make this point:

> A miracle is a violation of the laws of nature; and as a firm and un-alterable experience has established these laws, the proof against a miracle, from the very nature of the fact, is as entire as any argu-ment from experience can possibly be imagined. ... Nothing is es-teemed a miracle, if it ever happen in the common course of nature. It is no miracle that a man, seemingly in good health, should die on a sudden: because such a kind of death ... has ... been frequently observed to happen. But it is a miracle, that a dead man should come to life; because that has never been observed, in any age or country. There must, therefore, be a uniform experience against every miraculous event, otherwise the event would not merit that

[19]   In a long footnote (*E* 10.10 n. 22) discussing his Indian prince example, Hume sketches a distinction between *extraordinary* and *miraculous* events, on the basis that the latter are *contrary* to past experience while the former are merely *not conformable* to it. It is debatable how far he manages to make good this distinction – for example Campbell (1762, I §2, pp. 47–59), Burns (1981, pp. 166–9, 224–30), and Coady (1992, ch. 10) for-cefully attack it, while Coleman (2001, pp. 208–9) and Garrett (2002, pp. 321–3) attempt a defence. If Hume were concerned to treat miracles quite differently from extraordinary events, by ruling them out in principle either logically (cf. Norton below) or epistemologically (cf. §12 below), then this distinction would be crucial in defending him from the accusation of un-justified dogmatism against unfamiliar events. But if I am correct in main-taining that Hume's principles are the same as applied to both categories, then very little hangs on it. (And it does seem to have been an afterthought: the Indian prince paragraph was added in the 1750 second edition, and the footnote only while that edition was going through the press. For discussion of some of the intellectual context, see Wootton 1990, pp. 194–7.)

> appellation. And as an uniform experience amounts to a proof, there is here a direct and full *proof*, from the nature of the fact, against the existence of any miracle; nor can such a proof be destroyed, or the miracle rendered credible, but by an opposite proof, which is superior. (*E* 10.12)

The entire thrust of this paragraph is to urge, on the basis of what a miracle is understood to be, that any miracle must *ipso facto* be an extreme case of an extraordinary event: an event against which there is a strong *proof* from experience. Hence Hume's argument concerning reports of extraordinary events – already virtually completed before this paragraph starts, and culminating in his Maxim immediately after it – will automatically apply to any reported miracle story.

Some interpreters, however, have been misled by this paragraph to see Hume as proposing an entirely different kind of argument, based on the *concept* of a miracle:

> A miracle is a violation of the laws of nature; a law of nature is established by a firm and unalterable experience. The champion of miracles is arguing, however, that this experience is not firm and unalterable; at least one exception is, he claims, known. From this exception it follows, Hume reminds us, that there is no violation of a law of nature because there is no law of nature, and hence, there is no miracle. (Norton 1982, p. 299; cf. Wilson 1989, p. 260)

However this sort of reading – which interprets Hume's argument as demonstrative in force – cannot possibly be right, for at least two reasons. First, it would imply that his aim is not so much to undermine the evidence *for the very occurrence* of a given reported extraordinary event, but rather to deny that the event, *if it occurred, was a genuine miracle*. Hume, however, says nothing on the latter point, and the argumentative move that Norton describes in the quotation above, whereby Hume is supposed to countenance the possibility that *M* did occur after all, albeit non-miraculously, simply doesn't appear in the text here. The second and even more decisive objection to this sort of reading is that it makes a nonsense of Hume's situating his argument so firmly within the context of his treatment of probability. No account of his essay that pays significant attention to the earlier paragraphs can with any plausibility present it as turning on a contradiction in terms.[20] Indeed paragraph 12 itself makes clear

---

[20]   In Part 2 Hume does sometimes describe miracles as impossible, but then he means physical or causal rather than conceptual or logical impossibility – see §15 below.

that Hume takes "the proof against a miracle" to be an "argument from experience" rather than a priori, and potentially defeasible by "an opposite proof" rather than demonstrative.

11. What Does Hume Mean by a "Law of Nature"?

Hume famously characterises a miracle as an event that violates or transgresses a "law of nature" (by the agency of the Deity or some invisible agent).[21] But if – as is commonly assumed – he conceived of a "law of nature" as being a *true* universal generalisation about how things behave, then a miracle so characterised would be, after all, a contradiction in terms, notwithstanding §10 above. In fact, most of his uses of the term refer to *moral* "laws of nature", following in the tradition of Grotius, Pufendorf, and Locke. The *Enquiry* is Hume's earliest work to refer to *physical* "laws of nature", with most such references in Section 10 itself,[22] but nowhere does he spell out exactly what he takes such a law of nature to be. I suspect that the common assumption described above – that he can only have in mind a *de facto* exceptionless generalisation – is largely based on confusions about his theory of causation, which is supposed by many to imply that there is no such thing as a causal law beyond "a summation of a wholly uniform past experience" (Norton 1982, p. 298; cf. Wilson 1989, p. 259). This common view is mistaken, and Hume is entirely comfortable with causal science (including the notions of hidden causes and functional relationships between forces etc.),[23] so there is no obvious reason why he should have significantly more difficulty making sense of the concept of a miracle

[21] I call Hume's statement that "A miracle is a violation of the laws of nature" (*E* 20.12) a *characterisation* rather than a *definition*, because his full definition follows in a footnote attached to the very end of the paragraph: "A miracle may be accurately defined, *a transgression of a law of nature by a particular volition of the Deity, or by the interposition of some invisible agent.* A miracle may either be discoverable by men or not. ... The raising of a house or ship into the air is a visible miracle. The raising of a feather, when the wind wants ever so little of a force requisite for that purpose, is as real a miracle, though not so sensible with regard to us." (*E* 10.12 n. 23).
[22] The full catalogue of relevant paragraphs is *E* 4.9, 8.4, 8.14, 10.12, 10.12 n. 23, 10.31, 35, 37, and 38.
[23] This is not to imply that relevant philosophical difficulties cannot be raised for his position. For the interpretation of Hume on causal science, see Millican (2007b, pp. 232–3; 2009, §1). For the view that he is limited to an inadequate conception of a law of nature, see for example Flew (1961, pp. 204–6) and Gaskin (1988, pp. 160–2).

than other thinkers who have tried to explicate this delicate notion. The general idea, familiar at least since Aquinas (e.g. *Summa Contra Gentiles*, 3.101.1–2), is that of an intrusion into the natural order, whereby supernatural agency brings about some event that would not – and typically *could* not – have occurred in the ordinary course of things.[24] This presupposes that there is some set of default "laws" that determine how things behave in the absence of special supernatural intervention. And although filling this out in detail could be problematic, such problems belong more to the theist who appeals to miracles "to be the foundation of a system of religion" (*E* 10.36) than to his sceptical critic. Hume himself never suggests that the concept of miracle is incoherent, but if it turned out to be so, that would merely provide additional ammunition in his overall attack on the case for theism.

Hume's argument requires no more than a relatively vague interpretation of a "law of nature", as a description of behaviour that has virtually always – but maybe not universally – been observed in nature. Sometimes he uses the term in just this way, as for example its one occurrence in *The Natural History of Religion*, where he remarks on a "uniform law of nature" to which "few exceptions are found" (*NHR* 15.3). There are also plenty of other places where he seems to use "uniform" to signify something less than strict universality.[25] This casts a softer light on his frequently attacked assertion that "There must ... be a uniform experience against every miraculous event" (*E* 10.12). Many of Hume's critics (e.g. Lewis 1947, pp. 105–6; Purtill 1978, pp. 191–2; Johnson 1999, pp. 18–19) have seen this as crudely begging the question by taking for granted that no miraculous event has ever actually taken place. Others (e.g. Broad 1917, pp. 85–6; Gaskin 1988, pp. 159–60) have understood him to be assuming that an event can count as miraculous only if it reaches the absolute limit of improbability, as an entirely one-off violation of an otherwise strictly universal "law". In response to such criticisms, Garrett (2002, p. 320) rightly points out that the epistemological focus of Hume's discussion implies a *subjective* notion of a law of nature (i.e. relative to the experience of the observer) rather than *absolute* (i.e. descriptive of what actually occurs, whether observed or not). As remarked in §10, Hume's interest is

---

[24] Mackie (1982, pp. 19–23) gives a lucid defence and discussion of this general idea of a miracle.

[25] See for example *T* 2.3.1.4, *M* 5.45, "Of National Characters" paras 6, 18, 19, 20 n. 10 (*Essays*, pp. 199, 206, 207, 208), "Of the Standard of Taste" para. 17 (*Essays*, p. 237), *NHR* 6.2.

consistently in whether a particular event *actually happened*, not whether the event *would have been contrary to (unknown) natural laws*. And although a subjective understanding of a "law of nature" may run counter to most modern usage, it was certainly available in Hume's day (e.g. Sherlock 1729, p. 61). In this sense, someone yet to be convinced that anyone has ever been resurrected from the dead has (subjective) "uniform experience" for the "law of nature" that such events do not occur, but this does not logically rule out that a resurrection has (objectively) occurred *beyond* their experience. Nor does it imply that resurrections would cease to count as miraculous if they were repeated, as, for example, in the Gospel accounts of Lazarus and Jesus. Hume's own "accurate" definition of a miracle is clearly compatible with repeated violations of a natural law, as confirmed by this passage which immediately precedes it:

> ... if a person, claiming a divine authority, ... should order *many* natural events, which immediately follow upon his command; these might justly be esteemed miracles, because ... nothing can be more contrary to nature than that the voice or command of a man should have such an influence. (*E* 10.12 n. 23, my emphasis).

There is also an indication, near the end of the essay, that Hume intends his argument to apply not only to overtly religious claims, but also to "every thing new, rare, and extraordinary in nature ... that is to be found in the writers of natural magic or alchemy, or such authors, who seem, all of them, to have an unconquerable appetite for falsehood and fable" (*E* 10.39, quoting Francis Bacon). Were Hume alive today, he would no doubt include within this category many modern "New Age" claims, for example those associated with alternative therapies such as homeopathy whose alleged mode of operation seems to run wildly at odds with our established scientific understanding of the world. Such therapies characteristically claim to involve reliably repeatable phenomena, and yet Hume's argument can apply to them just as effectively as to the more typically one-off miraculous claims of religion (cf. n. 39 in §18 below).

12. Is Part 2 of the Essay Redundant?

Hume's main argument in Part 1 of the essay is commonly called his "a priori" argument concerning miracles, because it is based on general principles rather than the specific characteristics of actual historical testimony. Part 2 starts from four "a posteriori" arguments, drawing attention to the weakness, remoteness, and inconsistency of such testimony, and our tendency to be too easily seduced by it. Overtly, the Maxim with which Part 1 concludes appears to set a genuine threshold for credibility which is then addressed by the Part 2 arguments. But some scholars have instead read Part 1 as intended by itself to establish the incredibility of miracles, either by ruling out their very possibility (a reading rejected in §10 above), or more plausibly, by ruling out the possibility of testimony sufficient to establish a miracle.

This reading, which Burns calls the "classical" interpretation (1981, p. 143), seems to have been widely taken for granted until challenged by Antony Flew.[26] It is suggested by the statement in paragraph 12 that "the proof against a miracle, from the very nature of the fact, is as entire as any argument from experience can possibly be imagined". For if the proof against a miracle is as strong as "any argument from experience [that] can possibly be imagined", then presumably no argument from experience could possibly outweigh it. And such impossibility would then neatly explain Hume's apparently rather dogmatic denials of miraculous testimony in Part 2 (which we shall come to in §14, §15 and §17 below).[27]

On the other side, however, there are plenty of indications in the final text of the essay that Hume did not intend this extreme position. In Part 1, he supposes "that the testimony, considered apart and in itself, amounts to an entire proof [so] there is proof against proof" (E 10.11), and he goes on to consider what would follow were "the proof against a miracle" to "be destroyed ... by an opposite proof, which is superior" (E 10.12).[28] Likewise the second part of his

---

[26]   See Flew (1959, pp. 2–5, 12–14; 1961, p. 176), and cf. Gaskin (1988, pp. 153–4). Broad (1917, p. 94) exemplifies the earlier orthodoxy, while Burns (1981, pp. 142–58) gives the most sustained opposition to Flew's reading.

[27]   According to Burns, "scattered throughout the exposition of the four a posteriori arguments are a number of asides which can reasonably be interpreted only as out-of-context references to the a priori argument understood according to the classical interpretation", and he goes on to cite E 10.16, 22, 25, 26 and 27 (1981, p. 152).

[28]   This last passage occurs within *the very same paragraph* in which Hume has just stated that "the proof against a miracle ... is as entire as any argument from experience can possibly be imagined". So that statement has to be understood as less absolute that it initially appears, perhaps along the lines of his reference to a "*species* or *kind* of proof, which is full and certain when taken alone" but which yet admits of degrees (cf. §6 above).

Maxim ("And even in that case ...") is entirely focused on this eventuality (E 10.13). Part 2 starts by saying:

> In the foregoing reasoning we have supposed, that the testimony upon which a miracle is founded, may possibly amount to an entire proof ... But it is easy to shew ... that there never was a miraculous event established on so full an evidence. (E 10.14)

This does not give the impression that Part 1 has already settled the question. Later in Part 2, Hume states explicitly that, outside a religious context, "there may possibly be miracles, or violations of the usual course of nature, of such a kind as to admit of proof from human testimony" (E 10.36), and he gives an example of eight days of darkness across the world, witnessed worldwide and reported by travellers. Campbell – who presumed that Part 1 was intended to be decisive by itself – evidently thought this example quite contrary to that aim, devoting Section I § 3 of his *Dissertation*, entitled "*Mr Hume himself gives up his favourite argument*", to highlighting the inconsistency. But in his 1761 letter to Hugh Blair, Hume responded:

> Sect. III. There is no contradiction in saying, that all the testimony which ever was really given for any miracle, or ever will be given, is a subject of derision; and yet forming a fiction or supposition of a testimony for a particular miracle, which might not only merit attention, but amount to a full proof of it. For instance, the absence of the sun during 48 hours; but reasonable men would only conclude from this fact, that the machine of the globe was disordered during the time. (HL i 349–50; Hume 1748, p. 165)

Hume denies any contradiction, and implies that he is deliberately leaving open the possibility of "testimony for a particularly miracle, which might ... amount to a full proof of it".[29]

I conclude, therefore, that we should understand Hume's "a priori" argument as intended to do exactly what the text says: namely, to erect a theoretical hurdle that testimony for a miracle could *in principle* overcome, exactly in line with his general probabilistic framework (which, as we saw in §§5–7 above, leads very naturally to his Maxim). This then leaves a clear role for his subsequent "a posteriori" arguments – namely, to emphasise the extreme unlikelihood of any such testimony ever achieving this hurdle in practice – and thus

---

[29]   Here I disagree with Burns, who says that "no repudiation of the classical interpretation is attempted in any of the points raised against Campbell" (1981, p. 153), and fails to mention this passage.

Peter Millican

avoids the unpalatable assessment of them as philosophically gratuitous. But a nagging question might remain, given Hume's apparent shift of perspective from that of the "wise man" of the beginning of Part 1, who carefully weighs the relevant evidence (*E* 10.4), to that of the "wise", "judicious" and "learned" of Part 2, who treat any miracle story with scorn (*E* 10.21) and who "are contented ... to deride its absurdity" without serious consideration (*E* 10.22). We shall return to this question in §17 below.

13. How Does Hume Explain the Propagation of Miracle Stories?

Having erected an appropriate threshold of credibility by means of his Maxim, Hume moves on in Part 2 to argue that no actual testimony for a miracle has ever got close to reaching that threshold. While doing so, he also indirectly suggests his own explanation of how such false testimony could have propagated. His first "a posteriori" argument economically packs a wide range of points into a single sentence:

> For *first*, there is not to be found, in all history, any miracle attested by a sufficient number of men, of such unquestioned good-sense, education, and learning, as to secure us against all delusion in themselves; of such undoubted integrity, as to place them beyond all suspicion of any design to deceive others; of such credit and reputation in the eyes of mankind, as to have a great deal to lose in case of their being detected in any falsehood; and at the same time, attesting facts, performed in such a public manner, and in so celebrated a part of the world, as to render the detection unavoidable (*E* 10.15)

These points are later augmented by Hume's third argument, which follows a few paragraphs later:

> *Thirdly.* It forms a strong presumption against all supernatural and miraculous relations, that they are observed chiefly to abound among ignorant and barbarous nations; or if a civilized people has ever given admission to any of them, that people will be found to have received them from ignorant and barbarous ancestors ... When we peruse the first histories of all nations, we are apt to imagine ourselves transported into some new world; ... Prodigies, omens, oracles, judgments, quite obscure the few natural events ... (*E* 10.20)

Hume's explanation of this phenomenon – whereby miraculous stories "grow thinner every page, in proportion as we advance nearer the enlightened ages" (E 10.20) – is not that human nature has changed: "it is nothing strange ... that men should lie in all ages" or that "marvellous relations" should be started by those with vivid imagination (E 10.21). But in educated societies, such stories are "treated with scorn by all the wise and judicious" and "at last ... abandoned even by the vulgar", whereas those "sown in a more proper soil" – that is, in a culture of superstition and ignorance – are allowed to grow unchecked (E 10.20). It follows that the stories that become prominent tend to originate from ancient, remote and uneducated parts of the world.

Hume's second argument complements these others, by providing an explanation of why miracle stories are so popular in the absence of critical scrutiny:

> *Secondly.* ... The passion of *surprize* and *wonder*, arising from miracles, being an agreeable emotion, gives a sensible tendency towards the belief of those events ... But if the spirit of religion join itself to the love of wonder, there is an end of common sense; and human testimony, in these circumstances, loses all pretensions to authority. A religionist may be an enthusiast, and imagine he sees what has no reality: He may know his narrative to be false, and yet persevere in it, with the best intentions in the world, for the sake of promoting so holy a cause ... The many instances of forged miracles ... which, in all ages, have either been detected by contrary evidence, or which detect themselves by their absurdity, prove sufficiently the strong propensity of mankind to the extraordinary and the marvellous ... (E 10.16–19)

Hume might also usefully have added here some discussion from his *Natural History of Religion*, concerning humans' tendency to ascribe events to gods and spirits, which also helps to explain both why supernatural miracle stories seem so plausible to uneducated cultures, and why by contrast the progress of science tends to undermine them:

> ... We hang in perpetual suspence between life and death, health and sickness, plenty and want; which are distributed amongst the human species by secret and unknown causes ... These *unknown causes*, then, become the constant object of our hope and fear ... Could men anatomize nature, ... they would find, that these causes are nothing but the particular fabric and structure of the minute parts of their own bodies and of external objects; and that, by a regular and constant machinery, all the events are

produced, about which they are so much concerned. But ... the ignorant multitudes ... can only conceive the *unknown causes* in a general and confused manner ...

There is an universal tendency among mankind to conceive all beings like themselves ... We find human faces in the moon, armies in the clouds; and by a natural propensity, if not corrected by experience and reflection, ascribe malice or good-will to every thing, that hurts or pleases us. ... No wonder, then, that mankind, being placed in such an absolute ignorance of causes, and ... at the same time so anxious concerning their future fortune, should immediately acknowledge a dependence on invisible powers, possessed of sentiment and intelligence. ...

In proportion as any man's course of life is governed by accident, we always find, that he encreases in superstition ... All human life, especially before the institution of order and good government, being subject to fortuitous accidents; it is natural, that superstition should prevail every where in barbarous ages ... (*NHR* 2.5–3.3)

Obviously any such explanation of the origins of religion is to some extent speculative, but Hume's account seems generally plausible.[30] And that humanity has a love of "surprize and wonder" is evident enough: the propagation of "urban myths", conspiracy theories, paranormal and miracle cures, monster and alien sightings etc. over the Web and the more sensational media demonstrates sufficiently that this passion is still widespread today.

14. What is Going on in Hume's "Contrary Miracles" Discussion?

Hume's fourth "a posteriori" argument is less straightforward and convincing than the other three, though it provides him with a pretext for introducing material which is highly effective in his debate with Christian believers:

I may add as a *fourth* reason ... that, in matters of religion, whatever is different is contrary; and that it is impossible the religions of ancient ROME, of TURKEY, of SIAM, and of CHINA should, all of them, be established on any solid foundation. Every miracle,

---

[30] For an example of recent research confirming the tendency of both children and adults towards "promiscuous teleology", see Lombrozo *et al.* (2007), whose introduction also mentions a number of other relevant studies.

therefore, pretended to have been wrought in any of these religions (and all of them abound in miracles), as its direct scope is
to establish the particular system to which it is attributed; so
has it the same force, though more indirectly, to overthrow
every other system. In destroying a rival system, it likewise de-
stroys the credit of those miracles, on which that system was established; so that all the prodigies of different religions are to
be regarded as contrary facts, and the evidences of these prodigies, whether weak or strong, as opposite to each other. (*E* 10.24)

This argument, unlike the others, depends crucially on the idea that
each miracle claim is being used to support a specific religious belief,
from which Hume takes it to follow that where those beliefs conflict,
the miracle claims are in turn rendered indirectly contrary to each
other. Unfortunately, however, this argument works only if the evidential relationships between each miracle story and its corresponding religion are demonstrative: Hume, uncharacteristically, is here
failing to notice how differently things fall out if they are merely
probabilistic. Starting from a default position of naturalism, for
example, we might well consider that the genuine occurrence of a reported "Christian" miracle – by greatly raising the probability of
supernatural agency (even more than it raises the probability of
Christianity itself) – would thereby raise the probability *also* of a reported "Islamic" miracle, notwithstanding the conflict between the
two religious systems. So Hume goes too far when arguing that miracles "pretended to have been wrought" in contrary religions are cor-
respondingly "to be regarded as contrary facts".

Despite its logical flaws, Hume's "contrary miracles" argument
retains significant *indirect* persuasive force, by challenging the believer to distinguish the credentials of her own preferred miracle
stories from those she rejects. And this could explain why Hume
goes on to cite several miraculous accounts that are relatively well attested, and which might therefore superficially seem to weaken, rather
than strengthen, his overall case.[31] The point here may be not so much
that his Christian readers are *logically compelled to deny* the miracles of
rival religions (as the contrary miracles argument would suggest), but
rather, that such believers *will in fact want to deny* them. This denial
might be motivated simply by scepticism towards rival religious
beliefs, but it might also reflect an awareness that insufficiently

---

[31]   Indeed Hume exaggerates the strength of the evidence for these cited
miracles, as noticed by several of his early critics. See for example Campbell
(1762, II §§4–5, pp. 181–248) and Flew (1959, pp. 8–9).

discriminating acceptance of the miraculous, by putting the Gospel miracles on a par with others, both undermines any special claims for Christianity and also casts doubt on the entire collection (especially when contemporary forged miracles are "detected by contrary evidence", *E* 10.19). Thus the would-be discriminating believer is put in a bind: keen to explain away the host of alien miracle stories as fraudulent or delusive (perhaps by appeal to the sorts of tendencies we saw Hume emphasising in §13 above), while denying that the stories she herself endorses (e.g. from the Gospels) can be undermined in the same way. Seen in this light, Hume's abrupt dismissal of the alleged miracles of Vespasian ("so gross and so palpable a falsehood", *E* 10.25) and Saragossa ("carried falsehood upon the very face of it", *E* 10.26) becomes much easier to understand. Rather than attempting to *argue* for such rejection, he may simply be reporting a view that he expects others to share, and tacitly inviting his discerning reader to notice the difficulties this implies.

15. How Can Hume Describe Miracles as "Absolutely Impossible"?

Hume's dismissal of the Abbé Pâris miracles might seem less easy to condone:[32]

> Where shall we find such a number of circumstances, agreeing to the corroboration of one fact? And what have we to oppose to such a cloud of witnesses, but the absolute impossibility or miraculous nature of the events, which they relate? And this surely, in the eyes of all reasonable people, will alone be regarded as a sufficient refutation. (*E* 10.27)

He has often been criticised for this apparent dogmatism (e.g. Swinburne 1968, p. 323; Earman 2000, pp. 31-2), and accused of inconsistency in his talk of "the absolute impossibility ... of the events" (e.g. Gaskin 1988, pp. 161–4). Certainly he cannot consistently claim that these reported events are *conceptually* or *a priori* impossible (cf. *E* 12.29). But it is entirely consistent for him to claim that the supposed miracles are *causally* impossible, given the laws of nature that we have all learned from experience (and which, at this point in the discussion, he is taking to be generally agreed – hence there need be

---

[32] Note that the supposed miracles of Abbé Pâris, a Jansenist, would be rejected by the vast majority of Roman Catholic readers as well as Protestants.

no dogmatism here). Some commentators (including Gaskin *op. cit.*) have seen even this as problematic, apparently owing to the common assumption that Hume denies any genuine causal modality. But as we noted in §11 above, he is very committed to causal explanation and causal science; moreover he repeatedly and explicitly insists that necessity is essential to causation (e.g. *T* 1.3.2.11, 1.3.6.3, 2.3.1.18, *E* 8.25, 8.27). It follows that he must acknowledge such causal necessity, and this automatically brings with it a cognate notion of possibility (applying to anything whose contrary is not causally necessary in that sense).[33] Hence we should not be at all surprised to find Hume describing would-be miracles as "impossible" or even "absolutely impossible", precisely because they would violate established causal laws.[34]

16. Why Does Hume Strengthen his Maxim Against Religious Miracles?

Having rejected the supposedly well-attested stories that he expects his readers also to reject, Hume builds on his contrary miracles argument by itemising several other reasons for particularly doubting *religious* miracle stories. Some of these are strongly reminiscent of points made in his second "a posteriori" argument:

> what greater temptation than to appear a missionary, a prophet, an ambassador from heaven? ... Or if, by the help of vanity and a heated imagination, a man has first made a convert of himself, ... who ever scruples to make use of pious frauds, in support of so holy and meritorious a cause? ... the gazing populace, receive greedily, without examination, whatever sooths superstition, and promotes wonder. ... How many stories of

---

[33] Hume denies causal necessity *as other philosophers attempt to conceive of it* (indeed he denies that they achieve any such conception). But to treat this as an unequivocal denial of causal necessity is rather like supposing that if I reject the *vital force* theory of life and hence deny having any such force within me, then I am implicitly claiming to be dead.

[34] Hume also uses "absolutely impossible" in a causal sense at *T* 1.1.1.10, 2.1.5.3, *E* 2.8. Note that this impossibility is *not* epistemological: Hume is not suggesting that the miracles are impossible in that "their existence is ruled out by a proof" (Garrett 2002, p. 326), but rather, that they are impossible *causally* given the way nature works. This is a claim about what the laws of nature are, with which he thinks his readers will agree and for which he has strong evidence (in the form of inductive proof), but he is not claiming infallibility – there is no *epistemological* impossibility of error.

Peter Millican

this nature have, in all ages, been detected and exploded ... ?
Where such reports, therefore, fly about, the solution of the
phaenomenon is obvious; and we judge in conformity to
regular experience and observation, when we account for it by
the known and natural principles of credulity and delusion. (*E*
10.29–31)

Here we see again hints of the line of thought implicit in the contrary
miracles discussion, whereby all the countless religious miracle stories
are lumped together as equally deserving of a common dismissive
explanation. And Hume goes on to suggest that this particular human
weakness with respect to *religious* miracle stories, and their appalling
track record,[35] give reason for strengthening his Maxim in their case:

It is experience only, which gives authority to human testimony;
and it is the same experience, which assures us of the laws of
nature. When, therefore, these two kinds of experience are contrary, we have nothing to do but substract the one from the
other, and embrace an opinion, either on one side or the other,
with that assurance which arises from the remainder. But according to the principle here explained, this substraction, with regard
to all popular religions, amounts to an entire annihilation;[36] and
therefore *we may establish it as a maxim, that no human testimony
can have such force as to prove a miracle, and make it a just foundation for any such system of religion.* (*E* 10.35, my emphasis)

Here Hume approaches an attitude of immediate dismissal towards
such stories, an attitude which he clearly takes to be justified
inductively.

17. Is Hume's Dismissal of Miracle Stories Overly Dogmatic?

At several points in Part 2 of the essay, Hume suggests that any
miracle report will be taken seriously only by "fools" and the

[35]   Again, notice that even the Christian reader can be expected to acknowledge that there have been plenty of bogus miracle stories associated
with *contrary* religions.
[36]   Garrett (2002, p. 324 n. 25) interprets this as implying that "proofs
entirely obviate, or 'annihilate', considerations of probability", so that a
probability weighed against a proof will count as nothing. But when one
army annihilates another, this does not imply that it sustains no losses
itself, and likewise Hume's words here can perfectly well be understood as
meaning simply that the proof will always win easily, leaving no *net*
balance on the other side.

180

"weak", and will be "treated with scorn by all the wise and judicious", who "are contented, in general, to deride its absurdity, without informing themselves of the particular facts, by which it may be distinctly refuted" (*E* 10.21–2). Later he says that the profusion of bogus religious miracle stories should be "sufficient, with all men of sense, not only to make them reject" any such story, "but even reject it without farther examination"; he accordingly expresses a "general resolution, never to lend any attention" to such testimony (*E* 10.38). Is this just hyperbolic dogmatism, perhaps provoked by the ridiculous stories he has been considering, or can it be justified?

Hume makes some relevant points at *E* 10.32–34, when discussing religious miracles, which are anticipated in his (largely invented) description of the attitude of Cardinal de Retz:

> He considered justly, that it was not requisite, in order to reject a fact of this nature, to be able accurately to disprove the testimony, and to trace its falsehood, through all the circumstances of knavery and credulity which produced it. He knew, that, as this was commonly altogether impossible at any small distance of time and place; so was it extremely difficult, even where one was immediately present, by reason of the bigotry, ignorance, cunning, and roguery of a great part of mankind. He therefore concluded, like a just reasoner, that such an evidence carried falsehood upon the very face of it, and that a miracle, supported by any human testimony, was more properly a subject of derision than of argument. (*E* 10.26)

This attitude might well seem reasonable when the origins of a story are shrouded in mystery, but can we justify dismissing a story without bothering to investigate it even when we have a genuine opportunity to do so? Challenged by George Campbell in Section I §4 of his *Dissertation*, Hume responded with a more interesting and general consideration:

> *Sect. IV.* Does a man of sense run after every silly tale of witches or hobgoblins or fairies, and canvass particularly the evidence? I never knew any one, that examined and deliberated about nonsense who did not believe it before the end of his inquiries. (*HL* i 350; Hume 1748, p. 165)

Interpreted as an answer to Campbell's complaint (rather than just a bald reassertion that no man of sense would give any time to such stories), Hume seems to be suggesting that all of us are prone to lose sound critical judgement if we get drawn too much into the particularities of specific tales. That being so, experience can teach us that sometimes it is rational *not* to rely on careful and detailed critical assessment, but instead to prefer the verdict of a general rule without giving the matter too much thought. A modern example might be the persuasive and polished advertising (for investments, prize draws, novel therapies, conspiracy theories etc.) that regularly bombards us, where reading the advertiser's seductive arguments is typically not only a waste of time, but worse, carries the danger of being persuaded. Hume is suggesting that this same attitude is appropriate to miracle stories: that this is a case where, counter-intuitively, it can often be *more* rational to give *less* detailed consideration!

18. Can Divine Teleology Provide a Response?

After expressing his strengthened maxim (quoted in §16 above), Hume gives three examples to illustrate his preference for secular over religious miracle stories. The first of these (*E* 10.36) is the imagined eight days of darkness in January 1600, as mentioned in §12 above; the second (*E* 10.37) involves a reported resurrection of Queen Elizabeth I, also dated to 1600, and the third (*E* 10.38) is similar except that the resurrection is "ascribed to [a] new system of religion". However Hume's discussion of these examples is rather confusing, first because he suggests that the credibility of the universal darkness is due to its analogy with natural events (rather than to the absence of religious distortions), and secondly because his emphatic dismissal of the resurrection examples seems to be almost unaffected by the potential religious association – "the knavery and folly of men" provide an equally obvious explanation in both cases. The real contrast between the universal darkness and the resurrections, therefore, seems to lie not in anything to do with religion, but in the quality of the evidence (widespread and independent, as opposed to local and potentially colluding). So it is interesting to consider a modified example in which the relevant global celestial phenomenon is not eight days of darkness, but instead something transparently religious. Imagine, for example, a month-long appearance in 1600 of a new set of purple stars, spelling out across the sky the words "εγω ειμι η οδος και η αληθεια και η ζωη", New Testament Greek for "I am the way and the truth and the life" (*John* 14:6). The logic of Hume's discussion suggests that he would dismiss such testimony as more likely to derive from a powerful religious conspiracy than to be genuine. But Christians might well respond (cf. Locke, *Essay* IV xvi 13, quoted in §3 above) that the evident religious content of the celestial message makes it *more* likely to be explicable by supernatural

means than some non-religious alternatives (for example a comparable set of stars tracing out line diagrams of the Platonic solids). If
the testimony were to be as widespread and consistent as that for
the eight days of darkness, why should it not be credible?

Perhaps Hume himself had an inkling of this sort of objection,
because he provides an argument that seems calculated to address it:

> Though the Being to whom the miracle is ascribed, be ...
> Almighty, it does not, upon that account, become a whit more
> probable; since it is impossible for us to know the attributes or
> actions of such a Being, otherwise than from the experience
> which we have of his productions, in the usual course of
> nature. (*E* 10.38)

Though ingenious, this is too quick to be convincing. If correct, it
would imply that the belief in an omnipotent Deity can make no
difference to the credibility of *any* inference to the unobserved, on
the grounds that any such inference has to rely on induction, and
induction will apply in exactly the same way whether the experience
to which we appeal is taken to be expressive of brute laws of nature, or
expressive of the will of the Deity. But there is a crucial asymmetry
between these, because theistic explanation potentially has the
power to explain not only conformity to causal laws (which account
for the future in terms of the past), but also teleology (which accounts
for the past in terms of the anticipated future, appealing to goals as
well as to existing structures). And it is not difficult to *imagine* a
world in which explanation of natural events in terms of divine purposes would prove to be of special value (e.g. where wicked people
tend to get struck by meteorites).[37] Despite Hume's ingenious
argument, therefore, a Deity who intervened miraculously to fulfil
intelligible purposes (rather than working exclusively through
uniform causal laws that reveal no teleological pattern) could
indeed provide the theist with explanatory resources unavailable to
the atheist. And there seems to be no reason in principle why
sufficiently persuasive reports of miracles, displaying consistency
of apparent purpose, should not provide supporting evidence for

---

[37] Even if, as Hume will stress in *Enquiry* 11, our world does not seem to
be like that. Perhaps he has here been carried away by the force of his later
argument, to the effect that if we cannot discern any *moral* tendency in
this world, then it is illegitimate to infer any such tendency in the world
to come. That seems correct, but it does not imply in general that teleological considerations *could never* properly ground an inference beyond what is
observed.

"a system of religion".[38] Overall, we can conclude that although Hume is right to suggest that religious miracle stories deserve to be treated with extreme caution (because of their dubious track record), it remains true that the teleological aspect of religious explanation could in principle support such stories, if only the world were such as to make that teleological story plausible.[39]

19. Is Hume's Maxim Correct?

Having just seen the principal objection to Hume's arguments of Part 2, it is now time to return to Part 1 and consider again his central argument for his Maxim. Unfortunately, the Independence Assumption on which it depends is not universally valid, and as a result the Maxim itself fails. First, many forms of evidence will not yield a consistent general probability of error. Thus to take the example of §9 above, there is no particular reason why a test for some gene within a biological sample should have the same probability of giving a false-negative result when the gene is present, as it has of giving a false-positive result when the gene is absent. Indeed an exact equality here seems highly unlikely, given that any change in the test's sensitivity to the gene is likely to have opposite effects on the two probabilities. Likewise for the witnessing of marvels: there is no reason why someone, gazing over a foggy Scottish loch at twilight, should mistake a floating log for a sea monster with exactly the same probability as he would mistake a sea monster for a floating log. Moreover Hume himself is surely aware of this, because in Part 2 he repeatedly makes the point that

[38] See Swinburne (1996, ch. 7) and Houston (1994, ch. 11). Houston particularly emphasises (pp. 133–5) that it is question-begging against the theist to presume that everyday uniformity is *ipso facto* evidence against the miracle believer, because *that the dead always stay dead* in our experience, for example, is something she herself believes: for her, the resurrection of Jesus is precisely exceptional. The debate, therefore, cannot be decided by appeal to induction alone, but will depend on the relative general plausibility of the overall theistic account as compared with its rivals.

[39] These considerations suggest – rather ironically – that Hume's argument may be stronger against *non-religious* "miracles". For pseudo-sciences such as homeopathy, which run wildly contrary to our scientific understanding, aspire to capture repeatable, causal aspects of the world, which are not dependent on supernatural teleology and are therefore more straightforwardly testable by the inductive methods that Hume's argument presupposes.

human testimony is subject to various distortions depending on the subject-matter (marvellous, religious, favouring the vanity of the reporter, etc.). This might suggest that his Maxim is not intended as a final position so much as a stage on the way, showing that miracles are hard to credit even if we start from the Independence Assumption, as a prelude to arguing in Part 2 that the Assumption is if anything too generous to the believer.

Although such a strategy would have force against some of Hume's contemporary opponents, who themselves based their support for miracles on something like the Independence Assumption,[40] it does not suffice to vindicate his argument. As Campbell and Price pointed out,[41] his Maxim runs into major problems making sense of ordinary cases in which events (or combinations of events) that would antecedently seem hugely improbable are easily "established" by everyday testimony. Suppose, for example, that my son were to run indoors, shouting "A red lorry just bashed the wing-mirror off a yellow Mercedes at the corner". Collisions do occasionally happen there, but if I were invited to bet *in advance* on such a precisely specified event I would demand odds of thousands (if not millions) to one. My son's testimony, though generally reliable, is nothing like *that* unlikely to be false, and yet I would unhesitatingly believe such a report if told with apparent sincerity. His testimony is credible, even though it is *not* "of such a kind, that its falsehood would be even less probable, than the fact, which it endeavours to establish".[42]

Where, then, does Hume's argument go wrong? Much could be said here, but in brief, it is generally fallacious to calculate the probability of a "false positive" (where the event M does not occur, but is falsely reported as having occurred) by the formula used in §8 above:

$$Pr(\neg M \ \& \ t(M)) = Pr(\neg M) \times Pr(false \ report).$$

Even if we allow the assumption that my son has witnessed some collision, the probability that he will falsely report it as involving

[40] For example Price (1768, §2, pp. 413–6).
[41] See Campbell (1762, I §1, pp. 30–2) and Price (1768, §2, pp. 407–9), both of whom acknowledge Butler (1736, II ii 3, [§11]) as having anticipated this idea.
[42] It is tempting to suggest (as does Coleman 1988, p. 334) that such examples are irrelevant to Hume's argument because the events reported are not miraculous. But this response looks ad hoc and question-begging: *the burden would be on Hume* to show that miracles are a special case, and his argument claims to be based on generally applicable principles.

Peter Millican

precisely a red lorry and the wing-mirror of a yellow Mercedes is hugely overestimated by this formula. His report could be false in a myriad ways, of which this is just one. Hence a "false positive" of precisely this type is extremely unlikely, even less likely than a "true positive" (which is why his report is indeed credible).

Hume seems to have ignored this crucial objection, though he must have read of it. Perhaps he failed to appreciate the danger because the informality of his own text led him to misremember his Maxim as resisting refutation. Possibly, like so many later critics, he sometimes took himself to be proposing only the inoffensive triviality that "we cannot accept a miracle on the basis of testimony unless we regard the miracle, given the testimony, as more probable than its non-occurrence".[43] But there is also a more interesting possibility, which is close enough to his original Maxim to be expressible in very similar terms, resistant to refutation, yet also non-trivial:

Revised Humean Maxim

No testimony is sufficient to render a miracle M more probable than not, unless the testimony is of such a kind, that the occurrence of a false M report of that kind (*given that M does not in fact occur*) would be even less probable than M itself.

In the terms used above, this is roughly equivalent to saying that a report of M is credible only if a "true positive" would be more likely to occur than a "false positive",[44] which seems obviously right (and without having to depend on any Independence Assumption, as only M reports are being considered). But note that it involves a crucial shift in perspective from what Hume's argument for the Maxim led us to expect, because it compares the probability of M not with the general *epistemic probability* of a given type of testimony's falsehood, but instead with the probability of such false testimony, specifically for M, *being delivered*.[45] This Revised Maxim

---

[43] Quoted from Noonan (2007, p. 187), who adds "This is where Part 1 ends, and it does so on an incontrovertible, indeed, near tautological, point". For other references, see note 9 in §5 and note 15 in §8 above.

[44] It is not quite the same, but is implied as long as M's being unreported if true is at least as probable as M itself (which is almost certain to be the case if M is a miracle). The details of all this must wait for another occasion.

[45] Technically, this replaces inverse probability by direct probability: calculating *forward* from the envisaged events and propensity to report them, instead of attempting to calculate *backwards* from the delivery of a given report to the epistemic probability of the event reported.

186

thus moves from the abstract inductive epistemology of Part 1 of the essay to the more down-to-earth psychology of Part 2. With so much material in these later arguments stressing the human tendency to report miracles even in their absence, it would hardly be surprising if Hume sometimes mistook his original, faulty Maxim for this less vulnerable alternative.

20. What is the Enduring Significance of Hume's Essay?

"Of Miracles" is a rich, fascinating and insightful essay, though the lessons to be learned from it are not always quite those that Hume intended. Presented as a direct application of his theory of induction, its main weaknesses derive precisely from the inadequacies of that theory, which emphasises crude extrapolation from experience to the neglect of other considerations that are now often expressed in terms of "inference to the best explanation".[46] We saw this clearly in §18, where he overlooks the possibility of an integrated theistic framework in which miracles fit into a purposive account of the world. And a somewhat similar problem lies behind the main objection to his Maxim in §19, where his focus on the inductive evidence for and against a miracle claim apparently leads him to overlook that a report can be mistaken in many different ways. When a specific report has been presented, our assessment cannot just rely on a general abstract probability of error which is independent of the subject-matter; it has to look at the specifics, and compare the competing accounts of how that particular report is to be explained.

It is therefore somewhat ironic that the most enduring value of Hume's essay lies precisely in this explanatory direction, with his clear identification and investigation of ways in which our human cognitive failings can usefully be considered in the assessment of miracle reports. For Hume recognised the potential role of systematic "heuristics and biases" (as they are now called) within our cognitive functioning, nearly two and a half centuries before such research became fashionable through the well-known work of Amos Tversky and Daniel Kahneman.[47] This theme is obvious in Part 2,

---

[46]   I am not meaning to suggest that Hume is totally wedded to a crude inductivism. But his broader insights in philosophy of science (e.g. on analogy and hidden causes) are rather unsystematic and in any case play little role within "Of Miracles". For further discussion, see the references in footnotes 19 and 23 above.

[47]   Their best-known article is Tversky and Kahneman (1974), while Gilovich et al. (2002) is a major recent collection in honour of the research

Peter Millican

with its numerous references to flighty imagination, credulity, love of wonder, vanity, and motivated deceit, all of these magnified in the context of religion.[48] Less obvious is the extent to which Part 1 involves a similar theme, here directed not on those whose beliefs we investigate, but on ourselves as investigators. Indeed Hume's Maxim can be seen as intended precisely to correct for a powerful bias in our assessment of evidence, commonly called the *base rate fallacy*. This is clear in the diagnostic test example of §9 above, where we naturally find it all-too-easy to ignore the background "base rate" of the disease when assessing the significance of the test result. Such error is perhaps unsurprising, because the specific immediacy of the test itself – and its apparently impressive reliability of 99.9% – strike us with far more *force and vivacity* (as Hume would say) than the memory of the general "prior probability" of one in a million. But it turns out that people very commonly go wrong in this way with far less excuse.[49] Hume's Maxim – notwithstanding its weaknesses – is thus of considerable value as a vivid reminder of the need to take base rates into account. And although the Independence Assumption on which it relies is not always appropriate, where it is, the Maxim stands.

I ended §19 above by suggesting that Hume might have had in mind an alternative – and far more defensible – version of his Maxim, which is not the explicit goal of his main argument, but is readily suggested once the broader considerations of his essay come into play. This Revised Maxim nicely pulls together his initial emphasis on the inductive unlikelihood of miracles with his later stress on psychological explaining away of miracle reports. And it provides a potentially powerful response to the objection of §18, by focusing less on the improbability of miracles (which the theist can legitimately contest by appeal to divine teleology) and more on the relative

---

programme they began. Note that the original version of Hume's discussion of miracles seems to have been intended for the *Treatise* (Hume 1748, pp. 161–2; *NHL* 2), probably in Book 1 Part 3 together with his pioneering discussions of other human cognitive weaknesses (e.g. *T* 1.3.9.6–19, 1.3.10.4–9, 1.3.13.1–10).

[48] See §13 and §16 above, and note our natural teleological bias as made explicit in the *Natural History of Religion*.

[49] See for instance the striking example given by Tversky and Kahneman (1974, pp. 1124–5). Note that this same weakness seems to underlie Hume's observation in §17 above, that "I never knew any one, that examined and deliberated about nonsense who did not believe it before the end of his inquiries."

probability that false miracle stories will arise through natural processes. Thus equipped, Hume need not insist – with apparent inductive dogmatism – that the theist's stories are so intrinsically incredible as to be unworthy of consideration. Instead, he can wait for our empirical science of the mind to explain such beliefs away by appeal to cognitive dispositions that are manifest more generally, and thus render the hypothesis of divine action gratuitous.[50] Understood in this way, Hume's attack on miracles turns increasingly towards the psychology of *Treatise* 1.3 and the anthropology of the *Natural History of Religion*. But the spirit of his famous essay remains.

Hertford College, Oxford

References

Aquinas, Thomas (1258–64), *Summa Contra Gentiles*, translated by Vernon J. Bourke as *On the Truth of the Catholic Faith*, Doubleday and Co., 1956. Excerpt reprinted in Richard Swinburne (ed.), *Miracles* (Macmillan, 1989), pp. 19–22.

Broad, C. D. (1917), "Hume's Theory of the Credibility of Miracles", *Proceedings of the Aristotelian Society* 17, pp. 77–94.

Burns, R. M. (1981), *The Great Debate on Miracles*, Associated University Presses.

Butler, Joseph (1736), *The Analogy of Religion, Natural and Revealed, to the Constitution and Course of Nature*, ed. W. E. Gladstone, Clarendon Press, 1896 [bracketed § numbers are Gladstone's].

Campbell, George (1762), *A Dissertation on Miracles*, Edinburgh: A. Kincaid & J. Bell.

Coady, C. A. J. (1973), "Testimony and Observation", *American Philosophical Quarterly* 10, pp. 149–55.

Coady, C. A. J. (1992), *Testimony*, Clarendon Press.

Coleman, Dorothy (1988), "Hume, Miracles and Lotteries", *Hume Studies* 14, pp. 328–46.

---

[50] For some relevant recent work, see French and Wilson (2007). The point here is that if empirical work were to show that the propagation of false miracle stories is absolutely to be expected within relevant contexts (e.g. first century Palestine), then the atheist can easily contest such stories *without* having to insist that they are in themselves vanishingly improbable. The hypothesis of supernatural action simply becomes one for which there is no need, no compelling evidence, and which runs counter to all modern rigorous investigation.

Coleman, Dorothy (2001), "Baconian Probability and Hume's Theory of Testimony", *Hume Studies* 27, pp. 195–226.

Earman, John (2000), *Hume's Abject Failure: The Argument Against Miracles*, Oxford University Press.

Earman, John (2002), "Bayes, Hume, Price, and Miracles", *Proceedings of the British Academy* 113, pp. 91–109.

Flew, Antony (1959), "Hume's Check", *Philosophical Quarterly* 9, pp. 1–18.

Flew, Antony (1961), *Hume's Philosophy of Belief*, Routledge & Kegan Paul.

Fogelin, Robert J. (2003), *A Defense of Hume on Miracles*, Princeton University Press.

French, Christopher C. and Krissy Wilson (2007), "Cognitive Factors Underlying Paranormal Beliefs and Experiences", In Sergio Della Sala (ed.), *Tall Tales about the Mind and Brain: Separating Fact from Fiction*, Oxford University Press, pp. 3–22.

Garrett, Don (2002), "Hume on Testimony concerning Miracles", in Peter Millican (ed.), *Reading Hume on Human Understanding*, Clarendon Press, pp. 301–32. Adapted from Garrett, *Cognition and Commitment in Hume's Philosophy*, Oxford University Press (1997), chapter 7: pp. 137–62.

Gaskin, J. C. A. (1988), *Hume's Philosophy of Religion*, Macmillan, second edition.

Gillies, Donald (1991), "A Bayesian Proof of a Humean Principle", *British Journal for the Philosophy of Science* 42, pp. 255–6.

Gilovich, Thomas, Dale Griffin, and Daniel Kahneman, eds (2002), *Heuristics and Biases: The Psychology of Intuitive Judgment*, Cambridge University Press.

Holder, Rodney D. (1998), "Hume on Miracles: Bayesian Interpretation, Multiple Testimony, and the Existence of God", *British Journal for the Philosophy of Science* 49, pp. 49–65.

Houston, Joseph (1994), *Reported Miracles: A Critique of Hume*, Cambridge University Press.

Howson, Colin (2000), *Hume's Problem: Induction and the Justification of Belief*, Clarendon Press.

Hume, David (1739/40), *A Treatise of Human Nature: A Critical Edition*, vol. 1, ed. David Fate Norton and Mary J. Norton, Clarendon Press, 2007 (references indicated by "*T*" and given to book, part, section and paragraph number).

Hume, David (1741–77), *Essays, Moral, Political, and Literary*, ed. Eugene F. Miller, Liberty Classics, second edition 1987 (*"Essays"*, references given to paragraph number and to page number).

Hume, David (1748), *An Enquiry concerning Human Understanding*, ed. Peter Millican, Oxford University Press, 2007 (references indicated by *"E"* and given to section and paragraph number, except when giving page references for additional material such as Hume's letters).

Hume, David (1751), *An Enquiry concerning the Principles of Morals*, ed. Tom L. Beauchamp, Oxford University Press, 1998 (references indicated by *"M"* and given to section and paragraph number).

Hume, David (1757), *A Dissertation on the Passions and The Natural History of Religion*, ed. Tom L. Beauchamp, Oxford University Press, 2007 (references to Natural History indicated by *"NHR"*, and given to section and paragraph number).

Hume, David (1932), *The Letters of David Hume*, ed. J. Y. T. Greig, 2 vols, Clarendon Press (references indicated by *"HL"*).

Hume, David (1954), *New Letters of David Hume*, ed. R. Klibansky and E. C. Mossner, Clarendon Press (references indicated by *"NHL"*).

Johnson, David (1999), *Hume, Holism, and Miracles*, Cornell University Press.

Larmer, Robert (1996), "David Hume and the Miraculous" in Larmer (ed.), *Questions of Miracle*, McGill-Queen's University Press, pp. 26–39.

Lewis, C. S. (1947), *Miracles: A Preliminary Study*, Macmillan.

Locke, John (1690), *An Essay Concerning Human Understanding*, ed. P. H. Nidditch, Clarendon Press, 1975 (*"Essay"*, references given to book, chapter and section number).

Lombrozo, Tania, Deborah Kelemen and Deborah Zaitchik (2007), "Inferring Design: Evidence of a preference for teleological explanations in patients with Alzheimer's disease", *Psychological Science* 18.11, pp. 999–1006.

Mackie, J. L. (1982), *The Miracle of Theism*, Clarendon Press.

Millican, Peter (1993), "'Hume's Theorem' Concerning Miracles", *Philosophical Quarterly* 43, pp. 489–95.

Millican, Peter (2003), "Hume, Miracles, and Probabilities: Meeting Earman's Challenge", available online at http://www.davidhume.org/documents/2003 Miracles and Probabilities.pdf (as presented at the Las Vegas Hume Conference, July 2003).

Millican, Peter (2007a), "Humes Old and New: Four Fashionable Falsehoods, and One Unfashionable Truth", *Proceedings of the Aristotelian Society*, Supplementary Volume 81, pp. 163–99.

Millican, Peter (2007b), "Against the 'New Hume'", in Rupert Read and Kenneth A. Richman (eds), *The New Hume Debate: Revised Edition*, Routledge, pp. 211–52.

Millican, Peter (2009), "Hume, Causal Realism, and Causal Science", *Mind* 118, pp. 647–712.

Noonan, Harold (2007), *Hume*, Oneworld Publications.

Norton, David Fate (1982), *David Hume: Common-Sense Moralist, Sceptical Metaphysician*, Princeton University Press.

Price, Richard (1768), *On the Importance of Christianity and the Nature of Historical Evidence, and Miracles, Dissertation IV* of *Four Dissertations*, second edition (first edition was 1767), London: A. Millar and T. Cadell.

Purtill, Richard L. (1978), "Miracles: What if They Happen?" in Richard Swinburne (ed.), *Miracles* Macmillan, 1989), pp. 189–205. From Purtill, *Thinking about Religion*, Prentice Hall, pp. 65–79.

Selby-Bigge, L. A. (1894), "Editor's Introduction" to *Enquiries Concerning the Human Understanding and Concerning the Principles of Morals by David Hume*, Clarendon Press, pp. vii–xxxi.

Sherlock, Thomas (1729), *The Tryal of the Witnesses of the Resurrection of Jesus*, London: J. Roberts.

Sobel, Jordan Howard (1991), "Hume's Theorem on Testimony Sufficient to Establish a Miracle", *Philosophical Quarterly* 41, pp. 229–37.

Stroud, Barry (1977), *Hume*, Routledge & Kegan Paul.

Swinburne, Richard (1968), "Miracles", *Philosophical Quarterly* 18, pp. 320–8.

Swinburne, Richard (1996), *Is There a God?*, Oxford University Press.

Traiger, Saul (1993), "Humean Testimony", *Pacific Philosophical Quarterly* 74, pp. 135–49.

Tversky, Amos and Daniel Kahneman (1974), "Judgment under Uncertainty: Heuristics and Biases", *Science* 185, pp. 1124–31.

Wilson, Fred (1989), "The Logic of Probabilities in Hume's Argument against Miracles", *Hume Studies* 15, pp. 255–75.

Wootton, David (1990), "Hume's 'Of Miracles': Probability and Irreligion", In M. A. Stewart (ed.), *Studies in the Philosophy of the Scottish Enlightenment*, Clarendon Press, pp. 191–229.

Darwinism, Purpose and Meaning

MARY MIDGLEY

Researchers report that people who are asked to give their reason for converting to Creationism often say that they have done so because they see it as the only possible alternative to 'Darwinism' – something which they find intolerable and equate with scientific atheism.

What does Darwinism mean here? No doubt their idea of it often contains a good deal of bloody-minded 'Social Darwinism', a hardy weed which, like ground-elder, never really goes away. Much more recent sources are, however available to them. In *River Out Of Eden* – a book which he has deliberately subtitled 'A Darwinian View Of Life' – Richard Dawkins sums up what he believes to be its message;

> In a universe of blind forces and physical replication, some people are going to get hurt, others are going to get lucky, and you won't find any rhyme or reason in it, nor any justice. The universe we observe has precisely the properties we should expect if there is, at bottom, no design, no purpose, no evil and no good, nothing but blind, pitiless indifference. As that unhappy poet A.E. Housman put it,

> > For Nature, heartless, witless nature
> > Will neither care nor know.

> DNA neither cares nor knows. DNA just is. And we dance to its tune.[1]

Similarly on page 1 of *The Selfish Gene* he declares that 'we no longer have to resort to superstition when faced with the deep problems; Is there a meaning to life?[i] What are we for? What is man?' These questions have, he says, been given a final, unmistakeably negative answer in 1859 by the publication of *The Origin of Species*.

This is Dawkinsism, not Darwinism, but it should, I think, still be looked at seriously. For a start, we should ask what it means to say that the universe contains 'no evil and no good?' This is biologically odd because that universe does, after all, contain many living organisms, including ourselves, And for any living organism some things are

---

[1]   Dawkins, *River Out of Eden: A Darwinian View of Life* (New York: Basic Books, 1995), 155.

doi:10.1017/S1358246111000099   © The Royal Institute of Philosophy and the contributors 2011

necessarily evil, others good. Each species has its own natural needs, for which some things are useful, others harmful. When we humans call something 'good' or 'evil', we are not adding mysterious 'non-natural' qualities to the universe but merely reporting facts about how it affects ourselves.

Of course our peculiar kind of conscious awareness makes us register those facts in a particular way. It makes us specially aware of conflicts, especially of cultural differences. It also gives us a special interest in arguing borderline cases But it does not create the thing reported.

Next, what does it mean to say that the universe contains 'no purpose, no design'? This can scarcely be right because human beings – who, again, are a natural part of the universe – plainly do have purposes, among which the purpose of removing religion is just one typical example. And this purposiveness is not a peculiarly human trait. It is one that we share with other animals. Of course (again) the special, articulate, highly conscious form of planning that we use *is* uncommon, being made possible by our specially developed brains. But the purposivenss itself – the strong, persistent, systematic striving till a particular end is reached – plainly is not unique to us. The fact that Dawkins represents the Selfish Gene itself as relentlessly purposive shows how impossible it is to describe the workings of life without using such language.

A human trying to get out of a trap doubtless uses different means from a fox or a rat, and thinks differently about them. But the striving itself – the intense, persistent effort directed to that end – is surely the same for all. Human observers watching the animal will have no doubt about what it is doing, nor about its relation to our own striving. Similarly, seeds that germinate under paving-stones go to incredible lengths to grow past them, or even, if necessary to lift them out of place. As Aristotle noted, there is here a remarkable continuity that runs from our own fully conscious purposes right through the realm of life.

Teleology Is Not Optional

People who claim that there is no purpose in the natural world seem to conceive *purpose* as something peculiar to humans, a cultural construct which we have invented, a fancy that we anthropomorphically project onto neutral, directionless matter. This idea is intended to heal the rift between matter and mind by treating them both simply as matter, and inert matter at that – matter made of the kind of dead, billiard-ball-like particles that used to be believed in, not the highly versatile bundles of energy that physicists deal in today.

This kind of naïve materialism has, of course, raised great hopes over the last century and many scientists still embrace it. But for some time it has been running into great difficulties over the 'problem of consciousness' and also over this unrealistic attitude to purpose. The concept of matter turns out to be quite as puzzling as the concept of mind; indeed perhaps more so.

Some people are therefore now beginning to suspect that the rift may be better dealt with differently – perhaps in the way that Spinoza proposed, by not letting it arise in the first place. Perhaps there are not two radically different kinds of stuff, mind and matter, but just one great world which has both mental and physical attributes. This can then quite properly be viewed, without contradiction, from both these angles. And it would not be surprising if a single tendency, or *conatus*, runs through the whole, so that our kind of conscious purposiveness is only one part of it,

Such talk is, of course, out of fashion. But the current sweeping denial of purpose outside human life is certainly no less metaphysically ambitious. It only strikes us as less surprising because we are so used to it. Exclusive materialism is an extreme philosophical doctrine just as exclusive idealism is, not a scientific discovery. It is not economical because conceptual economy is not attained by using as few terms as possible but by using just the ones that work, ones that will actually explain the data in question. The proof of these puddings is in the eating. It is true that the concept of Purpose is not used in physics, but then physics is not in the business of trying to explain life. If our aim is to understand a world that includes ourselves, along with our thoughts, and the other organisms, we need concepts that will help us do this.

Purposive behaviour is not, then, something that we humans have invented or constructed but something universal among earthly organisms. Indeed it is hard to see how, if it had not been already there, we could ever have invented it. To innovate on this scale we would surely have had to be creatures unrelated to other life-forms, creatures drawing our capacities from some quite alien outside source. That, indeed, was Descartes' idea when he ruled that minds were pure spirits, unrelated to bodies, and that non-human animals were mere unconscious machines. But that isn't the way we think today.

Making the Best of our Evolved Minds

Purpose and value, then, aren't arbitrary colours painted onto the world by our vanity. They have grown up in that world and are natural aspects of it – emergent properties, shapes that appear as soon as its inhabitants become complex enough to need them. Just as there are no aeronautical properties till something starts to fly, and no musical properties till something produces music, so these life-patterns are not found in a lifeless world. But that does not make them any less real or natural. They are aspects of evolution which become steadily more complex as the organisms themselves do so.

These properties involve no fishy supernatural interference, nor – still more obviously – does meaning. To find the universe meaningful is not to decode an extra, cryptic message hidden behind it but simply to find a continuity between its patterns and those of our own lives – enough continuity to confirm that our presence here makes sense. *The point is not that the world belongs to us but that we belong to it.* We do not have to think that it was designed for our benefit, nor that we can understand it completely. We only need to see it as ordered in a way that makes our presence here intelligible. And, since we actually are a part of it, this is not a silly project. It explains why we are naturally disposed to respond to this world with the mixture of caution, trust and reverence that have proved appropriate for our ancestors over many aeons of hard experience.

People often suggest today that we should discount all such natural tendencies because they are merely a part of our evolved human nature. But, since we actually are humans and cannot become anything else, it is hard to see what this would achieve. Psychological surgery conducted on these principles could not be confined to a few special cases; it would call for a wider massacre. For instance, our human nature is also the source of our surprising conviction that the people around us are conscious fellow-beings, not mindless robots, and of our tendency to feel friendly and co-operative towards some of them. It is, too, the source of our remarkable belief that the material world is still there when we turn our backs on it, and of our strange habit of trusting other people's testimony – including, of course, the testimony of scientists – unless there is some special reason not to do so. It is, in short, the only tool-box that we have for living and thinking at all.

Of course we sometimes need to reject thoughts that come naturally to us. But we don't reject them just because they come from our evolved nature. We reject them because they conflict with others that are better supported. And in such cases we always try to reconcile the conflicting insights involved. Indeed, that reconciling is a central business of our intellectual life because we need to integrate our personalities as a whole. We cannot by-pass it by rejecting certain selected ideas simply for being natural.

The Dream of Infallibility

It is rather remarkable that this kind of sceptical argument is so often invoked specially for the case of religion, as if that were the only un-reliable part of the human equipment. Thus Charles Darwin, re-counting in his autobiography how his views on religion had developed, explained that he was still impressed by –

> the extreme difficulty, or rather impossibility, of conceiving this immense and wonderful universe, including man... as the result of blind chance or necessity. When thus reflecting, I feel com-pelled to look to a First Cause having an intelligent mind in some degree analogous to that of man, and I deserve to be called a Theist... [But then, he says] arises the doubt, can the mind of man, *which has, as I fully believe, been developed from a mind as low as that possessed by the lowest animal*, be trusted when it draws such grand conclusions?[2]

This discouraging idea led Darwin to remain agnostic on the matter – agnostic, as he often explained, in a literal sense; he was far too aware of mystery to be an atheist. But if evolutionary considerations took him that far they ought surely to have taken him further. He should surely have distrusted the whole mass of reasoning which made him reject the chance explanation – indeed, he should have dis-trusted the whole mass of thought, including scientific thought, that had caused his doubts. It all came from the same evolutionary source, and indeed from social sources as well. His complaint about the source suggests that there is some better alternative available, some direct revelation that would bypass these drawbacks. What would that oracle be?

This is surely a nostalgic vision, drawn from pre-evolutionary Platonic thinking, of a directly inspired hot-line to knowledge, a by-pass available only to our spiritually-privileged species. But, as he himself had showed, this is a dream. We know now that we are not purpose-built knowledge-machines but composite creatures who have acquired our intellectual capacities by the way as part of our general equipment for life. This does not, of course, mean that our brains are a mere helpless jumble, shaped haphazardly by any passing meme. But their powers are limited. They find it much harder to grasp some kinds of question than others, They find ques-tions about purpose and about our own relation to the world

[2] *Thomas Henry Huxley and Charles Darwin, Autobiographies* (London: Oxford University Press, 1974), 54.

Mary Midgley

particularly difficult. And there are very few questions, in science or anywhere else, to which they can give us a final answer.

What, then should we do about these strangely ambitious tendencies of our minds, such as the teleological one that Darwin noted? Simon Conway Morris, having laid out the tidy reductive answer which is so popular today, remarks –

> Yet, there are nagging doubts. Yes, it may all be due to a few misfiring neurons, perhaps an extra dollop of neuropeptide or whatever, but the fact remains that humans have an overwhelming sense of purpose. As a species we are strangely comfortable to find ourselves embedded in a teleological matrix.[3]

We need, he says, to ask why this is and whether this idea of a *telos* is really redundant. As he points out, such things are now usually explained by the methods of 'evolutionary psychology' by saying that these habits cheer people up, so they confer a selective advantage by preventing despair. But these answers, even if there were enough evidence for them, would still miss the point by a mile. The way in which they would miss it is perhaps best conveyed by citing a parallel.

Suppose that scientists from Alpha Centauri are studying human life and are wondering how to account for the practice of music, which of course they find pointless. Following prevalent doctrines, they decide that music cheers people up, perhaps by being bond-forming. And they cite research which seems to support this finding. In what sense have they now got an adequate explanation?

The trouble is, of course, that this story only provides an *outside* context – a causal framework inside which the puzzling phenomenon can occur – not a conceptual one. It does nothing to show just what work music does in people's lives. And if these researchers, encouraged by their success, go on to investigate other puzzling human activities such as laughter, flower-arrangement or football, they are surely likely to give the same explanation, Thus, all these activities really have the same function, and any one of them can always be substituted for any other.

Has something gone wrong here?

It has. When we ask about the point and meaning of an activity like music we want to understand what makes it worth doing – what is its importance, what place it has in life. This is a question that arises from the inside. I use the example of music because its role really

---

[3]   *Life's Solution; Inevitable Humans in a Lonely Universe*, (Cambridge: Cambridge University Press, 2003), 313.

does puzzle people. It isn't easy to spell out in clear terms just what music does for us. But nobody supposes this means that music doesn't do anything, that it is trivial, and need not be taken seriously. The trouble may be rather that it is too important – that it is so widely entangled in our lives that we can't easily see it as a whole.

How does this compare with the question about our natural leaning towards teleology? Unluckily, that question is mired in the history of past political and economic conflicts between scientists and the churches. That background has produced a situation where, for some time, many scientists have seen the issue as one of tribal warfare, a battle in their cold war against religion. Any notion of cosmic purpose or meaning strikes them as a dangerous superstition which will discredit science, so they avoid it. Paul Davies cites that great physicist Richard Feynman, who said that 'the great accumulation of understanding as to how the physical world behaves only convinces one that this behaviour has a kind of meaninglessness about it'.[4] And Steven Weinberg, taking a deep breath, blows up this sentiment to the full, declaring that 'The more the universe seems comprehensible, the more it also seems pointless'.

As Davies observes (18), Weinberg came in for some flak from his colleagues for writing this comment – not because he denied that the universe had a point, but for even suggesting that it could have a point. The odd thing here is, however, the conclusion that Weinberg draws from this pointlessness. The only thing that cheers him up on this wintry scene, where all normal value has been proved senseless, is the fact that people are still researching about astrophysics:

> If there is no solace in the fruits of our research, there is at least some consolation in the research itself. Men and women are not content to comfort themselves with tales of gods and giants... they build telescopes and satellites and accelerators and sit at their desks for endless hours working out *the meaning* of the data that they gather... The effort to *understand* the universe is one of the very few things that lift human life a little above the level of farce, and give it some of the grace of tragedy.[5]

But if the universe has already been shown to be pointless, why can it be important to study its workings? What is this *meaning* that the

---

[4]   Paul Davies, *The Goldilocks Enigma; Why Is The Universe Just Right For Life?* (London: Penguin, 2006), 17–18
[5]   *The First Three Minutes* (London: Andre Deutsch, 1977), 155. Emphasis mine.

researchers are looking for? Why are they doing science at all? Clearly Weinberg has cheerfully swallowed Jacques Monod's assumption that scientific truth can still survive as the only ideal left after a general holocaust of all other values, that science still makes sense in an alien universe of pure chance.[6] Paul Davies points out that this won't do:

> Doing science means figuring out what is going on in the world – what the universe is up to, what it is "about". If it isn't about anything there would be no reason to embark on the scientific quest in the first place... So we might justifiably invert Weinberg's dictum and say that *the more the universe seems pointless, the more it also seems incomprehensible.*[7]

This is a difficulty about the nature of understanding, one that arises from within science itself, not a criticism thrust on it by an alien religious tribe. And it is a problem that quite a lot of distinguished scientists have lately been raising. Many of them, like Davies, do so in reference to the remarkable coincidences which physicists have lately noted in the conditions that make intelligent life – or indeed any kind of life – possible in the universe The improbability of this happening by chance is, says Freeman Dyson, so startling that it becomes perverse to talk of our presence as due to chance. Plainly we are not alien creatures, as Jacques Monod thought, marooned in a universe that we cannot expect to understand. As Dyson puts it:

> I do not feel like an alien in this universe. The more I examine this universe and study the details of its architecture, the more evidence I find that the universe must in some sense have known that we were coming.[8]

This thinking does not, of course, involve commitment to any particular religious position. It simply declares the metaphysical and religious sphere open once more to scientists for serious discussion. Initially, of course, it points towards the territory of philosophers like Spinoza, Aristotle and Kant (none of whom can be suspected of being an agent for fundamentalist Christianity) but there are plenty of other directions in which it can be carried further. Davies, having described the cosmic coincidences and weighed the various possible interpretations, concludes:

---

[6] See Monod, *Chance and Necessity* (Glasgow, Collins, 1972), 154, 159.
[7] Davies, *The Goldilocks Enigma*, 18.
[8] *Disturbing the Universe* (New York: Harper & Row, 1979), 250.

It seems to me that there is a genuine scheme of things – the universe is "about" something. But I am equally uneasy about dumping the whole set of problems in the lap of an arbitrary god, or abandoning all further thought and declaring existence ultimately to be a mystery... Even though I do *not* believe *Homo Sapiens* to be more than an accidental by-product of haphazard natural processes... I do believe that life and mind are etched deeply into the fabric of the cosmos, perhaps through a shadowy half-glimpsed life principle.[9]

Similarly in biology, Simon Conway Morris sees the prevalence of evolutionary convergence as showing another set of apparent coincidences parallel to those revealed in physics, and just as hard to dismiss as mere chance. The idea that evolution is a wild, random casino is, he says, badly mistaken. Evolutionary convergences reveal both a clear order and a remarkable kind of creativity:

For all this exuberance and flair [in evolution] there are constraints; convergence is inevitable, yet paradoxically the net result is not one of sterile returns to worn-out themes; rather there is also a patent trend of increased complexity. Some cosmologists like to speculate that the universe is designed to be the home of life, to which some biologists might add "Yes, and not only that but we have a pretty shrewd idea of what was on the cards" [namely, the development of intelligence. We need, then, to ask] if some of our predecessors who saw their religious faith either ebb or haemorrhage were both misinformed and over-pessimistic, and to enquire whether some common ground can be regained.[10]

It is surely to be hoped that, instead of waging unprofitable cold warfare against all religion, scientists can indeed carry this kind of dialogue further.

Newcastle University

---

[9]   Davies, *The Goldilocks Enigma*, 302–3.
[10]   Morris, *Life's Solution*, 21 and 113.

Christianity and the Errors of Our Time: Simone Weil on Atheism and Idolatry[1]

MARIO VON DER RUHR

1. Introduction

In his 1985 book on philosophy and atheism, the Canadian thinker Kai Nielsen, a prolific writer on the subject, wonders why the philosophy of religion is 'so boring', and concludes that it must be 'because the case for atheism is so strong that it is difficult to work up much enthusiasm for the topic.'[2] Indeed, Nielsen even regards most of the contemporary arguments for atheism as little more than 'mopping up operations after the Enlightenment'[3] which, on the whole, add little to the socio-anthropological and socio-psychological accounts of religion provided by thinkers like Feuerbach, Marx and Freud, as any 'reasonable person informed by modernity' will readily acknowledge.[4] On this view, the answer to Kant's question – 'What may we hope?' – does not gesture towards a resurrection and personal immortality, but instead to the death of religious discourse itself:

> I think, and indeed hope, that God-talk, and religious discourse more generally, is, or at least should be, dying out in the West, or more generally in a world that has felt the force of a Weberian disenchantment of the world. This sense that religious convictions are no longer a live option is something which people who

[1] I am grateful to Mr John Kinsey, Dr Ieuan Lloyd, Prof. Anthony O'Hear, and the audience who attended a presentation of this paper on 27th February 2009 at the Royal Institute of Philosophy in London, for their generous and helpful comments. A slightly different draft of this paper has appeared in Lucian and Rebecca Stone (eds.), *The Relevance of the Radical: Simone Weil 100 Years Later* (Continuum: London, 2009). I am indebted to Continuum Publishers for permission to reprint it here.
[2] Kai Nielsen, *Philosophy and Atheism* (New York: Prometheus, 1985), 224.
[3] Nielsen, *Philosophy and Atheism*, 224.
[4] Ibid. 224–225.

doi:10.1017/S1358246111000130   ©The Royal Institute of Philosophy and the contributors 2011

Mario von der Ruhr

think of themselves as either modernists or post-modernists very often tend to have.[5]

A construal like this, which views religious belief as a phenomenon whose philosophical examination has been pretty much concluded, and which may therefore be handed over to the social scientist for general historiographic and anthropological archiving, certainly makes it hard to see what the philosopher of religion could have to contribute to the subject that, far from being 'boring', constituted a clarification of what is involved in the religious form of life, let alone one that could be recognized to *be* such, even by those who, unlike Nielsen, are religious believers.

However, the latter are likely to object that Nielsen's indictment of religious discourse is itself the product of problematic assumptions about the nature of religious belief, on the one hand, and the requirements of philosophical inquiry, on the other. The claim that the case for atheism is 'so strong' as to make religious convictions passé, for example, seems to imply, not only that both attitudes or forms of life are answerable to some Archimedean standard of intelligibility and rationality, but that the logical relation between religious belief and atheism must be roughly analogous to that between the affirmation of a proposition and its negation. Indeed, Nielsen thinks it obvious that, when religious believers affirm that there is a God, or that God created the world,

> they ... believe that [these] are *factual* assertions: that is to say that they have truth-values. It is a *fact* that there is a God; it is a *fact* that he created the world; it is a *fact* that he protects me and the like.[6]

But since all factual claims must, on Nielsen's view, be subject to public verification or falsification, and 'if we cannot even say what *in principle* would count as *evidence* against the putative statement that God created the world, then "God created the world" is devoid of factual content.'[7] Thus, the believer's avowal purports to assert a fact when, ironically, it does not even have a truth-value.[8]

---

[5] Kai Nielsen, 'Can Anything be Beyond Human Understanding?' in Tim Tessin and Mario von der Ruhr (eds.), *Philosophy and the Grammar of Religious Belief* (London: Macmillan, 1995), 179–180.
[6] Kai Nielsen and D. Z. Phillips, *Wittgensteinian Fideism?* (London: SCM Press, 2005), 31. (My emphasis).
[7] Ibid.
[8] Ibid.

Christianity and the Errors of Our Time

If this analysis adequately characterizes religious utterances *en gros*, then it looks as if the believer is, indeed, guilty of a semantic sleight of hand, in which the very conditions of a meaningful assertion are suspended no sooner than they have been acknowledged, thus turning the believer into what Oscar Wilde would have described as 'an adept in the art of concealing what is not worth finding'.[9]

That this conclusion would, however, be as hasty as Nielsen's identification of the truth-valued with the factual, and as unwarranted as his assumptions about what believers *must* mean by assertions whose surface grammar resembles that of empirical propositions, has been forcefully argued by the late D. Z. Phillips, whose detailed response to Nielsen in *Wittgensteinian Fideism?*[10] owes much of its inspiration to the works of Ludwig Wittgenstein and Simone Weil, two thinkers who not only shared a deep religious sensibility, but who rightly sensed that positivist or emotivist analyses of that sensibility were just as crude as the charge that all atheists suffer from an idolatrous aberration of the intellect.

Nielsen's own attitude towards Wittgenstein and Weil is guarded and sceptical. While he admits that Wittgenstein's remarks on religion, for example, are 'suggestive', he still dismisses them as 'too fragmentary and apocalyptic in tone to be much more than exasperating hints',[11] and thus as not being of much use in the debate. On the contrary, he finds that a Wittgensteinian conception of religion 'yields an utterly devastating view for Christianity', because it turns religion into

> a form of life that cannot be shown to have any superior rationality, authenticity, or justifiability to other incommensurable forms of life. But that is precisely what anyone who regards himself as a Christian, in any tolerably orthodox sense, cannot accept... With such Wittgensteinian friends, the Christian philosopher might remark, who needs enemies.[12]

Nielsen is, of course, right to caution the Christian thinker against false prophets in the philosophy of religion, but then a similar warning could be issued against those atheists whose condescending

---

[9]   Oscar Wilde, 'The Decay of Lying', in *Complete Works* (London: Collins, 1983), 973.
[10]   Nielsen and Phillips, *Wittgensteinian Fideism?* (London: SCM Press, 2005).
[11]   Kai Nielsen, *An Introduction to the Philosophy of Religion* (London: Macmillan, 1982), 45.
[12]   Nielsen, *Philosophy and Atheism*, 223–224.

Mario von der Ruhr

caricatures of religion undermine the very humanist cause they are ostensibly trying to defend. Moreover, the claim that 'tolerably orthodox' Christian philosophers should be able to demonstrate the 'superior rationality' of their religious convictions over alternative perspectives on life, seems to me neither warranted, nor defensible.

While it is true that, for such believers, *fides* and *ratio* form a symbiotic relationship in which the former can be inspired, helpfully expounded, and deepened by the latter – e.g. in natural and systematic theology – and while they may regard their faith as the deepest and most appropriate response to the existential questions that trouble them, they would surely not be so naïve as to think that they could rationally demonstrate the superiority of that response to atheists like Schopenhauer, Nietzsche, or Kai Nielsen.

Indeed, it is precisely because such an undertaking would be as formidable as that of trying to persuade a miser to be generous, on the miser's *own* terms, that Plato's depiction of Socrates' exchanges with the power-hungry orators in the *Gorgias*, for example, can emerge as a realistic and truthful account of what would be involved in the kind of persuasion that informed a radical reorientation of the spirit. In presenting us with a dialogue that does *not* culminate in an epiphanic ending for any of Socrates' interlocutors, Plato is not so much revealing Socrates' dialectic labours to be futile – in fact, as genuine expressions of concern for the spiritual welfare of his fellow citizens, they never are – as drawing attention to both the (psychological) obstacles that may get in the way of seeing things from Socrates' perspective, and the limits of *rational justification*. Far from giving offence to orthodox Christians, these limits are clearly acknowledged in their emphasis on the need for revelation, and summarized in the dictum *credo ut intelligam*.

Now, whether a Wittgensteinian analysis of key Christian concepts might nevertheless cause just such offence, is an altogether different matter, which I will not pursue here, save to note the following: On the one hand, even the more orthodox Catholics among, for example, D. Z. Phillips' commentators, agree that his account must not be understood as a unified theory of religious discourse, but represents a broad spectrum of philosophical positions and perspectives that range from the strictly orthodox to the 'heretical', and that this is also what one would expect of a philosopher who sees himself as a disinterested grammarian of *Lebensformen* (forms of life) and their distinctive, though by no means unrelated, conceptual and linguistic frameworks. Thus, as the Thomist scholar Brian Davies has pointed out in a recent, critical reappraisal of Phillips' work, much of it can simply be read as a straightforward attack on anthropomorphism, and his account of God-talk, in particular, as an unqualified endorsement of Aquinas' doctrine of divine simplicity – i.e. the view that God is not an object among objects, but unique, non-spatial, causally unaffected, changeless, etc. – according to which God's existence is *not* properly described as a 'fact' that might, for instance, lend itself to *a posteriori* investigation. If Phillips is theologically out of line here, then, as Brian Davies rightly insists, so is Thomas Aquinas,[13] whose place in the history of Biblical scholarship is hardly that of a non-traditionalist or revisionist. This is not to deny that there are features of Phillips' account of religion from which the orthodox believer would rightly withhold the *imprimatur*, including a construal of immortality according to which '[eternity] is not an extension of this present life, but a mode of judging it ... not *more* life, but this life seen under certain moral and religious modes of thought'.[14] But then, as has already been pointed out, Phillips' work was never intended as an exercise in religious apologetics to begin with, nor should he be criticized for diverging from official Church doctrine when alternative understandings of immortality, prayer, covenant, the idea of a chosen people, etc. seem to him deeper, both philosophically and spiritually.

Readers who have been struck by the close philosophical kinship between Wittgenstein and Simone Weil will not be surprised to learn that Nielsen views the latter with a mixture of admiration and incomprehension. On the one hand, he admits that he is impressed by the starkness of Weil's thought – on the subject of *hubris*, for example[15] – granting that it 'has insight' and acknowledging that it is 'sensitive to *some* of the conceptual perplexities' that also occupy his own thinking about religion. Indeed, Nielsen finds that his disagreements with her seem to arise from a shared universe of discourse:

> Miss Weil is not, after all, to me like the Azande with his witchcraft substance. We both learned 'the language' of Christian belief; only I think it is illusion-producing while she thinks

---

[13] Cf. Brian Davies, 'Phillips on belief in God', *Philosophical Investigations* **30.1** (July 2007), 219–244, esp. 229–230.

[14] D. Z. Phillips, *Death and Immortality* (London: Macmillan, 1972), 49. For a critical assessment of Phillips' view, see Mario von der Ruhr, 'Theology, Philosophy, and Heresy: D. Z. Phillips and the Grammar of Religious Belief', in ed. Andy Sanders, *D. Z. Phillips' Contemplative Philosophy of Religion* (London: Ashgate, 2007), 55–75.

[15] Nielsen and Phillips, *Wittgensteinian Fideism?*, 197.

Mario von der Ruhr

that certain crucial segments of it are our stammering way of talking about ultimate reality.[16]

Then again, Nielsen has to confess that 'what she can understand and take as certain, I have no understanding of at all', indeed that Weil 'blithely accepts what I find unintelligible', so that, apart from momentary flashes of agreement, 'a very deep gulf separates us'.[17] In what follows, I will not engage with Nielsen's assessment of Wittgenstein and Weil, but rather look at some of what Weil herself has to say about atheism and its relation to religious belief, not only for the sobriety her reflections bring to the polemic exchanges that have come to dominate much of the current debate about religion, but because of the impartiality with which she exposes the practitioners of idolatry on *either* side of the divide. In addition, her thought calls for the continuation of precisely the kind of dialogue that, in her own time (1934–1938) brought together such staunchly anticlerical movements as the 'Popular Front' and Christian thinkers like Yves Congar, Jacques Maritain, Jean Daniélou, and Henri de Lubac.[18]

2. Idolatrous Atheists and Idolatrous Christians

In *Gravity and Grace*, a series of notebook entries compiled by her friend Gustave Thibon after her death, Simone Weil claims that '[the] errors of our time come from Christianity without the supernatural',[19] and that the influences of secularism and humanism are the primary causes of this development. What she means by 'supernatural' in this context is not 'metaphysical', however, but rather a certain purity of character or motive, one that is uncontaminated by self-regarding desires or sentiments. Thus, Mother Teresa's love of the poor and afflicted, for example, could be described as supernatural, whereas a love directed solely at what is pleasing, attractive, or lovable, would count as 'natural' love. As for the 'errors of our time', Weil's catalogue includes blind faith in technological and

---

[16] Nielsen and Phillips, *Wittgensteinian Fideism?*, 31.
[17] Ibid., 30.
[18] For an excellent discussion of this dialogue and its aftermath, see Stephen Bullivant, 'From "Main Tendue" to Vatican II: The Catholic Engagement with Atheism 1936–1965', in *New Blackfriars* **90.1026** (March, 2009): 178–188.
[19] Simone Weil, *Gravity and Grace*, tr. Emma Craufurd and Mario von der Ruhr (London: Routledge, 2002) (references indicated by *GG*), 115

economic progress;[20] the prevalence of narrowly utilitarian conceptions of the good;[21] the idolization of religious, social or political bodies and institutions;[22] an uncritical deference to science as the only paradigm of true knowledge and understanding;[23] debased notions of compassion and gratitude;[24] a 'mutilated, distorted, and soiled' sense of beauty (e.g. in art, music, architecture, or literature);[25] the proliferation of pseudo-spiritualities;[26] a growing rift between secular life and religious practices;[27] the degradation of the sacraments to merely external rituals;[28] and an ever-growing scepticism about 'man's supernatural vocation'.[29] Now, even though Weil believes that secularism and humanism are the prime causes of these social ills, she also insists that a certain kind of atheism, far from undermining belief in God, may actually serve to deepen it.[30] If this is so, then the relation between religious faith and atheism is far more complex than the ready employment of terms like 'believer' and 'atheist' in ordinary discourse about religion might suggest, and merits further investigation.

What, then, does Weil have to say about the two kinds of atheism – the one which is directly antithetical to the Christian faith, and that which may contribute to its purification?

As she sees it, the former is typically materialist in orientation and idolatrous, taking as its object not only material goods,[31] but aspirations towards power, fame, and other variants of prestige, as well as

[20] GG, 162.
[21] Simone Weil, The Need for Roots, tr. A. F. Wills (London: Routledge, 2002) (references indicated by NR), 539.
[22] Simone Weil, Selected Essays, ed. and tr. Richard Rees (London: Oxford University Press, 1962) (references indicated by SE), 53.
[23] NR, 237.
[24] Simone Weil, Waiting for God, tr. Emma Craufurd (New York: Harper & Row, 1973) (references indicated by WG), 162–163.
[25] Ibid.
[26] NR, 273.
[27] Simone Weil, Intimations of Christianity Among the Ancient Greeks (London: Routledge, 1988) (references indicated by IC), 151. See also, NR, 118.
[28] Simone Weil, First and Last Notebooks, ed. and tr. Richard Rees (New York: Oxford University Press, 1970) (references indicated by FLN), 295.
[29] SE, 47.
[30] 'There are two atheisms of which one is a purification of the notion of God'.(GG, 114).
[31] Simone Weil, Notebooks, 2 vols., tr. Arthur Wills (London: Routledge & Kegan Paul, 1956) (references indicated by NB) vol. 1, 144.

Mario von der Ruhr

the attainment of absolute goods (justice, equality, liberty, etc.) through revolutionary change wrought by a worldy power:

> Atheistic materialism is necessarily revolutionary, for, if it is to be directed towards an absolute good here on earth, it has to place it in the future. In order that this impetus should have full effect there must therefore be a mediator between the perfection to come and the present. This mediator is the chief – Lenin, etc. He is infallible and perfectly pure. In passing through him evil becomes good.[32]

In Weil's *Notebooks*, the progress in whose name such revolutionaries are carrying out their sinister maneuvers is described as 'the outstanding atheistic idea', but of course she does not mean by this that faith in the betterment of the human condition is a vain hope and the relentless work for its realization a waste of time. Such an attitude would betray precisely the kind of un-Christian fatalism and quietism that Weil herself never tired of combatting, whether in her writings, in the classroom, or on the factory floor. The point of her remark is rather that the propagation of the 'progress' in question may be grounded in *hubris* and fuelled by idolization of an individual (Lenin, Hitler), a collective (the proletariat), or an abstract process (History). As Weil puts it:

> Even materialists place somewhere outside themselves a good which far surpasses them, which helps them from outside, and towards which their thought turns in a movement of desire and prayer. For Napoleon it was his star. For Marxists it is History. But they place it in this world, like the giants of folklore who place their heart (or their life) inside an egg inside a fish in a lake guarded by a dragon; and who die in the end. And although their prayers are often granted, one fears they must be regarded as prayers addressed to the devil.[33]

In this connection, Weil is also struck by the frequent combination of such unholy self-transcendence with an overly zealous reverence for science, or *scientism*. Her examples of this alliance include the French atheist Félix Le Dantec (1869–1917), and a well-known gang of anarchist terrorists:

> In France, people question everything, respect nothing; some show a contempt for religion, others for patriotism, the State, the administration of justice, property, art, in fact everything under the sun; but their contempt stops short of science. The

[32] *GG*, 173–174.
[33] *FLN*, 308.

crudest scientism has no more fervent adepts than the anarchists. Le Dantec is their saint. Bonnot's *bandits tragiques* took their inspiration from him, and the greatest hero among them, in the eyes of his comrades, was nicknamed 'Raymond la Science.'[34]

Weil is by no means opposed to scientific or technological progress *per se*, which would be an absurd position to take, nor does she reject automation if this would bring genuine relief to the worker. Her concern is rather with the crudely positivist gospel of writers like Le Dantec, whose ready dismissal of religious belief in *Athéisme* (1907) ends up doing just as great a disservice to the cause of science as it does to atheism.[35]

At this point, it would be tempting to conclude that the religious believer exemplifies the exact opposite of the atheist as here described, but Weil, ever suspicious of deceptively simple dichotomies, instead proceeds to show that the expression 'religious believer' is no less problematic and obscure than the label 'atheist', indeed that the latter provides a mirror in which the former can see the reflection of her own spiritual deformities. For while it is true that '[e]very atheist is an idolater – unless he is worshipping the true God in his impersonal aspect', there is (as yet) no reason for the believer to congratulate herself on her own moral and spiritual rectitude, because, as Weil insists in the *First and Last Notebooks*, '[t]he *majority* of the pious are idolaters'.[36] Her verdict is grounded, not only in personal encounters with fellow Christians, including priests and other leading representatives of institutionalised religion – e.g. she finds that 'most believers, including some who are really persuaded of the opposite, approach the sacraments only as symbols and ceremonies'[37] – but in her belief that, like any social collectivity, the Church is prone to idolatrous

---

[34]   *NR*, 236.

[35]   Félix Le Dantec, *Athéisme* (Paris: Flammarion, 1907). The following remark is characteristic of Dantec's outlook: 'Je crois à l'avenir de la Science: je crois que la Science et la Science seule résoudra toutes les questions qui ont un sens; je crois qu'elle pénétrera jusqu'aux arcanes de notre vie sentimentale et qu'elle m'expliquera même l'origine et la structure du mysticisme héréditaire anti-scientifique qui cohabite chez moi avec le scientisme le plus absolu. Mais je suis convaincu aussi que les hommes se posent bien des questions qui ne signifient rien. Ces questions, la Science montrera leur absurdité en n'y répondant pas, ce qui prouvera qu'elles ne comportent pas de réponse.' Quoted at http://agora.qc.ca/mot.nsf/Dossiers/Scientisme (Accessed on 18 Feb 2009).

[36]   *FLN*, 308. (My emphasis.)

[37]   *WG*, 45.

Mario von der Ruhr

self-adulation and, in this regard, no different from the worldly revolutionary movements that it has traditionally opposed.[38] Even her friend and spiritual mentor Fr Perrin, she thought, was not immune from the subtly suggestive powers of the religious institution of which he was himself a member. Reflecting on Perrin's attitude towards the affliction of those who are outside the Church, for example, she tells him:

> It also seems to me that when one speaks to you of unbelievers who are in affliction and accept their affliction as a part of the order of the world, it does not impress you in the same way as if it were a question of Christians and of submission to the will of God. Yet it is the same thing.[39]

Weil's comment reveals something about the subtle ways in which the believer's spiritual loyalties may be remodeled or directed away from its original object, with unwitting discrimination marking the early stage of a progressively deepening idolatry. Looking back at the history of her own country, Weil finds that even as well-intentioned a Christian as Cardinal Richelieu (1585–1642), prelate and minister to Louis XIII, was not immune to the allure of stately power, and that he presents a good example of a Christian who failed to see that 'the welfare of the State is a cause to which only a limited and conditional loyalty is owed'.[40] The attempt to make the church a department of the state is, for Weil, just as misguided as the Church's use of the Inquisition as a means of eradicating heresy, since both involve an idolatrous worship of a (political or religious) collective.

Equally alarming, for Weil, is the tendency of such misdirected loyalties to make the citizen, whether atheist or believer, a willing accomplice in the state's wider political designs, including the colonization of foreign cultures and, as far as the Church is concerned, missionary expeditions:

> The more fervent secularists, freemasons, and atheists approve of colonization ... as a solvent of religions, which in fact it is...

[38] WG, 54.
[39] WG, 95.
[40] NR, 115. Op. cit., For a different interpretation of Richelieu's motivations, see D. P. O'Connelli, *Richelieu* (London: Weidenfeld and Nicolson, 1968). Among other things, the author argues that, contrary to appearances, 'Richelieu's policy was not so much to make the Church a department of the state, as to make France a theocracy, with the church interlocked with the state and permeating secular activity with its moral authority' (139). Weil would certainly have applauded such a permeation of the secular with the religious, though she would probably not find O'Connelli's reading entirely convincing.

French colonization does indeed disseminate some Christian influence and also some of the ideas of 1789; but the effect of both is comparatively slight and transitory. It could not be otherwise, given the method of propagating those influences and the vast discrepancy between our theory and our practice. The strong and durable influence is that of unbelief or, more accurately, of scepticism.[41]

If the religious believer is prepared to condemn the militant atheist's use of colonization as a 'solvent' of religion, then how can she condone the Church's missionary ventures if these have similarly deleterious effects, both materially and spiritually? Readers familiar with the *Letter to a Priest* will recall Weil's personal response to the question: her confession that she would 'never give even as much as a sixpence towards any missionary enterprise';[42] her belief that, far from having Christianized the African and Asian continents, such enterprises merely 'brought these territories under the cold, cruel and destructive domination of the white race';[43] her disappointment at the Church's failure to condemn punitive expeditions to avenge the missionaries it had lost;[44] and her conviction that these missions have caused the irretrievable loss of valuable sources of spiritual illumination.[45]

Weil's concern for these uprooted cultures and peoples and her opposition to colonization and Christianization by force are rooted in her understanding of Christ's own mission, and the *manner* of his encounter with those who did not (yet) believe:

> [It] was in any case never said by Christ that those who bring the Gospel should be accompanied, even at a distance, by battleships. Their presence gives the message a different character; and when the blood of the martyrs is avenged by arms it can hardly retain the supernatural efficacy with which tradition endows it. With Caesar as well as the cross, we hold too many aces in our hand.[46]

It is clear to Weil that, insofar as the cross is crucially important for an understanding of Christ, it must also inform the believer's conception of her relation to God. Among other things, this means that '[one] may not debase God to the point of making Him a partisan

---

[41]   *SE*, 197.
[42]   Simone Weil, *Letter to a Priest*, tr. A. F. Wills, with an introduction by Mario von der Ruhr (London: Routledge, 2002) (references indicated by *LP*), 18.
[43]   *LP*, 17.
[44]   *LP*, 18.
[45]   *LP*, 19.
[46]   *SE*, 197.

in a war',[47] whether in the Old Testament, by the Church of the Middle Ages,[48] or in Jeanne d'Arc's letters to the King of France.[49] Indeed, contemplating even a short excerpt from one of these letters, one finds it difficult not to agree with Weil that, in spite of the saintly aspects of her character, 'there is something essentially false' about her story, something bound up with *prestige*:

> I am sent by God, the King of Heaven, to chase you one and all from France... If you refuse to believe these tidings from God and the Maid, when we find you, we shall strike you and make a greater uproar than France has heard for a thousand years... And know full well that the King of Heaven will send the Maid more strength than you could muster in all your assaults against her and her good men-at-arms. We shall let blows determine who has the better claim from the God of heaven.[50]

The pertinence of Weil's observations for religious fundamentalism, especially the more militant and fanatic kind, need hardly be pointed out. For her, all atrocities conducted in the name of God or any other deity constitute a *reductio ad absurdum* of any pretensions to religious witness, an ironic lapse into the very idolatry that is ostensibly being attacked. Here, the atheist who worships God 'in his impersonal aspect', i.e. lives just as much in the *spirit* of Christ as Weil herself was doing until she discovered the truth of the cross, is surely at one with the believer here.

But isn't the *language* of religious belief – i.e. talk of divine creation, original sin, angels and saints, incarnation, intercessionary prayer, atonement, grace, eternal life, etc – so radically at odds with the terms in which an atheist would couch her experience of the world that it would be seriously misleading to amalgamate the two? Surely, someone who engages in 'God-talk' is *ipso facto* expressing a different conception of reality from someone who does not?

Weil is not denying that the world of a Christian like Francis of Assisi is radically different from that of an atheist like Arthur Schopenhauer, nor is she asking us to let the Stoic detachment and self-effacing attitude of the latter make us oblivious to the wider conceptual framework of which it forms a part. But she is asking how much, if anything, a speaker's employment of religious vocabulary

[47]   *NB*, Vol. 1, 55.
[48]   *NB*, Vol. 2, 502.
[49]   *NB*, Vol. 1, 25.
[50]   *The Trial of Joan of Arc*, tr. and ed. Daniel Hobbins (Cambridge, Mass.: Harvard University Press, 2005), 134–135.

can reliably reveal about his attitude to life and the world at large. Even Félix Le Dantec begins his book *Athéisme* with a dedication (to his mentor Alfred Giard) in which he resorts to the very language whose meaning his book is designed to undermine:

> Dieu merci, mon cher maître (voilà, je l'avoue, un début bizarre pour un livre sur 'l'athéisme, mais il faut bien parler français), Dieu merci, l'on n'est plus brûlé aujourd'hui pour ses opinions philosophiques; on n'a plus besoin d'héroïsme pour dire ce que l'on pense.[51]

When Dantec insists that one must, after all, speak French, he is, of course, merely generalizing about a common practice in any language whose historical development involves religious associations, as the casual use of expressions like 'Thank God!', 'For Christ's sake!', 'Jesus!', 'Bloody hell!', or 'I'll be damned!' readily illustrate. Nor should Dantec, descended as he was from a devout Catholic family in the Bretagne, be reprimanded for preferring the more emphatic '*Dieu merci*' to '*heureusement*' or, even worse, advised to consult an *index verborum prohibitorum* compiled especially for atheists like him. And while Dantec's linguistic habits are part of, perhaps even reinforce, the kind of profanation in which religious symbols become mere fashion accessories and holy sacraments are diluted into 'lifestyle options', they neither intend to deceive, nor are they mistaken for a religious confession. However, there are other and more sinister examples of God-talk, by comparison with which Dantec's '*Dieu merci*' seems trivial and harmless. Consider, for instance, the following:

> Come what may, I shall always love God, pray to Him and adhere to the Catholic Church and defend it, even if I should be expelled from it.[52]
>
> [All] that there was and is on this earth was created by God and animated by God. Foolish ... people have created the fable, the fairytale, that our forefathers worshipped gods and trees. No, they were convinced, according to age-old knowledge and age-old teaching, of the God-given order of this whole earth, the entire plant- and animal-world.[53]

---

[51]   Daniel, *Athéisme*, 1: 'Thank God, my dear Maître (there, I admit it, a strange opening for a book on "atheism", but one had better speak French), thank God that we are no longer burnt for our philosophical opinions, that it no longer requires heroism to say what one thinks.' (My translation)
[52]   Peter Padfield, *Himmler: Reichsführer – SS* (London: Mcmillan, 1990), 3. Entry in Himmler's diary, dated 15.12.1919.
[53]   Ibid., 176.

Mario von der Ruhr

No, ... don't talk to me about this sort of hunting. I don't care
for so crude a sport. Nature is so wonderfully beautiful, and every
animal has a right to life.[54]

These remarks were all made by the same individual, over a period of
twenty years. Taken on their own, they seem to reflect different
aspects of a continuous and admirable devotion to the Catholic
faith, including the firm belief in a divinely-ordained natural order
in which animals are accorded a prominent place. Unfortunately,
the character of this spiritual narrative – which, incidentally,
belongs to Heinrich Himmler (1900–1945) – underwent a radical
transformation, from fervent profession of Catholicism (1919) to
wholesale rejection of Christian ritual (1936):

> I should like to say some things about all the festivals, all the cel-
> ebrations in human life, in our life, whose Christian forms and
> style we cannot accept inwardly, which we can no longer be a
> party to, and for which, in so and so many cases, we have not
> yet found a new form.[55]

Having attended his own father's Catholic funeral in the previous
year, Himmler admitted that he had merely done so out of respect
for his father's beliefs, even though he did not share them himself:

> I myself, in my personal case, have acted in that way. My father
> was – according to the tradition of our family–a convinced
> Christian, in his case a convinced Catholic. He knew my views
> precisely. However, we did not speak on the religious issue ... I
> never touched on his convictions and he did not touch on mine.[56]

As for the religious practices of his parents' generation, he knew that
it would be difficult for them to become accustomed to the modified
baptismal, burial and other public rites which he envisaged for the
new *Reich*:

> Please! *Jawohl!* One cannot change people of seventy. There is no
> point in upsetting the peace of mind of people of sixty or seventy.
> Destiny does not require that, nor our own ancestors of the ear-
> liest times – who merely want us to do it better in the future.[57]

It was not long before Himmler and his fellow *Gruppenführer* did
begin to do it 'better', by instituting new birth or name-giving

[54] Padfield, *Himmler: Reichsführer – SS*, 351.
[55] Ibid., 172.
[56] Ibid., 172.
[57] Ibid., 172.

ceremonies in which a 'sponsor' would hand the child a silver birth tankard from which she could drink as she was growing up, and solemnly declare: 'The source of all life is *Got*... From *Got* your knowledge, your tasks, your life-purpose and all life's perceptions flow. Each drink from this tankard be witness to the fact that you are *Got*-united.'[58] Commenting on the Nazis' use of the word '*Gott*', the Himmler biographer Peter Padfield rightly points out that '[the] word was given only one 't' in the transcription, allegedly the old Germanic spelling, but it was chiefly useful, probably, to distinguish the SS God from the conventional Christian *Gott*.'[59]

Simone Weil's reaction to this example would, I believe, have at least three aspects. First, she would agree with Padfield that it illustrates a defilement – in every sense of the word – of God's name. Second, she would ask us to recall the equally idolatrous demeanour of the Ancient Romans and draw our attention to various structural analogies between their thinking and Nazi ideology. In fact, *The Need for Roots* contains a highly illuminating remark in which she does exactly that:

> [The Romans] felt ill at ease in their all too vulgar idolatry. Like Hitler, they knew the value of a deceptive exterior of spirituality. They would have liked to take the outer coverings of an authentic religious tradition to act as a cloak for their all too visible atheism. Hitler, too, would be pleased enough to find or found a religion.[60]

Third, her thoughts would linger on the nineteen year old Himmler's profession of undying loyalty to the Catholic faith, noticing both its ironic and, considering the rest of Himmler's biography, more tragic aspects. In this context, one is not only reminded of Saint Peter's betrayal of Christ, but of Weil's penetrating comments on its genesis:

> St. Peter hadn't the slightest intention of denying Christ; but he did so because the grace was not in him which, had it been there, would have enabled him not to do. And even the energy, the categorical tone he employed to underline the contrary intention, helped to deprive him of this grace. It is a case which is worth pondering in all the trials life sets before us.[61]

---

58   Padfield, *Himmler: Reichsführer – SS*, 174.
59   Ibid., 175.
60   *NR*, 273.
61   *NR*, 180–181. See also, *FLN*, 161.

Mario von der Ruhr

Unlike St Peter's betrayal of Christ, Himmler's betrayal of the Catholic faith was neither acknowledged nor atoned for, the cult of the *Führer* drawing him ever further away from the God of his father.

3. 'Purifying' Atheism and Orthodox Christianity

In light of Weil's observations about (idolatrous) atheism and its alliance with scientism, her harsh verdict even on the spiritual condition of the faithful – '[t]he majority of the pious are idolaters' – and her conviction that, unless our faith is deep, we ourselves will be 'creating by contagion men who believe nothing at all',[62] her assessment of our relation to the Cross must appear both sobering and disheartening.

If her diagnosis is accurate, then how are 'our diseased minds'[63] to be cured of these ills, and what role could a 'purifying' atheism play in this cure? Weil's answer must be pieced together from remarks scattered across her oeuvre, and since her whole way of thinking is inimical to systematizing and theorizing, one must not expect a comprehensive and unified account of the matter. Even so, the general direction of her thought may be summarized as follows:

(i) Apart from the idolatrous kind discussed above, there is a species of atheism that purifies the notion of God by, for example, purging it of anthropomorphism and thus highlighting the nature and radical otherness of God's being:

> A case of contradictories which are true. God exists: God does not exist. Where is the problem? I am quite sure that there is a God in the sense that I am quite sure my love is not illusory. I am quite sure that there is not a God in the sense that I am quite sure nothing real can be anything like what I am able to conceive when I pronounce this word. But that which I cannot conceive is not an illusion.[64]

The atheist rejects belief in a personal God, whether he be conceived as a giant policeman in the sky, an entity whose existence and whereabouts might be determined by empirical evidence, or a being who might be held to account for his actions, who might get angry and vengeful, or change over time, etc.[65] For Weil, proper contemplation

[62] *SE*, 197.
[63] *NR*, 266.
[64] *GG*, 114.
[65] Simone Weil, *Oppression and Liberty*, tr. Arthur Wills and John Petrie (London: Routledge, 2002) (references indicated by *OL*), 168.

of the atheist's rejection of such a god can give the believer a deeper understanding of what 'God' means, and is therefore to be welcomed.

(ii) Purifying atheism gives its complete assent to the necessity governing the visible world *without*, however, mistaking the order of that world for a proof of God's non-existence.[66] This attitude not only mirrors the *amor fati* of the Stoics, but is analogous to the Christian believer's loving acceptance of God's will:

> Whatever a person's professed belief in regard to religious matters, including atheism, wherever there is complete, authentic and unconditional consent to necessity, there is fullness of love for God; and nowhere else. This consent constitutes participation in the Cross of Christ.[67]

When Weil speaks of necessity, she has in mind the impersonal and mechanical relations of cause and effect in the physical world, as well as the psychological propensities that characterize us in our interactions with each other. It is an important part of her understanding of creation that, even though 'God has entrusted all phenomena, without any exception, to the mechanism of this world',[68] it would nevertheless be wrong to conclude from this that suffering is specifically sent to particular individuals as ordeals. Rather, '[God] lets Necessity distribute them in accordance with its own proper mechanism.'[69] Human suffering, in other words, must not be justified or explained (away) by God's arbitrary interference in his own creation. Instead, it should be seen as an ineliminable part of the material 'veil' between God and man, one whose mechanism expresses a kind of obedience to the divine will. Weil uses the example of a shipwreck to illustrate her thought:

> The sea is not less beautiful in our eyes because we know that sometimes ships are wrecked by it. On the contrary, this adds to its beauty. If it altered the movement of its waves to spare a boat, it would be a creature gifted with discernment and choice and not this fluid, perfectly obedient to every external pressure. It is this perfect obedience that constitutes the sea's beauty.[70]

It may be difficult to hold on to this perception of the sea when it causes the sailors difficulties or even costs them their lives, but

---

[66] *NR*, 266.
[67] *IC*, 184.
[68] *NB*, Vol. 2, 361.
[69] *WG*, 73.
[70] *WG*, 129.

Mario von der Ruhr

Weil still insists that, just as a man should cherish the needle handled by his departed wife, so the material world, 'on account of its perfect obedience', deserves to be loved by those who love its Master.[71] Weil does not see in this attitude a recipe for passivity and quietism vis-à-vis human affliction, however. On the contrary, she would commend an atheist like Docteur Rieux in Camus' *La Peste* precisely for his Stoic and courageous struggles against such affliction, no matter how much they may be thwarted by forces beyond his control. Weil died too young (1943) to have read *La Peste* (1947), but it is worth noting that, when Camus himself began to read Weil's work while on a lecture tour in New York, in 1947, he was so impressed by it that he soon began to publish it in his *Collection Espoir,* a book series he had founded with Gallimard. Over the years, nine volumes of Weil's work would appear in this series. Camus' interest in Weil is, perhaps, not surprising when one considers the intellectual affinities between the two authors. Like Weil, Camus had a deep appreciation of Ancient Greek culture and civilization; was familiar with, and highly respectful of, Christian thought – he even wrote a Master's thesis on 'Christian Metaphysics and Neoplatonism' – supported political activism without placing his faith in the revolutionary movements of his day; and counted among his best friends such thoughtful and serious believers as the poet René Leynaud, a Resistance comrade who would be executed by the Germans in 1944, and Jean Grenier, who had been a fellow student at the University of Algiers.[72] Moreover, Camus always thought of his atheism as an entirely *personal* affair, not as the only tenable conclusion to be drawn from sober and impersonal philosophical reflection. As he emphasized in a speech at the Dominican monastery of Lautour-Maubourg, in 1948: 'I wish to declare ... that, not feeling that I possess any absolute truth or any message, I shall never start from the supposition that Christian truth is illusory, but merely from the fact that I could not accept it.'[73]

(iii) The purifying atheist does not believe in his own, continued existence beyond the grave – or what the late D. Z. Phillips has aptly called 'a transcendentalized version of 'See you later',[74] – but nevertheless views the world he inhabits as a home. As Weil puts it:

---

[71] *WG*, 128.
[72] James Woelfel, *Albert Camus on the Sacred and the Secular* (Lanham, MD: University Press of America, 1987), 25.
[73] Ibid., 27.
[74] D. Z. Phillips, 'Dislocating the Soul', in *Can Religion Be Explained Away?* D. Z. Phillips (ed.) (London: Macmillan, 1996), 247.

220

Not to believe in the immortality of the soul, but to look upon the whole of life as destined to prepare for the moment of death; not to believe in God, but to love the universe, always, even in the throes of anguish, as a home – there lies the road toward faith by way of atheism.[75]

On Weil's account, the idea of death as complete annihilation is preferable to a belief in the soul's temporal progression beyond the grave because it highlights the significance of *life*, of what the individual becomes, and of what she will (eternally) remain when her life has expired. 'The thought of death', Weil says, 'gives a colour of eternity to the events of life. If we were granted everlasting life in this world, our earthly life, by gaining perpetuity, would lose that eternity whose light shines through it.'[76] Thus, an atheist who takes this attitude towards death will not be indifferent to the way her life goes, but will instead want to prepare herself for the final hour, similarly to the way in which a believer would prepare for it by 'dying' to the world and detaching herself from all that might get in the way of her salvation. Both would agree on the significance of a life's narrative unfolding one way rather than another, and on what it would mean to speak with any depth about the meaning of death.

(iv) Our atheist will reject false consolations, including the hope of future compensations for sufferings undergone and losses sustained in the past. Contrary to common assumptions about the psychological 'benefits' of religious belief, Weil takes the view that 'religion, in so far as it is a source of consolation, is a *hindrance* to true faith,'[77] and that this is also why the atheist's rejection of such hopes *may* reveal a deeper appreciation of human suffering and bereavement. These must not be cheapened or absorbed into a general theory in which their meaning is diluted – something that theodicists are unwittingly doing as they grapple with the problem of evil – but recognized for what they are. In his moving memoir *A Grief Observed*, C.S. Lewis captures well the spirit of Weil's own thinking on the subject. Contemplating the loss of the woman he loves, Lewis records:

> You tell me, "she goes on", But my heart and body are crying out, come back, come back... But I know this is impossible. I know that the thing I want is exactly the thing I can never get. The old life, the jokes, the drinks, the arguments, the lovemaking, the tiny, heartbreaking commonplace. On any view whatever,

[75] *NB*, Vol. 2, 469.
[76] *FLN*, 275.
[77] *GG*, 115. (My emphasis)

to say, "H. is dead", is to say, "All that is gone". It is a part of the past. And the past is the past and that is what time means, and time itself is one more name for death, and Heaven itself is a state where "the former things have passed away". Talk to me about the truth of religion and I'll listen gladly. Talk to me about the duty of religion and I'll listen submissively. But don't come talking to me about the consolations of religion or I shall suspect that you don't understand.[78]

(v) Atheists or 'infidels' who are free from self-adoration, whose relation to their fellow men is marked by pure compassion, and whose love demands nothing in return, are, in Weil's view, 'as close to God as is a Christian, and consequently know Him equally well, although their knowledge is expressed in other words, or remains unspoken.'[79] As we saw in connection with Himmler, the use of religious symbolisms or utterances no more vouches for true, Christian discipleship, than its absence from a person's life and thought signifies its opposite. If 'infidels' exhibit supernatural virtue, then, as Weil rightly insists, 'such men are surely saved.'[80]

A good illustration of the kind of atheism Weil has in mind here is provided by the literary character of Axel Heyst, in Joseph Conrad's novel *Victory*. While Heyst's restless travels and conscious avoidance of close personal attachments suggest an uprootedness and anxiety that do not entirely fit Weil's requirement that one love the universe 'as a home', and even though Heyst's general conception of the world bears a much closer resemblance to the pessimist outlook of a Schopenhauer than it does to an agnostic humanist, he nevertheless responds to his neighbour's plea for help with an admirable spontaneity and generosity, expecting nothing in return. Conrad already draws our attention to these traits early on in *Victory*, as Heyst is approached by an acquaintance called 'Morrison', who is about to lose his livelihood – an old brig – unless he can pay the fine that will keep it from falling into the hands of the Portuguese authorities. Having just described his predicament to Heyst, Morrison adds:

Upon my word, I don't know why I have been telling you all this. I suppose seeing a thoroughly white man like you made it impossible to keep my trouble to myself. Words can't do it justice; but since I've told you so much I may as well tell you more. Listen. This morning on board, in my cabin, I went

---

[78] C. S. Lewis, *A Grief Observed* (San Francisco: Harper, 2001), 24–25.
[79] *LP*, 22. See also, LP, 20.
[80] *LP*, 20. See also, FLN, 84.

down on my knees and prayed for help. I went down on my knees![81]

The ensuing exchange, apart from touching on the notion of prayer, also reveals much about the character of Morrison's relation to God:

'You are a believer, Morrison?' asked Heyst with a distinct note of respect.

'Surely I am not an infidel.'

Morrison was swiftly reproachful in his answer, and there came a pause, Morrison perhaps interrogating his conscience, and Heyst preserving a mien of unperturbed, polite interest.

'I prayed like a child, of course. I believe in children praying – well, women, too, but I rather think God expects men to be more self-reliant. I don't hold with a man everlastingly bothering the Almighty with his silly troubles. It seems such cheek. Anyhow, this morning I – I have never done any harm to any God's creature knowingly – I prayed. A sudden impulse – I went flop on my knees; so you may judge – '[82]

Heyst's response to Morrison's confession is unhesitating and generous: 'Oh! If that's the case I would be very happy if you'd allow me to be of use!' he tells the latter, leaving him greatly bewildered by this unexpected offer. Such things do not, in Morrison's experience, happen very often, so this must either be a miracle and Heyst has been sent from God, or it is a case of deception and Heyst is, in fact, an emissary from the Devil. But Morrison's fears are soon allayed:

'I say! You aren't joking, Heyst?'

'Joking!' Heyst's blue eyes went hard as he turned them on the discomposed Morrison. 'In what way, may I ask?' he continued with austere politeness. Morrison was abashed.

Forgive me, Heyst. You must have been sent by God in answer to my prayer. But I have been nearly off my chump for three days with worry; and it suddenly struck me: 'What if it's the Devil who has sent him?'

'I have no connection with the supernatural', said Heyst graciously, moving on. 'Nobody has sent me. I just happened along.'

'I know better,' contradicted Morrison. 'I may be unworthy, but I have been heard. I know it. I feel it. For why should you offer–'

---

[81]   Joseph Conrad, *Victory* (Oxford: Oxford University Press, 1986), 65.
[82]   Ibid., 65.

Heyst inclined his head, as from respect for a conviction in which he could not share. But he stuck to his point by muttering that in the presence of an odious fact like this, it was natural.[83]

4. Atheists, Believers, and Divine Judgment

Looking back on Weil's remarks about atheism and idolatry, some of her Christian readers might well agree with her condemnation of the first, idolatrous kind of atheism, and yet wonder whether her attempted *rapprochement* between the 'purifying' type of atheist and the Christian believer does not come at too high a price, even for those who are prepared to give their atheist neighbors a sympathetic hearing. After all, Axel Heyst is not – despite the phonetic similarity and certain aspects of his demeanour – an incarnation of Christ, someone who could truly *save* a man like Morrison, not just from bankruptcy, but from despair over his suffering, or over the point of his life as a whole.

Heyst's gesture may have led Morrison to place his trust in this particular man, Axel Heyst, perhaps it has even restored his faith in humanity at large, but none of this seems to cut to the *core* of his religious convictions. Imagine, for the moment, a Morrison who, instead of being helped by Heyst, is callously dismissed by him, subsequently losing his precious brig to the Portuguese and, through no fault of his own, receiving the kind of beating that leaves the victim permanently crippled in body and soul. Would even the most compassionate atheist be able to offer an innocent sufferer like Morrison any *hope* that will speak to his need for the restoration of justice? And would such hope, if it could be given, not have to involve the kind of consolation Weil would reject? The question is pertinent because of the light its answer would shed, not merely on the atheist's (or Axel Heyst's) conceptual distance from the believer, but on Simone Weil's relation to orthodox Christianity. Suppose further that we asked a character like Morrison, for example, how he had managed to retain his faith in the face of all the injustices he had endured, and he replied as follows:

This innocent sufferer has attained the certitude of hope: there is a God, and God can create justice in a way that we cannot conceive, yet we can begin to grasp it through faith. Yes, there is a resurrection of the flesh. There is justice. There is an 'undoing'

---

[83]   Conrad, *Victory*, 67.

of past suffering, a reparation that sets things aright. For this reason, faith in the Last Judgment is first and foremost hope.[84]

Would Morrison's belief in the resurrection of the flesh be just as clear an instance of 'false consolation' as his belief in an 'undoing' of past suffering? Would it not depend on how these beliefs informed Morrison's life and thought more generally – for example, whether they deepened his love of his neighbors, or cheapened his sense of what their affliction meant to them? And couldn't Weil agree that an adequate elaboration of the affirmation '*Spes mea in Deo*' should contain the thought that

> Grace does not cancel out justice. It does not make wrong into right. It is not a sponge which wipes everything away, so that whatever someone has done on earth ends up being of equal value... Evildoers, in the end, do not sit at table at the eternal banquet beside their victims without distinction, as though nothing had happened.[85]

While I do not think that Simone Weil would have an unequivocal response to these questions – she was not a dogmatist, either philosophically or religiously – the general tenor of her answer is disclosed in two remarks concerning the resurrection. One of these occurs in a letter to her Dominican friend Fr Perrin, written shortly before her departure from Marseille, on April 16, 1942:

> Once I have gone, it seems to me very improbable that circumstances will allow me to see you again one day. As to eventual meetings in another world, you know that I do not picture things to myself in that way. But that does not matter very much. It is enough for my friendship with you that you exist.[86]

The second appears in correspondence with the French priest Fr Couturier, to whom she wrote in the autumn of the same year:

> [If] the Gospel omitted all mention of Christ's resurrection, faith would be easier for me. The Cross by itself suffices me.[87]

In an interview, Albert Camus once confessed that, while he had a deep sense of the sacred, he did not believe in a future *life*.[88] It is

---

[84] Benedict XVI, *Saved in Hope* (San Francisco: Ignatius Press, 2008), 90.

[85] Ibid., 92.

[86] *WG*, 59.

[87] *LP*, 34

[88] Woelfel, *Albert Camus on the Sacred and the Secular*, 18.

Mario von der Ruhr

because, for him, untiring revolt against affliction and suffering do *not* come with the prospect of a future life and rewards in heaven, that Weil would think herself closer to him than to many of her fellow Christians. Their faith, she would insist, has yet to be purified through an encounter with just such an atheist.

Swansea University

Spirituality for the Godless

MICHAEL MCGHEE

1. How to be spiritual without being religious[1]

'Godless' was never a neutral term: in 1528 William Tindale talked of 'godlesse ypocrites and infidels' and a 'godless generation' is one that has turned its back on God and the paths of righteousness. An atheist, by contrast, a *new* and self-conscious atheist perhaps, might now wear the term as a badge of pride, to indicate their rejection both of belief and the implication of moral turpitude. Traditionally, though, those who declared themselves 'atheist' had a hardly better press than the 'godlesse', since 'atheism' was and in some cases still is considered a form of intellectual and moral shallowness: thus Sir Francis Bacon offers a bluff refinement of the Psalmist's verdict on the fool who says in his heart that there is no God:

> The Scripture saith, *The fool hath said in his heart, there is no God*; it is not said, *The fool hath thought in his heart*; so he rather saith it, by rote to himself, as that he would have, than that he can thoroughly believe it, or be persuaded of it.

In these sentences from his essay *On Atheism*[2] Bacon expresses the irritated commonsense one associates with a certain kind of believer, who cannot take non-belief quite seriously, but treats it as a kind of wishful thinking or self-deception. Bacon, however, goes further: 'as atheism is in all respects hateful, so in this, that it depriveth human nature of the means to exalt itself above human frailty'.

I shall in what follows speak up for the secular humanist project and defend it against the charge of shallowness *and* the charge that it leaves us without the resources to overcome our human frailty – though I shall also suggest that the plausibility of the defence depends upon the appropriation of some of the phenomena covered by the term 'spirituality'. This may seem at first sight

---

[1] Many of my reflections in this paper run in tandem with my 'Spirituality and Humanism: or How to be a Good Atheist' in Cornwell & McGhee (eds.) *Philosophers and God* (Continuum, 2009).
[2] I have used Brian Vickers (ed.) *Francis Bacon: A Critical Edition of the Major Works* (Oxford, Oxford University Press, 1996), 371–73.

doi:10.1017/S1358246111000087   ©The Royal Institute of Philosophy and the contributors 2011
Royal Institute of Philosophy Supplement **68** 2011   227

Michael McGhee

incompatible with the project, which is to develop and promote a conception of ethics independently of religious belief, and surely, it will be said, 'spirituality' cannot be disentangled from such belief since it has to do with our relationship with God or the things of the spirit – though the clue to what can be retrieved lies in the implicit opposition, viz., with the things of the world or the flesh: an opposition which reveals an ethical estimate of two ways of living *from the point of view of one of them*. I wish to recommend the notion as a repository of wisdom and experience as we seek to understand and confront the conflicted moral condition which gave rise to that distinction between spirit, world and flesh in the first place. Some secularists have a faintly absurd antipathy to anything that sounds 'religious' and may react against my suggestion. Such reactivity, though, is to be found also in their opponents, and it would be unfortunate if all believers and non-believers had in common was an unjust and inaccurate estimate of each other's position. If dialogue between believers and non-believers is to prosper, then it must be premised on the correction of false perceptions.

ii

The opening verses of Genesis draw on the imagery of artistic production and appreciation and convey a judgment of artistic success. They draw on our experience of the moment when the artist knows their work is achieved and loves it as their offspring – God saw that what he had made was *good*. But the image of an artist or creator expresses a sense of wonder and delight in the earth's beauty and, crucially, in the original beauty and innocence of humanity. This sense of wonder, at the earth and at ourselves, takes the imaginative form of delight in what the artist has created and represents the impulse of protective care towards it – towards humanity and the earth. It is the sense expressed in Blake's thought that 'everything that lives is holy'. The verses express, but also promote, a common but fugitive human experience, that of inclusive love and benevolence, and this universal sense becomes the half-remembered measure of moral endeavour. It is the felt *Sorge* that motivates the diverse phenomena that we collect under the term 'morality', an experience of the moral sentiments in their universal expression. Now it is certainly true that this is a suspect way of talking – 'he loves humanity but doesn't like people' – but, as I shall suggest in the conclusion, this inclusiveness or universality may be expressed in and precipitated *by* the particular, and doesn't so much embrace all as *any*. Nevertheless, and this is really our theme, there is a gulf between the acknowledgment, even the love, of the ideal or measure, and the ability to live by that standard.

These moral sentiments are not only independent of 'religious belief', but they *inform* its narratives, and, in the case of the theistic traditions, therefore, have determined (changes in) how God has been conceived in those narratives, both in terms of what he commands and what he sanctions, as exemplified in the familiar difference in conception between the wrathful Jehovah and the 'still small voice'. Some theists may want to say that we have over time come to a better understanding of God's will because he has disclosed it gradually and according to our lights, but secularists will simply note the moral improvement enshrined in how that will has been conceived.

In any case, that we describe the moral sentiments as 'moral' in the first place indicates our cultural approval of them, and it will be asked what the grounds of that approval might be. It is not as though we exist as a neutral consciousness impartially judging the merits of opposing tendencies: we find, rather, that we have already taken sides. Our approval seems to rest in this underlying but evanescent attitude of inclusive benevolence which I suggested informed the opening of Genesis. It is a fundamental orientation that is, however, often overlain, though its bass note is audible even when most muffled or distant, in the form of disquiet or remorse. I would call it a primal and ungrounded moral vision or perspective, an internal moral ideal, a *conscience*, perhaps, though I use that term with caution since 'conscience' is liable to manipulation and perversion, particularly by what John Buchan called dogmatic enthusiasm, and by creeds that attract (because they express) intemperate mentalities in conflict with this moral ideal. Certainly we cannot give an account of the moral sentiments independently of critical scrutiny of their proposed intentional objects – and the moral sentiments are not, alas, the only human sentiments or impulses to inform the scriptural narratives.

But if we have already taken sides, what are we to make of the idea of *metanoia* or moral conversion? Surely this is the idea of a *re*-orientation *from* a life of crime, as it were, and towards the good. In one sense this is right – in the sense that it represents a self-conscious *renunciation* of the inner forces that stand in the way of the good, a renunciation motivated by *concern* for the good, not as an abstract entity, however, but in the sense of concern to avoid the harm and damage one finds oneself doing. The metaphor of the 'still small voice' is an apt representation of the phenomenology. *Metanoia* represents a moment of self-conscious commitment and renunciation that *strengthens* an orientation that is already in place and is its motivating force. This commitment is activated by the vivid sense of what is endangered by what needs therefore to be renounced. To put it another way, and to draw on diverse sources, *metanoia* takes the form of a commitment to the processes of self-overcoming or inner *jihad* – commitment, in other words, to the disciplines of a spiritual life.

To use the language of the state of nature, human beings are capable of sympathy, benevolence and generosity of spirit, though these are limited in scope and force by contending impulses of cruelty, vindictiveness and the ruthless pursuit of power and territory at the expense of others. The antagonism between these fundamental attitudes is also part of the scriptural narrative, though as we shall see the narrative often enough *compounds* what its history has also sought to resolve. Nevertheless it is a narrative that has plenty to recommend it to humanists since it represents the progress of moral struggle, and spirituality is as it were a body of knowledge that treats of the contours and limits of that struggle. As I have already indicated, and to reassure the more suspicious secularists, the moral sentiments, albeit in contention with our darker nature, are not only independent of religious belief but also inform it, so that religion might be thought of as in debt to morality rather than the reverse.

iii

However, there are two things that the promoters of a humanist ethic would quite rightly dissociate themselves from. The first is that form of allegedly 'religious' consciousness and practice which reflects, reinforces and seeks to justify conduct that flows from the dark side of our nature.[3] Recent secularist writers have done this emphatically, but have tended, with a lamentable absence of critical judgment, to tar all religion with the same brush. The second is those 'moral beliefs' or 'moral convictions' that are determined by credal beliefs or 'metaphysical commitments'. Needless to say, certain creeds, particularly those which operate with a simple-minded cosmogony, can

---

[3]   John Buchan remarks of the divines of the Seventeenth Century Scottish Kirk that 'Finding little warrant for force in the New Testament, [they] had recourse to the Old Testament, where they discovered encouraging precedents in the doings of Elijah and Hezekiah and Josiah', *Montrose* (Cornwall: House of Stratus, 1928/2008), 29.

so represent things that an act of torture becomes a sort of higher kindness and requires one to 'overcome' the natural human sentiments even as they appeal to them – they appeal to them, but alter and pervert their objects. One needs to make a distinction here. Humanists would not wish to be associated with a certain kind of justificatory theology or metaphysics even though it endorses moral positions that they hold independently. But nor would they associate themselves with casuistic moral beliefs that are determined by a particular theological or metaphysical position. One thinks for instance of the alleged (but not often self-ascribed) 'objective disorder' of homosexuality, and of certain other precise delineations of sexual and reproductive ethics that one associates with the official teaching of the Catholic Church, and to which a rhetoric of moral sentiment is often attached, even though the objects of these sentiments are metaphysically determined and remote.

There is another side to this story, however. In the first instance, 'being religious' is quite obviously not all one thing and the resources for a critique of its malformations are available within the history of the traditions themselves, as we have seen and as evinced in Buchan's wry remarks about the Seventeenth Century Kirk – *available* even if they are occluded or perverted in certain cultural and political contexts (giving rise to protests and reactions later recognised as 'movements of renewal'). But even religiously-minded people who would join in the secularist repudiation of religious zealotry will complain that secularists who express admiration for some of the moral teachings of the Bible can in the nature of the case appropriate those teachings only in an incomplete form, and that it is an error to minimise the sharp differences between secularists and 'people of faith'. It is indeed an error, but there is plenty of common ground, if not about what ultimately constitutes human well being, at least about the justice of striving to establish and maintain the conditions for the possibility of any kind of flourishing at all, and if secularists do not share the hope of eternal life and the conquering of death, they will also note the promise that such a life can be tasted here.

There is, then, a moral content independent of 'metaphysical commitment' and 'religious belief' that plays an original and determining role in the formation of religious narrative and theology, and is not their outcome – and this notwithstanding the pitiless vein of *Realpolitik* that also runs through the scriptures, and sometimes distorts and sometimes overwhelms the moral vision. But the articulation and expression of this moral vision requires an account of the conditions for its fulfilment, conditions which are both interior and

Michael McGhee

intersubjective, and I suggest that the concept of spirituality belongs to such an account. Now, the same religiously-minded people who insist that secularists can only partially appropriate the New Testament message will also routinely charge them with a 'shallow' and optimistic view of human nature and the possibilities of human progress. This criticism is well-deserved in some cases. It applies to certain polemical writers who have expended their intellectual energies in the refutation of belief and are then too tired or ill-equipped to offer more than a glad gesture towards a glorious future. Nevertheless, the moral vision that the older generation of secular humanists endorsed is precisely a humanist one in its passion for justice and its condemnation of hypocrisy and corruption. But, to return to the issue of spirituality, the humanist movement needs not only to re-endorse this defining moral vision, but also to take seriously the reality of a divided self by incorporating an account of the kind I have just mentioned of the conditions for the fulfilment of that vision.

iv

In his *Treatise* (Book III Section V) David Hume remarks that

> Tho' there was no obligation to relieve the miserable, our humanity would lead us to it; and when we omit that duty, the immorality of the omission arises from its being a proof, that we want the natural sentiments of humanity.

Hume makes the want of these 'natural sentiments of humanity' an object of moral criticism and you might think that he relies in that case on what appears to be the moral judgment that we *ought to have them*. I have elsewhere[4] tried to defend the view that this kind of ought judgment is an epistemic rather than a practical one – roughly, 'being possessed of certain sentiments' describes a *condition* rather than an action, and there is a shift in the logic of ought as it applies to the two kinds of case. A practical ought judgment is one which implies that there is a reason to *do* something, whereas an epistemic ought judgment is one which implies that there is a reason to *believe* something. In the present case the judgment that someone *ought to have* the 'natural sentiments of humanity' implies that there is reason to believe that they *will* have them, on the grounds that human beings generally *do*. To have this expectation, though,

---

[4]   See 'Facing Truths' in McGhee (ed.) *Philosophy, Religion and the Spiritual Life* (Cambridge University Press, 1992).

is relatively naïve since experience shows us all too well that human beings often don't. But it still makes sense in the face of their absence to insist that they *ought* to be there – and we thus imply that there must be a special explanation of their absence – and indeed we are usually ready to offer such explanations, usually of a psychosocial nature. But the *tone* of these judgments depends upon disappointed *empirical* expectations which have a practical impact – if someone lacks these sentiments then they are dangerous or frightening. There are probably only very few who want these natural sentiments entirely, but we now know well enough how easily they are subverted and overlain or stifled, and not simply by 'selfishness' which we have traditionally thought of as the natural contrary of benevolence or sympathy. As we now know a bureaucratic conscientiousness as well as deference to voices of authority can cancel these sentiments in the sense that they cancel awareness of what naturally attracts their attention, and have disastrous consequences for human well-being.

But the idea of 'having' or 'possessing' the moral sentiments is ambiguous. One can have them in the sense that at least intermittently they provide a perspective on the world, or one can have them in the sense that they dominate consciousness and action in their light flows naturally and without effort. The transition from the one state to the other represents the programme for spirituality.

The problem with the moral sentiments has always been their reliability and their scope since if we are naturally benevolent we are also naturally selfish, fearful and deferential and we anyway exhibit in our sympathy a bias to the near. But, as Hume indicates, we are wanting in the natural sentiments of humanity if we are indifferent to the plight of the miserable, *whoever* they may be. To be moved to act in the presence of human or other animal misery indicates a widening of the scope of the relevant sentiment of sympathy or compassion. Indeed the very idea of *universality* as a necessary and 'objective' component of morality is in reality a reflection of the internal moral ideal that represents our collective memory of protective care such as informs the opening verses of Genesis. The significant point about them from the point of view of spirituality is that the perspective is easily lost and even when lost we are too full of human frailty to act in its light.

As I have said, we don't stand over against these opposing forces as a neutral consciousness wondering how to choose, but are, rather, constituted by the struggle – and precisely *haunted* by one pole of the opposition. The sense of the whole and of an inclusive rather than partial benevolence is not a possibility of our nature that

Michael McGhee

stands on all fours with our appetites, for instance. The latter present themselves already in the form of *temptations*. The sense of the whole expresses an orientation that determines what we take our nature to be and in the light of which we make judgments about what our demeanour in particular circumstances ought to be, and we explain the absence of that demeanour in terms of desires that we count as wayward just to the extent that they are obstacles.

v

It may be helpful here to consider a suggestion made by the Catholic theologian, Nicholas Lash, to the effect that we should think of the various religious traditions as 'schools':

> ...we would do well to think of Judaism, Christianity and Islam, of Buddhism and Vedantic Hinduism, not as "religions" but as *schools*, schools whose pedagogy ... "has the twofold purpose – however differently conceived and executed in the different traditions – of weaning us from our idolatry and purifying our desire".[5]

I want to suggest that secular humanism is also a school in this sense, one whose pedagogy would also in that case have 'the twofold purpose ... of weaning us from our idolatry and purifying our desire'. You do not need to be a theist to warn against idolatry, and not all the 'schools' mentioned here by Lash are theistic. Theologians and religious leaders often warn us against the worship of false gods, and there is a long tradition, already invoked in this paper, that laments the unconscious propensity of believers to fashion God in their own (unregenerate) image, and it is often just these conceptions of deity that are the target of secularist criticism (though some secularists are justly criticised in turn by theologians who think that the real nature of theism has eluded them). But the notion of idolatry also has a moral content: it involves turning away from the paths of righteousness.

In suggesting that secular humanism is also a school, I imply that it is more than an intellectual position, and humanists in any case think of themselves as involved in a *movement* defined by its concern for

---

[5]   Lash, 'The Impossibility of Atheism' – page 29 of *Theology for Pilgrims* (Darton, Longman & Todd, 2008) in which he quotes from page 21 of his *The Beginning and the End of 'Religion'* (Cambridge University Press, 1996).

234

human flourishing. Richard Norman, for instance, has talked of the need to give an account of how we should live, but without religion, and he sees humanism as 'the positive affirmation that human beings can find from within themselves the resources to live a good life without religion'.[6] Notice, however, the collision between Norman's talk of finding the resources within ourselves and Bacon's complaint that atheism 'depriveth human nature of the means to exalt itself above human frailty'. We shall have to return to this, though I think the issue turns on an equivocation about what we are calling human nature, about what belongs to our nature and what belongs to 'the means' that exalts it above frailty.

The idea of the purification of desire does not present itself in a vacuum and without context. The premise is that unless desire is purified it is inimical to our ends, eclipses our vision, undermines our power of action – the moral notion of purification is predicated on the lived experience of a divided self. This gives us the agenda for the training and *ascesis* of the spiritual life. In bringing secular humanism into connection with the religious traditions through the common notion of a school I do not seek to *assimilate* it to religion any more than I should wish to do in the case of the ancient Stoic or Epicurean schools that Lash no doubt draws his inspiration from. But once we take seriously the idea of secular humanism as a movement and as a school, we introduce the notion of the cure of souls, the well being of its members, and all this invites the question whether humanism should see itself, not as a religion among other religions, but at least as a spiritual community (the suggestion is probably too close to the idea of a church or sangha for some humanists to stomach, though it might also give them reason to reconceive such institutions). In any event, I suggest that what we are talking about are schools of *spirituality*.

For quite different reasons secularists and religionists will resist this term as applied to a humanist movement. But secular humanists can appropriate an operational notion, not only of spirituality, but also of 'transcendence', without being committed in either case to religious belief. Both notions can be understood in moral terms, though they also put pressure on our notion of what it is to be moral at all. Transcendence may be understood in the light of our experience of inner conflict *and the state of our self-knowledge*. This is important because it lies at the heart of doctrines of grace and accusations of humanist pride. Thus we tend to identify ourselves with our familiar 'unregenerate' impulses (we make our frailty our nature, if I might contend against Bacon), impulses which determine the horizon

---

[6] See Richard Norman, *On Humanism* (London, Routledge, 2004), 18.

Michael McGhee

within which our attention ranges – and our more regenerate ones are therefore experienced and received as *visitations* from beyond that horizon, as opposed to being thought of as the promptings of a 'higher' but not yet integrated self. This is the point at which believers invoke the notion of grace and Spirit, both of which are attempts, in a theistic setting, to make sense of the phenomena of *metanoia*, that switch in the balance of forces when we identify with universal and disinterested ends but find that they are not under our conscious control, or part of our conscious repertoire, part of the habitual and therefore effortless formation of our will. Richard Norman's talk of humanism as 'the positive affirmation that human beings can find from within themselves the resources to live a good life without religion' needs to be qualified by integrating into that conception precisely this experience of transformation as included within what we take our resource *to be*.

Nicholas Lash is surely correct in his criticism of *some* talk of 'spirituality', and he puts his finger on the reason that makes me at least feel uneasy about using the term at all:

> Nor is it surprising that, since the term [religion] nevertheless still carries ancient overtones of public life and conduct, of established norms and practices, many people prefer to describe the games they play in the private playgrounds of Cartesian consciousness not as religion but as "spirituality".

However, what Lash draws attention to is a profound misunderstanding of the term. Spirituality does not properly belong within a private inner space but has an essentially public application. It relates precisely to 'public life and conduct' rather than to a Cartesian consciousness, and, although it is concerned with the development of the conditions for both vision and action, as a moral category it governs the nature of the relationships *within and between communities*. When St Paul distinguished between the gifts of the flesh and the gifts of the spirit he was referring to the sentiments and impulses that governed the conduct of an allegedly *exemplary* community.

2. How to be godless without being shallow

'I had rather believe all the fables in the Legend, and the Talmud, and the Alcoran', declares Sir Francis Bacon, as his producer turns down the sound on his Elizabethan cultural perceptions, 'than that this universal frame is without a mind ... God never wrought miracle, to convince atheism, because his ordinary works convince it ...'

The atheist will notice the sleight of hand in the invitation to look upon the world as someone's 'work' in the first place, even though, as we have seen, in a contemplative mood a person's mind might well turn towards the *imagery* of making, to the image, indeed of a wonderful artist. But the vivacity of an image, and even the state of wonder induced by good story-telling, can mislead us into taking it 'literally' – and yield what we now call 'creationism', though when we say that creationists take the text 'literally' we actually mean, I think, that they read it as belonging to the language game of information, historical reportage, rather than as the narrative which is creatively derived from and takes the form of that language game. However, to claim, by contrast, that we are dealing with metaphors and stories does not by itself imply that they are about *us* as opposed to a transcendental reality, dimly thus apprehended. And so we come to the very edge of the common ground between secularists and believers.

The idea of a maker comes from a movement of the imagination, and to conceive it or hold the image in one's mind is hardly by itself to be 'convinced' that there really is a wonderful artist at work. To return to Bacon, it is this image of 'work', mediating between the world and our wonder, rather than the world itself, that might 'convince' someone, who might see in it a revelatory symbol of our dependence on God.

Now, in defence of believers, I should want to deny that this kind of conviction is 'blind' and I do so because the linguistic stage-setting that would support that adverse judgment is absent. A belief is 'blind' when someone holds it without reference to evidence, whether confirming or disconfirming, and the judgment is adverse just because evidential avenues are open and determining. But where we are talking about the world as such rather than about contingent features *within* the world, then talk of evidence, or indeed of explanation, is misplaced. This is one reason why some philosophers have claimed, without adverse judgment, that such beliefs are ungrounded rather than 'blind', though I would myself rather not call them beliefs at all, mostly because of the way we conflate the notion with that of empirical belief and then confuse this with the quite separate notion of 'trust'.

'It is true', Bacon goes on, 'that a little philosophy inclineth man's mind to atheism; but depth in philosophy bringeth men's minds about to religion':

For while the mind of man looketh upon second causes scattered, it may sometimes rest in them, and go no further; but when it beholdeth the chain of them, confederate and linked together, it must needs fly to Providence and Deity.

But is it *true* that 'the mind of man' *must* 'fly to Providence and Deity'? I think that the obvious answer is no, and that Bacon fails to see a middle position between his shallow atheist who rests in second causes and the deeper philosopher who flies to Providence and Deity – viz that of someone who beholds the chain of causes confederate and linked together but does not fly to Providence and Deity.

However, the ethical *form* of the impulse to fly thither *can* be shared by the atheist. As we have seen, part of the interest of the Creation story is that it presents the Creator in terms that rely on the experience of aesthetic achievement and protective care, a natural widening of the moral sentiments, a universal benevolence.[7] What informs the narrative is, if you like, an ethic of care – except that patriarchy enshrines a contaminated conception of protective care that we have still not overcome. The story embodies a *conception* of its subject-matter – it expresses an ethical perspective, endorses the providential care that it narrates, and informs us that we are made in the image of the God who extends to us that providential care, and thus commends this attitude to its hearers. It then laments our moral failure, and our tendency to live lives in conflict with this ideal, lives that are destructive and careless rather than creative of this care. The theologian James Mackey[8] has written very powerfully about how the Hebrew Bible and the Christian New Testament together testify to the history of this struggle between the contending impulses of benevolence and ruthlessness – contending impulses with which the history of philosophy is also familiar.

But the particular interest of Mackey's analysis lies in his insistence that this heterogeneous collection of writings testifies to the progress of these contending impulses in more than one way: they give expression to and celebrate the original ideal; they record, from the point of view of that ideal, its conflict with our tendency to self-aggrandisement, to use Mackey's word, but they are also in many places contaminated and overwhelmed by that tendency and its distortions of vision. In other words, the scriptures reveal the divided self, in the sense of exposing it but also in the sense of betraying it.

[7] See Richard Norman, 'Secularism and Shared Values', in Cornwell & McGhee (eds.), *Philosophers and God* (Continuum, 2009).
[8] See his *Christianity and Creation: The Essence of the Christian Faith and its Future among Religions: A Systematic Theology* (Continuum, 2006). I should like to record here my indebtedness to his writing more generally.

ii

But now, before reflecting further on spirituality and ethical ideals, I want to say more about the role of wonder in philosophical theism, since the idea of the world as God's creation is already an imaginative expression of wonder: some god has done this![9] Bacon's complaint was that atheists are shallow because they do not press their questions far enough, and this sentiment is frequently echoed by theistic philosophers. But though it might be thought that the very existence of things is as plausible an object of wonder as the *suchness* of things, wonder at the existence of things does not naturally take the form of or lead to the question *why* there is anything at all. It is not even clear that the idea of wonder at the existence of things isn't simply a variant expression for wonder at what exists rather than at that it exists. Wonder at the suchness of things, by contrast, *can* express itself in the form of the idea of an artist Creator. Theistic faith consists in taking this image as a revelation or intimation of the nature of things. However, it is only in the light of this idea, already formed and furnishing the mind, that it makes sense to raise the question *why* is there anything at all – and it makes sense to raise it, the question suggests itself, because we now have an answer ready to hand. To someone who is not already a theist, however, it is not obvious that the question is well-formed.

The late Fr Herbert McCabe is associated with a revival of interest in the question – and he certainly thought, in the spirit of Francis Bacon, that it is a failure of rationality not to raise it. Those who pursue this line of inquiry tend to treat the question as though it were the most general form of – and had the same logic as – the question, why are things thus rather than so, where the implication is already that things could have been otherwise, and are as they are because of the nature of the conditions which have given rise to them. But the latter kind of question is raised in the context of, and is predicated upon, an already acknowledged experience of contingency: that things come into existence that might not have done if the conditions had been different, that things fall out in a particular way and we can find an explanation for this by inquiring into the conditions. The significant thing in such cases is that we presume, take ourselves to be justified in assuming, that there *is* an explanation even if we do not yet know what that explanation is. But such a presumption applied to the existence of the totality of contingent things

---

[9]   To say this is to remain neutral about the question whether the world 'really is' God's creation.

Michael McGhee

lacks its original conditions of intelligibility and simply begs the question, though it is the conclusion that the line of questioning invites.

However, I am inclined to think that the real point of this line of questioning is not so much to compel us to a conclusion as to invite us to think in a way congenial to a confession of theistic faith. In other words, it invites us to *think the possibility* that the totality of contingent things – 'creation' – is contingent upon the activity of a creator, to think the possibility that there *might be* an explanation even if we cannot assume in advance that there must be. Someone who professes belief in God already sees humanity and the world we live in as dependent creation, as contingent upon God's sustaining and creative power, but there is no rational failure in not thus flying to Providence and Deity. But, to repeat, whereas in the case of an empirical feature of the world that we seek to explain we presume that there *must be* an explanation even if we do not know what it is, this presumption is not available to us in the case of the world itself – we cannot presume that there must be an explanation. This does not imply that there isn't one, but the question is pressed by those who think there is one – but not because they originally asked this question themselves.

A more plausible route to theism derives from wonder at the suchness of things. Thus we might have a sense of wonder at the *immensity* of the starry heavens or at the *loveliness* of a meadow in early May, or at the *charm* of a young child. And the point about the wonder is that it is an experience associated with rejoicing and care. *Genesis* expresses wonder, not at the existence of things but at the *suchness* of things, the *glory* of Creation, and tells of its fashioning. It is a story about how things came to be as they are rather than about how anything came to be at all – specifically a story about how *we* came to be as we are, and how we became divided and wayward beings. The categories are moral and aesthetic. The story *invokes* divine agency but does not argue to (the very idea of) a divine agent. In the face of wonder at the beauty of the world the idea of the work of a creative intelligence suggests itself as a natural metaphor, as I said earlier. So, then, what is in favour of Bacon's claim that God's ordinary works 'convince' atheism?

I have no doubt that the original Genesis story can strike a person with what we call 'the force of truth' *and* change their lives. It does the latter partly because its conception of Deity already embodies a conception of human ideals, and it can awaken or recall the hearer to their deepest impulses. But there are two things here. In certain contemplative moods the image of a maker naturally suggests itself, and

240

might do so for *anyone* because we are naturally anthropomorphic. But, as I just suggested, it can also strike someone as a revelation or intimation of the ultimate nature of things.

I use the phrase 'strike with the force of truth' to imply that for those who are struck in this way, the story, at least initially, *compels assent* and this is what is called 'Faith' – which is also the natural arena of religious doubt. Those who struggle with this doubt struggle precisely with whether what was received as a revelation is genuinely so. However, the reference to an assent that is 'compelled' implies that there is no voluntarism involved here (as distinct from the theological virtue of 'belief in God' that consists in an attitude of trust in God's saving power). The story impresses itself upon someone as a revelation of how things are, whether it is understood as a mythopoeic or symbolic representation of the providential care of an eternal being, or, more naively, as a likeness of what it represents. Thus, if I might repeat my earlier remarks about 'blind' belief – it might be objected that just because something strikes you as true it doesn't follow that it is true! That is surely right, but the model invoked by the objector is that of a hunch about a particular, contingent feature of the world that actually stands in need of independent verification, and where this necessity is being disregarded. But there is no such empirical context here, only an ungrounded vision of the world seen as a whole. I do not share this vision, but calling it a vision, or a picture', does not imply that it cannot be a revelation of how things ultimately are – but 'faith' is the bottom-line, faith in the form of a compelled assent. The assent can wax or wane, can appear less than compelling, and then be restored – or dissipate entirely. As far as religious doubt is concerned, it can take the form of a scepticism directed at a literal interpretation in favour of the symbolic, or, more radically, of the symbolic representation also. In either case doubt, like assent, dawns over the whole system of propositions and doubting the existence of God in that case should not be construed on the model of doubting the truth of a single existential proposition – doubt is cast on the revelatory nature of the whole vision.

3. Conclusion

Bacon's ancestral voice lingers on, but it is worth seeking to accommodate it to some degree. There *is* a sense in which attention only to 'second causes' is in some way shallow, and that to behold them confederate and linked together requires reflection and depth. The

Michael McGhee

shallowness Bacon complains about is that of someone who lives a life of unreflective immediacy, *resting* in second causes, immersed 'in the world', which expression implies moral criticism of the associated formation of subjectivity – one that determines the horizon within which one ranges. Depth, by contrast, is found in the *contemplation* of the world as a whole that belongs to wonder and its associated attitudes. Our immersion in what we call the world distracts us from what lies beyond that horizon of interest, and when we do see beyond it this comes, as I said earlier, in the form of a visitation, and traditionally, and following Paul, the visitation has been taken to be from the Spirit and its influence. Spirituality is the derived term that refers to the discipline of protecting the conditions for the possibility of that distinctive perspective on the world.

I should like to be more precise and emphatic about this idea of contemplating the world as such. Elsewhere I have described it as 'aesthetic perception' and have cited Paul Valery's remark about how poetry gives us 'the sense of a universe'. I have also cited Kant's notion of aesthetic ideas[10] in order to indicate the interplay between universal and particular. The thought is that in both art and nature universals can be evoked in and by particulars which are their instantiations. So the beauty of *this* landscape may sometimes be perceived in its exemplary as well as individual presence as disclosing the beauty of the world itself. The terrified face of this child in Gaza evokes in its particularity the dreadful political world in which it is trapped, and all such worlds. But the interesting thing here is that one is at once moved by the plight of the individual child *and* by the state of the world that its plight discloses. These kinds of aesthetic perception can be startling because they happen to us and change our mood. By contrast, under the influence of Hamlet's depression, this goodly frame the earth becomes a stale promontory, this most excellent canopy the air becomes a foul and pestilent congregation of vapours. What we have here is an example of Nietzsche's symptomatology of emotions. It is not so much that here are two equal options as that here are two aetiologies, a condition in which one's inner disposition determines how one sees the world – as precisely contaminated by that disposition – and one in which the sight of the earth's glories determines one's inner condition, or, more realistically, gives one a sense of that possibility.

What I have tried to do is present a picture of a moral vision that *informs* the religious picture we associate with the Abrahamic

[10] McGhee, *Transformations of Mind: Philosophy as Spiritual Practice*, (Cambridge University Press, 2002).

religions. I suggested that this moral vision informs theology, and I should like to end with a few comments on that.

It is hardly surprising that the scriptures reflect the moral attitudes and self-understanding of their authors, though we know that in so doing they also endorse and justify some of our most brutal tendencies. But nor is it surprising that the engulfing urgency to revenge that follows carnage and slaughter and is perceived as justice, should give way to calmer reflection on the atrocious consequences of escalation, reflection that engages compassion for the human condition. It is hardly surprising, in other words, that what we think of as the ethical development of human beings and the changing conceptions of Deity that reflect that development, should be expressed and even worked out in the history of scriptures that represent some of our earliest forms of self-consciousness. These latter changes are the product of creative imagination and calm reflection, this time on the perceived dissonance between our conceptions of the divine and our experience of dreadful realities. Thus the Lisbon Earthquake in the eighteenth century and the Holocaust in the twentieth have occasioned creative but existentially fraught theological renewal as thinkers have tried to make sense of the problem of evil. But these reflections are arenas for the development of moral insight. Thus the question where was God in the Holocaust finds resolution for some in the thought that God can only act through human hands, a reflection which turns (deflects?) the attention of the believer to the moral condition of humanity. It seems to me that the doctrine of *kenosis*, the doctrine of God's 'self-emptying', or of Christ's making himself powerless, is precisely a way of fixing or projecting *a moral insight* about the nature of power, specifically power over others. When we have someone in our power, so that we can do with them just what we want to do, or when we know that they are eclipsed by our power, then that power needs to be renounced if compassion, or any other moral virtue that allows others to *be*, is to emerge or flourish. The religions are, then, among other things, expressions of the state of moral insight, and it is obvious that moral reflection can be disconnected from what we call religious belief. But a religious picture that belongs to story-telling about origins can be undermined when it is confronted by the phenomena of natural and human evil, and theologians seem to be people who make adjustments to the story in the light of events and in accordance with their own moral judgment.

A moral philosopher will typically defend an intellectual position, make distinctions that are liable to be overlooked, describe and seek to resolve conceptual difficulties and confusions, and then stand aside.

Michael McGhee

However, as I said in the body of this paper, secular humanism presents itself as more than an intellectual position about the independence of ethics from religion. It also seeks, as a movement, to promote a moral vision. In that case it needs to take seriously the responsibilities of its role as a school of (godless) spirituality.

University of Liverpool

Living in the Light of Religious Ideals[1]

CLARE CARLISLE

As a 'poet of the religious', Søren Kierkegaard sets before his reader a constellation of spiritual ideals, exquisitely painted with words and images that evoke their luminous beauty. Among these poetic icons are ideals of purity of heart; love of the neighbour; radiant self-transparency; truthfulness to oneself, to another person, or to God. Such ideals are what the 'restless heart' desires, and in invoking them Kierkegaard refuses to compromise on their purity – while insisting also that they are impossible to attain. It is the human condition which makes them impossible, and he is willing to describe this in dogmatic terms as original sin – sin being the refusal and loss of God, and thus also the loss of a self that has its ontological ground in its relationship to God – but he is more concerned to explore it in psychological terms. The human condition is for Kierkegaard characterised not merely by ignorance, but by wilful self-deception.

One of the most striking aspects of Kierkegaard's philosophy of religion is his elucidation of a tension at the centre of Christian teaching: between an insistence on the limits of the human being, and an unconditional command or an irresistible impulse to transcend these limits. This would render the human situation utterly tragic were it not for grace, and indeed the difficulty of recognising and receiving this grace makes it tragic enough. The religious life seems to be a sort of spiritual rollercoaster: the beautiful ideals are glimpsed, and they elevate and inspire; one falls short of them, and despairs; a gift is offered and despair is transfigured; the gift slips away and leaves one empty-hearted. 'Christianity is as paradoxical on this point as possible', writes Kierkegaard: 'it seems to be working against itself by establishing sin so securely as a position that now it seems utterly impossible to eliminate it again – and then it is this same Christianity that by means of the Atonement wants to eliminate sin so completely as if it were drowned in the sea.'[2]

---

[1] A version of this essay was first published under the title 'Ideals and Idealism' in John Cornwell and Michael McGhee (eds.), *Philosophers and God* (London: Continuum, 2009) and is re-printed here by kind permission of Continuum.

[2] Søren Kierkegaard, *The Sickness Unto Death*, tr. Howard V. Hong and Edna H. Hong (Princeton: Princeton University Press, 1980), 100.

doi:10.1017/S1358246111000026   © The Royal Institute of Philosophy and the contributors 2011

Royal Institute of Philosophy Supplement **68** 2011   245

Clare Carlisle

In this essay I want to reflect on the structure as well as the content of the kind of impossible ideals that are invoked in many of Kierkegaard's texts. I want to consider the shape of a life lived in relation to these ideals, to trace the twists and turns of the spiritual path as it gains and loses sight of God. There is perhaps something specifically 'religious' about the structure of the ideals in question: on the one hand an absolute impossibility, tied to an interpretation of the human condition as such; and on the other hand an absolute demand, an irresistible claim exerted by these ideals that admits of no compromise. I think that this kind of logic can be found in Buddhist teachings, too, and I suspect that it may be shared by other traditions; Jacques Derrida has found the same paradoxical structure in ideals such as justice, democracy, forgiveness and so on – and it may be that these ideals are in some sense religious, perhaps the apparently secularised residue of a essentially theological way of thinking.

In considering on the structure of impossible ideals, I will try to respond to the important and influential critique advanced by Friedrich Nietzsche. Nietzsche famously criticizes the content of Christian ideals: he regards them as symptoms of *ressentiment*, and as hypocritical insofar their valuation of pity and compassion masks a covert will to power – but he also criticizes idealism itself as a negation of the world we live in. Put in very general terms, this critique rests on the view that if we live according to ideals that could not be instantiated in this world, then we subject this world to values that are not *of* it, and when life inevitably falls short of these impossible standards it is, as a whole, denigrated. This is an important aspect of what Nietzsche calls nihilism, the essence of western metaphysics, of idealism, of Platonism, of Christianity: 'A nihilist is a man who judges of the world as it is that it ought *not* to be, and of the world as it ought to be that it does not exist.'[3] In his lectures on Nietzsche during the late 1930s, Martin Heidegger explained that 'the cause of nihilism is morality, in the sense of positing supernatural ideals of truth, goodness and beauty that are valid "in themselves". The positing of the highest values simultaneously posits the possibility of their devaluation, which already begins when these values show themselves to be unattainable. Life thus appears to be unsuitable and utterly incompetent for the realisation of these values.'[4] This Nietzschean analysis

---

[3]   Friedrich Nietzsche, *The Will to Power*, tr. R. J. Hollingdale and Walter Kaufmann (New York: Vintage, 1967), §585.

[4]   Martin Heidegger, *Nietzsche*, tr. David Farrell Krell (San Francisco: Harper & Row, 1979–87), vol. III, 206.

should be taken seriously, and one way of responding to it would be to compromise on the purity of moral and religious ideals, and on the desire or demand for them, and thus to find a new and less difficult logic of becoming, for example, a Christian – to straighten out the spiritual path. But this is certainly not Kierkegaard's way, for he seeks to accentuate the difficulties – both intellectual and existential – of Christianity. I want to suggest that Kierkegaard is right to regard the invocation of impossible ideals as an indispensable aspect of Christian teaching, and I also want to argue this does not make it, nor any other teaching that is structured in this way, nihilistic. The Kierkegaardian version of ethico-religious idealism can be interpreted as aiming precisely at understanding and enhancing *this* life, *this* world. Setting aside Nietzsche's attack on the content of Christian morality, then, we can read Kierkegaard in a way that addresses the general, structural issue of idealism.

*

The theme of impossible ideals pervades Kierkegaard's authorship as a whole, although it is naturally most prominent in his more explicitly religious texts. In *Fear and Trembling* (1843) the pseudonym-poet Johannes de silentio expresses his awe and admiration of Abraham, the 'father of faith', and repeatedly confesses his own inability to do what Abraham did: 'The poet or orator can do nothing that the hero does; he can only admire, love, and delight in him... I cannot make the final movement, the paradoxical movement of faith.'[5] Johannes de silentio suggests that Abraham's greatness consists precisely in the absolutely paradoxical character of his response to God's command to sacrifice his son Isaac; 'He who expected the impossible became the greatest of all',[6] writes the pseudonym in his 'Eulogy on Abraham'. When a person 'examines the conditions of his life', these 'explain that [faith] is an impossibility', but the Kierkegaardian Christian is a 'knight of faith' who 'acknowledges the impossibility, and in the very same moment...believes the absurd, for if he wants to imagine that he has faith without passionately acknowledging the impossibility with his whole heart and soul he is deceiving himself'.[7]

---

[5] Søren Kierkegaard, *Fear and Trembling/Repetition*, tr. Howard V. Hong and Edna H. Hong (Princeton: Princeton University Press, 1983), 15; 51.
[6] Ibid., 16.
[7] Ibid., 42; 47.

Clare Carlisle

Kierkegaard thought that the assumption that one is a Christian easily and as a matter of course was the most pervasive and dangerous malaise within Christendom, and in *Fear and Trembling* he seeks to challenge this perceived complacency by raising the question of whether faith is even possible. The implicit question posed by his interpretation of the story of Abraham is: *Would you, could you do what Abraham did? could anyone? And if not, do you really have faith? could you? could anyone?* Johannes de silentio presents the reader with a beautiful ideal of faith, but at the same time he shows it to be so monstrous, so repellent, that it becomes impossible not only to attain it, but even to wish to attain it. 'Let us then either cancel out Abraham, or learn to be horrified by the prodigious paradox that is the meaning of his life, so that we can understand that our age, like every other age, can rejoice if it has faith.'[8]

The 1846 discourse *Purity of Heart of to Will One Thing*, written in Kierkegaard's own name, invokes the ideal of a pure heart – and yet most of the text is devoted to detailing all the different forms of *impurity* of heart. Desire for reward, fear of punishment, pursuit of a personal victory over impurity, and fluctuations in persistence and effort are all variations of the self-interest that prevents a person from willing the good 'in truth', solely for its own sake. Kierkegaard emphasises that 'the separation of sin lies in between' a person's resolution to live purely and the successful realisation of this ideal: 'each day, and day after day, something is placed in between: delay, blockage, interruption, delusion, corruption.'[9] Similarly, in *Works of Love* (1850) he outlines only to deconstruct a distinction between pure and impure love; between Christian, agapeistic love and preferential, erotic love.[10]

Another important example of the impossible Christian ideal is the characterisation of faith in Kierkegaard's 1849 text *The Sickness Unto Death*. Here the pseudonym Anti-Climacus insists that faith, rather than virtue, is the opposite of sin, and of the despair which constitutes the spiritual 'sickness' of sin. He describes faith as a state in which 'the self rests transparently in the power that established it' – that is to say, in God. But Anti-Climacus goes on to suggest that despair is universal, implying that the clear, untainted, self-present, restful

---

[8]   Ibid., 52–3.
[9]   Søren Kierkegaard, *Purity of Heart Is To Will One Thing*, tr. Douglas V. Steere (New York: Harper and Row, 1956), 31; 218.
[10]   See Vanessa Rumble, 'Love and Difference: The Christian Ideal in Kierkegaard's *Works of Love*' in Elsebet Jegstrup (ed.) *The New Kierkegaard* (Bloomington: Indiana University Press, 2004).

state of faith is never actually reached: 'anyone who really knows mankind might say that there is not one single living human being who does not despair a little, who does not secretly harbour an unrest, an inner strife, a disharmony, an anxiety about an unknown something or a something he dare not even try to know, an anxiety about some possibility in existence or an anxiety about himself...'.[11] The real author of the text certainly includes himself among those who suffer from despair; this is why the pseudonymous voice of Anti-Climacus is needed, for faith can only be known, and thus described, from this fictional perspective. Kierkegaard, who is named as the editor of *The Sickness Unto Death*, considered emphasising his distance from his pseudonym by including an editorial note in which he states that the book's description of despair and sin 'applies to me in many ways... I, the editor, am not the physician, I am one of the sick'.[12]

But why offer a description of faith if such faith is impossible to attain? Why invoke the ideal of purity of heart if this is unrealisable? What purpose is served by these ideals of transparency and purity? What do these ideals *accomplish*?

The obvious answer to this question is that 'resting transparently in God' presents the reader with a goal to strive after. But surely the profound 'rest' of faith must be the opposite of all striving? It is true that Kierkegaard sometimes emphasises the importance of striving. However, if we interpret his ideals as merely regulating a striving for perfection, in the way that Kantian ideals are regulative, this does not respond to the Nietzschean accusation of nihilism – for why should we 'regulate' or judge this life according to ideals and standards that can never be found within it?

Kierkegaard's ideals are not just untouchable guiding stars to help us progress from bad to better. The light of these ideals is not a reminder of a remote heaven, but a means of illuminating *this* world, *this* life, *this* human condition. The notion of transparent rest in God, for example, works to bring into relief essential features of sinfulness: the anxiety and restlessness, the concealment and deceit. It is in living with the ideal, in the light of the ideal, that these phenomena of sin come into view – and they need to be uncovered, pointed out, because otherwise the ubiquity and totality of sin, and therefore of its symptoms, hides it from view. (The theological doctrine of original sin conveys precisely these qualities of ubiquity and totality; another way of putting this is to say that the condition of sin, and

---

[11] Kierkegaard, *The Sickness Unto Death*, 22.
[12] See ibid., 162.

its concomitant suffering, is ontological rather than psychological.) Kierkegaard suggests in *Purity of Heart* that the chief reason for practices such as prayer and confession is the exposure of the individual's sinful condition: 'The all-knowing One does not get to know something about the maker of confession, rather the maker of confession gets to know about himself... The prayer does not change God, but it changes the one who offers it... Much that you are able to keep hidden in darkness, you first get to know by your opening it to the knowledge of the all-knowing One.'[13] As Kierkegaard observes in this discourse, delusion 'is unable to check itself.'[14] Continual anxiety is like a low continuous sound – the humming noise of a refrigerator, for example – that is usually unnoticed until it stops. The concealment inherent in sin deceives itself as well as others. Anti-Climacus' description of rest and transparency serves to expose, by delimiting and rendering recognisable, an inability to rest and to see clearly. In fact, *the notions of rest and transparency serve to expose the condition of their own impossibility*: the condition of sin. Similarly, the ideal of 'willing one thing', crystallized in *Purity of Heart*, exposes the many different varieties of 'double-mindedness' which contaminate even the sincerest attempt to live a good Christian life.

This exposure, this detection of sin, is accomplished by a kind of *testing*: the ideals of rest and transparency *test* the anxiety and opacity of sin; the concept of purity of heart *tests* 'double-mindedness'. 'Testing' here means tapping against something to sound it out for faults and weaknesses, to find whether or not it 'rings true' – what Nietzsche, in fact, describes as 'philosophising with a hammer' in order to 'sound out' idols.[15] While Nietzsche uses tools such as vigorous critical thinking and, in the 1880s, the doctrine of eternal recurrence to test ideals and values in the name of 'life' and 'affirmation', Kierkegaard uses ideals to test human life. But the aim of this testing is not to *judge* life in accordance with a transcendent value, but rather to *know* life, to gain a more intimate and honest acquaintance with one's own inner life. Both Kierkegaard and Nietzsche exhibit a critical brilliance that has its roots in a much older religious tradition of scrupulous self-examination before God.[16]

13   Kierkegaard, *Purity of Heart Is To Will One Thing*, 50–51.
14   Ibid., 39.
15   See the Foreword to Nietzsche's *Twilight of the Idols*.
16   See Don Cupitt, *Above Us Only Sky* (Santa Rosa: Polebridge Press, 2008), 15.

To some extent, Kierkegaard's view of ideals echoes Luther's view of the law, which the German reformer presents in his interpretation of Romans 3.20: 'By the law is knowledge of sin'. For Luther, the law is 'impossible of attainment', and thus 'the entire design and power of the law is just to give knowledge, and that of nothing but sin'. Kierkegaard follows Luther in emphasising the delusion and self-deception that characterize the human condition, and which thus provide the conditions of Christian practice. Luther writes that 'the Scripture sets before us a man who is not only bound, wretched, captive, sick and dead, but who, through the operation of Satan his lord, adds to his other miseries that of blindness, so that he believes himself to be free... But the work of Moses is the opposite of this – namely, through the law to open to man his own wretchedness.'[17] Kierkegaard, however, seems to be far more conscious than Luther of the possibility that his writing might be an exercise in testing or sounding out the hidden weaknesses in the reader's inner life, and indeed in his own life too; the impossibility of Christian ideals not only preoccupies his reflections on 'the task of becoming a Christian', but often also dictates the style of his texts, especially his use of pseudonyms. As Vanessa Rumble writes, 'Kierkegaard sets the Christian standard so high that no human could work to attain it and no human consciousness really wish it, so high that...so many of his pseudonymous texts disintegrate into the paired roles of...the observer/poet caught up in submissive wonder before the inaccessible hero of immediacy.'[18] We have seen how this literary structure is exemplified in *Fear and Trembling*.

If ideals merely served to expose the human condition as it really is, they might yet seem to be nihilistic, to be orientated to the condemnation of life in the name of an impossible ideal. The important question here is the quality, the 'how' of this exposure; the attitude or spirit of the testing, the bringing-to-light. If an ideal helps a person to understand herself and others better – and this involves grasping precisely why the ideal is impossible – then this knowledge can promote compassion, toleration, forgiveness, humility... the very ideals that are impossible to realize in their purity. In all its formulations, the Christian ideal is basically the ideal of love: self-love, love for the neighbour, love for God. There must be, then, a kind of 'double movement' involved in the invocation of the Christian

[17]   See Martin Luther, *The Bondage of the Will*, tr. J. I. Packer and O. R. Johnston (London: James Clarke, 1957), 158–62.
[18]   Rumble, 'Love and Difference: The Christian Ideal in Kierkegaard's *Works of Love*' in *The New Kierkegaard*, 164.

Clare Carlisle

ideal: first, an uncompromising questioning in the name of a ideal that has to be preserved in its pristine purity; and second, a profound and loving acknowledgement that *this is where we are, this is who we are*: it is here, now, under these less-than-ideal conditions that one tries to practise justice, or Christianity, or selflessness, and indeed it is these very conditions that invite or even impel one to practise them. Kierkegaard's attack on the complacency of Christendom is certainly harsh and uncompromising, and it is tempting to regard this as evidence of an intolerant refusal to give Christendom a chance. But on the other hand, his insistence that we are absolutely mired in the state of sin, so much so that only a god can save us, means that we are stuck in Christendom and that therefore our 'practice in Christianity' *has to* take place here.

Practising Christian love involves a double gesture: of challenge and forgiveness, of discrimination and open-hearted welcome, of vigilant self-examination and unconditional acceptance. This implies double-mindedness, and thus impurity, only if the first gesture does not already contain the second, and draw its energy and motivation from it. There is certainly a *moment* of condemnation when the ideal of purity is invoked: in *Purity of Heart*, for example, Kierkegaard states that 'the apostolic admonition "purify your hearts ye double-minded" is condemning, namely, *double-mindedness*.'[19] However, he also implies that any condemnation (or even testing) in the name of an ideal of pure love *violates the ideal*, since the judgment exhibits precisely the 'double-mindedness' that purity of heart is supposed to exclude. This very scenario is, in fact, described in *Works of Love*:

> With the one ear you hear what he says and whether it is wise and correct and penetrating and brilliant etc., and, alas, only with the other ear do you hear that it is the beloved's voice. With the one eye you look at him, testing, searching, criticising, and, alas, only with the other eye do you see that he is the beloved. Ah, but to divide in this way is not to love the person one sees.[20]

The second moment of the double gesture of testing in the name of the Christian ideal, then, means *looking with love* on imperfection, on impurity. One can only look with love on what has been made visible, exposed by the first moment of testing. It is important to

---

[19]   Kierkegaard, *Purity of Heart Is To Will One Thing*, 53. He is commenting on James 4:8.
[20]   Søren Kierkegaard, *Works of Love*, tr. Howard V. and Edna H. Hong (Princeton: Princeton University Press, 1987), 165.

recognise that this compassionate attentiveness is just as opposed to *over*looking faults indulgently as it is opposed to criticism and condemnation.

Sin, for Kierkegaard, is the reality of human life, and as such it has the highest claim on our attention. The purpose of the ideal of purity is to shed light on sin, helping Christians to see it more clearly within themselves. Kierkegaard knew that focusing on the ideal of purity, rather than on the reality of sin, can be one of many ways to overlook – and in overlooking, to avoid – one's own sinfulness. A genuinely Christian ethic, he insists, 'does not ignore sin, and its ideality does not consist in making ideal requirements, but...in the penetrating consciousness of reality, of the reality of sin... The new ethics...presents ideality as a task, not however by a movement from above down, but from below up.'[21] According to Kierkegaard, the task of Christianity is not primarily a matter of believing that certain historical events took place, nor even a non-rational confession of faith, but the continual deepening of a person's inward, heartfelt understanding that she is a sinner. This bare self-identification is given by dogmatics, but Kierkegaard's communicative task is to explore more fully the condition of sin: its phenomenology and its psychology; its modes of operation and its effects; its various manifestations and disguises. The self-discovery of sin does not just accomplish greater intellectual truthfulness, but opens up *within sin itself* the possibility of becoming a Christian, the possibility of faith, the possibility of a loving life – the possibility of loving life itself in its weakness, its blindness, its impurity.

*

I find in Kierkegaard's works an insight into the religious life that is not confined to a Christian context. Or, to put it another way, if this insight is specifically Christian, it expresses a truth that applies to anyone who aspires to live in accordance with ideals that surpass their present human condition. Philosophers outside the Christian tradition, such as Plato and Spinoza, have also recognised that an essential aspect of the task of living in such a way is to bring together love and knowledge, kindness and understanding, acceptance and awareness, compassion and wisdom (*philo–sophia*). These qualities are like the wings of a bird: they must be equal in size and equal in strength, for otherwise the bird will not fly. Neither knowledge without love,

---

[21]   Søren Kierkegaard, *The Concept of Anxiety*, tr. Reidar Thomte (Princeton: Princeton University Press, 1980), 18.

Clare Carlisle

nor love without knowledge will allow what Kierkegaard calls the human 'spirit' or 'inner being' to grow and flourish.

But doesn't this just present us with yet another impossible ideal? Isn't the perfect balance of awareness and acceptance the narrowest of narrow paths, like a walk along a tightrope that requires super-human precision, delicacy and concentration? Is anything in nature perfectly symmetrical?

From Kierkegaard's point of view, acknowledging the impossibility of such an ideal effects the transition from a merely-human 'ethical sphere' of existence to a 'religious sphere'. In the religious sphere the individual is 'before God', and the movement into this sphere is one of surrender and receptivity to God's love. Kierkegaard insists that this movement must be continually renewed, constantly repeated, since sin comes into being afresh at every moment. By oneself, one cannot maintain the balance of knowledge and love – either of oneself or of others – but to exist before God is to be known and loved infinitely, and thus in equal measure. It is in this light that the traditional doctrine of divine omniscience, benevolence and omnipotence comes to life: God knows all, loves unboundedly, and saves what seems irredeemable.

Here, however, we find ourselves in a circle, because this relationship to God, which constitutes the religious sphere, is precisely what is defined as faith – the faith that is impossible, humanly speaking. And how can we speak other than humanly? People sometimes ask me how I can be a Kierkegaardian without being a Christian, and this is not an easy question to answer, but perhaps it is equally difficult to say how one might be a Kierkegaardian *and* a Christian. Not only does Kierkegaard follow the Lutheran interpretation of the Sermon on the Mount, according to which Jesus does not teach an ethic that we can actually live, here and now, but rather sets an impossible standard that exposes the depth of sin and thus shows us that salvation can come only by faith and by an unmerited gift of grace – but he seems to go even further in accentuating the paradox and impossibility of faith itself. To know and love others is difficult enough, but, according to Kierkegaard, 'it is far more difficult to receive [love] than to give [it]'.[22]

Faith as Kierkegaard describes it can seem to be an abstract vanishing-point, so highly spiritualised that it is more divine than human. However, his remarks about the practices of prayer and confession, quoted earlier in this essay, indicate a way out of the circle that philosophical thinking alone cannot follow. These practices

[22] Kierkegaard, *Fear and Trembling*, 104.

can bring a person – whether in solitude or in a community – before a knowing, loving God in a more concrete sense, for they involve the whole being in an attitude of the body as well as of the mind, and engage the imagination and emotions as well as the intellect. Likewise, in the Buddhist tradition meditation practices bring together *sati* (mindfulness) and *metta* (loving-kindness). For example, the technique of *metta-bhavana* (cultivation of loving-kindness) meditation involves a kind of attentive well-wishing: the practitioner seeks to channel love to herself, to friends, to those whom she has harmed or been harmed by, to all beings; the technique of *vipassana* (insight) mediation is the practice of attentive awareness of whatever arises from moment to moment, combined with acceptance of this. In the case of both these techniques, the inevitable failure to maintain mindfulness and *metta* or acceptance is just another aspect of the self, or just another passing phenomenon, to be observed with understanding and love. The Christian and Buddhist traditions are alike in incorporating very powerful figures of human beings – Jesus and Gotama – who not only symbolise the qualities of wisdom and compassion, but overflow with them in an excess that transcends their historical existences, repeating itself in lineages of teaching, and in liturgical, devotional, and meditative practices.

Kierkegaard writes that 'in order to pray, there must be a God', but he immediately adds that (in other words) 'there must be a self plus possibility'.[23] Here, a 'self' is conceived as determinate, limited, whilst its 'possibility' transcends its limitations and yet is in some way related to it. Possibility in this sense is difficult to distinguish from *im*possibility, that is, from what the individual cannot reach or accomplish by herself. I cannot say what is possible; I do not know what *my* possibilities might be. I do not even know who I am. But I have encountered in other human beings qualities of wisdom and love that at once reflect back to me my own limitations and show me, with an ephemeral clarity and certainty, that there is much more than I now know beyond them.

University of Liverpool

---

[23]   Kierkegaard, *The Sickness Unto Death*, 40.

Sacrifice, Transcendence and 'Making Sacred'

DOUGLAS HEDLEY

Varieties of Sacrifice

Despisers of religion throughout the centuries have poured scorn upon the idea of sacrifice, which they have targeted as an index of the irrational and wicked in religious practice. Lucretius saw the sacrifice of Iphigenia as an instance of the evils perpetrated by religion. But even religious reformers like Xenophanes or Empedocles rail against 'bloody sacrifice'.[1] What kind of God can demand sacrifice? Yet the language of sacrifice persists in a secular world. Nor does its secularised form seem much more appealing. One need only think of the appalling and grotesque cult of sacrifice in numerous totalitarian regimes of the twentieth century. The perversion of the Jihad in radical Islam in contemporary Europe would provide another sombre instance. Throughout Europe in the last few years we have seen the revival of a classical Enlightenment atheism, a movement that, far removed from Nietzsche's pathos for the Death of God, pursues a vigorous and relentless policy of Écrasez l'infâme! Indeed, contemporary polemicists like Dawkins and Hitchens wish to emphasise precisely this dimension of Christianity: not just false but nasty! The modern cultured despisers of religion are the self confessed descendants of Hume and Voltaire. Religion is the product of the period of ignorance in the superstitious and terrified fearful infancy of humanity, and is the crude attempt to face the natural human longing for knowledge, consolation and emotional support. How can one strive to defend the concept of sacrifice against such cultured despisers? I think we need to start by reflecting upon why the slaughter of an animal, say, makes holy – sacra facere? The root meaning of 'sacrifice' has a basis in ritual practice, as its Latin etymology suggests. Though in common parlance it communicates a giving up or rejection, the word as we are going to understand it

---

[1] Sylvana Chrysakopoulou, *Théologie versus physique dans la poésie présocratique de Xénophane à Empedocle* (Thesis at the Sorbonne, Paris IV, 2003), 318–328.

doi:10.1017/S135824611100004X   © The Royal Institute of Philosophy and the contributors 2011
Royal Institute of Philosophy Supplement **68** 2011   257

Douglas Hedley

signifies the *substitution*, or more perhaps *sublimation*, of an item or interest for a higher value or principle. St Augustine speaks of the outward symbol of the true sacrifice of spiritual offering that God requires in the altar of the heart – a sacrifice of humility and praise.[2] The metaphor works because his audience was familiar with the literal sense of the term.

Three Phases of Sacrifice: Ancient, 1st Millennium and Enlightenment

Our culture possesses an inherited concept of sacrifice, largely from Christianity and the Graeco-Roman world. The near sacrifice of Isaac by Abraham or the sacrifice of Iphigenia by Agamemnon (though she is spirited away in one major version) are instances. The death of Jesus Christ is understood by the gospel writers as a sacrifice and St Paul enjoins Christians to become living sacrifices.

Sacrifice was immensely important within the Graeco-Roman world. Judaism and Christianity marked the end of that kind of literal sacrifice. Animal sacrifice was part of the expected behaviour of the Roman citizen, a contribution to the sustaining order of the universe. When Christians refused to submit to Imperial power and offer sacrifices to him, they seemed to be challenging the very cosmic order supported by the sacrificial system.[3] Whereas animal sacrifice was a fundamental part of the ritual method of attaining communion between the divine and the human in the Graeco-Roman world, the destruction of the Temple in A.D. 70 meant that animal sacrifice disappeared in Judaism. One might note the argument of Guy Strousma concerning the end of public sacrifice.[4] Christianity rejected both the sacrifices of the Jews and the 'Pagans'. The religion of the Rabbis, like Christianity, was a radical transformation of sacrifice. The period between Christ and Mohamed was an age of transition that prepared for the great metaphysical theologies of medieval Islam and Christendom.

However, the potency of the figurative meaning of sacrifice did not end there. Throughout its history, Christianity has been fascinated by the idea of sacrifice and the battles of the Reformation are

---

[2]   Augustine, *City of God*, X, 5.

[3]   Heyman, G., *The Power of Sacrifice, Roman and Christian Discourses in conflict*, Catholic university of America, (Washingon, 2007).

[4]   G. Stroumsa, *La fin du sacrifice: Les mutations religieuses de L'Antiquité tardive* (Paris, 2005).

incomprehensible without reference to it. Much of this debate is about the levels of the symbolic, figurative and literal. In the early modern period we have the development of a radical critique of sacrifice *tout court*. Philosophers of 'self preservation' such as Machiavelli, Hobbes and Spinoza have criticised the very idea of sacrifice. The key question is no longer just whether the relationship between literal and figurative sacrifice is one of continuity or rupture. It is now: has sacrifice hitherto 'imagined' become unimaginable. Is the very language of sacrifice a barbaric vestige of antiquated cruelty and superstition? As Girard observes in his own terminology: '(T)he phrase "modern world" seems almost like a synonym for the sacrificial crisis.'[5] If we take that to mean the problem that post Enlightenment European culture confronts in the legacy of sacrificial language, then Girard's point is most apt.

Sacrifice and Imagination

There is a considerable literature consisting of anthropological approaches to sacrifice, a body that has developed since the late nineteenth century.[6] E.B. Tylor on sacrifice as a gift to the gods within a context of animism; W. Robertson Smith on sacrifice as a ritual of communion; James Frazer on sacrifice as liberating spirit from body with a context of magic and fertility, Henri Hubert and Marcel Mauss (sacrifice as a oscillation between the profane and sacred); E.E. Evans-Prichard, who presents sacrifice as a process of ritual substitution in his work on the Nuer Religion. Others have argued for a pure pragmatic account of sacrifice: eminent scholars of religion and antiquity have argued that 'sacrifice' is the product of the fancy of other scholars. The distinguished French scholar Marcel Detienne famously considers sacrifice as merely a political and sociological phenomenon. Others have doubted whether any rational explanation for such an irrational activity can be given.[7] Walter Burkert's *Homo Necans* and Girard's *La Violence et Le Sacré* in 1972 represents a momentous period in the literature on scholarship. Among the manifold and wildly incompatible theories

---

[5]   Girard, *Violence and the Sacred*, (New York: Continuum, 2005), 199.
[6]   Strenski, I., *Theology and the First Theory of Sacrifice*, (Leiden: Brill, 2003).
[7]   Joseph Henninger, 'Sacrifices', in Mircea Eliade (ed.) *Encyclopedia of Religion* (New York: Macmillan, 1987).

of sacrifice, Girard and Burkert produce clear explanations of the nature of sacrifice.

Sacrifice explained: Burkert and Girard

Burkert and Girard are of particular note because of the scope and vigour of their theories of sacrifice. Both draw upon longer traditions: Burkert is the inheritor of the magnificent tradition of German Classical philology together with wider philological concerns, (I am thinking especially of Nietzsche); Girard is clearly standing within a tradition of French speculation about sacrifice that goes back to the spirituality of counter-Reformation. Both are proponents of grand and provocative theories of sacrifice.

Walter Burkert notes that even the great age of Aeschylus to Euripides possesses striking archaic elements within sacrificial contexts. If one thinks of the paradigmatic tragic cycle of the *Oresteia*, it is structured by a succession of failed sacrifices: from the sons of Thyestes through Iphigenia to Orestes' killing of his mother, Clytemnestra. The ubiquitous nature of sacrifice through Ancient Greek religion can be explored in various texts: however Burkert pursues the ritual of sacrifice into the Palaeolithic age of our hunter-gatherer ancestors, and beyond. He is inspired by the ethology of Konrad Lorenz, especially his *On Aggression* of 1963. Thus animal behaviour is the paradigm for understanding human behaviour. On the assumption that 90% of the evolutionary history of *homo sapiens* was in the Hunter/gatherer state and must have at least vestigial influence in later civilisation, Burkert pursues the roots of sacrifice in the hunting practices of our ancestors.

It is a moot point whether the Palaeolithic evidence is as convincing as Burkert avers. Perhaps there was more gathering than hunting, and more scavenging than heroic killing. That aside, my concern is that Burkert gives inadequate weight to the imaginative dimension of human culture. Is culture, in this case specially a cultural milieu with certain religious rites, merely the conventional shape of universal natural instincts? This seems to be Burkert's assumption. For example, Burkert's theory requires the generation of myth by ritual, which in turn is grounded in biosocial factors. The myths of gods and heroes are derived from ritual of sacrifice, which in turn are derived from ritualised hunting practices. If culture were a level of life that rests neatly upon biological structures, then a biological account of 'religion', like Burkert's, would be feasible. However, perhaps human culture is not the conventional shape of passions that are universal in human nature. Rather, the distinctively human passions are shaped by cultural traditions and history. This, I think, is a subtle and intriguing critic of naturalism in ethics. Man is made by society, by institutions and rituals, and as such human nature is irreducible to the stimulus-response model of the crude naturalists and barely explicable by the more sophisticated versions of naturalistic theory. As Vico, Burke and Maistre insisted with profundity: art is man's nature.

Girard cannot be accused of naturalism. His inspiration is not biology but imaginative literature and he is scathing of those who deny great literature the capacity to convey real truth. Furthermore, his theory of mimetic desire is consciously anti-naturalistic. The imagining of the desires of others shapes desires. The object of human desires is thus moulded by the imagination and imitation of the desires of others. In Girard's theory the social psychology of desire cannot be reduced to the push and pull of raw instincts, inclinations and aversions.[8] Girard's theory of mimetic desire is derived from literature and quite incompatible with ethology.[9] Whereas Burkert's theory is naturalistic in the sense that sacrifice emerges out of the natural need to kill for food, Girard's theory is based on a monstrous act of murder. This arises from a mimetic desire that is inherently competitive and which generates an upsurge of violence with the community. Girard uses the term 'mimetic doubling' for this process by which rivalry for the mediated desires generates the monstrous double: the competitor locked into conflict over the desired objects, and the ensuing violence Rivalry is not the product of the fortuitous convergence of two agents desiring the same object. The one subject yearns for the object precisely *because* the rival wants it. Violence is not an unfortunate by-product of clashing desires, but the necessary upshot of mimesis:

> ...the original act of violence is the matrix of *all* ritual and mythological significations.[10]

Mimetic doubling generates the mimetic crisis, in which swelling violence threatens social breakdown (Girard depicts as the erosion of hierarchy and distinction). The resolution of this mimetic lies in

---

[8]   There is no truth 'not mediated by culture', Girard, *Violence and the Sacred*, 240.

[9]   Though Girard has become very interested in the evolutionary dimension of mimesis. See *Evolution and Conversion: Dialogues on the Origins of Culture*, Girard, Pierpaolo Antonello and de Castro Rocha, J.C.

[10]   Girard, *Violence and the Sacred*, 117.

Douglas Hedley

the redirection of the violence of the mob to a single victim. The society almost destroyed by conflict can unite itself by concentrating its ire upon a scapegoat. Hence the murder of single victim both releases the violence of the mob and unites the many.

Religion is a complex attempt to obscure the terrible truth of victimisation at the root of human culture, sacrificial ritual the inadequate attempt to resolve the problem of violence at the root of all human relations, and myth is a language of concealment. The *Bacchae* of Euripides plays an important role for Girard since the relations between myth, ritual and literary reflection are so porous. Girard's thesis rather oddly makes the surrogate victim, the scapegoat rather than God the sacred, or indeed as Girard writes: 'the sacred is violence'.[11]

If Burkert with his enthusiasm for ethology fails to do justice to the crucial role of imagination in human culture, Girard sees mankind as almost universally condemned to a perversely overactive imagination: creating saviour figures out of ritual substitutes. Briefly, I think that Girard is wrong about myth as a process of concealment and is an attempt to divorce Christianity from any mythic component. Christians, according to Girard, become the Gnostic few who have grasped the secret curse of human culture.

Making Sacred

What is the 'sacred'? It is often contrasted with the profane. In the popular imagination the sacred or the holy is associated with a sacred place and a time: a temple, a festival, or perhaps a place that seems to evoke awe. There is a dimension of the sacred that is often remarked upon: its ambivalent status. The 'making sacred' of sacrifice is both a source of terror and consolation. It holds society together and yet induces anxiety and horror. This is true of theories of sacrifice from Maistre to Girard. The obvious point of reference is to the seminal work of Rudolf Otto's *Das Heilige* of 1917. Otto employs for his motto the lines from Goethe:

Das Schaudern ist der Menschheit bestes Teil.
    Wie auch die Welt ihm das Gefühl verteuere,
    Ergriffen fülht er tief das Ungeheure

These lines are very difficult to translate. 'Schaudern' is cognate with the English shudder. 'Ungeheuer' has connotations of massive scale

---

[11]   Girard, *Things Hidden Since the Foundation of the World* (Stanford University Press: Stanford, 1987), 32.

262

and the uncanny. 'Ergriffen' is a state of being grasped. It means that awe is the best part of mankind, even if not valued by the world; it is grasped in the depths by the sense of the numinous. But I don't know how to translate it into poetry. The difficulty is to find words that resonate in a similar manner. Burkert in his effort to produce an ethology of Greek religion clearly thinks that Otto's influence is baneful.[12]

A good example of the numinous is one of the seminal discussions of sacrifice in modern philosophy: Kierkegaard's *Fear and Trembling*. The title itself points to that experience of the non rational *Schaudern* of Goethe and Otto. Abraham is famously silent in Kierkegaard's account: he cannot conceptualise his experience. For Kierkegaard – and I think this is a plausible interpretation of the position presented in *Fear and Trembling* – it is the fact of transcendence, of the 'absolute relation to the absolute' that justifies the idea of sacrifice. This, of course, makes any rational-ethical justification impossible. Kierkegaard's idea of the teleological suspension of the ethical is highly suggestive and problematic.[13] It challenges any cosy domestication of religion – like Arnold's famous 'morality touched with emotion'. But Kierkegaard's rejection of an identification of religion with the ethical has the unwelcome effect of furnishing warrant for fanaticism.

Whereas many modern writers, whether for against, assume the absurdity of the practice of sacrifice, the Savoy Count de Maistre does not. In the text *Enlightenment on Sacrifice*, he noted the oddity of the phenomenon that sacrifice is a universal and intractable element in human societies. He claims that the ritual of sacrifice furnishes institutions with both awe and terror: it makes them sacred. For Maistre, Christianity fulfils rather than denies the principle of sacrifice that forms the basis of the partial truth of heathen piety.[14] The pagans demand regularly repeated 'communion in blood', while Christ sacrifices his divinely innocent blood so that the heathen sacrifice, 'redemption through blood', can find its telos. Maistre's account is specifically aimed at the rationalism of the French revolution and the optimism of its theorists. Maistre thought that a failure to

[12] See the useful discussion, Burton Mack: 'Introduction: Religion and Ritual', in Hamerton-Kelly (ed.), *Violent Origins: Ritual Killing and Cultural Formation*, (Stanford, 1987), 1–70.

[13] See Rudd, A., *Kierkegaard and the Limits of the Ethical*, (Clarendon: Oxford, 1993).

[14] St. Petersburg Dialogues, or Conversations on the Temporal Government of Providence, ed. and tr. Richard A. Lebrun (Kingston and Montreal, 1993).

Douglas Hedley

recognize human limits, frailty and finitude would create terror.[15] Maistre's own vision is an apocalyptic view of the whole earth as a gigantic altar upon which there is a continual and terrible sacrifice of life until the final eradication of evil. The world is a vast altar on which each being must sacrificed until the final purification of evil: evil is not a refutation of Divine purpose and providence but rather reveals the necessity for sacrificial expiation and redemptive substitution as part of a process of cosmic return to Divine Unity. This return is a divine education of mankind realised through pain and sorrow.

There was a tradition that fed upon the vigorous rhetoric of Maistre through Donoso Cortés up to Carl Schmidt, and which used this apocalyptic vision to justify violence and war. The attempt of a thinker like Girard to distance Christianity from the very principle of sacrifice is doubtless both inspired by and in revolt against Maistre. Yet Maistre's own philosophy is better understood within a tradition of Christian theodicy than as some sombre irrationalism of the kind diagnosed by critics like Isaiah Berlin. Indeed, theologically Maistre is attached to the Greek Orthodox tradition of Origen and universalism. The ultimate interest of Maistre is in Christus consummator rather than violence, and his theodicy is an ingenious attempt to re-imagine sacrifice in a profane age. I cannot here defend such a reading of Maistre, but his is a brilliant reading of the relationship between literal and figurative sacrifice as one of continuity not rupture.

Sacrifice and the Crucified Holy One

Maistre was a Chrisian Platonist. Plato's description of the discussion between Glaucon and Socrates concerning the just and the unjust man. The just man as an image of eternal justice is contrasted with the unjust man who is concern with courting the mere appearance of justice. The initial comparison begins with the famous ring of Gyges, which makes its wearer invisible and free from approbation or disapprobation. The most unjust man is one who feigns the appearance of justice: he practices immorality while attaining the appearance of righteousness. By way of contrast, the truly just man cares not for the appearance but the substance of justice. Since *apparently* just acts may be motivated by the desire for honour or gifts, it is not always evident whether the motive lies in justice itself or the

---

[15]   Bradley, Owen, *A modern Maistre: the social and political thought of Joseph de Maistre* (London: University of Nebraska, 1999).

desire for reputation. Thus in order for his justice to be evidently motivated for the right reasons, he should be mocked and held in disregard. Hence Glaucon is intent on placing the 'simple, good man' where his stubborn love of justice can be proved. Thus the depiction of the perfectly unjust man as hailed for his justice and the truly righteous man is lonely and despised. Socrates observes that the two figures are like polished statues. Glaucon goes further and claims that the righteous man will be humiliated and tortured, bound, blinded and crucified:

> They will say that the just man, as we have pictured him, will be scourged, tortured, and imprisoned, his eyes will be put out, and after enduring every humiliation he will be crucified, and learnt last that one should want not to be, but to seem just.[16] (*Republic*, 362)

Evidently these lines were composed after and in the light of the death of the suffering and execution of Socrates. Socrates had been publically humiliated by Aristophanes, the most popular writer of comic plays in Athens. Yet he had to endure not merely the mockery and humiliation through the wit of the poet, but also a vicious attack on his piety and the accusation of corrupting the youth in court. The actual death of Socrates was not as described – it was in fact the serene death of a free citizen. The description of the suffering of the just is closer to the violence and humiliation of Golgotha. The King of the Jews, descendant of King David, executed through a slave's death.[17]

In his *Religion within the Boundaries of Mere Reason* Kant discusses the crucifixion of Christ as the sacrifice 'Holy One' of the Gospel, especially in the section concerning the evil principle's rightful claim to dominion over the human being, and the struggle of the two principles with one another'.[18] Kant is here drawing upon his theory of 'radical Bose' in humanity as expressing the innate disposition to evil. Kant, like Plato, emphasises the manner in which the righteousness of Christ provoked the 'prince of this world' to humiliate and kill him:

> He finally pursued him to the most ignominious death, without achieving anything in the least against him by this onslaught by

---

[16] Plato, *The Republic* (Harmondsworth: Penguin, 1987), tr. D Lee, 49.

[17] Benz, E. 'Der gekreuzigte Gerechte bei Pato, im Neuen Testament und in der alten Kirche', *Akademie der Wissenschaften und Literatur in Mainz*, **12** (1950), 1–46.

[18] *Religion within the Boundaries of Mere Reason*, eds. Allen Wood and George di Giovanni (Cambridge, 1998). All text references are to this edition.

unworthy people upon his steadfastness and honesty in teaching, and example for the sake of the good. (*Religion* 6:81)

Christ's death serves to manifest goodness. It reveals the capacity of the free agent to exhibit autonomy and the power of the moral law over inclination: the contrast between the freedom of the children of heaven and the bondage of a mere son of earth (*Religion* 6:82). It is a paradigm of the capacity of the virtuous agent to prevail over the most difficult of circumstances. Moreover, within Kant's rational theology, Christ's death can convey a powerful awareness of mankind's moral vocation, the potential for liberation from bondage to inclination, and as the perfect representation of holiness: the utter correspondence of disposition to the moral law.

> It means that sacrifice is unavoidable: those in the world who adhere to the good principle should always be prepared for physical sufferings, sacrifices and mortifications of self-love. (*Religion*, 6.83)

This suggests a difference of emphasis at least between the *Groundwork* and Kant's *Religion*. The motivational rigorism of the *Groundwork*, the thesis that actions are only morally good if prompted by duty rather inclination. On this thesis the special value of ethical sacrifice is that it can be an index of the sovereignty of the moral law: 'the sublimity and inner worth of the command is the more manifest in a duty, the fewer are the subjective causes for obeying it and the more there are against...' (*Groundwork*, IV 425).[19] Thus virtue 'reveals itself most splendidly in suffering' *Critique of Practical Reason* V 156).[20] From being an indication of the sublime power of the moral law, sacrifice becomes an unavoidable aspect of the free agent's experience in the Religion:

> The emergence from the corrupted disposition into the good is in itself already sacrifice (as "the death of the old man" "the crucifying of the flesh") and the entrance into a long train of life's ills which the new human being undertakes in the disposition of the Son of God. (*Religion* 6:74)

Kant quotes St Paul's notion of being crucified with Christ. If we bracket the complex and opaque idea of grace in Kant as a surplus

---

[19] *The Moral Law.* H.J. Paton (ed.) (London: Hutchinson, 1981), 88.
[20] *Critique of Practical Reason* (ed.) Mary Gregor (Cambridge: Cambridge University Press, 2004).

imputed via Christ's death, the dominant idea is the symbolic crucifixion of the inclinations and sharing in the sufferings of the just man
par excellence: an idea that is strikingly akin to Plato's vision of the
innocent suffering of the righteous man in the *Republic*. Here we
have the language of 'Sacrifice' is, of course, often employed when
considering the core meta-ethical problem of moral worth. What
reasons can one give for a rational interest in the moral?

Let us bracket the arguments in the social sciences (especially
psychology, evolutionary biology and economics) concerning cost-
benefit analysis of action towards others and expense to the agent.
The typical arguments about reputational altruism, reciprocal
altruism or the hedonistic account of altruism reduce morality to
some form of egoism. Plato and Kant produce an account of self-
sacrifice as an index of the freedom of the agent to pursue the good.
They both explicitly use the language of ethical sacrifice to express
the sublime power of a transcendent goodness. Both envisage the re-
ception of the power in terms of a dualism of a phenomenal and nou-
menal, sensible and intelligible domain. Both envisage the good life
in metaphysical terms as proper subordination of the former to the
latter. Both present the fulfilment of that good life as a life of sacrifice.
Maistre makes this thought explicit: mankind's proper relation to the
physical cosmos is a sacrificial rite, a 'making sacred'. Through sacrifice, the hidden seed of the Divine is brought out of potentiality into
actuality. As such, the renunciation of the will, the sacrifice of self for
an absolute good must remain an integral element of human self-
realisation. Maistre, with Burke the most eloquent polemicist
against Enlightenment, saw himself as the inheritor of the great philosophical inheritance of Europe and the relentless adversary of the
trivialisation and banalisation of Western philosophy in so called
'philosophes' like Voltaire. Yet Maistre was no mere polemicist: he
was an astute reader of Plato and the Platonic tradition, and his reflections upon the relevance of the concept of sacrifice reflect his deep
immersion in the European philosophical canon.

Conclusion

I have reflected upon philosophers of very different temperaments, to
suggest why I do not think that sacrifice is merely 'constructed'.
The idea of sacrifice exhibits the natural and legitimate human
sense of the sacred dimension of life. Here I think Plato, Kant and
Maistre, are better guides than socio-political pragmatists like
Detienne. Sacrifice traditionally concerns usually a relation to gods

or a God. Its ritual forms often reflect or point to the violence that pervades the animal kingdom and human culture: the threat of death and the violent origins of cultures. Yet it also points to humanity's abiding desire for renewal: to 'make sacred' and participate in the very source of life. Religious thinkers, from Vico to Maistre and Girard know that society is not a product of human contract. If sacrifice is ambivalent in the sense that it a transcendent dimension to human experience, it is an index of a double obstacle for the naturalist. For the naturalist can neither provide a satisfactory reduction of the irreducible hermeneutical dimension of sacrifice, its role in our stories about ourselves as creatures aware of life *and* death. One only need think of the power of many tragic and, by implication, 'sacrificial' themes in Western art: from Wagner to Mann, from George Eliot's *Middlemarch* to Melville's *Moby Dick*. This is why the Romantic legacy is still so important for our age. The greatest minds of that period had both a deep sense of cultures as wholes: we cannot ignore the particularity and contingency of any human culture. Yet neither can we ignore the sacred and the eternal impinging upon human consciousness: the transcendent source of the gift of life.

Clare College, Cambridge

The Incarnation: divine embodiment and the divided mind

ROBIN LE POIDEVIN

1. 'And was made man'

The central doctrine of traditional Christianity, the doctrine of the Incarnation, is that the Second Person of the Trinity lived a human existence on Earth as Jesus Christ for a finite period. In the words of the Nicene Creed, the Son is him

> who for us men, and for our salvation, came down from heaven, and was incarnate by the Holy Ghost of the Virgin Mary, and was made man.

The idea was developed in 451 by the Council of Chalcedon, who insisted, in the course of an extended statement on the doctrine, that in Jesus Christ two natures, one wholly human, the other wholly divine, combined in a single person:

> we all with one voice confess our Lord Jesus Christ one and the same Son, the same perfect in Godhead, the same perfect in manhood, truly God and truly man, the same consisting of a reasonable soul and body, of one substance with the Father as touching the godhead, the same of one substance with us as touching the manhood, *like us in all things apart from sin*; begotten of the Father before the ages as touching the Godhead, the same in the last days, for us and for our salvation, born from the Virgin Mary, the *Theotokos* [the God-bearer], as touching the manhood, one and the same Christ, Son, Lord, Only-begotten, to be acknowledged in two natures, without confusion, without change, without division, without separation; the distinction of natures being in no way abolished because of the union, but rather the characteristic property of each nature being preserved, and concurring in one Person and one subsistence, not as if Christ were parted or divided into two persons,

doi:10.1017/S1358246111000129   © The Royal Institute of Philosophy and the contributors 2011

Royal Institute of Philosophy Supplement **68** 2011

Robin Le Poidevin

but one and the same Son and only-begotten God, Word, Lord, Jesus Christ;[1]

The divine, in other words, became embodied, and that embodiment took a human form. But *can* the divine be embodied? The Chalcedonian definition, as it is often called, highlights a fundamental paradox at the heart of the doctrine of the Incarnation: the idea of an individual that is at once both limited in power and understanding (by virtue of being in a human body) and unlimited (by virtue of being divine). The intellectual challenge to us as the inheritors of Christian tradition is to articulate in detail what would have to be the case in order for the Chalcedonian statement to be true.

For many philosophers, and theologians, that is just the *wrong approach*. The fact, they say, that the doctrine, literally construed, is transparently self-contradictory gives us the clearest indication that we should understand it as a metaphor, or see it as expressive of our feelings towards the man Jesus. Here, for instance, is John Hick's comment:

> orthodoxy insisted upon the two natures, human and divine, coin-hering in the one historical Jesus Christ. But orthodoxy has never been able to give this idea any content. It remains a form of words without any assignable meaning. For to say, without explanation, that the historical Jesus of Nazareth was also God is as devoid of meaning as to say that this circle drawn with a pencil on paper is also a square...It therefore seems reasonable to conclude that the real point and value of the incarnational doctrine is not indicative but expressive, not to assert a metaphysical fact but to express a valuation and evoke an attitude.[2]

Perhaps this is right, and it is better to talk, as John Robinson does, of Jesus as 'the human face of God' Robinson, *The Human Face of God* (London: SCM Press, 1973) much as we might describe Lenin as the acceptable face of communism. But, to make a historical point, since the Chalcedonian statement was intended to distinguish orthodoxy from heresy, on which much depended, it is most unlikely that it was intended by the Council of 451 simply as a metaphor, or an expression of a valuation, or a means of evoking an attitude. And to make a theological point, only by *really* being made man could

---

[1]   J. Stevenson, *Creeds, Councils and Controversies: Documents illustrating the early history of the church 373–561*, rev. W. H. C. Frend (London: SPCK, 1989), 35–3

[2]   Hick, 'Jesus and the World Religious', in Hick (ed.) *The Myth of God Incarnate* (London: SCM Press, 1976), 178

The Incarnation: divine embodiment and the divided mind

God enter into a uniquely close relationship with us. Finally, to make a philosophical point, an examination of the coherence of the doctrine, literally construed, is prior in the order of inquiry to the question of whether we should construe the doctrine non-literally. The surface contradiction may hide a deeper truth.

From now on, then, we shall set aside the metaphorical approach, and take an unapologetically literal view of the Chalcedonian statement. That is not to say that it requires no interpretation. It may be that we have to recognise differences between the way we are embodied and the way the Son can be embodied. So it is perhaps better to talk, not so much of a 'literal' view of the Chalcedonian statement, one that allows no reinterpretation, but rather a 'realist' one: one, that is, that takes it to be an attempt to articulate, though not necessarily in wholly transparent terms, how things actually are.[3]

We will look at two accounts of embodiment, both of them plausible in ordinary (or at least non-divine) contexts, and ask of each whether it offers a suitable model for divine embodiment, while at the same time doing justice to Christ's human nature. The answer

---

[3]   In an illuminating essay ('What Does Chalcedon Solve and What Does it Not? Some Reflections on the Status and Meaning of the Chalcedonian Definition', in Davis, Kendall and O'Collins (eds.) *The Incarnation* (Oxford: Oxford University Press, 2002), 143–63), Sarah Coakley outlines three approaches to an understanding of Chalcedon to be found in the literature, and finding them all wanting in some respect, proposes a fourth. The first interpretation takes the definition to lay down the terms in which the Incarnation is to be described, but makes no ontological claims. A second takes the definition to be metaphorical. Both of these Coakley finds implausible. The third approach is one found in analytic philosophical treatments of the Incarnation, typified by Brown (*The Divine Trinity* (London: Duckworth, 1985) and Morris (*The Logic of God Incarnate* (Cornell: Cornell University Press, 1986). In these, the Chalcedonian statement is taken to be, or intended to be, a literally true description of the Incarnation. Coakley applauds the recognition in this approach that the statement does intend to be truly descriptive of an actual state of affairs, but points out that 'literal' has additional connotations that may not appropriately represent the intentions of those who originally constructed the statement. Her own proposal is that Chalcedon, in her words, 'sets a 'boundary' on what can, and cannot, be said, by first ruling out three aberrant interpretations of Christ...second, providing an abstract rule of language for distinguishing duality and unity in Christ [i.e. two natures but one person], and third, presenting a 'riddle' of negatives by means of which a greater (though undefined) reality may be intimated'. (Coakley 'What Does Chalcedon Solve and What Does it Not?', 161.)

in each case, I suggest, is 'no'. The situation is not improved, it turns out, by what is otherwise a promising approach to the dual nature, namely the 'divided mind' hypothesis, according to which Christ's mind exhibited two parallel streams of consciousness. Where this inquiry leads us, I suggest, is to the *kenotic* approach to the Incarnation: the Son gave up (at least some of) the characteristics of divinity in order to become incarnate.

2. Two accounts of embodiment

'Veiled in flesh the Godhead see', says the Christmas hymn. But if the suggestion is that the divine is *merely* veiled in human flesh, this runs counter to the thinking enshrined in the Chalcedonian statement: the Son did not merely take on the *form* of a man, but was, in the words of the statement, 'truly man, the same consisting of a reasonable soul and body...like us in all things apart from sin.' There must be an intimate connection between the divine person and the human body, one that is not adequately captured by the concept of simple containment. For containment hardly captures our own relation to our bodies. As Descartes puts it:

> Nature...teaches me by these feelings of pain, hunger, thirst, etc., that I am not only lodged in my body, like a pilot in his ship, but, besides, that I am joined to it very closely and indeed so compounded and intermingled with my body, that I form, as it were, a single whole with it. (Meditation VI)

So what is it to form 'a single whole' with one's body?

The first of the two accounts of embodiment we will consider is distinctly unCartesian, in that it rejects the idea that the mental and the physical are two distinct ontological categories. Recent orthodoxy in the philosophy of mind ('recent' here meaning within the last 50 years) has favoured a physicalist approach: the mind is a physical entity, just as the body is; or, if we prefer not to reify talk of 'the mind', mental events are identical to physical processes in the brain. This at once distances us from the metaphor of the pilot and his ship, for the pilot is not (in any literal sense) part of the ship: he is merely in it. Physicalism shows us how the mind and the body are indeed one. This, then, looks like a promising account of embodiment: a person is embodied if all the states of that person (including all the mental states, indeed *especially* the mental states) are states of a body. We will, perhaps, need to restrict this to intrinsic states, that is, states of the person that are logically independent of any other object. A person may be the focus of a revolution, for example, but it would at the very least be odd to consider this as a state of the body. Here then is our first account of embodiment:

The physical realisation account: a person P is embodied in body B if and only if all the (intrinsic) states of P are wholly realised by (intrinsic) states of B

The second account is ontologically neutral: that is, it does not make any assumptions about whether the mental and the physical constitute a single ontological category or two. It defines the embodiment relation in terms of causal connections of certain kinds. This account is articulated by Jonathan Harrison, who defines embodiment in terms of five conditions:[4]

  (i)   effects on B are felt by P
  (ii) P feels the inside of B
  (iii) P can move B directly
  (iv) P's perception of the environment is spatially centered on B
  (v) P's thoughts and feelings are affected by B's state

Richard Swinburne, in discussing Harrison's conditions, expresses some doubts about (v), remarking that although it may well be true that we are typically affected by B's state, this is not obviously part of what is meant by embodiment.[5] And indeed, it seems plausible that some at least of what happens in or to our bodies need have no conscious consequences, a consideration that extends to (i) and (ii). But we do have knowledge of some of the states of our bodies that is denied to anyone else, in that it is direct, not inferred from behaviour. And (iii) and (iv) are both clearly central to our feeling of being embodied. (iv) contains two ideas: that the body is the mediator of perceptual knowledge of the world, and that that knowledge is presented in a spatially perspectival way, as a result of the body's location in space. Disparate though these criteria might seem, the key idea is *causal connection* rather than realisation, which means that P need not be identified with B.

Given that each of the criteria is logically independent of the others, it is possible for a person-body pair to satisfy some of these criteria but not others. (Indeed, as Harrison also points out, we could contemplate the possibility of a person satisfying each criterion in relation to a *different* body.) What should we say of such a case? That the person in

---

[4] 'The Embodiment of Mind, or What Use is Having a Body?', *Proceedings of the Aristotelian Society* **74** (1973–4), 33–55.
[5] Swinburne, *The Coherence of Theism* (Oxford: Clarendon Press, 1977), 103.

question is only partially embodied, that embodiment, as Harrison puts it, admits of degrees. This then paves the way to the idea of a person being embodied to zero degree – i.e. not being embodied at all.

Our second account of embodiment, then, is this:

> *The causal account*: P is embodied in B if and only if (a) P has direct knowledge of some of B's states; (b) P is able to move B directly, as a result of P's intentions; (c) P's perceptual knowledge of the world is mediated by B; (d) P's perception of the environment is spatially centred on B.

Given that mere spatial containment is not an adequate account, for reasons we have already considered, the physical realisation and causal accounts have a reasonable claim to be exhaustive as ways of capturing embodiment. They are not, however, exclusive. Indeed, if physicalism is correct, human beings, in ordinary circumstances, fulfill the criteria of both accounts. Only when conditions are unusual do they come into conflict, a fact amusingly explored in Daniel Dennett's *tour-de-force* 'Where am I?' Here he tells the (fictional!) story of being persuaded by Pentagon officials to undergo an operation in which his brain is removed but connected via radio links to the rest of his body, so as to enable him to undertake a mission exposing to him to an unusual form of radiation that is harmless to most body cells but damaging to brain tissue. By leaving his brain behind in the laboratory (but still in control of his body) he avoids the dangers that would otherwise have ensued. The operation is a success. But where is he?

> When I came out of anesthesia, I opened my eyes, looked around, and asked the inevitable, the traditional, the lamentably hackneyed post-operative question: "Where am I?" The nurse smiled down at me. "You're in Houston", she said, and I reflected that this still had a good chance of being the truth one way or another..."I gather the operation was a success", I said, "I want to go see my brain." They led me (I was a bit dizzy and unsteady) down a long corridor and into the life-support lab. A cheer went up from the assembled support team, and I responded with what I hoped was a jaunty salute. Still feeling lightheaded, I was helped over to the life-support vat. I peered through the glass. There, floating in which looked like gingerale, was undeniably a human brain, though it was almost covered with printed circuit chips, plastic tubules, electrodes and other paraphernalia. "Is that mine?" I asked. "Hit the output transmitter switch there on the side of the vat and see

for yourself", the project director replied. I moved the switch to OFF, and immediately slumped, groggy and nauseated, into the arms of the technicians, one of whom kindly restored the switch to its ON position. While I recovered my equilibrium and composure, I thought to myself: "Well, here I am, sitting on a folding chair, staring through a piece of plate glass at my own brain... But wait," I said to myself, "shouldn't I have thought, 'Here I am, suspended in a bubbling fluid, being stared at by my own eyes'?" I tried to think this latter thought. I tried to project it into the tank, offering it hopefully to my brain, but I failed to carry off the exercise with any conviction. I tried again. "Here am *I*, Daniel Dennett, suspended in a bubbling fluid, being stared at by my own eyes." No, it just didn't work. Most puzzling and confusing. Being a philosopher of firm physicalist conviction, I believed unswervingly that the tokening of my thoughts was occurring somewhere in my brain: yet, when I thought "Here I am," where the thought occurred to me was *here*, outside the vat, where I, Dennett, was standing staring at my brain.[6]

On the physical realisation account, the answer to Dennett's question 'Where am I?' is that I am wherever my brain is, since it is my brain whose states realise the aspects I most closely identify with myself. But in Dennett's story, this is not where the hero locates himself. He locates himself exactly where the immediate sensory input is coming from, right next to the things he can see and touch. It is that experience that is captured by the causal account.

Since they can give different results in cases like this, it is natural ask which of the two accounts is the correct one. But this, arguably, is not an appropriate question. Once we have specified where the body that I directly control is located, and also where the states that realise *my* states (especially my mental states) are located, there is no further question where *I* am located. As Dennett's story shows, we might feel some conflict, but it is not a conflict that is resolved by any metaphysical considerations. There is a sense in which I am located *here*, and also another in which I am located *there*. What is important is that satisfying the criteria of either account would justify talk of embodiment.

So let us turn now to the question of whether they can be applied to the case of divinity.

---

[6]   Dennett 'Where Am I?', in *Brainstorms* (Harvester Press, 1978), 311–12

Robin Le Poidevin

3. Divine embodiment and omnipresence

Consider the physical realisation account: can we account of the Son's embodiment in Christ's human body in these terms? Admittedly, it is the anti-physicalist Cartesian conception that is more readily identified with theological orthodoxy, for the existence of the Word predated the taking on of flesh: it had, as it were, a pre-physical existence. This dualistic picture of the mind and body as distinct categories of being is not, however, forced on us either by the Scriptures or the Creeds. The Chalcedonian definition talks of 'a reasonable soul and body', but does not specify the relation between them. Hud Hudson has proposed that a physicalist outlook is suggested by the doctrine of the resurrection of the body.[7] Why, unless our mental lives were essentially bound to a physical form, should the raising of the dead require bodily resurrection?

As an account of the embodiment of a divine being, however, the physical realisation account seems to be a complete non-starter, for it is just not plausible that the states of an omniscient and omnipotent person should wholly be realised by the physical states of a finite – indeed very limited – body. Anything recognisable as a human body will have finite capacities for action, and limited mechanisms for deriving and storing knowledge of the world.

Does this mean that we cannot understand the Incarnation unless we accept a dualistic picture in which mind and body belong to completely different ontological categories? This does not follow at all. We could certainly suppose the divine mind of Christ to be realised in *some* physical form, it is just that the boundaries of this physical form would not precisely coincide with those of any human body.

What of the causal account? This immediately looks more promising: a divine being could certainly directly control a human body, and be able, when they desired to do so, to perceive the world via the sense organs of that body. Note that this does not imply the restriction of all knowledge of the world to that obtained via the body, just knowledge of a sensory kind (or more specifically of a kind characterised by the five human sense modalities). But difficulties soon emerge over the 'direct control' component of the account. An omnipotent being will not only be able to bring about any logically possible state of affairs, but will also be able

---

[7] Hudson, *A Materialist Metaphysics of the Human Person* (Ithaca: Cornell University Press, 2001); cf. P. F. Strawson, *Individuals* (London: Methuen, 1959), 116.

to do so directly, without the mediation of any other object. But then this would imply that such a being satisfies the first criterion, at least, of the causal account, in respect of every object in the cosmos.

This ability directly to control every object in the cosmos is what, for Aquinas, underlies the doctrine of divine omnipresence.[8] Does it justify the, possibly stronger, view that God is actually embodied in the cosmos? Swinburne suggests that it justifies what he calls limited embodiment, but full embodiment would entail the satisfaction of other conditions. One way in which we could strengthen the account is to drop the modal character of criterion (b) – P is *able* to move B directly – and replace it with the condition that P does in fact move B directly. In this way, we can combine the Thomistic conception of omnipresence with the idea of the divine becoming embodied in a particular human body.

4. Two minds or one?

So far, then, we have been able to use the causal account to make sense of the embodiment of the divine in a limited human body. But this is not yet to make sense of the Incarnation, as it is understood by Christian tradition. The Chalcedonian statement insists that Christ has a dual nature, human and divine, and that the humanity is not merely confined to his body. To be 'perfect in manhood', humanity must also extend to the mind of Christ. And now we have the central mystery of the Incarnation: how can a mind be both human and divine without somehow mixing or, in the words of Chalcedon, 'confusing' those natures? How can one and the same mind be omniscient and limited in knowledge? And if we can make sense of that, can we do so in such as way as not to disturb our understanding of what it is for the divine to be embodied?

One way of making sense of the dual nature is to view the mind of Christ as composite, having divine and human parts. We are familiar with the idea of a composite object having contradictory properties as a result of having different parts with those properties. A coin may have a representation of the Queen's head on one side and a representation of Britannia on the other; a Zebra's hide may be black in some parts and white in others, and so on. Thus the human part of Christ's mind is limited in knowledge and the divine part omniscient.

---

[8] Aquinas, *Summa Theologiae*, Vol. II (Blackfriars edition) Ia.8.3.

Robin Le Poidevin

Though parts of the same mind (in some sense yet to be explained), they are, necessarily, very independent of each other. The human mind has no access to most of the contents of the divine mind. And the knowledge available to the divine mind is obtainable without the mediation of the human mind, with the possible exception of perceptual knowledge. Equally, the human mind can acquire beliefs about the world without the mediation of the divine mind. There is also a moral difference: though Christ is 'without sin', his human mind is subject to temptation in a way that his divine mind is not.[9]

This division of the mind of Christ into two parts, however, though allowing us to make sense of his dual nature, obscures our understanding of divine embodiment. For it now looks as if only the human part satisfies the criteria of the causal account of embodiment, for it is the limited human mind that actually directly controls Christ's body, even though the divine mind could do so. It is human, not divine, decisions that determine Christ's actions. The voice that is heard in the prayer in the garden of Gethsemane, for example, and the cry of dereliction from the cross, is very recognisably a human voice.[10] And although the divine mind may have a spatial perspective on the world that is centred on Christ's body, it does so only in a way that is mediated by the human mind. The divine mind has access to that perspective only because the human mind does. The conclusion must be that on the composite model, only Christ's human mind is embodied, not the divine mind. So, given the dual nature, the Incarnation appears not to be the paradigm example we took it to be of divine embodiment.

But there is another model of the dual nature that seems to avoid this problem, and that is the 'divided mind' account proposed by

[9]   The composite view has been articulated and defended both by Eleonore Stump ('Aquinas' Metaphysics of the Incarnation', in Davis, Kendall, and O'Collins (eds.) *The Incarnation*, 197–218) and by Brian Leftow ('A Timeless God Incarnate', in Davis, Kendall, and O'Collins (eds.) *The Incarnation*, 273–99). Both find the roots of this view in Aquinas.
[10]   According to St Matthew's narrative:

> And he went a little farther, and fell on his face, and prayed, saying O my Father, if it be possible, let this cup pass from me: nevertheless not as I will, but as thou wilt. (26.39)
>
> And about the ninth hour Jesus cried with a loud voice, saying Eli, Eli, lama sabachthani? That is to say, My God, my God, why hast thou forsaken me? (27: 46)

The Incarnation: divine embodiment and the divided mind

Thomas Morris and Richard Swinburne.[11,12] There are cases where consciousness appears to be divided, or dissociated. Swinburne offers self-deception as an example.[13] I persuade myself that p even in the face of conflicting evidence, because it is important to me that p be true (that cherished scientific hypothesis has been vindicated, my novel is brilliant, Hermione loves me, etc.) while still recognising that p is, of course, false. Somehow I have managed to compartmentalise these beliefs, so that they do not come into conflict. Morris offers lucid dreaming as another instance.[14] You are quite convinced that you are in the middle of a castle, in the dark corridors of which some nameless horror is roaming, while being aware at the same time that this is really a dream. A more dramatic instance, also mentioned by Morris, is provided by multiple personality disorder (or dissociated personality syndrome), in which one body appears to contain utterly different personalities that emerge at different times: Here is Jonathan Glover's description:

> Some people seem to be possessed at different times by different personalities. These 'personalities' can vary in voice, mannerisms and handwriting. They can call themselves by different names. One may be left-handed when others are not. In an American case, one personality spoke with an English accent and knew Arabic, while another knew Serbo-Croat and spoke English with a Yugoslav accent. And, notably, each of them has a very different general style. One thirty-nine-year-old woman had six of these personalities, including Mary, 'a nun who preached sacrifice', and Deborah, a 'screaming lady who recounted the many traumatic incidences of sexual molestation and perverse rituals at the hands of the patient's aunt and grandmother'.[15]

---

[11]   See Morris, *The Logic of God Incarnate*, 103–7; Swinburne, 'Could God Become Man?', 64–6; *The Christian God*, (Oxford: Clarendon Press, 1994), ch. 9. cf. Brian Hebblethwaite, *The Incarnation: collected essays in Christology* (Cambridge: Cambridge University Press, 1987), 31, 68.

[12]   Whereas I have talked of 'accounts' of embodiment, I have followed writers such as David Brown in talking of 'models' of Christ's nature. The implication, I take it, is that any theory we come up with concerning the divine must at best be an approximation.

[13]   Swinburne, 'Could God Become Man?', in Godfrey Vesey (ed.) *The Philosophy in Christianity*, (Cambridge: Cambridge University Press, 1989), 64–5.

[14]   Morris, *The Logic of God Incarnate*, 104–5.

[15]   Glover, I: *The Philosophy and Psychology of Personal Identity* (Harmondsworth: Penguin, 1989), 1.

One mind, then, can contain parallel streams of consciousness. What, given this dissociation, justifies us in talking of a single mind? According to Swinburne, the unity stems from the fact that the streams of consciousness arise from a single set of cognitive powers. It is this principle of unity that distinguishes the divided mind model from the composite model: the human and divine minds are not *parts* of Christ's mind, but different expressions of the same set of powers. So either the whole mind is embodied, or none of it is: there is no room for the thought that only one part (the human part) is embodied. This allows the divided mind model to avoid an awkward consequence for the composite model, which is that, if only a part of Christ's mind is embodied, then Christ, *qua* embodied individual, is not a person

So far, then, it appears that we can combine the causal account of embodiment with the divided mind model of Christ's dual nature to explain how a person who is both human and divine can be wholly embodied. But a difficulty remains.

The introduction of the notion of cognitive powers should prompt us to revisit the question of what it is to be embodied. What would it be for the *cognitive powers themselves* to be embodied? Here the physical realisation account seems more immediately applicable than the causal account: a set of cognitive powers is embodied in B if and only if they are realised by states of B. Our cognitive powers, for instance, are realised by states of our brains. But the cognitive powers of an omniscient being far outstrip anything that could be realised by a human brain. So, at best, the cognitive powers of Christ can only be partially be realised by states of Christ's brain: it is just the human powers that are so realised. The divine powers are realised by something else entirely. Conceding this, however, undermines the notion that we have a single set of cognitive powers here. Rather, we have *two* sets: a set of human powers, realised by brain states, and a set of divine powers, not so realised. Perhaps we could think of these two sets as forming a larger whole, but this then looks indistinguishable from the composite account, in which the human and divine aspects of Christ's consciousness are simply parts of a whole.

Swinburne himself rejects physicalism in favour of interactionist dualism, so this is not a route he would be led down. But then what account would he give of the embodiment of cognitive powers? Again, it is the causal link between those powers and the states of a body that underlies our ordinary talk of embodiment: those powers are expressed through the actions of the body, including utterances which express beliefs. And, conversely, the powers of acquiring knowledge are constrained by the capacities of the body. However, in Christ's case, the link is only partial: his cognitive powers are only partially expressed through his body. That ought to mean, then, that the person of Christ is only *partially embodied*, though not in the sense that only a part of Christ's person is embodied. Defenders of the divided mind view do not typically think of Christ's person as composite. But as Harrison's discussion shows, it is possible to be partially embodied in a different sense: as satisfying some of the criteria of embodiment but not others. And I think we can identify a third sense of partial embodiment, that of having powers *only a part of the range of which* is constrained by, and expressed through, that body. The full range of those powers goes well beyond what could be expressed through, and constrained by, a human body. And the part of the range that transcends those limitations is precisely what distinguishes the divine from the human mind. So the divided mind model has not, after all, allowed us to explain how the divine nature of Christ is embodied, but only how the human nature is embodied. That conclusion is reinforced by further considerations about the different perspectives that the human and divine minds must have, to which we now turn.

5. Perspectival knowledge

Consider the following conundrum: the Son satisfies one of conditions of embodiment (as set out by the causal account) by being directly aware of states of Christ's body. But the Father, being omniscient, also directly knows the states of Christ's body: it would be a limitation on his omniscience if any aspect of his knowledge had to be mediated, or inferential. So either we say that the Father partially satisfies the requirements for embodiment in Christ, or this particular condition is irrelevant to embodiment. Either conclusion seems uncomfortable.

There is, however, this difference: although both the Son and the Father know the states of Christ's body, only the Son entertains those contents in the first person (in the form of 'I' beliefs). The Son, that is, has a unique perspective on Christ's experiences. Both the Son and the Father can know that Christ is suffering on the cross, and know this directly, but only the Son can express that knowledge by saying, or thinking, '*I* am suffering on the cross'. The Father has to think '*He* is suffering on the cross'. The difference between first-person and third-person knowledge is one of perspective rather than content, so the fact that the Father's knowledge that Christ is suffering is not expressed by the thought 'I am not suffering' does not undermine the Father's omniscience, if omniscience is a matter of knowing all true propositions.

Sometimes, however, a change in perspective *can* be a gain in knowledge. John Perry tells the story of pushing a trolley around a supermarket and noticing that there was a trail of sugar on the floor.[16] He thought 'someone is making a mess', and set off with his trolley in pursuit. The sugar trail soon became two sugar trails. Eventually, Perry realised that the sugar was leaking out of a bag in *his* trolley, and experienced a sudden change of perspective, from 'he or she is making a mess' to '*I* am making a mess'. This is a gain in knowledge, and not simply a perspectival shift. Some knowledge, it seems, has to be entertained perspectivally. If you are making a mess, you can only know this if you can express the knowledge by thinking 'I am making a mess'. Christ can only know he is suffering if he is able to frame his knowledge by the thought 'I am suffering'. Does that mean there is something that the Father cannot know? No, just that the Father can only express that same knowledge by thinking 'He is suffering'. Christ's divine mind is embodied in Christ's body because that mind can have the thought 'I am suffering' as a direct response to the experiences of Christ's body. To reflect this, we should amend the first clause of the causal account of embodiment in the following way:

P is embodied in B if and only if (a) P has direct knowledge of some of B's states, *and* entertains that knowledge in the form of first person beliefs...

And we should add to this account a further clause (or an elaboration of criterion (b)), that P's beliefs concerning the states of P's body and the contents of P's mind can be expressed by B's first-person communicative acts.

Unfortunately, this move, which distinguishes between the Father and the Son, also drives a wedge between the human and divine minds of Christ, for there are thoughts that only Christ's *human* mind can have, as a result of its lack of omniscience. Thoughts like 'It is possible for me to sin', and 'I do not know whether I will be crucified'. The divine mind cannot have these thoughts, because, being omniscient and therefore knowing that its own nature includes moral perfection, it knows that Christ cannot sin. It also knows, being omniscient, that Christ will be crucified. So the human mind has thoughts that the divine mind cannot have (since the divine mind cannot have false beliefs or entertain doubt). But the divine mind knows the contents of Christ's human mind: it knows that the human mind is

[16] Perry, 'The Problem of the Essential Indexical', *Nous*, **13** 3–21.

thinking 'It is possible for me to sin', and 'I do not know whether I will be crucified'. So how will it express those thoughts? It cannot express them in the first person, because the divine mind knows those beliefs to be false. Nor can they be expressed impersonally ('Christ thinks it is possible for Christ to sin'), for, as we noted before, some knowledge, to be complete, has to be entertained perspectivally: it must intimate whether it is *me* that is in such and such a state. It seems that the divine mind can only think '*He* thinks it possible that he will sin', and '*He* does not know that he will be crucified'. The divine mind, in other words, is compelled to take a third-person perspective on those thoughts, so distancing it from the subject of those thoughts. But Christ, as human, cannot be both 'I' and 'He' from the perspective of the divine mind: that would involve a contradiction.

Perhaps there is another possibility. The divine mind could think 'There is a part of my (i.e. Christ's) mind, a level of consciousness, in which the thought 'It is possible for me to sin' is being entertained.' But this is far from the divine mind acknowledging a belief as its own – it simply locates it at some sub-personal level, much as we might, in cases of perceptual illusion where we recognise the illusory nature of the experience, locate the illusory belief at some sub-personal level.

What this shows is that the dissociation between Christ's human mind and divine mind is sufficiently radical that the divine mind, although aware of the human mind's beliefs, will not acknowledge some of those beliefs as its own, but think of them in third-personal terms. These thoughts, of course, will not be expressed through Christ's body, putting another obstacle in the way of understanding how Christ's divine mind can be embodied.

6. An alternative model: kenosis

It is time to consider a completely different model of the relation between Christ's human and divine natures. On this alternative model, the Son gives up certain, if not most, of the divine attributes in order to share our condition, and become incarnate in Jesus Christ. He completely ceases to be omniscient and omnipotent. This process is referred to as *kenosis*, or emptying, hence the name the 'kenotic model' for this view. The notion of kenosis has its origins in certain passages in the New Testament, especially one verse from Paul's letter to the Philippians:

> Let the same mind be in you that was in Christ Jesus, who, though he was in the form of God, did not regard equality with God as something to be exploited, but emptied himself, taking the form

of a slave, being born in human likeness. And being found in human form, he humbled himself and became obedient to the point of death – even death on a cross. (2:5–8)

The idea, however, was only developed in the nineteenth century, by theologians such as Charles Gore, who made it the subject of his 1891 Bampton Lectures at Oxford.[17]

What are the objections to the kenotic model? First, that it is unorthodox; second, that it undermines Christ's claim to divinity.

Perhaps the main stumbling block to accepting the kenotic view as orthodox is that it seems to be explicitly ruled out by Chalcedon's insistence that Christ's exhibiting divine and human properties must be 'without change'. Thomas Morris takes this line. David Brown, whilst recognising a conflict, suggests that the phase is only of secondary importance. The essence of the Chalcedonian definition is an identity claim: that a single person was both human and divine. The phrase 'without change', in Brown's words, 'earned its place not in its own right but because the Fathers at the Council believed that [it] was the only way of preserving the divine nature; for them divinity was taken necessarily to imply immutability'.[18] But what is so valuable about immutability? Perhaps the capacity to change, to give up his exalted status, for love of humanity, is a measure of the Son's moral perfection. What matters is that the Son does not change in the crucial respect: he does not cease to be a divine being.

Or does he? The second objection seems hard to resist. After all, if the Son gave up the characteristic properties of divinity, how could he continue to be divine? It is true that the connection between divinity and the 'omni-properties' (omniscience, omnipotence, etc.) cannot be severed entirely. An individual who at no stage in their existence exhibited *any* of the traditional set of divine properties would have a weak claim to divinity. But Christ's claim to divinity lies in his divine origins. A being who had all the omni-properties, but voluntarily gave them up, would not thereby cease to be divine, anymore than a human being, who began life in the way normal for our species would not cease to be human, however limited an existence

[17] Gore, *The Incarnation of the Son of God* (London: John Murray, 1891). The kenotic model is defended at length in Brown (*The Divine Trinity* (London: Duckworth, 1985)). For recent discussion see Peter Forrest's 'The Incarnation: a philosophical case for kenosis' (*Religious Studies* **36** (2000), 127–40), and Stephen C. Evans' *Exploring Kenotic Christology: The Self-emptying of God* (Oxford: Oxford University Press, 2006).
[18] Brown, *The Divine Trinity*, 227.

The Incarnation: divine embodiment and the divided mind

he subsequently lived – perhaps without the characteristic, in the sense of typical, attributes of humanity. And the Son need not have given up all his divine properties. His moral perfection remains: Christ is without sin.

At first sight, the divided mind model seems to have the advantage over the kenotic model, but actually both involve a dissociation between human and divine minds. On the divided mind model it is *synchronic*: the human and divine streams are contemporaneous. On the kenotic model, in contrast, it is *diachronic*: the divine mind evolves into the human mind. It is not immediately obvious that synchronic dissociation gives Christ a firmer claim to divinity than diachronic dissociation. For it is part of the divided mind model that Christ's actions are causally insulated from his divine mind. In fact, the considerations of the previous sections give us reason to think that it is the kenotic account that has the advantage. The essence of the doctrine of the Incarnation is that a divine being became embodied. The divided mind model, as we have seen, is not able, ultimately, to explain this, in that the divine mind does not satisfy all, or even any, of the criteria of embodiment. In contrast, if we allow that divine status is not lost with the temporary and voluntary loss of omniscience and omnipotence, then a divine being can become fully embodied in a human body. The kenotic model, I submit, offers the way to a better understanding of divine embodiment than does the hypothesis of the divided mind. For given kenosis, we can see how the whole of the Son's mind can express itself through, and be informed by means of, the body of Christ.

University of Leeds

285

Religious Tolerance, Diversity, and Pluralism

PETER BYRNE

Introduction

The theme of this paper can be introduced in this way: does a pluralist approach to religion entail a pluralist approach to religion? My theme is not *that* odd, because I have two notions of pluralism in mind. There is what I will call 'tolerant pluralism' and what I will call 're-ligious pluralism'. And thus my question is 'Does tolerant pluralism re religion entail religious pluralism?'

In more detail, the problem I wish to explore begins from the rec-ognition that tolerance toward and by religious believers is a highly desirable virtue, one that should be cultivated in any liberal state. Religious tolerance involves a form of pluralism: that is, the welcom-ing and fostering of religious diversity. Religious believers should be pluralists in this sense. Given that conclusion, the following ques-tions arise. Can religious individuals be tolerant and exhibit plural-ism while retaining full commitment to the truth of their own religious beliefs? Or, is it the case that society's demand for religious tolerance, and the pluralism that grows out of it, is really a call for re-vision of how believers see their faith? Is a demand for tolerance and the welcoming of diversity a demand to see all religious convictions as uncertain to a substantive degree? As I shall explain, the stance in the philosophy of religion that is labelled 'religious pluralism' contains a core commitment to agnosticism about the truth of religious beliefs. Is such agnosticism the necessary price of religious tolerance?

In two recent articles,[1] the late Philip Quinn offered an argument for the following claim: tolerance between believers of the major world religions may be based on an appeal to religious scepticism. Appeal to religious scepticism, Quinn contends, is a sound means of dealing with opposition to religious difference fuelled by religious demands to create uniformity in belief and practice. Behind his argu-ment is the portrayal of a clash between, on the one hand, injunctions

---

[1]   Quinn 'Religious Diversity and Tolerance', *International Journal for the Philosophy of Religion* 50 (2001), 57–80; 'On Religious Diversity and Tolerance', *Daedalus* 134 (2005), 136–39.

doi:10.1017/S13582461110000014   © The Royal Institute of Philosophy and the contributors 2011

Peter Byrne

in such religions to compel the whole of humanity to accept the religious truth and, on the other, our awareness of moral principles that forbid the visiting of harm and coercion upon others. A religious obligation to compel or persecute confronts the moral obligations bound up with the thought that tolerance is a virtue. Quinn aims to show the way out of this tension. A central plank in his method of dealing with the clash between religious demand and moral principle is the assertion that the very problem generating the tension – the diversity of religious belief in the world – provides the resolution. The following quotation introduces his path out of the tension: 'there is a clear connection between the epistemological problems posed by religious belief and the political problems posed by diversity'.[2] In other words, we must move toward *religious* pluralism, and the thought that no religion has a monopoly on the truth, in order to support the *tolerant* pluralism that welcomes diversity. Is Quinn's underlying thought correct?

Tolerance and tolerant pluralism

In order to discuss the questions I have raised so far it is necessary to lay out in a brief, and therefore somewhat dogmatic, manner the main elements of tolerance as a virtue of individuals and communities. I am interested in 'tolerance' as the name of a serious moral or political virtue – not merely in tolerance as the disposition to put up with that which is found disagreeable. As a serious virtue of individuals and societies, tolerance has the following separately necessary and jointly sufficient conditions. A person tolerates some opinion or behaviour when there is:

1. *difference*
2. *importance*
3. *opposition*
4. *power*
5. *non-interference*
6. *requirement*.[3]

Difference: agents who tolerate other people's behaviour, words, or thoughts note that others' behaviour etc. is different from their own. Importance: the difference between the tolerators' mode of

---

[2] Quinn, 'On Religious Diversity and Tolerance', 136.
[3] Adapted from C. McKinnon *Toleration* (London, Routledge, 2006), 14.

behaviour, speech, and thoughts and the tolerateds' is not minor or trivial. The difference matters, at least potentially, to the tolerators. Opposition: in noting the fact of difference they also note that the behaviour etc. is not something they like or approve. Power: the others' behaviour is something they could do something about. If they do not have the means to suppress or change it altogether, they can take steps towards its suppression. Non-interference: they in fact take no steps to interfere with that which they oppose. Indeed, a tolerant person may even act to protect and encourage another in behaviour that he or she thinks is mistaken. Requirement: tolerant behaviour is, in general, morally right and tolerant attitudes are good. Tolerance is a virtue, something that we can recommend to all and something for which an agent is prized and praised.

Much can be said about the separate elements in this analysis of tolerance. For example, we may wonder what exactly is meant by 'opposition'. Is mere dislike of someone's behaviour enough to fulfil this necessary condition of tolerance? I dislike the way my elder son rises late each morning (hours after I am up and active). If I don't use my power over him to get him to be more like me in his daily habits, do I count as being tolerant toward him and this fact of difference? Arguably not: for I cannot represent even to myself that my son's different way of starting the day is wrong from any objective point of view. By the same token, I would find it hard to view it as an important difference – at least not on one of my rational days. This is linked to requirement. If my leaving him to get up late and go to bed late manifest tolerance on my part, I deserve praise for it. But if I can find nothing in the difference of habit but something that is mildly irritating and another example of the sad fact that Peter Byrne's way of going about things is not generally followed by the rest of humanity, then I don't deserve any commendation for not badgering number one son.

It has to be admitted that there is a gradation in ordinary talk of tolerating that stretches from tolerating that which we merely dislike to tolerating that which we disapprove of from a moral, objective point of view. But if 'tolerance' is the name of a serious moral and political virtue, it seems that both the importance and opposition conditions for tolerance entail that one can, by definition, tolerate only that which one disapproves of. Disapproval in this context must amount to thinking that the thing to be tolerated is objectively and non-trivially wrong or mistaken. If it is opinions or expression, they must be thought of by the tolerator as mistaken, false, or significantly short of warrant. If it is practice, then it must be thought of as morally wrong or based on false beliefs, so that it is likely to be productive of harm – at least to the

Peter Byrne

individual performing it. Moreover, the line of reflection that takes us toward this conclusion and that is influenced by the thought that tolerance is *required* bids us go one step further. It is not enough for the evincing of tolerance that the agent regards that which is opposed but not interfered with as objectively wrong. The would-be tolerator must hold the relevant beliefs marking out this objective wrongness in a reasonable manner. This point is demonstrated by the stock example in the literature of the 'tolerant' racist.

Suppose we have a man who is racially bigoted. He may nonetheless behave toward members of racial minorities in a manner which exhibits difference, importance, opposition, power, and, crucially, non-interference. He obviously recognises difference. He may think racial difference is important and feel that 'racial pollution' is a pressing matter. But for reasons other than sheer laziness he does not use such power as he has to harass those who are 'polluting White civilisation'. It is highly plausible to say that, whatever may be true of this 'gentle racist', he is not a tolerant man. His non-interference is not an expression of tolerance the virtue. True, his non-interference may make him better, or less bad, than an active member of some neo-Nazi grouping, but he is not possessed of one of the virtues. His sense of others and of his relation to them is thoroughly corrupt from the moral point of view.

Suppose we find an agent exhibiting what appears to be tolerant behaviour to another. We find key conditions of tolerance present: difference, importance, opposition, and power. These go along with non-interference, and we detect that opposition is based upon disapproval of something perceived as objectively wrong or mistaken. There are then at least two stances we can take toward this agent. One involves attacking the fact of opposition. We judge the agent's disapproval of the other's behaviour (or whatever it may be) to be unreasonable. The agent's beliefs and attitudes need to be changed. Her attitudes toward that which she opposes need to change. Opposition is not a reasonable position for her to take up. In this light, her non-interference is not part of an ensemble of attitudes and thoughts which is commendable and virtuous. The other stance is to accept the agent's opposition as entirely reasonable and right, given her background beliefs and attitudes. But she deserves all due praise for allowing others to think and live as they see fit. Now our agent is judged as truly tolerant and that means we feel no inclination to get her to re-think the opinions and attitudes that produced her opposition. She is perfectly entitled to them. They are not the result or expression of mere prejudice, palpable ignorance, or moral blindness. They are reasonable. That does not mean, of course, that we who praise this tolerant person agree with her. To say that her opposition-producing opinions are reasonable, warranted, or in some other way justified, is not to declare that they are true. But they may have all that belief requires in order to be knowledge, save truth. No epistemic, or other, vices are manifested in the holding of these beliefs. It is only the agent with reasonable opinions defining her opposition who can be truly tolerant.

Tolerance as a significant moral virtue is revealed to be more than putting up with behaviours, opinions, etc. that are different than ours. The tolerator has to be opposed, in a principled manner, to that which she puts up with. Given this, the way is open to argue that it is an impossible virtue.[4] Toleration has been defined so that it is inherently paradoxical and impossible of manifestation in a coherent style of life.

The paradox of toleration is summed by Susan Mendus thus:

> where toleration is based on moral disapproval, it implies that the thing tolerated is wrong and ought not to exist. The question which then arises is why, given the claim to objectivity incorporated in the strong sense of toleration, it should be thought good to tolerate.[5]

Matters are worse when we remind ourselves, as Mendus does, that to see something as morally wrong is to see it as wrong from a universal, impartial standpoint. So, the would-be tolerator believes the behaviour to which she is opposed is, from a universal and impartial point of view, better absent from the world than present. It is something that should be interfered with from this standpoint. Why then is it virtue not to interfere with it?

Non-interference with that which agents regard as objectively wrong can only seem to be something that leads in the long run to indifference about good and evil, or to a detachment by agents from their convictions about goodness and truth. An attitude of 'live and let live' toward difference can only be a 'virtue' in a society that has encouraged its members to have no strong convictions about what is right and wrong, true and false, from an impartial, objective standpoint. Thus it is no virtue at all. If toleration is a paramount virtue in liberal societies, that can only be further evidence that liberalism encourages the privatisation of conceptions of the good.

---

[4] For this phrase see B. Williams 'Toleration: an Impossible Virtue?' in Heyd, D. (ed.) *Toleration: an Elusive Virtue* (Princeton,Princeton University Press), 18–27.

[5] S. Mendus *Toleration and the Limits of Liberalism* (Basingstoke, Macmillan, 1989), 19.

Peter Byrne

It may thus appear to be unacceptable for liberal individuals and communities to press those with strong religious convictions to tolerate the religious beliefs and practices of others. For that now seems to be tantamount to pressing religious individuals with the demand to give up, or at least weaken, the religious convictions that gave rise to the thought that what others believe and do is mistaken and wrong.

The air of paradox surrounding the virtue of tolerance can be dispelled quickly if we accept this thought: the would-be tolerator faces a conflict of goods and evils. It may be good if behaviour which is seen as morally wrong and opinions which are seen as objectively mistaken did not exist, but it is a bad thing if their suppression is brought about by the means of interference in the lives of others. The tolerator sees the liberty and autonomy of others as a good. Out of respect for that good the tolerator does not interfere, having the power to do so, because the loss of that good outweighs the good of removing error from the world. Toleration can be seen in this light to be a doctrine of means. The would-be tolerator can be as keen a champion of moral rectitude and truth as anyone, but she has equally strong commitments to a doctrine of the proper means for promoting these things. They are only to be properly promoted amongst adult, compos members of the community by persuasion, debate, and example – not by forceful interference. This is because amongst the tolerator's moral commitments are ones to the integrity of persons. That means she is committed to respecting others as having the right to form their own opinions and choose their own life-styles. Tolerance is a virtue in a complex world. In this world we have strong commitments to goodness and truth. We face a conflict between aspects of those commitments. Given the fact of human diversity, then those commitments bid us respect the ability of others to function as autonomous agents while they also entail that we enter judgements about the success and failure of their efforts to determine what is good and true. Recognition of these facts by the tolerant does not mean that they cease to attempt to judge conduct and opinions from an objective standpoint. It means instead that they prosecute the differences they have with others that arise from such exercise of judgement in a certain way, namely by persuasion, debate, and example. Difference is thus not met with indifference.

There is therefore no paradox in toleration, merely recognition that it is one of those areas in which the complexity of the good and its pursuit manifests itself.

I am now going to make a concession to the idea that there is a paradox of tolerance. Once we see the other's behaviour as the expression of their nature as an autonomous being, its wrongness from an impersonal standpoint has to undergo alteration. To see it as the expression of another's selfhood, a selfhood that we respect and wish to foster, is to see a value in it that cannot be present to reflection when it is viewed in the abstract. The value in this other person that resides in their embodiment of autonomous selfhood permeates what they do, think, and say. In this way, it is not quite right to say that the tolerant weigh the good of respect for persons against the bad of wrong behaviour etc. in others. The value in persons leaks into the value of that which displays a person's nature and characteristics. This is a dimension to behaviour and expression that the tolerant will be particularly alive to because they see others as worthy of respect.[6]

It is still the case that the tolerant also need to have a clear sight of the wrongness in that which they tolerate to avoid toleration degenerating into a form of vice. We should also note that acts of toleration should, on occasion, properly be the outcome of genuine struggle. The tolerant are individuals with strong convictions about the good and the true. So they should feel the wrongness, from a detached point of view, of that which they tolerate. If they do not feel it, then they practise live and let live out of indifference, laziness, or the like. Then they do not deserve any commendation for their so-called 'tolerance'. So, whatever perspective they have upon the persons they tolerate, it cannot blank out the fact of opposition.

The above account of tolerance needs to be related to Oberdiek's three-fold distinction between bare toleration, mere toleration, and full toleration.[7] This is how he explains his classification. Bare toleration is found when the tolerator puts up with the tolerated but has no respect for them as persons. The tolerated are a nuisance. The barely tolerant have no interest in them as persons and would rather they go away. We may say that the barely tolerant have only a grudging recognition of the fact of difference. The merely tolerant, by contrast acknowledge the existence of others and their deep interest in living lives of their own choosing. They do not wish that the fact of difference go away. But they have no interest in the alternative ways of living or opinions of those they tolerate. They are not prone to reflect on their own ways of living and opinions in the light of the

---

[6]   For the idea that tolerance involves a change of perspective towards belief and behaviour see D. Heyd 'Introduction' in Heyd, D. (ed.) *Toleration: an Elusive Virtue* (Princeton, Princeton University Press, 1996), 11–14.

[7]   H. Oberdiek *Tolerance: Between Forbearance and Acceptance* (Lanham, Rowman and Littlefield, 2001), 28–33.

Peter Byrne

recognition of difference. The fully tolerant, however, are prepared to see value in difference. They welcome the fact that others have the freedom to choose a way of life of their own. Alternative ways of life gain value because of the manner in which they express the autonomous choices of human beings. Because of this, the fully tolerant will be prepared to facilitate other persons' choices of alternative ways of living. While not endorsing that which they tolerate, they will support institutions and social structures that foster the development and expression of difference – within the limits of that which is tolerable. Moreover, the fully tolerant will be prepared to go further and examine whether the different life-styles and opinions they confront provide grounds for re-examining the worth of their own life-styles and opinions.

Oberdiek's full tolerance is consonant with the notion that tolerance is based on respect for others as autonomous persons in their own right. It is evident that full tolerance brings with it a form of pluralism. The fully tolerant do not merely put up with the fact of difference; to some degree or other, they welcome difference and wish it to be enabled and cultivated. Difference of opinion and life style is a means whereby the integrity of individuals as autonomous beings can be fostered. Pluralism and full tolerance do, however, bring the paradox of tolerance into sharper relief. The fully tolerant individual – the pluralist – enables and cultivates that which she regards as wrong and mistaken. How can that be? Is not this stance incoherent? But recall, that which is wrong and mistaken from a detached point of view may be seen as of value insofar as it is the authentic expression of a respect-worthy person's mode of living. The value of autonomy leaks into that which displays it. And then there is a further value in cultivating difference and thus things one disapproves of. Through doing so a variety of opinions, values, and life-styles exist in the community. This variety facilitates the choices of individuals and enables a market-place of ideas and values to exist. This in turn promotes necessary discussion and debate about what is good and true.

Religious tolerance and religious pluralism

Let us remind ourselves of the list of necessary conditions for the presence of tolerance as a serious moral virtue: *difference, importance, opposition, power, non-interference,* and *requirement.* The demand for non-interference in the religious beliefs and practices of others may seem straightforward *if* we have made the move toward religious

294

scepticism or indifference typical of many modern liberal thinkers. (See for example Locke on religious certainty in Book IV of the *Essay concerning Human Understanding*.) But very many religious believers do not sign up to such a picture of religious truth. For them, religious diversity presents differences with others that pertain to matters of supreme importance and are associated with confidently held beliefs that give rise to strong, compelling judgements of opposition. This makes restraint upon the exercise of opposition to difference especially hard to justify. What can compel a religious believer with compelling convictions to exercise such restraint? Can respect for the other as an autonomous agent with a life of her own to lead be sufficient to justify non-interference by the religious in the 'mistaken' opinions and practices of those who do not belong to the faith?

The above question can be sharpened. Can religious believers ever attain to full tolerance of the opinions and practices of those of other faiths, or of no faith, and remain true to the commitments that define their own religious allegiance? If a religious believer lives in a liberal society, she may be forced by the structure of its laws and institutions to a bare tolerance of those outside the faith. Laws and institutions may force the believer to put up with the non-faithful even while she cannot respect them as persons. Bare tolerance of non-belief will be encouraged if the perception that someone has 'turned their back' on the Truth and the Way, indeed upon God, produces a damning indictment of their worth as a human being. In being an infidel (or whatever) they are lost. If a barely tolerant believer had her own way – not possible in a liberal state – measures would be taken against unbelief. The merely, as opposed to the barely, tolerant lack such hostility to those outside the faith. They are simply indifferent to them. Not possessing the Truth and the Way, the opinions and life-styles of unbelievers are not worth of study or reflection. They provide no occasion for the faithful to re-examine their beliefs. For the merely tolerant believer, alternative religions or world views are in no sense a challenge. So, in a similar manner, one might not hate or wish to shut up the person who goes around saying that the world is flat, but their stance is not respect-worthy enough to make one think again about matters geographical and astronomical. In contrast, the fully tolerant religious believer will actually see value in the rival systems of belief and unbelief of others. The value will reside in the perception that these others are able to express their autonomous selfhood via these alternative systems. This tolerant believer will want society to provide the means and opportunity for 'other faiths' to exist and for their members to engage in their own forms of worship. Crucially, the fully tolerant believer will see in the alternative belief systems of others something of potential value to herself. This is the opportunity to engage in critical reflection on the truth and value of the tolerator's own convictions. That respect-worthy human beings are capable of living in accordance with contrary beliefs and apparently of living fulfilled lives guided by those beliefs is occasion to join with them in debate as to what is true in religion, and perhaps to modify the tolerator's own opinions, even if the modification is only of how she understands her own faith.

The full tolerant individual is, we said, a pluralist. Without abandoning her own beliefs, she wishes to enable and encourage the adoption and outward expression in speech and action of alternative ones. Pluralism welcomes diversity. Pluralists, though not having to abandon their beliefs, as some readings of the paradox of toleration maintain, inevitably put themselves in a position whereby their opinions are open to the possibility of revision. Crudely put, they implicitly take up a second-order stance of fallibilism. Tolerant pluralists who are religious see in religious diversity the occasion for a worthwhile, perhaps necessary, re-examination of their faith commitments.

Tolerant pluralism vs. religious pluralism

It is important to note that the pluralism in the religious sphere defined above (let us call it 'tolerant pluralism') is different from the kind of pluralism picked out in many discussions of the challenges posed for religious diversity (let us call it 'religious pluralism'). It is common to distinguish four main responses to the issues around the interpretation of religion provoked by religious diversity: scepticism, exclusivism, inclusivism and pluralism. The fact of religious diversity gives rise to such questions as: Which, if any religion is true? Which, if any, contains the genuine path to salvation? The sceptical response concludes that there is no way any one religion can be shown to be true or salvific and that the best explanation of religious diversity is that all religions are fictions. Notice that the sceptical response affirms a mode of equality between the faiths: they are all false. An exclusivist response by contrast affirms that there is truth and salvation in one religion, but it is exclusive to that one. An inclusivist response to diversity affirms that there is truth and salvation in one religion, but that other religions can partake of these. Usually, inclusivists are keener on asserting that their religion is uniquely true but that salvation is available to folk in other faiths and through those faiths. A simple version of an inclusivism-in-salvation view is found in those Jewish theologies that state that, whilst Judaism has the truth about the Almighty, people in other faiths can still be saved. They can so be if they know of, and adhere to, the seven Noachide laws (a set of fundamental socio-ethical norms). Other religions may be of use and value if they preach the Noachide laws, for all that the definitive truth about God is in Judaism.[8] A religion may also be inclusivist about the truth, as when some Islamic theologies affirm that Judaism and Christianity are 'Religions of the Book', containing knowledge of the one true God, albeit that it is not perfect or complete. Both exclusivist and inclusivist views are founded upon a judgement of inequality. Religious pluralism, by contrast, affirms a rough equality of the faiths, but it is an equality of success not of failure. Pluralism views all, or at least the major, religions as partial successes. It can be summed up in the following three propositions. (1) All major forms of religion are equal in respect of making common reference to a single, transcendent sacred reality. (2) They are likewise equal in respect of offering some means or other to human salvation. (3) All religious traditions are to be seen as containing revisable, limited accounts of the nature of the Ultimate; none is certain enough in its specific dogmatic formulations to provide the means of interpreting the others.[9]

Pluralism with respect to religions of this kind is an epistemic and interpretive stance toward religions. Epistemically, it is a form of agnosticism toward religions. In contrast to the religious sceptic, the pluralist affirms that, between them, the religions provide enough grounds for postulating a religious ultimate. In contrast to religious exclusivists and inclusivists, the pluralist concludes that the grounds for the specific doctrinal claims of the religions cancel each other out. Adherents of different religions may be entitled to their religious convictions, but no set of creedal claims is objectively more certain than another set. Different versions of religious pluralism will provide different pictures of the overall character of human religion. The most well-known version of pluralism is that advanced by John Hick in his *An Interpretation of Religion*. This account of pluralism centres on Hick's 'pluralist hypothesis', according to which we must distinguish between two ways of thinking about the ultimate reality (styled by Hick 'the Real'). We may consider it as in itself and as it appears to human beings. In the former guise it is

[8]   See N. Solomon 'Is the Plurality of Faiths Problematic?' in Sharma, A. (ed.) *God, Truth and Reality* (Basingstoke, Macmillan 1993), 189–99.
[9]   See P. Byrne *Prolegomena to Religious Pluralism* (Basingstoke, Macmillan, 1995), 12.

Peter Byrne

unknown and unknowable. The Real is only known to human beings as it appears to them in one stream of human culture or other. Each of the gods or ultimates that belong to a particular religion's pattern of worship or contemplation is but an appearance of the Real. The distinction recalls Kant's distinction between the world as it is in itself and as it appears to human beings. Hick's distinction is based on the Kantian thought that human modes of cognition (in this instance the conceptual structure supplied by a culture or a religious tradition) shape our awareness of reality. Since we cannot but cognise the Ultimate via the concepts furnished by a given human tradition, we cannot have an unmediated apprehension of it. All this is set out at length in chapters 14–15 of *An Interpretation of Religion*. With the pluralist hypothesis there goes a re-interpretation of truth in religion. At one level, different religions have pictures of the divine that are true of different things, for there are many ways that the Real appears to human beings in history and the different religions contain true accounts of those different phenomenal manifestations. At another level, different religions contain metaphorically true accounts of the Real as it is in itself, and for that metaphorical truth the incompatibilities between their accounts when literally interpreted do not matter. This is because metaphorical truth in this context is, for Hick, a form of pragmatic truth. A religion is true of the Real in itself insofar as its concepts and practices provide a successful way of orienting its followers in behaviour; that is: it puts believers on a path toward genuine moral and spiritual transformation. Hick calls this theory of religious language and truth a 'mythological' reading of them.[10]

It will be seen immediately that tolerant pluralism and religious pluralism both entail that religious citizens should not actively oppose or interfere with, but rather welcome, the divergent beliefs and practices of fellow citizens who belong to other religions. Oppositional attitudes or behaviour towards others' religious beliefs is absurd given religious pluralism, since this stance toward religious diversity concludes that all religions (or all the main ones) have an equal claim to truth and salvific efficacy. All religions are partners in a common enterprise; all worship or contemplate the same ultimate reality, albeit indirectly. While there are differences between one religious citizen and another, there can be no meaningful opposition. If religious pluralism is true, then the beliefs and practices of those of other faiths cannot be judged to be objectively wrong by a religious

---

[10]   See J. Hick *An Interpretation of Religion* (Basingstoke, Macmillan, 2004), ch. 19.

Religious Tolerance, Diversity, and Pluralism

citizen. Though the behaviour of the tolerant pluralist and the religious pluralist towards those in different religions may be similar in many respects, they would not both manifestations of tolerance. The religious pluralist would not have anything to tolerate in the manifestations of religious difference. No more would the citizen who notes that her neighbour takes his holidays in a different location from hers have anything to tolerate in this fact of difference.

Both religious pluralists and tolerant pluralists do more than simply accept, without active opposition, the divergent religious beliefs of others. Both will welcome and encourage the expression of religious difference. Both will be interested in learning about the beliefs of others. But note that it is only the tolerant pluralist who will see in the different religious beliefs of others the occasion to re-examine her own. The beliefs of religious others (excluding the beliefs of the non-religious) cannot challenge those of the religious pluralist, for there is no opposition between the beliefs of religions covered by a pluralist hypothesis. The religious pluralist can learn from the beliefs and practices of other faiths, but not by way of finding them a challenge to her own; rather they might provide supplements and additions to her inherited beliefs. The tolerant pluralist facing religious difference sees in the opposing and conflicting religious positions of others reason to question the certainty and truth of her own. For her, the thought 'But what if they are true?' has the implication 'I need to re-examine my own beliefs; they may be false'.

Tolerant pluralism and religious exclusivism

Is it possible for fully tolerant religious believer to be a religious exclusivist? Must she, by virtue of having the attitudes of the fully tolerant, be embarked upon a journey that moves her inexorably toward religious inclusivism, if not to pluralism and then scepticism? This question has no simple answer. We need to be sensitive to the dimensions of religious exclusivism. We need in particular to distinguish doxastic exclusivism from soteriological exclusivism. Doxastic exclusivists make a stand on the truth and warrant of their religious beliefs. They hold that their beliefs are exclusively true and possessed, to the exclusion of other sets of rival beliefs, of genuinely truth-indicative grounds. Truth and warrant belong to their religion, but not to others.

Prima facie the religious exclusivist who is a tolerant pluralist need not give up the affirmation that her beliefs are exclusively true. She recognises and respects the selfhood of individuals who are religiously different. She welcomes the expression of these individuals' religious convictions and is prepared to re-examine her own beliefs in the light of them. But that does not mean that she is unsure of her religious beliefs or that the re-examination of them will lead to the conclusion that they need modifying, still less that they are false. Like all those who exhibit full tolerance and tolerant pluralism, she sees value in the differing and opposing convictions of others, but the value is an expressive one. The value is discerned through considering such convictions not in the abstract or from an impersonal point of view. It resides rather in the way opposing convictions express the autonomous life of others. A sense of this value can be reinforced by reflection on the way in which these convictions support and direct important forms of life that are evidently rich in cultural meaning. In all this a religious exclusivist exhibiting full tolerance is in the same position as the atheist who nonetheless fosters and respects the expression of religious belief. None of this need seem paradoxical if we recall that the set of attitudes in question is similar to those found in many walks of life. Consider the historian who, while having her own firm historical convictions, supports a structure in her discipline that promotes a rich diversity of opinion.

In the above we have argued that there is nothing in the attitude of full tolerance per se that undermines doxastic exclusivism. That contention does, however, connect with an important issue in epistemology. It is the issue of whether recognition of disagreement between epistemic peers leads to agnosticism/scepticism. There is a thriving literature in both general and religious epistemology on the epistemic significance of disagreement.[11] A key question in the literature on the epistemic significance of disagreement is this: if we find two individuals who are epistemic peers with respect to some proposition, who recognize this fact, but who disagree over the truth of that proposition, does it follow that their stances toward the proposition's truth should thereby be weaker? It is tempting to conclude that confrontation with someone who is recognised as an epistemic peer but who disagrees with one over the truth of some proposition ought to lessen one's confidence in its truth. The notion of an epistemic peer in this argument needs spelling out. It

---

[11] For a survey of the issues in general epistemology see T. Kelly 'The Epistemic Significance of Disagreement' in Gendlier, T. Z. and Hawthorne, J. (eds) *Oxford Studies in Epistemology*, vol. 1 (Oxford, Clarendon Press, 2006), 167–95, and for survey of the issues in the epistemology of religion see J. Kraft, 'Religious Disagreement, Externalism, and the Epistemology of Disagreement: Listening to our Grandmothers', *Religious Studies* **43** (2007), 417–32.

is someone whose cognitive equipment is functioning as well as one's own – they are not, for example, suffering from defective memory, senses, or reasoning powers. It also includes the acceptance that they are as well informed about matters other than the truth of p as oneself. These conditions entail that disagreement between epistemic peers cannot be diagnosed by reference to either party being ignorant of general matters, or through either party suffering from defective reasoning or information-gathering powers. Recognition that there is epistemic disagreement of this sort over the truth of a given proposition suggests agnosticism/scepticism with regard to that proposition because it makes the following inference highly tempting. There is disagreement in such a case because the matter is undecidable and opinions on both side of the case are objectively uncertain.

There is a great deal more to be said about the implications of epistemic peer conflict. The important question for us is whether full tolerance/tolerant pluralism in the face of religious diversity entails a verdict of uncertainty that would in turn undermine doxastic exclusivism. A provisional, initial answer is that it need not because believers who opt for full tolerance/tolerant pluralism do not have to admit that those who differ from them on religious matters are their full epistemic peers. What is needed for full tolerance is respect for the other as a person. In exploring the nature of that respect we have employed a set of notions surrounding the value of autonomy that in turn point to a commitment to a basic form of humanism. This humanism bids us to respect all human beings as having an interest-based right to live a life of their own. The exclusivist could maintain this necessary respect for religious others while not judging them to be her full epistemic peers. Adherents of other religions may lack epistemic parity with the exclusivist believer because they have not been inducted into a revelation that provides the divine's only genuine self-disclosure. Or they may be ignorant of an array of apologetic arguments demonstrating that the only true faith is indeed true. How can they know of such an array if they have been brought up in a different religious tradition? There are ways, then, in which the religious other can be a person of integrity, generally well-informed, and possessed of the standard set of cognitive faculties (that function normally), but still be someone who misses the one, exclusive religious truth by a mile. This is to make the same distinction between *general* epistemic parity and *specific* epistemic parity that Kelly uses to block the move from disagreement to uncertainty.[12] The exclusivist stops the inference to uncertainty from the fact of disagreement

[12] See Kelly 'The Epistemic Significance of Disagreement', 179.

Peter Byrne

by asserting that unbelievers cannot be the full epistemic peers of
believers.

Doxastic exclusivist intolerance

In very general terms, the defence of full tolerance as a virtue in this
paper prevents any inference that might be drawn from 'crime, to
criminal, sin to sinner'. That is to say: opposition to that which is
different is noted; the fact of error on behalf of the other is thereby
recorded; but the 'crime' does not make the other a 'criminal'. The
other to be tolerated retains worth as a person despite the verdict of
error. Thus they are not due coercion but become partners in a
debate about the true and the good. I have contended thus far that
the perception of, what is to the believer, major religious error may
still allow sin and sinner, crime and criminal to be separated.

'May still allow sin and sinner, crime and criminal to be separated.'
It has to be conceded that some doxastic exclusivist perspectives may
not allow sin and sinner to be kept apart. Let us cite the commentary
by an Iranian theologian on article 18 of the Universal Declaration of
Human Rights (this clause grants freedom of thought, conscience and
religion to all human beings, including the freedom to change
religion):

> No man of sense, from the mere fact that he possesses intelli-
> gence, will ever turn down the better in favour of the inferior.
> Anyone who penetrates beneath the surface to the inner essence
> of Islam is bound to recognise its superiority over the other reli-
> gions. A man, therefore, who deserts Islam, by that act betrays
> the fact that he must have played truant to its moral and spiritual
> truths in his heart earlier. If he pleads doubt as his reason, he
> must be saved from uttering falsehoods by a calm discussion.
> Other motives may be operative: e.g. another religion has been
> bribing him with material gain or with false promises; or he
> may feel that some wrong or injury has been done to him
> within Islam and drop his religion out of spite against the man
> who he fancies is the cause; or he may have been led astray by
> carnal lusts into actions he knows Islam forbids.[13]

The upshot of this way of analysing religious difference is that apostates born into Islam are to be executed without possibility of

[13] S. Tabandeh *A Muslim commentary on the Universal Declaration of
Human Rights*, Goulding, F. J. tr, (Guildford, F.J. Goulding, 1970), 71–2.

repentance. Apostates are to be given three days for repentance before being done to death.[14]

Tabandeh's analysis of the religious apostate evidently excludes the possibility of separating the sinner from the sin. The only way he can explain the change of heart over the truth of Islam is by an account which entails that the decision and its author cannot be respected: 'he must have played truant to its [Islam's] moral and spiritual truths'. Respect for other human beings with a right to live lives of their own does not enter into this account. It has been excluded from the picture by the dominant thought that apostates have done violence to their own nature as human beings – they are human beings who have heard God's call and then turned their backs on that call. In this instance, the minimal humanism on which liberal tolerance rests is being implicitly rejected. Rather than viewing human beings as having interest-based rights to live autonomously, they are viewed primarily as having an interest in achieving right relation to God. There can be no value in a wilful, conscious decision to withdraw from that relationship – seen in the case of Islam as a relationship of submission and obedience – because such a decision can only stem from a perverted will. There cannot be any genuine reasons for the acts of apostates, since the truth they abandon must be evident to them. Only a sick perversion of the chief mark of humanity (our ability to know of and submit to the Almighty) can explain what they do. Their decisions are thus not respect-worthy.

Tabandeh is in effect contending that unbelievers are not the full epistemic peers of believers. They are unbelievers because they are ignorant of the grounds of Islam, or because they have been distracted by non-rational factors from acknowledging its truth, or because they have wilfully hardened their hearts against its obvious truth. Unbelief is either the result of non-culpable ignorance of Islam or of culpable rejection of its truth. So we can say that here we have religious exclusivism with a rejection of full epistemic parity between believer and unbeliever.

Acceptance of full epistemic parity between believer and unbeliever creates problems for doxastic religious exclusivism because it prompts the inference 'if there is disagreement the matter must be objectively uncertain'. It is just this inference that a religious pluralist such as Hick wants to rely on. A central pillar of Hick's pluralism is the claim that the universe is religiously ambiguous.[15] Religious

---

[14]   Tabandeh, *A Muslim Commentary on the Universal Declaration of Human Rights*, 72–3.
[15]   See Hick *An Interpretation of Religion*, Part II and also R. McKim 'On Religious Ambiguity', *Religious Studies* **44** (2008), 373–92.

ambiguity is shown by the very fact that equally reasonable individuals can belong to different religions or none. They can be equally reasonable because there are no neutral facts about the world that objectively show one major religious tradition to be true and the others false. Pluralism and some doxastic exclusivists are, in this regard, playing the same game; both accept the hypothesis that equal reasonableness plus equal information on the part of those with conflicting religious opinions entails uncertainty. The exclusivist then denies that religious others have equal reasonableness and equal information. That can lead, as we have seen, to an intolerant stance toward some religious others.

To maintain that full tolerance does not entail the denial of doxastic exclusivism we need to show that the inference from epistemic peer conflict to uncertainty does not hold in the case of religion. Tolerance in this area need not be based on a form of scepticism. As we noted above, the religious exclusivist might be able to point to a variety of factors that explain why individuals who are epistemic peers in general are differently situated with regards to the perception of the exclusive religious truth. Further grounds for questioning the inference from epistemic peer conflict to uncertainty can be provided if we accept the following plausible account of the justification of religious beliefs: successful justification depends upon a cumulative case. I will outline this account very briefly.

The idea of a cumulative case is neatly encapsulated in John Wisdom's analogy: in some arguments different pieces of evidence are the like the legs of a chair, not like the links in a chain.[16] Each leg of a chair plays some part in keeping the chair upright, but it cannot keep the chair up by itself. Moreover, though each leg separately contributes to keeping the chair upright, its power to do so is dependent on the contribution of the other legs. In similar vein, it is plausible to suppose that the various truth-indicative grounds for any one religion each function to provide some evidence for that religion's truth, but none on its own makes it more probable than not. Moreover, the epistemic force of any one ground depends on it being seen in the context of the other. Likewise, the fact that the suspect in a murder case was seen at the scene of the crime shortly beforehand may in itself be of little probative significance, but becomes so when taken with the discovery that she had a motive to kill the victim. The grasping of a cumulative case for a religion's truth may

[16] J. Wisdom 'Gods' in Wisdom, J. *Philosophy and Psychoanalysis*, (Oxford, Blackwell, 1953), 157. See also B. G. Mitchell, *The Justification of Religious Belief* (London, Macmillan, 1973).

thus be a matter of a *Gestalt*, like seeing an aspect in Wittgenstein's famous discussion of puzzle pictures in the *Philosophical Investigations*.[17] Someone might be aware of the individual pieces of evidence but not grasp the pattern that connects them all. The ability to acquire the *Gestalt* that enables the full force of the cumulative case may itself be something that is acquired only by of induction into a way of judging and experiencing. Another analogy: I may be able to explain to a birding novice each little visual difference that enables a mistle thrush to be distinguished from a song thrush. It is another matter whether the novice is then able to make the discrimination in the field. To do that, the way these individual differences form a pattern of difference that enables discrimination must be grasped. And that takes time and practice. The practice may only be acquired through training by an expert whose judgement can be trusted. A way of seeing must be created.

The application of this model to judging the truth of religious world views should be clear. When applied it gives force to Kelly's distinction between general and specific epistemic parity. The religious other may not see the religious truth the religious exclusivist advances, but she need not be in general less well-informed or cognitively defective. The religious other lacks that training, that inwardness with a way of seeing, that allows an accumulation of individual phenomena to be seen as probative. She may be the exclusivist's general epistemic peers and be guilty of no epistemic sin or moral failing; her personal worth need not be in question. This model would permit the doxastic exclusivist to retain the thought that religious matters admit of objective certainty. To re-use one of my analogies: it may appear, quite properly, objectively certain to the experienced birder that this is a mistle thrush and not a song thrush even though lots of equally intelligent and generally well-informed people just cannot 'see it'.

Soteriological exclusivism and tolerance

A liberal defence of tolerance rests on an appeal to rights, and rights, as resting upon needs and the fundamental conditions for human well-being, generally trump the opposition condition in tolerance. Provided the person in question is not thereby violating the mutual respect for others as persons with a life to make for themselves

---

[17] L. Wittgenstein *Philosophical Investigations*, tr. Anscombe, E. (Oxford, Blackwell, 1963), 193ff.

Peter Byrne

found in a tolerant society, his or her conduct is simply off limits to interference and control. If we accept the linking of tolerance to the core liberal insistence on respect for the value and worth of others as persons with a life to make for themselves, then we must acknowledge that there is a further question to be raised about the compatibility of exclusivist religious convictions and tolerance. Do the exclusivist religious beliefs on matters of soteriology found in many of the world's religions destroy the perception of all as due a minimal respect? We have noted that doxastic religious exclusivism need not go hand in hand with soteriological exclusivism. But it often does. The link is frequently made between having right beliefs and being in a position to be saved. Only those who live and die in the right faith (where that includes having the right beliefs) have a chance of salvation. Those who do not are lost to God. With the move to soteriological exclusivism unbelief and apostasy take on new dimensions. Full tolerance is now under threat. Here we allude to the stigmatising effect of categories that grow out of exclusivist forms of religion. Many things can block off the awareness of rights that respect for others creates. The perception of racial difference, or of sexual orientation, or of disability can result in the other being perceived not as a fellow human being with a life to make for him- or her-self, but as a non-person who merits only hatred and persecution. In a similar fashion, the perception of someone as hated by God, lost to him, fated only for damnation may block off interpersonal recognition and acceptance. We might ask whether the switch to hatred and disrespect that may follow perception of religious difference is avoidable or not. Is it at all possible for one human being to look at another, see him or her as damned and hated by God because of unbelief or apostasy, and yet still see him or her as deserving of respect, as having value and worth as a person with a life to make for him/herself? Rousseau certainly thought that the answer to this question can only be 'no':

> Those who distinguish civil from theological intolerance are, to my mind, mistaken. The two forms are inseparable. It is impossible to live at peace with those we regard as damned; to love them would be to hate God who punishes them: we positively must either reclaim or torment them.[18]

There is continuing debate in the philosophical literature on religious diversity over whether religious exclusivism is or is not

[18]   J. J. Rousseau (1968) *The Social Contract*, tr. Cole, G. D. H. (London, Dent, 1968), 114.

306

'arrogant'. I suggest that the question to which Rousseau gives so clear an answer is the more important one: is soteriological exclusivism necessarily destructive of respect for persons? Soteriological exclusivism does have its contemporary defenders. In Christian thought, it goes with the assertion that only if individuals have explicit faith in Christ can they be saved.[19] Whether or not it is arrogant, it threatens mutual, interpersonal respect. The question at issue is, of course, not whether as a matter of fact folk with exclusivist religious views have the stance toward 'the other' notable in the racist or the homophobe, but whether an attitude of respect and acceptance of others makes sense alongside the opinion that the other is God-hated and damned for eternity.

The case can be made that soteriological exclusivists are not seeing others as fellow human beings but as unbelievers, the damned, traitors to God, or as vermin. Soteriological exclusivism, as opposed to mere doxastic exclusivism, surely has the power to undermine a liberal defence of tolerance. A liberal defence of tolerance rests on the perception of the other as due respect in virtue of being a fellow human being. As noted, this could be described as a minimal kind of humanism: the view that each and every human being has an intrinsic and high value just in being a human being. In soteriological exclusivism we have the view that those not 'of the faith' do not merely have wrong beliefs but are cut off from God. It is evident that this kind of exclusivism may end up denying the value claim in my minimal humanism. The unbeliever, the faithless one, may be incapable of being pictured as having intrinsic value as a human being if s/he has forsaken God or been forsaken by him. Behind such a thought may lurk another: in forsaking God, the unbeliever has spurned any chance of partaking in human flourishing. Only through being rightly, soteriologically aligned to God can there be any chance of sharing in the human good. On such a perspective, far from liberty of thought, speech, and action being intrinsically and instrumentally important for the human good, the reverse is true. For liberty may lead to wrong belief and thus estrangement from God. Such exclusivist beliefs are opposed to my minimal humanism. They will tend to divide human beings into an in-group and an out-group. The out-group are not deserving of the fundamental respect due to those in the in-group. There is no value in them as human beings. They are cut off from the only source of value there is:

[19]   As in William Lane Craig '" No Other Name": A Middle Knowledge Perspective on the Exclusivity of Salvation through Christ', *Faith and Philosophy* **6** (1989), 172–88.

right relation to God. From such a perspective, we do not serve any one's good or acknowledge anything respect-worthy in human beings by allowing unbelievers liberty of thought and expression. Their very existence may be a standing temptation to the weak, enticing them by example into losing that faith which alone will give any hope of participation in the sole thing that makes human life of value: right relation to God.

Soteriological exclusivism thus appears to be the potential enemy of full tolerance. It also appears to be something that liberalism and its minimal humanism will be hard put to argue with. Insofar as soteriological exclusivists cannot respect religious others as persons with their own lives to lead, then they seem to live in a different moral universe than the liberal humanist. Of course, it does not have to be the case that a soteriological exclusivist is opposed to bare or mere tolerance. The barely tolerant exclusivist may actively regard unbelievers with contempt but consider that it is not worth doing anything about them. They may reason that it is impractical to 'compel them to come in' or that punishment of the lost is for God and not for human beings. Or the exclusivist may be merely tolerant of religious others, regarding them with indifference. This exclusivist may simply be content to let each work out their own salvation; if some are lost to God in so doing, then that is their funeral. Rousseau may then be wrong: we may be able to 'live at peace' with those we regard as lost to God. But he is right that it will be difficult to have that respect for their welfare that goes along with an active sense of shared citizenship. We might also fear that a view of unbelievers as lost to God is always liable to disrupt an attitude of 'live and let live'. The soteriological exclusivist may regard it as pragmatically expedient not to interfere with the ability of others to express and propagate their religious beliefs. But it would be hard to see how such a person could see the expression of what is unbelief to her as valuable in itself. Indeed, it surely must be seen as harmful in itself. There can be no value in the fact of religious difference.

If Quinn, Hick, and McKim are correct on the epistemic effects of diversity, are correct in thinking that diversity points to substantive uncertainty in religious beliefs, and if we could convince some doxastic exclusivists of this, then we might shake them out of soteriological exclusivism. They may make the move: 'if all religious beliefs are to a substantial degree uncertain, perhaps having the correct ones is not necessary for salvation'. Even if we do not think that the doxastic brand entails the soteriological brand, many exclusivists do. And we must use whatever strategies are to hand to wake them up.

But there is an air of unreality in the above suggestion. The persecutors and killers in the name of religion might be better, more directly, woken from their nightmarish visions by being asked to stop and appreciate their potential victims as human beings. Perhaps then they will see through their religious delusions.

King's College London

Index of Names

Index of Names

Index of Names

Royal Institute of Philosophy Supplements

The Royal Institute of Philosophy Supplements are published twice a year. Institutional subscribers to the journal *Philosophy* receive the supplements as part of their subscription. The following supplements are available to purchase as books.

Volume 37	1994	Philosophy, Psychology and Psychiatry	(ISBN 0521469023)
38	1995	Philosophy and Technology	(ISBN 0521558166)
39	1995	Karl Popper: Philosophy and Problems	(ISBN 0521558158)
40	1996	Philosophy and Pluralism	(ISBN 0521567505)
41	1996	*Verstehen and Human Understanding*	(ISBN 0521587425)
42	1997	Thought and Language	(ISBN 0521587417)
43	1998	Current Issues in Philosophy of Mind	(ISBN 0521639271)
44	1999	German Philosophy since Kant	(ISBN 0521667828)
45	1999	Philosophy and Public Affairs	(ISBN 0521667844)
46	2000	Logic, Cause & Action	(ISBN 0521785103)
47	2000	Philosophy, the Good, the True and the Beautiful	(ISBN 0521785111)
48	2001	Philosophy at the New Millennium	(ISBN 0521005086)
49	2001	Naturalism, Evolution and Mind	(ISBN 0521003733)
50	2002	Time, Reality & Experience	(ISBN 0521529670)
51	2002	Logic, Thought and Language	(ISBN 0521529662)
52	2003	Philosophy and the Emotions	(ISBN 0521537347)
53	2003	Minds and Persons	(ISBN 0521537339)
54	2004	Modern Moral Philosophy	(ISBN 0521603269)
55	2004	Agency and Action	(ISBN 0521603560)
56	2005	Philosophy, Biology and Life	(ISBN 0521678455)
57	2005	The Philosophy of Need	(ISBN 0521678447)
58	2006	Political Philosophy	(ISBN 0521695597)
59	2006	Preferences and Well-Being	(ISBN 0521695589)
60	2007	Narrative and Understanding Persons	(ISBN 9780521714099)
61	2007	Philosophy of Science	(ISBN 9780521718967)
62	2008	Being: Developments in Contemporary Metaphysics	(ISBN 9780521735445)
63	2008	Kant and Philosophy of Science Today	(ISBN 9780521748513)
64	2009	Epistemology	(ISBN 9780521138581)
65	2009	Conceptions of Philosophy	(ISBN 9780521138574)
66	2010	Philosophy as Therapeia	(ISBN 9780521165150)
67	2010	The Metaphysics of Consciousness	(ISBN 9780521173919)

From Volume 13 onwards the Series is published by Cambridge University Press and some earlier titles are also available.

For EU product safety concerns, contact us at Calle de José Abascal, 56–1°,
28003 Madrid, Spain or eugpsr@cambridge.org.

www.ingramcontent.com/pod-product-compliance
Ingram Content Group UK Ltd.
Pitfield, Milton Keynes, MK11 3LW, UK
UKHW020339140625
459647UK00018B/2216